ETHICAL
EXCELLENCE

ETHICAL EXCELLENCE

Philosophers, Psychologists, and Real-Life Exemplars

Show Us How to Achieve It

HEIDI M. GIEBEL

The Catholic University of America Press

Washington, D.C.

Library of Congress Cataloging-in-Publication Data
Names: Giebel, Heidi M., author.
Title: Ethical excellence : philosophers, psychologists, and real-life
exemplars show us how to achieve it / Heidi M. Giebel.
Description: Washington, D.C. : The Catholic University of America
Press, [2021] | Includes bibliographical references and index.
Identifiers: LCCN 2020041969 | ISBN 9780813233338 (paperback)
Subjects: LCSH: Excellence. | Conduct of life.
Classification: LCC BJ1533.E82 G45 2021 | DDC 170/.44—dc23
LC record available at https://lccn.loc.gov/2020041969

For Maysel Rose,
who has far more virtue than can be
credited to my parenting

CONTENTS

ACKNOWLEDGMENTS

To the many people who made this project possible, I owe enormous debts of gratitude. Most obviously, this book could not have been written without the stories and insights provided by the sixteen featured exemplar interviewees: Judy Berry, Cathey Brown, Susan Burton, Cathy Heying, Pam Koner, Noah Levinson, Gloria Lewis, Margaret Martin, James McCormick, Mauricio Miller, Lisa Nigro, Estella Pyfrom, Don Schoendorfer, Toni Temporiti, Patty Webster, and Andy Wells. I am most grateful to each of them for taking the time to share their life stories with me.

The support and advice I needed to arrange the interview portion of the project came from a generous grant from the Beacon Project at Wake Forest University and the Templeton Religion Trust. (Naturally, the views expressed in this book are my own and do not necessarily reflect those of the Beacon Project, Wake Forest University, or Templeton Religion Trust.) And I owe special thanks to Christian Miller, the Beacon Project's philosophy project leader, and to core team members Anne Colby and Daniel Russell for their amazingly helpful advice. I also owe thanks to many past teachers and mentors for their guidance over the years; although these are too numerous to list, I'm particularly grateful to Steve Angle for introducing me to Confucian philosophy, to my undergraduate adviser Scott Schreiber and my graduate adviser Kristin Shrader-Frechette for sharing their wisdom, and of course to my wonderful parents—my first teachers—for raising me to care about virtue.

I am grateful to John Martino at CUA Press for the interest he has shown in this project from its beginning, to the anonymous reviewers who supported the book and offered suggestions for its improvement, and to Anne Needham, whose excellent copy editing significantly improved the manuscript. Many thanks to Bill Ferry of William Ferry Fine Art Photography for this book's cover image.

I thank the University of St. Thomas for providing the sabbatical leave during which I drafted most of the book. Several of my colleagues and students in the Philosophy Department—far too many to list, I'm afraid—helpfully commented on my sketchy drafts and descriptions of various chapters. My student research assistant, Maria Hill, was an incredible blessing—finding (and explaining!) just the right psychology articles to illustrate and add to several of the concepts I was trying to address. And I don't think I could have written this book without the help and advice of my psychologist colleague Tonia Bock, who (in addition to pointing me to relevant psychology research and helping me hire Maria) spent countless hours coding and discussing the interview transcripts with me. It will take me years to return the favor.

On a more personal note (and, speaking of owing years' worth of favors), I am hugely indebted to my husband, Jerry—for helpful discussions regarding many of the book's topics, for tolerating the extra time this project has taken, and especially for exemplifying on a daily basis so many of the virtues about which I've written.

Above all, and as always, Deo gratias.

INTRODUCTION

I T WAS a cold, dreary day last February, and I was exhausted and a little cranky: in addition to being not quite over a nasty cold, I had given birth less than forty-eight hours earlier. Reluctantly, I fished my voice recorder and ear bud microphone out of my desk drawer. It was time to call one of my "exemplars"—someone who had won a national award for outstanding service to the community. She had already rescheduled our phone interview once, and I didn't want to risk losing her as a participant, so I didn't dare ask her to reschedule again. Dutifully, I dialed her number, thinking, "At least it will probably be a short interview—judging from the length of her emails, she's probably not much of a talker." Almost five hours and half a bag of cough drops later, with my arms cradling a sleepy newborn and my head nearly bursting from the almost-too-fascinating-to-be-true stories and the genuinely helpful advice my interviewee had shared, I hung up the phone. Once again, I had loved every minute of it.

This book is about ethical excellence—and about how ordinary people like us can achieve it. Over the course of its chapters, we'll see advice and stories from sixteen amazingly good people whose life stories I had the privilege of learning about and recording: people who have won awards like the Citizen Honors Medal, the Purpose Prize, and CNN Hero of the Week. My interviewees, who are so much like the rest of us in most ways, show us how to live deeply satisfying lives—and to do great things for our communities—through ethically excellent actions. In addition to seeing a bit of their life stories, we'll see how they illuminate and embody important ethical virtues like gratitude, justice, and self-discipline.

We'll also see concrete advice for developing the character traits that are so striking in each of these exemplars' stories—and the time-tested principles behind that advice. The principles come from two ancient and hugely influential traditions: those started by famous philosophers Socrates and Confucius. While these classical thinkers and their successors offer some helpful practical guidance as well, much of the best concrete advice regarding how we can apply the philosophical principles to achieve ethical excellence comes from contemporary psychologists: researchers who study the methods that work best for acquiring the traits and life skills related to ethical excellence—things like self-knowledge, perspective-taking, and willpower. When combined with and guided by the time-tested ethical principles of great philosophers, this empirical research can be put to work providing helpful insights into everyday ways to put those principles into practice. And my award-winning interviewees give real-life examples of this ethical excellence in action—along with inspiration for the rest of us to achieve it.

Why This Book?

Philosophical wisdom is inspiring—I've been hooked on it since the first day of my freshman year in college. A classic work of philosophy—say, from Plato or the Confucian thinker Mencius—is the sort of text you can come back to again and again and get something new and profound from each reading. Well, at least you can if you understand it and know how to apply it. But of course, that part is far from automatic: philosophy is an abstract discipline— it deals in things like logic and principles—and sometimes understanding it can be hard work. And even when our work is rewarded by a good grasp of the abstract principles, we still have to apply them to our lives: theory without any application risks uselessness.[1] These classical philosophers, as wise and profound as their writing was and still is, were writing in a time and place very different from ours. Sometimes their own applications of their theories seem obscure or old-fashioned, leaving us with incomplete guidance. For example, Mencius asks whether it is better, ethically speaking, to pursue a career in shaman-healing or coffin-making. Although with a bit of effort we can see his point—that the healer's success depends on helping people live, while the coffin-maker's depends on their deaths—it would be clearer and more easily applicable to our lives if we had some concrete, modern-day examples.

Psychology research, on the other hand, is very tangible and specific: if you read an article in an academic psychology journal, it will tell you exactly how many people participated in the study, what they did, and what the results were. There will be several charts giving you as much hard data as you could possibly ask for. And in the bigger picture, psychology can give us great insight into how people's minds work—and what methods, at least in general or on average, will be effective for things like forming or breaking habits or taking control of our emotions. And that's great too—but, like philosophy, it has its limits. The limitations of an empirical discipline like psychology become especially apparent—and problematic—in the area of ethical development. I've seen far too many articles attempting to show that this or that method is especially effective (or not) for promoting ethical development in the group studied—but the authors didn't bother to define (or maybe even to think about) what ethical development actually is. What kinds of change in our beliefs, values, or behavior count as ethical development (progress), and what kinds leave us ethically stagnant—or even regressing? What is the ultimate goal of ethical development? These aren't empirical questions; they are philosophical ones. Leaving them unanswered—or merely guessing at the answers—can put us on a very efficient path to a bad place. In other words, just as principle without application risks uselessness, technique without principle risks recklessness.

Suppose, thanks to strategic reading in philosophy and psychology, we have an adequate grasp of the theory and the application of ethical development—the principle and the technique. Will that be enough to get us started on our own journeys toward consistently acting on those good ethical principles? Not quite—at least not unless we're extraordinarily optimistic and self-motivated. Without accessible real-life examples of how people like us have enacted and embodied our most important principles and values, most of us will be left not knowing where to start—and not at all confident that our goal is even achievable. Even if we bypass the two dangers of uselessness and recklessness, we may not be able to escape a third: hopelessness.

And that's why we need a book like this one: a book that combines insights from philosophy, psychology, and biography. With the help of classical Confucian and Socratic philosophers,[2] we can find true and helpful principles to guide our ethical development: principles related to ethical excellences (virtues) like gratitude, justice, and benevolence. Once we understand the nature of these virtues and the reasons to pursue them, we can apply the findings of contemporary psychologists to help bring them to fruition in ourselves. For example, recent research on willpower can help us develop self-discipline, perseverance, and, less directly, a host of other virtues. Finally, lest we give up when we see how high the standards for ethical excellence really are—and they are quite high—we can benefit greatly from specific, real-life examples of otherwise ordinary people embracing and embodying the virtues. These exemplars provide us with inspiration and hope—and, in many cases, with a concrete model we can readily apply in our own lives.

Why I Get to Be the One to Write This Book

Writing this book, and the process leading up to writing it, has been an incredible journey of ethical and intellectual development. (Occasionally, I'll tell you about some of my adventures—and misadventures—on that journey.) How did I come to be so fortunate?

That story might be told beginning as far back as my sophomore year in college, when I was struggling to decide whether to major in psychology or philosophy. (Although I ultimately chose philosophy, I never lost interest in psychology.) But the trajectory toward this book began to pick up speed about twelve years ago, when I was about five years into my job as a philosophy professor. I'd dutifully mined my dissertation for publishable articles and was ready to start thinking about something else. My colleague Tonia Bock in the Psychology Department downstairs knew I was interested in exploring connections between our fields; she invited me to join her and a few students for a reading group focused on ethical development. As much as I've enjoyed and benefited from the psychology articles we've read together over the years (a few of which are featured in this book), as a philosopher I couldn't help but be frustrated occasionally at the apparent lack of theory behind many of the practices they detailed. (And where there does seem to be a coherent theory in the background, it often looks like a watered-down, seldom-acknowledged version of Aristotle.) Clearly, more careful and explicit connections could do both disciplines—and the people who stand to benefit from their research—a lot of good.

Another milestone on my journey to writing this book was a seminar that took place ten years ago, sponsored by the National Endowment for the Humanities and led by philosophers Steve Angle and Michael Slote, on Confucianism and contemporary (mostly Aristotelian) virtue ethics. For six fabulous weeks I got to be a student again, learning enough about classical Confucianism to develop a healthy admiration for the tradition, to see many connections between it and the more familiar Socratic tradition, and to start teaching the two traditions side-by-side in my Introductory Ethics course.

As a result of the reading group (and Tonia's help), I regularly give talks and write papers at the intersection of philosophy and psychology. And thanks to the seminar and its outstanding leaders, I also regularly speak and write at the intersection of Confucian and Socratic philosophy. So this book has been a fun and fruitful opportunity to bring those two pairs of overlapping interests together, extending and developing my thoughts in a fuller way. But, as I noted above, as valuable as the combined insights of philosophy and psychology might be, their real-life implementation is limited without concrete examples of the ethical heroes who embody them. I needed to take an in-depth look at the lives of exceptionally ethical people.

The opportunity to study the ethically exceptional came in the form of a generous grant from the Beacon Project, which supplied funding for me to conduct interviews with people who have won national awards for doing good.[3] These wonderful people each took two to five hours out of their busy lives (most of them run successful nonprofit organizations) to tell me their life stories.[4] And in the details of those stories, I saw—as you will soon see—theories about virtue and ethical development come to life. I saw how gratitude, as the Stoics had taught, is connected to many other virtues. I saw that Confucian philosopher Xunzi was right about how we can cultivate mental unity and stillness to overcome our unhealthy tendencies toward narrow-minded obsession. And with every interview I saw in vivid detail what Aristotle told us thousands of years ago: Even in far-from-ideal circumstances, the most virtuous people are the happiest people.

Part 1

FOUNDATIONS OF
ETHICAL EXCELLENCE

Chapter 1

THEORETICAL FOUNDATIONS

Ethical Excellence and the Good Life

IMAGINE you have entered a talent competition with a billion-dollar prize. Naturally, like everyone else, you want to win. The good news is that no contestant—including you—can bribe the expert judges: they are perfect models of fairness and objectivity. So to win the contest, you simply have to display more talent than any of the other contestants. The bad news is that there are thousands of other contestants and only one prize. So how can you improve your chance of winning?

Of course, there are a few obvious strategies you'll want to use: for example, pick an area in which you have some natural ability and practice your act diligently. But everyone else is doing those things too. To take your talent to the next level, you'll also have to do something that sounds a bit paradoxical: *Stop caring so much about the billion-dollar prize.*

I don't just mean that worrying about the prize could cause performance anxiety—although that might also be true. What I mean is that to be the sort of performer who really excels, who outshines the competition, you'll have to care more about the activity itself than about the external reward. You'll have to care more about the beauty of your dance, or the harmony of your piano keys, or the form of your bicep curl (or whatever—you get the idea), than you care about a billion dollars. In psychological terms, you'll have to develop intrinsic motivation.[1] In philosophical terms, you'll have to focus on the goods internal to the practice of your craft or skill.[2]

According to the famous philosopher Aristotle, life is a little like that contest: We all want the "prize" of an excellent life—a life that is enjoyable, successful, fulfilling, and meaningful. But if we just focus on that prize, we won't win it: a life focused primarily on rewards for ourselves actually is *not* enjoyable, successful, fulfilling, or meaningful. To achieve an excellent life, we need qualities like kindness, fairness, and gratitude—qualities that shift our focus away from what's in it for us and toward the rightness of our actions and the wellbeing of others. Like the talents displayed in the competition, these qualities—the ones philosophers call ethical virtues—have internal standards of excellence. In fact, the word "virtue" means "excellence." And caring about and developing these excellences is what gives us the best chance at an excellent life.[3] (Fortunately, life is *not* like that talent contest insofar as the excellent life is not competitive: the "prize" is available to all of us, and the more we help others to win it, the more likely we are to achieve it ourselves.)

In preparation for writing this book, I interviewed sixteen people who seem to have developed those ethical excellences, people who have won national awards for their significant and long-term service to others. Over and over, they demonstrated the truth of the connection between ethical excellence and an excellent life overall. These people were not born saints or moral heroes. In fact, most of them started out living in ways that were quite ordinary—or, in some cases, even noticeably *lacking* in ethical excellence. Like many of us, they cared primarily about themselves and perhaps a few close friends and family members. But they didn't find their lives nearly as meaningful, joyful, or fulfilling then as they do now that they have shifted their focus away from themselves and toward helping others flourish. Their service to others has given them a sense of purpose and meaning, they have experienced deep and lasting satisfaction with their paths in life, and their interpersonal relationships have blossomed. One interviewee summed it up this way: "The points when I have felt the best about my life have been when I've been able to help others."[4]

When asked what they thought was the most important value in life, none of the exemplary people I interviewed mentioned self-focused values like pleasure, wealth, or recognition. Instead, three chose the golden rule—

"do unto others as you would have them do unto you," an ethical principle focused on the treatment of others—and the rest chose outward-focused excellences such as love, justice, and compassion. These excellences of character—or, again, ethical virtues—are the primary focus of this book. Maybe you're reading it because you want to be a good person or do right by other people. That's great. Maybe you're hoping there's also something in it for you. No problem; there *is* something in it for you. In fact, the very best thing: an excellent life—but only if you develop an intrinsic motivation to be ethically excellent. For example, Gloria Lewis, founder of Care in Action USA and one of my interviewees, put it like this:

I have compassion and understanding for others who don't know how to cope with all the different struggles that life brings them—every time they lose a material thing they feel like it's the end of the world, because this society that we live in tells us that these things actually describe who you are, that having material things is what really makes you, and that if you don't really have material blessings or accolades to show for your life that your life is worthless and you really haven't accomplished anything in life.

But for me accomplishment is really, "Who have I helped? How have I made a difference in someone's life? Although I don't have much, how is it that I can do one little thing and still lift that person up?" It's not about me; it's about who I can lift today. Who can I be a shoulder to? Who I can give a kind word to? By doing that it lifts you up. I learned that the less you worry about you, the more you're blessing yourself, and your problems just somehow take care of themselves. By feeding into another person who doesn't have the strength, the courage, and the understanding that you have, they can look to you and feel like, "Wow, you know what? I can do this." And just a few kind words can really turn a person's life around.[5]

As we'll see throughout this book, classical philosophers and contemporary psychologists confirm that she's right: when we care about others and develop excellent traits like compassion and generosity, our lives really do become significantly better—or, as Lewis says, "blessed."

Aristotle on the Excellent Life

Despite his arrival on the scene at least two generations after its beginning
(he was the star pupil of Plato, who in turn was the star pupil of Socrates),
Aristotle is often considered the father of Western virtue ethics. Why? Compared to his predecessors, he provides much more explicit and systematic
discussions of the nature of virtue, how it is acquired, and which qualities
count as virtues. And they tend to align well with intuitive, commonsense
approaches to the virtues. So for purposes of the big-picture account of virtue ethics in this chapter, we'll rely primarily on his general account of virtues and of the excellent human life; occasionally we'll also note relevant
comparisons to the theories of the other Socratics and of the Confucians.

Aristotle quite reasonably begins his main ethical work, the *Nicomachean
Ethics*, at the beginning: with the goal of human life. "Wait a minute," you
might immediately protest: "Isn't the goal the *end* of any process rather than
its beginning?" In the chronological sense, yes: achieving the goal of an activity is the last part that takes place—once it's achieved, you're done. (For
instance, it seems to me that when people report finding some lost object "in
the last place I looked"—as though that were somehow surprising—they are
being silly. Of course the object was in the last place: once they found it, they
stopped looking.) The goal is also the end in what I'll call the "teleological"
sense (from the Greek *telos*, "purpose" or "goal"). We can use terms "end" and
"goal" synonymously, as Aristotle and many other philosophers do, to designate the purpose of a thing or activity. For example, as Aristotle observes at
the very beginning of *Nicomachean Ethics*, "as there are many actions, arts,
and sciences, their ends also are many; the end of the medical art is health, that
of shipbuilding a vessel, that of strategy victory, that of economics wealth."[6]

However, when we're *reasoning* about the achievement of some good, the
end or goal should be the beginning, for without a clear view of where we
want to go, we'll be unable to develop an effective travel plan. For example,
suppose I want to reside in my (as yet nonexistent) dream house. To accomplish my goal, I must begin by working backward: I think first of the goal
itself (the house). Next, I identify the goal's most immediate means, then the
means to those means, and so on until I reach something I can do here and
now: the first step(s) in the goal-achievement process. So a simplified version
of my plan might look like the pyramid in figure 1.1, with the one main goal

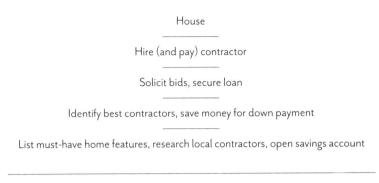

House

Hire (and pay) contractor

Solicit bids, secure loan

Identify best contractors, save money for down payment

List must-have home features, research local contractors, open savings account

Figure 1.1. Means-end pyramid: Building my dream house

at the top and the several means to achieve the goal appearing at various levels depending on the proximity of their relationship to the end.

As Thomas Aquinas, among the most celebrated of Aristotle's later followers, has succinctly observed,[7] the first thing in the order of intention—the goal or end that initiates the planning process—is the last thing in the order of execution or action, for, as we noted above, we stop pursuing the goal once it's achieved. Thus, in my means-end pyramid, the dream house appears alone at the top; the things I can do here and now to begin working toward it—the last things I came to intend—appear together at the bottom.

Similarly, as Aristotle explains, questions about ethics and moral education—about the best kind of human life and how we can help ourselves and others achieve it—must begin with the end or "chief good" of life in general: "Shall we not, like archers who have a mark to aim at, be more likely to hit upon what is right? If so, we must try, in outline at least, to determine what it is."[8] If a chief good or ultimate goal of human life really exists, then it is the thing we ultimately desire: it is at the top of our life's overall means-end pyramid. In Aristotelian terms, we call such a goal "final without qualification." That means we desire the chief good not for the sake of some other, more final, good, but solely for its own sake.

The Big-Picture Goal

But is there really such a thing as an ultimate goal of human life? Aristotle answers in the affirmative: our final end, he argues, is *eudaimonia*. This

Greek term, commonly translated "happiness," actually designates something more lasting. More helpful translations and descriptions include "fulfillment," "human flourishing," "wellbeing," "a meaningful life," and "having a good human life overall." Unlike with happiness as the term is commonly used in English, it is one's life as a whole, not one moment or day or even year, that has (or lacks) *eudaimonia*. As we consider the following passage, in which Aristotle defends his claim that "happiness" is the chief good, we will do well to keep the long-term meaning of *eudaimonia* in mind:

> Now [as final without qualification] happiness, above all else, is held to be; for this we choose always for itself and never for the sake of something else, but honour, pleasure, reason, and every virtue we choose indeed for themselves (for if nothing resulted from them we should still choose each of them), but we choose them also for the sake of happiness, judging that through them we shall be happy. Happiness, on the other hand, no one chooses for the sake of these, nor, in general, for anything other than itself.[9]

Thus, according to Aristotle, we could draw an overall means-end pyramid for each of our lives; while some of the means might differ, especially toward the bottom, at the top of each we would find the well-lived life: *eudaimonia*. A greatly simplified version of such a pyramid might look like figure 1.2.

As Aristotle points out, although everyone wants *eudaimonia*—who wouldn't want an excellent life?—not everyone agrees about exactly what it is or how to achieve it. So he starts with two points of consensus: First, *eudaimonia* is the highest goal in life. It's not a means to a higher end; it *is* the

Eudaimonia

Virtue, honor, pleasure, reason, etc.

Means to the virtue, honor, pleasure, reason, etc.

Figure 1.2. Means-end pyramid: Eudaimonia

ultimate end. That is, saying, "I want to achieve *eudaimonia* so that I can ..."
wouldn't make sense—no matter how we finished that sentence. Second, the
excellent life is self-sufficient; achieving it makes life desirable and lacking
nothing of importance. So no one could reasonably say, "I've achieved *eudaimonia*—my whole life is truly excellent—but it would be so much better
if...." Such a statement would show that the speaker hadn't achieved *eudaimonia* after all—and in fact didn't really know what the word meant.

Unfortunately, the consensus about *eudaimonia* ends with those gen-
eralities. To figure out its more specific nature, Aristotle first eliminates a
few popular but inferior candidates for the excellent life: A life focused on
pleasure isn't particularly excellent—it's fulfilling enough for lower animals
like pigs, but it can't ultimately satisfy human beings. (As pleasant as eating
apples and taking mud baths—or drinking champagne and taking bubble
baths—may be, imagine spending the rest of your life doing and pursuing
only that sort of thing.) A life of wealth can't be the ultimate end either,
because wealth by its nature is a *means* to other goods: we want money primarily so that we can buy things. And, as with pleasure, people have a lot of
trouble determining when they have the right amount of wealth—as soon
as they obtain what they thought they wanted, they find it doesn't satisfy
them and they want more. A life centered around honors or recognition is
too superficial to be the highest good: those things can't satisfy us all the
way down, so to speak. And any honor I receive is too external to me—other
people and situations actually determine and supply it—to be *my* highest
good. Besides, an honor is worthwhile only if it recognizes some genuine
excellence or virtue—*arēte*, the Greek word we translate "virtue," actually
means "excellence" more generally. To see this last point, think about a kin-
dergarten graduation: it honors six-year-olds for the accomplishment of surviving a year of ABCs and playing together. A cute photo opportunity, to
be sure, but not a celebration of genuine academic excellence. Now imagine
a life centered around trivial "honors" like that—would it be fulfilling? If
you're a normal human being, the answer is "no."

Since an honor's goodness depends on the virtue for which it's bestowed,
Aristotle reasons, perhaps *eudaimonia*—the excellent life—has a lot to do
with having virtue or excellence. Just equating the two turns out to be too
simplistic. Someone may have a character of extraordinary virtue but still
not have an excellent life—for example, because he has a physical ailment

that leaves him miserable, or because she is isolated from other people and has no one with or toward whom to exercise most of her virtues. But still, virtue must be a significant part—probably the largest part—of the answer to the question, "What is *eudaimonia*?" After all, how could living in excellent ways fail to be a major contributor to achieving an excellent life?

Excellence and Function

"Hold on," the skeptic in you might protest. "How do you know the *eudaimonia* at the top of each person's pyramid is really the same? Can it really be that the same version of *eudaimonia* or flourishing is pursued by everyone—regardless of personality, culture, or beliefs?" According to Aristotle, the answer is clearly "yes."[10] We all share a "human function" or uniquely human activity associated with our common human nature, and achievement of our chief good lies in the fulfillment of that human function. To put the matter simply, if we understand our function, we'll understand our nature (i.e., what it is that makes us human), which will tell us how to fulfill that nature; this fulfillment is *eudaimonia*.

At this point, it may seem, Aristotle has merely pushed our skepticism about a common *eudaimonia* one step back: now we might wonder whether all human beings, with our vastly different ways of life, could possibly have the same function. Such an idea may seem surprising, but for those who follow Aristotle's argument, it would be even more surprising if there were *not* some general function common to all human beings. As Aristotle points out, we take for granted the functionality of our parts and activities. For example, our eyes are for seeing and our ears are for hearing; eating is for nutrition and flute-playing is for music. Wouldn't it be odd, he suggests, if our parts and activities all had functions but *we* had none? Probably, then, there *is* a human function: some significant and characteristically human activity.

After eliminating life itself and perception, both of which we share with many other beings, Aristotle identifies our human function as "life of the rational element"—that is, exercising our unique ability to reason. This we do in two ways: (1) by engaging in the reasoning process itself, and (2) by reason's influence on our desires, emotions, and activities. Since acting on our reason is our function, then, *good* use of our reason will be the key to *eudaimonia* or human flourishing. Fulfilling our function well will make our lives good; it will also make *us* good. Just as the difference between a good pen and a not-so-good pen is that the good one performs its pen-function well (i.e., it is good for writing), the difference between a good human being and a not-so-good one is that the good person does the characteristically human activity well—he or she does a good job of (1) reasoning, and (2) applying reason to his or her decisions and actions. Excellence in reasoning is called "intellectual virtue" or "virtue of thought"; excellence in applying reason is called "moral virtue," "ethical virtue," or "virtue of character."[11] With that in mind, Aristotle settles on the following definition of *eudaimonia*: the "human good turns out to be activity of psyche in accordance with virtue … in a complete life."[12] So in the good human life—the life of fulfillment, meaning, and long-term satisfaction—the psyche consistently functions well: our feelings and desires align with our reason, which will translate into excellences of character such as generosity, courage, and justice.

Some Practical Implications

No doubt you want a fulfilling, meaningful life—it's hard to deny that something like the *eudaimonia* Aristotle describes is indeed our ultimate end or goal. But as we might notice when we begin to consider Aristotle's account of *eudaimonia*, we often *don't* see the big-picture goal of our lives. In fact, until quite recently (maybe even until you started reading this chapter), it may not have occurred to you to think much about your life's overall goal at all. We tend to focus primarily—often even exclusively—on the more immediate demands of our daily activities. This focus is sometimes good; after all, if we fail to take time to focus on the relevant details, we will have difficulty in our jobs, our studies, and our relationships. However, we should not become so focused on the details of life that we lose sight of the bigger picture. Imagine, for example, a portrait painter who takes great pains to depict each part of your face beautifully but fails to notice that she is painting most of them in the wrong places: your left ear appears where your nose should be, your nose has migrated to the middle of your forehead, and your lovely eyes gaze out at the viewer from inside your mouth. So while each part of your face looks even better than you had imagined, the total picture is positively monstrous. Similarly, when we fail to put the big pictures of our lives in order, they can be profoundly unsatisfying—even despite their apparent success.

Indeed, this failure to strive toward an overall purpose may in part explain the prevalence of depression in affluent societies. In the 1984 postscript to his famous work *Man's Search for Meaning*, Viktor Frankl—a psychologist, physician, philosopher, and Nazi concentration camp survivor—observed that "people have enough to live by but nothing to live for; they have the means but no meaning."[13] From his experience both in Auschwitz and as a therapist, he found that when people's meaning orientation is lost, focus on immediate pleasure takes over. For example, in the concentration camp those who gave up on life smoked their cigarettes rather than trading them for things like food or privileges. Among today's youth (particularly in the United States, where he had relocated), he suggested, many think they have no future and turn to the immediate gratification of drugs. In fact, he argued, there are three common reactions to a loss of the sense of purpose or meaning in life: depression, aggression, and addiction. He cites studies finding that over ninety percent of alcoholics and drug addicts believe their lives are meaningless.[14]

While Frankl acknowledged that depression isn't always caused by a sense of meaninglessness, he found that it still can be overcome through an awareness of meaning. For example, he tells a story of an elderly doctor who was suffering from depression after the death of his wife. Frankl asked him what his wife would have done had he passed away first; he replied that she would have suffered terribly from the loss. And that, as Frankl helped the man see, was the key to finding meaning in his own pain: "You see, Doctor, such a suffering has been spared her, and it was you who have spared her this suffering—to be sure, at the price that now you have to survive and mourn her."[15]

A second and related practical upshot of Aristotle's focus on *eudaimonia* is its connection to human nature. As we saw above, to achieve wellbeing or fulfillment is to be fulfilled in one's human nature or function. That function—the feature that differentiates humans from other beings—is our use of reason both in itself and in guiding our behavior. The connection between nature and fulfillment is both important and practical: we won't flourish by continually doing things for which we are not well suited. It is easy to see how this general rule applies to individual personalities and talents. For example, an introvert would be miserable in a sales or public relations career; an extrovert would be similarly unhappy to devote his workdays to updating spreadsheets or studying fruit flies.[16] The rule also applies to human nature in general: I will not live a good human life if I spend most of my energy pursuing activities and ends that aren't a good fit for me as a human being—things that ignore my natural reasoning ability or keep me from using it with excellence.[17] As Aristotle has argued, it's obvious that we all want to live well—the question is not *whether* but *how* to pursue *eudaimonia*. When we consider our human function, the answer to the "how" question becomes clearer. At the very least, we are able to rule out career and lifestyle choices that either (a) interfere directly with our ability to reason (e.g., a life of drug abuse), or (b) thwart or override our reason's ability to guide our actions, desires, and emotions.

As we noted above, *eudaimonia* is largely caused and constituted by excellences (virtues) of thought and character. So, as Aristotle suggests, "we must examine virtue; for that will perhaps also be a way to study *eudaimonia* better."[18] In addition to being a proximate means to *eudaimonia*, each type of excellence is very valuable and "choiceworthy in its own right."[19] In this book we'll focus—as our classical authors do—primarily on the moral excellences: the virtues of character.

Virtues of Character

The virtues of character, Aristotle explains, perfect and fulfill the part of the human psyche that can (but doesn't always) follow reason: the "appetitive" part—or, in more modern terms, our desires and emotions.[20] As Aristotle argues, our lives will be much better if we train our emotions and desires in "listening to reason as to a father" than if we do the opposite, enslaving reason to our nonrational whims and passions. When our appetitive part is guided by reason, we develop and strengthen those excellences of character that cause and partly constitute our flourishing or *eudaimonia* as a whole.

Virtues of character don't arise in us naturally. If virtues were natural to us, Aristotle explains, we wouldn't be able to form the vices that are their opposites. "Rather, we are adapted by nature to receive them, and are made perfect by habit."[21] So our repeated actions form corresponding habits; these habits form our character. We develop good habits such as generosity and courage, then, in just the way you'd expect: by consistently performing good actions—actions in accordance with good reasoning about things like giving and danger.

Although we'll consider several of these good habits—excellences of character—in more detail as the book progresses, for now let's note some important general patterns. As Aristotle and the Confucians independently observed, each virtue of character has not just one but two opposing vices: one of excess and the other of deficiency. The virtuous action or character trait is always found between these vices or extremes. It lies in the mean. Aristotle gives the following handy examples to illustrate the mean of virtue:

If, for instance, someone avoids and is afraid of everything, standing firm against nothing, he becomes cowardly; if he is afraid of nothing at all and goes to face everything, he becomes rash. Similarly, if he gratifies himself with every pleasure and abstains from none, he becomes intemperate; if he avoids them all, as boors do, he becomes some sort of insensible person. Temperance and bravery, then, are ruined by excess and deficiency, but preserved by the mean.[22]

As we can tell by thinking about these two example virtues, though, the "mean" of virtue is not identical with the arithmetical mean—courage is not halfway between fearing everything (even butterflies and paper clips) and fearing nothing (not even oncoming trains). Similarly, temperance is not halfway between never doing anything pleasant and nonstop sex, booze, and cheesecake.

To use an imperfect but helpful visual illustration, we can think of the mean of virtue as the high point on a skewed bell curve: It's at the top of the goodness scale, which runs up the y-axis; and, as represented by its position on the x-axis, it's somewhere between the maximum and minimum amounts of the relevant action or feeling—but not exactly in the middle. While the vice further from the virtue on the x-axis is at the lowest point on the y-axis, the other vice is not—representing the fact that one extreme (the virtue's commonsense opposite) is worse than the other. So we could represent the virtue of generosity as nearer the excess of giving using a skewed bell curve, as in figure 1.3.

Temperance or self-discipline, on the other hand, would be nearer the deficiency—with self-indulgence, its commonsense opposite, at the excess (see figure 1.4).

And we could make similar graphs for each of the other virtues of char-

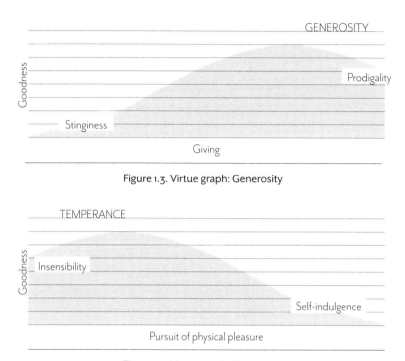

Figure 1.3. Virtue graph: Generosity

Figure 1.4. Virtue graph: Temperance

acter, keeping in mind that (1) they are skewed so that the long tail of the curve ends with the worse vice—normally the commonsense opposite of the virtue; (2) while the action or feeling will vary with each virtue, the y-axis always represents goodness (not frequency!); and (3) in addition to the right amount (as shown on the graph), virtuous behavior includes less-quantifiable things like the right time, place, and motive.

To sum up our account so far: We all want an excellent life, and excellent habits help us get there—and stay there. Each excellence of character (moral virtue) lies on a mean or right amount between the excess and the deficiency of a feeling or action. Once we figure out where the mean lies, we can acquire the relevant virtue (good habit or character trait) by repeatedly performing actions corresponding to that mean. How long does that take? Well, it depends on you, the habit you want to form, and the obstacles you face. The common notion that it takes twenty-one days for a habit to develop may be approximately right for small, easy habits like flossing our teeth; but don't lose heart if it takes much longer than that to form habits that are bigger and more complex—like the ones you need if you want to improve your character!

Aristotle has much more to say on both virtue in general and the particular ethical virtues; we'll consider parts of his account, and those of the other Socratics and the Confucians, as the book progresses. But already we can see how virtue makes our lives better. Being good is good for us—not just for those around us. According to Aristotle, there is not a sharp dividing line between behaving ethically and furthering my own interest, because virtue quite literally is excellence, and although developing a virtuous character requires some short-term sacrifices, it makes for an excellent human life. And as he observed, virtuous people enjoy performing virtuous activities. Once virtue has been developed, exercising it is not only objectively good but also subjectively pleasant—not in the instant-gratification way we might find cheesecake pleasant, but in a much deeper and more valuable way. (That is, even if there is not quantitatively more pleasure in exercising virtue than in eating cheesecake, virtue brings a qualitatively better pleasure.) As Confucian philosopher Xunzi put it, when someone "has truly learned to love what is right, his eyes will take greater pleasure in it than in the five colors; his ears will take greater pleasure than in the five sounds; his mouth will take greater pleasure than in the five flavors; and his mind will feel keener delight than in the possession of the world."[23] Thus, as we'll see in the stories of my interviewees throughout this book, the virtuous life is clearly worth pursuing, even for those of us who are motivated (at least at first) primarily by the prospect of the "prize."

Aristotle's Advice to Start Our Journey

Up to this point in Aristotle's account, becoming virtuous may sound almost suspiciously easy: it's good for us, it's (eventually) pleasant, and it's as simple as forming the habit of letting our reason guide our emotions and desires. But, at least for most of us, life experience tells us that developing virtue is far from easy. Was living virtuously that much easier for Aristotle, or was he just oblivious to life's challenges?

As it turns out, neither: Aristotle knew as well as any of us that achieving ethical excellence is hard—especially at the beginning. After explaining that a virtue of character is a mean between excess and deficiency in feelings and actions, he makes this observation:

> That is why it is also hard work to be excellent. For in each case it is hard work to find the intermediate; for instance, not everyone, but only one who knows [how to calculate it], finds the midpoint in a circle. So also getting angry, or giving and spending money, is easy and everyone can do it; but doing it to the right person, in the right amount, at the right time, for the right end, and in the right way is no longer easy, nor can everyone do it. Hence doing these things well is rare, praiseworthy, and fine.[24]

So, it appears, being virtuous is not nearly as easy as one might have thought. In fact, it appears nearly impossible: How can we possibly get the person, amount, manner, time, and reason right every time—or even enough of the time to form a virtuous habit? Fortunately, however, our prospects for good character aren't as bleak as they might seem in the quote above. In the rest of this chapter, we'll consider Aristotle's practical advice for achieving ethical excellence.

First, Avoid the Worst-Case Scenario

Like each ethical virtue, moral development, by Aristotle's account, is found in an intermediate position between two extremes. We might call the relevant extremes "suspiciously easy" and "practically impossible," and we might label the mean "appropriately challenging." Throughout the *Nicomachean Ethics*, Aristotle provides several good pieces of advice for our moral development; indeed, immediately after the passage just quoted he gives the first such practical tip: "Anyone who aims at the intermediate condition must first of all steer clear of the more contrary extreme … for one extreme is more in error, the other less. Since, therefore, it is hard to hit the intermediate extremely accurately, the second-best tack, as they say, is to take the lesser of the evils."

At first, we might be tempted to dismiss that advice as belonging to the "suspiciously easy" category: Why settle for second best? Is Aristotle—supposedly one of the greatest ethical minds of all time—really suggesting that we just go for the not-quite-as-bad vice and call it a day? Fortunately, the answer to that second question is definitely "no": The avoid-the-worse-extreme strategy (a) is preliminary—as suggested by the advice to *first of all* avoid the more contrary extreme—and (b) probably will not result in your hitting the less-contrary extreme anyway. In the following paragraphs we'll take a closer look at each of these two points.

To see why Aristotle suggests avoidance of the more contrary extreme as a first step toward acquiring virtue, recall that this extreme generally is both *much* worse than the other and much more common: that's why it's the commonsense "opposite" of the virtue. For example, recall the generosity graph from the last section. As we saw, prodigality is much closer than stinginess to the mean of generosity on both axes—its actions are more like those of generosity (hence their proximity on the *x*-axis), and it is correspondingly higher (represented on the *y*-axis) than stinginess in goodness. So heading toward prodigality is a reasonable preliminary strategy: it is fairly close to generosity, which (as we realize all along) is the real goal. Further, the fact that the worse extreme is more common—along with the fact that most of the possible ways of being are closer to the worse extreme than the better one (as represented by the amount of space to the left of that virtue on the graph)—makes it quite likely that one starting on the path of virtue development will improve ethically by heading in the direction of the less-bad extreme rather than in the other direction, or, as Aristotle put it, by first of all steering clear of the more contrary extreme.

Further, for at least three reasons, a person employing this aim-for-the-less-bad-extreme strategy is unlikely to succeed in developing that less-bad vice. First of all, he or she may not even succeed in *aiming* at the extreme: to someone near the worse extreme, the mean will likely be indistinguishable from the less-bad extreme. Sticking for the moment with the example of generosity and its opposing vices, to someone who tends to be rather stingy, the mean of generosity will look a lot like prodigality—both because prodigality really is fairly close to the mean of generosity and because stinginess is so far from both of those qualities that the stingy person is unable to see either of them clearly. Consider, for example, someone like the character Scrooge from Charles Dickens's *A Christmas Carol*: to someone too miserly to heat his house properly despite his wealth, a generous gift would seem ridiculously extravagant.

Second, even if she or he does succeed in aiming at the less-bad extreme, someone tending (as most of us do) toward the worse extreme will find progressing toward that less-bad target quite unpleasant—thus, she or he will likely be deterred well before arrival. We can see this deterrent effect quite easily with the case of generosity. If, like Scrooge, I tend toward stinginess (even though I like to think I'm not as far gone as he was), I prefer to keep my goods for the purpose of enjoying them myself; so I'll be pained at giving away even non-necessities—I'll be very unlikely to go yet further and start giving away the things I really need.

Finally, if (as Aristotle presumably hopes) one aiming for the less-bad extreme does succeed in making progress toward it, he or she will have to pass the mean on the way there. But upon becoming habituated to the mean, he or she has developed the relevant virtue; and having the virtue, he or she is in the right state to recognize that virtue. And recognizing the virtue for what it is, he or she will have no reason to continue progressing (or regressing?) toward vice. One who has finally succeeded in the ultimate goal of attaining virtue will be wholly unmotivated to pursue the intermediate goal; doing so would be not just unnecessary but downright detrimental.

Set Realistic Expectations

Although the "first, aim for the less-bad extreme" strategy doesn't represent a call to mediocrity, Aristotle does caution us against expecting perfection. Near the very end of his practical advice in book 2 of the *Nicomachean Ethics*, he gives the comforting assurance that "we are not blamed if we deviate a little in excess or deficiency from doing well, but only if we deviate a long way."[25] As he has already acknowledged, the precise mean of virtue can be difficult to determine; of course, it can be even more difficult to achieve.

Like Aristotle, Confucian philosopher Mencius discourages us from forming the expectation that we'll become moral saints or heroes overnight—if we try to force our character to develop too rapidly, our budding virtues may wither and die under the pressure of unreasonable demands: "One must work at it, but do not assume success. One should not forget the heart, but neither should one 'help' it grow. Do not be like the man from Song. Among the people of the state of Song there was a farmer who, concerned lest his sprouts not grow, pulled on them. Obliviously, he returned home and said to his family, 'Today I am worn out. I helped the sprouts to grow.' His son rushed out and looked at them. The sprouts were withered."[26] An interesting analogy for the balance of nurturing—but not pulling—the sprouts of our budding virtues might be found in psychoanalyst Donald Winnicott's famous discussion of the "good-enough mother": a mother (or caregiver) who is genuinely devoted to her child but doesn't aim to be the "perfect mother" who immediately grants all of her child's desires—such a mother allows enough frustration of the child's desires to allow him to develop independently as a person.[27]

Further Advice for Achieving Excellence

Aristotle gives two additional pieces of helpful advice at the end of his general account of virtue. First, to maximize our chances at attaining virtue, we must "examine what we ourselves drift into easily."[28] We will know our own tendencies, Aristotle says, "from the pleasure or pain that arises in us" when we perform or consider the activities corresponding to each virtue or vice. To develop virtue, we must set off in the direction that is opposite of our current negative tendencies: "for if we pull far away from error, as they do in straightening bent wood, we shall reach the intermediate condition."[29] To take just one example from my interviews, Cathey Brown (whose story we'll see in chapter 13) learned that she, like several of her family members, had a tendency toward alcoholism. After achieving sobriety herself ("straightening" through a twelve-step program), she started Rainbow Days, an alcohol and drug prevention program for at-risk youth. Through that program, Brown has helped hundreds of children who (because of family history and other factors) were at risk of becoming "bent" toward alcoholism as well.

Second, in pursuing virtue we should "beware above all of pleasure and its sources; for we are already biased in its favor when we come to judge it." People who are physically sick—or just habitually eat poorly—may have unreliable perceptions regarding the quality of food; similarly, if our character is lacking, we may judge pleasure incorrectly by assuming it is good in situations in which it is not. We also may err by finding things "pleasant" merely because they distract us from pain or distress—not because we're enjoying the attainment of some worthwhile good. In fact, we may even be mistaken regarding whether the activity to which we're drawn will be pleasant *at all*. To return to the example of poor eating, if I decide to go ahead and eat that tasty-looking pizza in the break room even though I've already had lunch, I may quickly find that doing so isn't pleasant after all: in addition to making me uncomfortably full, it doesn't even taste very good.

A related lesson, then, is that to attain virtue we need to take the right approach to pleasure. As Aristotle noted in book 2, the prospect of pleasure entices us to do bad actions, just as fear of pain motivates us to omit good ones. In book 10, Aristotle reminds us that although pleasure is *a* good, it's not *the* good. It is a "consequent end"—what we might call a "bonus" or a good side-effect—of achieving some other good. Although we are rightly pleased that we have attained the good thing we were pursuing (e.g., a promotion at work or an "A" on our history exam), the pleasure we get from doing so is neither the good thing itself nor its achievement. This principle applies to *the* good as well: although the excellent life (*eudaimonia*), because it is the highest good achievable, is the most pleasant life, the pleasure that results from it should not be confused with the goal itself. (Unfortunately, even though we recognize at an intellectual level that pleasure is not *the* good, or even an appropriate object of pursuit in a particular situation, our attraction to pleasure can lead us to pursue it despite our better judgment. We'll discuss that pitfall—and how to avoid it—later in this book.)

As we have seen in this chapter, achieving the mean of the virtues of character is difficult. But Aristotle has given us some helpful advice regarding the avoidance of a few main pitfalls. To avoid the worst-case scenario of developing the worse vice, we can start by aiming for the less-bad one. In fact, doing so can be a helpful preliminary strategy for attaining the virtuous mean. As we come to recognize and aim for that mean, we next need to beware of unrealistic expectations in our ethical development: we should keep in mind that, although the mean does indeed represent the good state for which we should aim, failure to hit it *exactly* is not immoral or blameworthy. Especially at first, good-enough is, well, good enough. Also, since we are all susceptible to pleasure, we need to be particularly aware of its tendency to unduly influence—and even override—our practical reasoning. A final starter lesson might be linked to the Socratic dictate "know thyself": if we are self-aware, we can be on guard against the temptations to which we are especially susceptible. With Aristotle's starter advice in mind, then, we're ready to turn to the more in-depth ideas and examples in the rest of this book. We'll start with a consideration that may serve to improve our self-awareness: our innate potential to become ethically good—or not-so-good.

Chapter 2

PRACTICAL FOUNDATIONS

Recognizing Your Potential

DON SCHOENDORFER seemed to have it all. He was a successful bio-medical engineer with a PhD from MIT, numerous patents, and a good job. His goals were similar to those of most people in his social circle: become even more successful, make even more money, and send his kids to Ivy League colleges. But after his daughter developed an eating disorder that proved resistant to treatment, Schoendorfer and his wife experienced a profound change of perspective: a shift in priorities away from material success and toward more meaningful pursuits, along with a religious conversion toward dependence on God to help them with things beyond their control. After his conversion experience, Schoendorfer felt a responsibility to help his fellow human beings, but at first he wasn't sure how to go about it:

> While going to church, I was learning a lot of stuff, but then on Monday when I'd go back to work things weren't really different. So I tried volunteering as a school tutor. We have a lot of Hispanics in Orange County, close to the border of Mexico; they're having a hard time conforming even to our language and definitely having a hard time in school. I figured, I have a math and physics background; I can help these kids. Well, they're really good to work with, and they're great kids just to talk to, but their

language skills were very basic, and the only value that I had there was just to sort of be friends with them.

I wasn't doing a very good job at tutoring, so I figured maybe I could mentor some kids. And so they lined me up with a couple of kids, and one of them had been in and out of jail and he was sleeping in the backseat of a car. I went to visit him, and the last thing he wanted was some fifty-five-year-old engineer who didn't have a clue what life was like living in the hood. And so it was almost like one day I got this message from God saying, "Don, what are you doing? You hate psychology. Do you remember how you barely passed that class? You're an introvert; you don't like being with people. You're terrible at this stuff. Why don't you use your tools that I gave you?"[1]

Schoendorfer eventually did find a way to use his unique ability in biomedical engineering to do great things for other people; I'll tell you about it later in this chapter. But first I'll ask you to consider a philosophical question. We are accustomed to speaking of individual potential when it comes to non-moral traits like strength, musicality, or mathematical ability. I'm sure you weren't surprised to hear that Schoendorfer had abilities—abilities most people lack—in engineering. But what about our character, our potential for ethical development? Should we expect to find individual differences there, too? To answer that question, let's first look at our shared potential as humans, and then consider whether we might have unique individual potential beyond that baseline.

The Potential We Share

Among the most famous of Confucian philosopher Mencius's recorded conversations concerns a certain king's potential to become a benevolent and effective leader—a "true King." As the king knows, despite Mencius's patient instruction, thus far he has fallen far short of true rulership; he is not optimistic. But Mencius sees a glimmer of hope. He recalls a conversation reported by one of the king's attendants. Upon seeing an ox being led to slaughter so that its blood could be used to consecrate a new bell, the king had commanded, "Spare it. I cannot bear its frightened appearance, like an innocent going to the execution ground." From this report, Mencius concludes that all is not lost: the king has potential to rule benevolently. When the king asks why he made this inference, Mencius explains:

> Suppose there were someone who reported to Your Majesty, "My strength is sufficient to lift five hundred pounds, but not sufficient to lift one feather. My eyesight is sufficient to examine the tip of an autumn hair, but I cannot see a wagon of firewood." Would Your Majesty accept that? ... In the present case your kindness is sufficient to reach animals, but the effects do not reach the commoners. How is this different from the examples I just gave? Hence, one fails to lift a feather only because one does not use one's strength. One fails to see a wagon of firewood only because one does not use one's eyesight. The commoners fail to receive care only because one does not use one's kindness. Hence, Your Majesty fails to become King because you do not act, not because you are unable to act.[2]

As we see, the glimmer of hope that Mencius found in the king came with a sting of rebuke. The king's *ability* to govern with kindness directly results in a *responsibility* to do so—a responsibility he is consistently failing to fulfill.[3] As we'll discuss later in this book, Mencius offers the king some practical advice for living up to his potential—advice that applies to all of us. For now, we'll notice that honest self-examination should lead to a recognition of both our weaknesses and our strengths—and, with respect to our strengths, further recognition of our as-yet-unfulfilled potential.

Mencius isn't claiming that there is anything exceptional about the king's potential for greatness. All of us have the potential to become highly virtuous, because we all share in human nature—and that nature, Mencius argues, is fundamentally good. He describes each human heart as having the beginnings, or "sprouts," of four important virtues:

> The reason why I say that all humans have hearts that are not unfeeling toward others is this. Suppose someone suddenly saw a child about to fall into a well: anyone in such a situation would have a feeling of alarm and compassion—not because one sought to get in good with the child's parents, not because one wanted fame among one's neighbors and friends, and not because one would dislike the sound of the child's cries. From this we can see that if one is without the feeling of compassion then one is

not human. If one is without the feeling of disdain, one is not human. If one is without the feeling of approval and disapproval, one is not human. The feeling of compassion is the sprout of benevolence. The feeling of disdain is the sprout of righteousness. The feeling of deference is the sprout of propriety. The feeling of approval and disapproval is the sprout of wisdom. People having these four sprouts is like their having four limbs. To have these four sprouts, yet to claim that one is incapable (of virtue), is to steal from oneself.[4]

There is great insight in Mencius's description of a defeatist attitude about developing virtue—telling ourselves that ethical excellence is too difficult and we might as well aim lower—as stealing from ourselves. Cutting corners in ethical development really is similar to doing so in other areas of life: although by failing to reach our potential we'll certainly fail to make the positive impact we could have made on others, we ourselves are the primary persons negatively affected by our falling short.

As we notice in the passage above, Mencius doesn't claim that we are born with fully developed virtues. A little later in his conversation, when a disciple brings up examples of sages and tyrants who seem to have dramatically different natures, he puts it like this: "As for what [people] are inherently, they can become good. This is what I mean by calling their natures good. As for their becoming not good, this is not the fault of their potential.... Some differ [in ethical development] from others by two, five, or countless times— this is because they cannot fathom their potentials."[5] As we saw in chapter 1, developing this potential requires care and nourishment but not force:

Those who abandon them, thinking it will not help, are those who do not weed their sprouts. Those who "help" them grow are those who pull on the sprouts. Not only does this not help, but it even harms them.[6]

The care that helps or harms our development of virtue, according to Mencius, takes two main forms: our own actions and our environment. (However, these influences aren't entirely separate: our environment, at least when we are adults, is in large part the result of our choices and actions.) Ever fond of agricultural analogies, Mencius compares the destruction of our potential through our own choices to the repeated destruction of vegetation on a once-beautiful mountain that now appears barren: "When we consider what is present in people, could they truly lack the hearts of benevolence and righteousness? The way they discard their genuine hearts is like the hatchets and axes in relation to the trees. With them besieging it day by day, can it remain beautiful?"[7]

Similarly, he compares negative environmental influences on moral development to the effects of frost: "Do not be surprised at the king's failure to be wise. Even though it may be the easiest growing thing in the world, if it gets one day of warmth and ten days of frost, there has never been anything that is capable of growing. It is seldom that I have an audience with the king, and when I withdraw, those who 'freeze' him come. What can I do with the sprouts that are there?"[8]

The Downside of Our Potential

Unfortunately, as rival Confucian philosopher Xunzi took great pains to point out, human nature doesn't always seem as attractive a picture as Mencius portrays. In fact, Xunzi describes our nature as outright evil. By "evil" Xunzi doesn't necessarily mean cruel or malicious—but he does mean that many of our natural tendencies, if not corrected, will lead to vice:

> The nature of man is such that he is born with a fondness for profit. If he indulges this fondness, it will lead him into wrangling and strife, and all sense of courtesy and humility will disappear. He is born with feelings of envy and hate, and if he indulges these, they will lead him into violence and crime, and all sense of loyalty and good faith will disappear. Man is born with the desires of the eyes and ears, with a fondness for beautiful sights and sounds. If he indulges these, they will lead him into license and wantonness.... Hence, any man who follows his nature and indulges his emotions will inevitably become involved in wrangling and strife, will violate the forms and rules of society, and will end as a criminal.[9]

Xunzi goes on to compare our nature to warped wood and blunt metal. Like those inferior materials, what we need to correct our nature is a lot of work—through rules, teachers, and conscientious efforts to follow them. What Mencius might describe as weeding (or, if taken to excess, pulling) our sprouts, then, Xunzi would likely call sharpening our blunt instruments or straightening our warped planks.

In theory, then, Xunzi doesn't disagree with Mencius's claim that we are all capable of becoming good. As he acknowledges, "any man in the street has the essential faculties needed to understand benevolence, righteousness, and proper standards, and the potential ability to put them into practice."[10] But this theoretical potential is a far cry from practical ease—as Xunzi puts it, "a person with two feet is theoretically capable of walking to every corner of the earth," but that doesn't mean it's easy, or perhaps even possible, for me to accomplish that feat in practice.[11] And walking the path to virtue, if Xunzi is correct, involves fighting the strong wind of our nature at every step. As I'll argue in the next section, the most reasonable assessment of human nature seems to be that it's a mixed bag: while we do (as Mencius argued) have natural tendencies that, if nurtured, can grow into virtues, we also (as Xunzi observed) have some innate tendencies that should *not* be nurtured, lest they become vices.

Psychological Support for Mencius's Theory *—and Xunzi's*

When babies approach a year of age, in my fairly extensive experience (I've hung out with dozens of babies, including my own), they like to engage in an activity known in my family as the "Sharing Game." Though delightful for an infant, the game is maddeningly simple for anyone else. It consists of handing a small, baby-safe object back and forth, cheerfully saying "Here you go" and "Thank you" until the baby gets bored. And although an infant of that age is supposed to have an attention span of only about a minute, this game can go on for almost half an hour—if the older player's patience holds out!

Babies' affinity for the Sharing Game would seem to be evidence for Mencius's view—from infancy, we are able and willing to be kind and generous, right? Further, as soon as they can walk, babies and toddlers want to help with routine household tasks like sweeping the floor and putting things away. My youngest child was especially keen on turning the lights on and off for us—not noticing that it was more work for us to carry her to the light switch than to flip it ourselves.

But of course, infants and toddlers aren't known only for their generosity and helpfulness. As Augustine famously noted in his autobiography *Confessions*, they tend to be quite demanding.[12] And as I've noticed with those same babies and toddlers who like the Sharing Game and housework, young children are also prone to hitting, taking toys away, and throwing tantrums. And even the Sharing Game has an evil twin called the "Taunting Game": it's played just like the Sharing Game, except that the baby only pretends she's going to share, yanking the object back at the last moment and laughing gleefully at the other player's misfortune—or perhaps just at her own cleverness. So there is definitely some anecdotal data to support Xunzi's theory too.

And speaking of data, a series of fascinating studies in the infant cognition lab at Yale University has shown similarly mixed results regarding our ethical starting place. On the one hand, babies well under a year old clearly prefer to be with and to imitate those who are kind and helpful toward others,[13] and children as young as three years old actively intervene when someone else is being harmed.[14] So we seem to be born with some tendency toward developing virtues like generosity and justice. On the other hand, babies favor those who share their preferences—even very trivial ones such as dry cereal versus graham crackers or yellow versus orange mittens—suggesting we're hard-wired to adopt an us-versus-them mentality.[15] And as researchers (and parents everywhere) have observed, young children have a strong tendency to favor themselves in distributions of goods.[16] So while we may have *some* good in our human nature on which to build, clearly we're not natural-born saints and heroes.

Using Our Individual Abilities for Good

Perhaps Mencius would describe Don Schoendorfer's shift in priorities as a weeding or thawing of his sprouts of kindness and generosity. Like everyone, Shoendorfer possessed them all along, but they couldn't grow much when he focused most of his attention on his career and finances. Once he made more room for relational and spiritual pursuits, however, his sprouts began to flourish. But he still wrestled with the question of how he—an introvert with engineering skills—could best exercise his newly discovered ethical qualities. As it turned out, he had encountered the answer decades earlier:

We went on a vacation to Morocco in 1979, and that was the first experience I had with poverty in the developing world. There's this woman crawling, trying to cross the dirt road into Tétouan—and this is a decent-sized city in Morocco—and trying not to be stepped on and trying not to be noticed. And everybody was doing their job; it was almost like nobody wanted to notice her, to recognize her presence. And it was like, "This is appalling; I've never seen somebody crawling on the ground like that before; and obviously—she's not begging—she must be doing that because she has to." And … I'm thinking, "Can we find a wheelchair for her? Where would I even look for one?" And next thing I know, she's gone, and all she wanted to be was to be invisible. And in Morocco, this is nothing surprising to them; they're used to this, so they weren't offering any assistance either, and I just kind of had to walk away from that whole scene.

Thinking back to that experience, Schoendorfer wondered how he might use his ability in biomedical engineering to provide free wheelchairs for people in the developing world. First, he researched what was already being done. In short, distribution of new or refurbished wheelchairs was expensive and inefficient, which meant that only a fraction of a percent of the need was being met. It was time for a new approach. From his background in the medical industry, he knew that the key to increasing efficiency was mass production and standardization—more specifically, given his limited resources, repurposing of components already mass produced for another product. So Schoendorfer designed and manufactured one hundred inexpensive, easily assembled wheelchairs using bicycle wheels and resin outdoor chairs he'd found on sale for four dollars each.

After meeting with initial resistance to his idea from both colleagues and on-the-ground organizations, he managed to bring just four of his wheelchairs to India on a medical mission trip. On the first day of his group's clinic, Schoendorfer—the only member of the team who was not a doctor or a nurse—was setting up tables and moving supplies. Then he noticed two people walking toward the clinic, struggling to carry something—or, as it turned out, someone: their son with cerebral palsy. Schoendorfer wasn't able to speak to the family and had no translator, but he set one of his wheelchairs in front of them. Immediately, the mother put the young man in the chair, managed to secure him in it, and began pushing him—first just rocking forward and back, then making figure eights, then pushing him farther, even successfully navigating a curb. And all of this with no instruction or training at all. His wheelchair was a resounding success!

That success, along with the unexpected loss of his job due to the bankruptcy of his employer, led Schoendorfer to a new chapter in his career and his life. He founded the Free Wheelchair Mission, which by 2017 had distributed over one million wheelchairs in the developing world. And he has found that he is helping people with more than just their physical disabilities:

They also have a cultural disability, a sociological disability, and a spiritual disability, because the explanation for the cause of the disability is not scientific. It's not based on medicine; it's based on black magic. "It's a curse": That's the only explanation that people can come up with that everyone else buys. And so there's a reason for this society not to help a disabled person—because it's a curse. And then the person with a disability hears this and the family hears this and they believe it, so they keep their loved ones alive, but they try to hide them. They don't want people to know, because it's a reflection on them, and so they're embarrassed.

And we give wheelchairs to people, and all of a sudden we get this person out of their home and neighbors come over and say "Where'd he come from? I didn't know that they had a child twenty-four years ago." And the family's done their best, but they kind of constrained their life to keep it a secret and not tell anybody. So they're not allowed to join the society, there's a limitation in the family. And then this whole thing about it being a curse: "There's a God, but the God that we have doesn't like you." So they have this spiritual disability, so it seems very appropriate for us that a Christian missionary would take this chair and try to break that curse. You get somebody who's living in a dark room and who's going to die in a dark room, and you give them a wheelchair and it cost us eighty dollars—it's a significant thing.

Schoendorfer has used his unique skills and abilities in biomedical engineering toward ethical ends, exercising kindness and generosity through the design, manufacture, and distribution of wheelchairs to those who need them most. In doing so, he provides us with an excellent model for using our own unique talents and abilities in ethically virtuous ways. But do we each have unique potential for virtue itself? I don't think the answer to that question is clear from Schoendorfer's story. He clearly developed and exercised his potential for generosity by using his unique strengths, but that doesn't imply that his potential *for generosity itself* was different from anyone else's.

But that's not to say that some people *aren't* ethically gifted, so to speak, with greater-than-average potential for—or, at least, tendency to develop—particular virtues. To see what I mean, let's look at one more example.

An Example of Unique Ethical Potential?

Unlike Schoendorfer, Cathy Heying knew from an early age that she wanted a career in human services and social justice. After graduating from college with a degree in social work, Heying accepted jobs as a caseworker for elderly people in rural Appalachia and as an assistant at a free legal clinic before landing her dream job as Director of Social Justice at her church. As with many churches—and probably more than most because of its location in a low-income urban neighborhood in Minneapolis—people would frequently drop by seeking assistance with personal and financial crises. Heying and the other staff would do their best to help, but she had a nagging sense that someone—maybe even she—should do more:

> And so many people were saying, "Can I get $300 or $500, because my car broke down and I work second shift, and there's no bus that runs when I get off at 11:00 o'clock on Saturday night. If I don't get the car fixed, I'm not going to be able to get to work, and I'm going to lose my job, and I just got out of the shelter and I don't want to go back into the shelter." So we would help them if we could, but I just kept thinking, "Somebody should do something about this. We're a big enough city; why don't we have free or low-cost car repair for low-income folks?" I was still paying off grad school student loans, and I had a completely happy life, but I kept thinking about car repair.[17]

Also unlike Schoendorfer, Heying *didn't* have a natural aptitude or affinity for the everyday, practical aspects of the work she had in mind: She was a social worker and public policy advocate with no car repair experience. But she saw an unmet need; so, reluctantly, at age thirty-eight she enrolled in an automotive repair program at a local technical college:

> It was absolutely terrifying. I walked in the door, and it's me and forty 18-year-old boys. [Laughs.] No idea what to do whatsoever, no idea. And I knew nothing about cars. I mean, I'd changed the oil in my motorcycle and a few things like that, but it was a huge learning curve. My brain does not work like that—honestly, it was like, "Can we just talk about how the cars are feeling? Can I facilitate a group about this?" [Laughs again.] It was so hard for me, and that was a huge blow to my pride—because I was all cocky, like, "I have a master's degree; I can go to tech school," and I just got my ass kicked. And I cried so many times, and I was *this* close to quitting so many times, because I was embarrassed and I felt stupid and I could not get it. And to this day, I would say I'm not a good tech. I mean, it does not come easily to me; I have to be like, "How exactly does the starter work inside again?" and "How do we diagnose this?" I have to work really hard at it.

After graduating from the automotive program and gaining a bit of experience in the field, Heying opened The Lift Garage, a nonprofit shop that provides affordable car repair for people with low incomes. Interestingly, she finds in her shop frequent opportunities to use her social work background. In addition to car repair, Heying and her team take care to provide welcoming hospitality and a listening ear: "It's so much more than fixing cars. I always say that we're social workers and grief counselors and financial counselors and resource specialists, and that we fix cars on the side. It's complicated, and people are coming to us with lots and lots of needs. Their car is just the presenting problem."

That preview of Heying's story (at which we will look in more depth in chapter 19) brings us back to the question with which we began this chapter: Do individual people have differing inherent qualities or traits that affect their potential to develop ethical virtues? For example, might Cathy Heying's development of the kindness and generosity that led her to sacrifice a comfortable and rewarding career to take on the challenge of The Lift Garage be explained by a greater-than-average natural inclination toward compassion?

Socratic philosopher Cicero argues that the answer to the general question is "yes"—at least to some extent. Like both Mencius and Aristotle, he argues that we are all potentially virtuous; he appeals to our nature as a standard and teacher of what is virtuous and "becoming" for human beings. He begins with our common nature: "Since the parts of consistency, moderation, self-restraint, [and] modesty are assigned to us by Nature, and since the same Nature teaches us not to be indifferent as to the manner of our conduct toward men, we may thus see how broad is the scope, both of that becomingness which belongs to all virtue, and of this which is made manifest in each several kind of virtue."[18] While we all share this common nature as human beings, Cicero argues, each of us also has an individual nature that may have a stronger tendency toward excellence in some areas than in others:

It is to be borne in mind that we are endowed by nature as it were with two characters, one of which is common to us with other men, inasmuch as we all partake of reason, and of the traits which raise us above the brutes, from which all that is right and becoming is derived, and from which we seek the method of ascertaining our duty; while the other is that which is assigned to each of us individually. For as in bodies there are great dissimilarities—we see some excelling in speed for the race, others in strength for wrestling; also in personal appearance, some have dignity, others grace—so in minds there are even greater diversities....

Every one ought to hold fast, not his faults, but his peculiarities, so as to retain more easily the becomingness which is the subject of our inquiry. We ought, indeed, to act in such a way as shall be in no respect repugnant to our common human nature; yet, holding this sacred, let us follow our individual nature.[19]

Interestingly, Cicero later adds to common and individual nature two more "characters" or "natures": what is given or imposed on us externally (e.g., wealth, honor, and even certain positions of authority), and what we choose to do or pursue (including careers, hobbies, and even character traits). Occasionally, circumstances require pursuits that don't fit well with our indi-

vidual natures—in such cases, we simply must do the best we can. But to
a great extent the activities we pursue are up to us; we should take care to
select the ones that don't violate our common human nature (by leading us
astray from what our reason knows is true and good) and that fit well with
our individual nature. "It will be each man's duty to weigh well what are his
own peculiar traits of character, and to keep them in serviceable condition,
and not to desire to try how far another man's peculiarities may be becoming to him; for that is most becoming to each man which is most peculiarly
his own. Let each of us, then, know his own capacities and proclivities, and
show himself a discriminating judge of his own excellences and defects."[20]

Finding Our Strengths

How do we know our excellences and defects—particularly those related to
our character traits? We might start with the self-examination methods we'll
discuss in chapter four: for example, daily self-questioning, seeking honest
feedback from close friends, and taking opposing views and critiques seriously. Establishing a habit of reflection and receptivity to feedback is essential for a better understanding of ourselves.

In addition to these everyday reflection aids, occasionally we might consider seeking more formal and systematic feedback. Psychologists Christopher Peterson and Martin Seligman, leaders in the positive psychology
movement, have developed an assessment for that purpose: the VIA (Values
in Action) Character Strengths survey. They and their colleagues have made
the survey available free of charge online.[21] Its purpose is to help people identify their greatest ethical strengths—and to encourage them to use those
strengths in their daily lives, including as a means to compensate for their
weaknesses.[22]

Peterson and Seligman made considerable effort to provide a theoretical
background for their classification of character strengths. Utilizing philosophical, theological, and literary depictions of virtues as well as feedback
from numerous other researchers in various fields, they classified twenty-
four different character strengths under the headings of six (nearly) universally recognized key virtues: wisdom, justice, courage, temperance, humanity, and transcendence. Some of the strengths—for example, gratitude and
kindness—are themselves typically recognized as important ethical virtues;

others—for example, leadership and humor—are not.[23] What *does* unite the various character strengths, according to Peterson and Seligman, is a "family resemblance" based on their meeting most or all of ten criteria, including contribution to fulfillment and the good life, desirability both in themselves and for their benefits, and presence in the lives of obviously virtuous exemplars.[24]

As Peterson, Seligman, and their colleagues at the VIA Institute on Character have noted in several studies, character strengths can be strong indicators and predictors of a person's self-perceived wellbeing. For example, one study found that among adolescents other-directed strengths predicted fewer symptoms of depression; transcendence-related strengths predicted greater life satisfaction.[25] And in a sample of almost four thousand adults, several character strengths were found to be highly related to life satisfaction—including hope, gratitude, and love.[26] In fact, across several studies, these strengths as measured using the VIA inventory consistently show a strong relationship with life satisfaction.[27]

Peterson and Seligman argue that if we recognize and use our individual character strengths, they can help us improve—and make up for—our not-so-strong areas. For example, suppose I'm not naturally very brave: I am disinclined to take risks, even for the sake of an important good. If I am prudent and creative, I can usually find ways to promote important goods without taking scary risks—and, with a bit of effort, I can put my prudence and creativity to work thinking of gradual ways to work up to developing bravery. Or suppose I'm not very generous by nature; giving up my time or money usually seems undesirable or even painful. If I am grateful and loving, I can start by devoting more of my resources to those whom I love or who have benefited me in the past; I can gradually work my way outward to those to whom I'm less close or less indebted.[28]

Another strategy for recognizing and working toward our potential for virtue focuses on the way our identities might develop. Mencius, we recall, says that by "human nature is good" he means that we all have the potential to *become* good; Xunzi begins his essay on human nature by describing the vices we'll develop if we let our natural desires call the shots. In analyzing our potential to build on our nature and become good—or not-so-good—Mencius and Xunzi are discussing what psychologists have come to call our "possible identities" or "future selves": "that part of self-concept focused on the self one might become."[29] In particular, the rival Confucian theories seem to address the "ideal self" and the "feared self"—the identity we most hope for and the one we most dread. Oyserman and James helpfully summarize the research in this area: people with more balanced future identities—that is, people who think about both positive and negative ways in which they might develop—tend to be more well-adjusted and successful.

When considering our strengths and how we might develop them if we wish to become more like our ideal self, perhaps we should pay more attention to how we imagine ourselves in the future. When you picture what sort of person you'd like to be at the next stage of your life, what characteristics does that ideal self have? And how are those traits related to the traits you have already? As Oyserman and James explain, the motivational impact a future self has on our current behavior depends on three known factors: connection, congruence, and interpretation of difficulty. First, the more connected we feel to our ideal future self, the more motivated we are to become that self—that's why I suggested thinking about the next stage of your life rather than about the distant future. The more clearly we can envision the future and the closer it seems to the present, the stronger its motivational power. Second, the better the fit between our ideal future self and important aspects of our current identity, the more likely we will be to work toward achieving the ideal—and, I think, the stronger the evidence that the ideal self really *does* represent our individual strengths and potential. So, for example, suppose your ideal future self is a collaborative team player, but you and your social group have always prided yourselves on being cutthroat competitors. In that case, you may need to do a little more soul-searching regarding who you are and what you really want before you determine that collaboration is—or even reasonably *could* be—your personal strength. Third, and related to both connection and congruence, we're most likely to make the effort necessary to realize our potential when we perceive that task to be challenging but not *too* challenging: If we see the attainment of our ideal as a sure thing, we may well put off indefinitely the work needed to make it happen. But if we see it as nearly impossible, we may just give up before we even start.[30]

On a final and related note, as I learned in a philosophy class long ago, if some scenario is *actual* then, necessarily, it is also *possible*. (I think I knew that intuitively all along, and you probably did too—if something *weren't* possible, how could it actually happen? But the class gave me the terminology to express it.) If we apply this simple principle to our potential to become ethically excellent, it suggests an equally simple strategy for discovering our potential for particular virtues: try exercising them. If you wonder whether you have a natural tendency toward kindness, make a point of trying to be kind—see if it comes more easily than you'd expected. If so, great—consider it a strength and work to develop it further, perhaps using it to shore up your weaker areas. If not, well, keep working on it anyway: we all have *some* potential to develop it, and—as philosophers, psychologists, and ordinary people in all times and places have found[31]—it's worth the effort.

Chapter 3

PERSONAL FOUNDATIONS

Willpower

ESTELLA MIMS PYFROM is a formidable woman. Growing up in the
1940s in Belle Glade, Florida, she was disadvantaged financially and
racially—she was the daughter of African-American farm laborers, and
segregation was in full swing. But as her parents made clear to her from an
early age, she did enjoy one key advantage: the power to make good choices.
While still a child, Pyfrom learned important skills like budgeting, prioritizing, and delayed gratification. Unfortunately, as she learned soon after mar-
rying, her husband (who had grown up more financially advantaged) lacked
these life skills:

Like most young families, we started off very with little. Our spending
habits were different. He was used to having anything he wanted; he
didn't have to work for it. And I knew the value of stretching a dollar. So
having gone through those challenges growing up, I learned how to make
it work, how to deal with having to postpone things that we could not
afford and accept that—I mean, if you can't do it, you just can't do it. But
the challenge basically was: How do I get him to understand that we just
can't have it? So my favorite phrase was, "We can't afford it. Here's what
we make. Now if you want to afford it, I'm OK with that. Get another
job." But that didn't happen.[1]

Pyfrom also had to get a job to make ends meet. She decided to go into education, returning as a teacher to the public schools in her childhood city of Belle Glade, a city known for having the highest AIDS rate in the United States in the 1980s and the second-highest violent crime rate in the nation in the early 2000s. After nearly fifty years teaching the children there, Pyfrom retired from the school system—but not from education. She poured her retirement account and other personal funds into a mobile technology education lab for underserved kids: a lab (and organization) known as Estella's Brilliant Bus. She encountered obstacles at every stage—due to health, finances, and even an attempt to co-opt her idea by the company she had contracted to construct her bus: "They held all my money. They waited until we got halfway through; then they tried to charge me more than the contract. And when the project was nearly finished, they said, 'You have to give us another $31,000 before you can get your bus.' And I changed the date of the open house for that project so many times, because they kept coming up with ways to hold it. It turned out that behind my back—because they thought it was such a great idea—they were trying to promote and advertise my project as their own." And while all this was going on, Pyfrom was spending most of her time keeping vigil over her husband, who had been critically injured because of a medical error, at the understaffed local hospital. With persistence, determination, and a few delays to her open house date, Pyfrom made her bus-turned-technology-lab a reality.

In an interesting twist, Pyfrom raised the necessary funds to build the bus partly thanks to the simple lifestyle that her husband—the former overspender in the family—had eventually developed. When their grown children advised the couple to sell some assets and use the funds to enjoy their retirement rather than worry about leaving an inheritance, Pyfrom's husband said, "You know, all that makes sense. But I don't want to do a damn thing." Having lost his earlier taste for extravagance, he simply wanted to stay close to home and enjoy listening to music—so with his support, Pyfrom directed their resources into her bus project. And now, in her eighties, she continues to take a very active role in running the organization—in fact, she had to discontinue our interview and reschedule it for later in the day because of an unexpected opportunity to meet with potential collaborators. When people—including her husband—try to tell her she has too much on her plate, she simply tells them, "I put it on there because I figured out a way to make it work."

When talking with her about her accomplishments and the obstacles she has overcome, one gets the impression that Estella Pyfrom can accomplish just about anything she wants to through the sheer strength of her will. She credits her parents with her ability to focus, persevere, and follow her dreams:

Growing up, my dad said, "You're not losing. You can't fail; just work on it a little bit longer." Then I had to think: Working at something a little longer—really, what does that mean? What do you have to do in order to not be a failure? If you undertake a task, you see it through. You keep working; you make it happen. Little by little, you improve until you get where you want to get with that project. I look at challenges as what I have to do something about. And I'm not one to just sit and not do something. I learned in the past with greater challenges to regroup and try again. If it's something important, I want to make it happen. And I don't know if it's bad or good, but I can't think of anything outright that I started to do and failed. I have setbacks and challenges, but I overcame those and moved on to the next level. It's almost like if you have to jump hurdles. I learned that if I'm too close to the hurdles that I have to jump over, I just back up and get another running start so I can jump over.

In the rest of this chapter, we'll learn how to be a little more like Pyfrom: by resisting temptations and distractions, overcoming obstacles, and persevering until we achieve our goals. First we'll take a look at voluntariness—roughly, the functioning of our wills—and the ways in which we can fail to use our wills well. (A very effective way to improve our own willpower is to understand how and why it can fail.)[2] Then we'll examine a few different types of practical strategies to boost our willpower—and to avoid overtaxing it.

Voluntariness: The "Will" in "Willpower"

As Pyfrom's story illustrates, willpower is closely related to two virtues discussed later in this book: perseverance and temperance. That is, through the strength of our wills, we—like Pyfrom—can keep going when the right path isn't the easy one, and we can resist temptations like junk food and overspending.

Although an explicit notion of the will as a distinctive faculty of the mind wasn't developed (in the East or the West) until centuries later, we see in Xunzi's "Dispelling Obsession" that the importance of this mental function—the mind's ability to choose and control its own activities and those of the body—was clearly recognized by the ancients: "The mind is the ruler of the body and the master of its god-like intelligence. It gives commands, but it is not subject to them. Of its own volition it prohibits or permits, snatches or accepts, goes or stops. Thus the mouth can be forced to speak or to be silent; the body can be forced to crouch or to extend itself; but the mind cannot be made to change its opinion."[3]

As contemporary philosopher Aaron Stalnaker demonstrates, Xunzi discussed in some depth the mind's ability to form intentions, assenting to (or dissenting from) various ways of acting and being, regardless of whether those ways accord with our desires.[4] We can choose, among other things, what we allow our minds to accept and what we allow them to dwell upon; and in doing so, we can choose whether to cultivate the desirable qualities of emptiness, unity, and stillness—and, ultimately, whether to follow the Way of virtue. Such a process isn't necessarily easy, of course, but it *is* within our control. That's good news—we're capable of achieving mental and moral excellence—but it also comes with a bit of bad news: if we fail, we have ourselves to blame. (There's more good news on the flip side of that, though: if we succeed, the credit is also ours.)

Aristotle begins his discussion of the nature of voluntary actions and passions—those under the control of what we now call our will—by noting that it is only for these (not involuntary actions or passions) that we are praised or blamed.[5] Since virtue is a praiseworthy state involving actions and passions, voluntariness forms a sort of boundary around the ones that help develop virtue—and that count as evidence of it. Inside this boundary of the voluntary are the actions and feelings that we ourselves produce in ordinary, non-misleading situations; outside the boundary are actions and feelings that arise through compulsion or ignorance.

Fortunately, the dividing line between voluntariness and compulsion is fairly clear and is familiar to all of us—even those of us who haven't spent much time thinking about it. Voluntary actions and passions are those that the agent herself causes; compelled ones are those entirely caused by things external to her. As John Searle helpfully explained in his discussion of free will, voluntary actions are those we would describe by saying, "I am making this happen"; compelled actions are those about which we would instead say, "This is happening to me."[6] So while my showing up for class by walking across campus is voluntary even if really I don't feel like going today, my showing up thanks to being carried there by a strong wind or by overly eager students would be compelled.[7]

Although these paradigm cases of nonvoluntariness through compulsion are fairly straightforward, the relation between ignorance and voluntariness is more complex: not just any sort of ignorance exempts the agent from praise or blame. For example, ignorance that arises through drunkenness doesn't render the resulting stupid actions involuntary—if anything, it results in *more* blame, not less. (In Aristotle's day, apparently, legal penalties were doubled for drunkenness.) Similarly, as Thomas Aquinas later elaborated, ignorance resulting from deliberately or negligently failing to obtain relevant information does not render the corresponding acts involuntary.[8] Further, knowledge of every aspect of one's action isn't necessary for voluntariness: "It is not mistaken purpose [e.g., motives like greed or malice] that causes involuntary action (it leads rather to wickedness), nor ignorance of the universal [principle] (for that men are blamed), but ignorance of particulars, i.e. of the circumstances of the action and the objects with which it is concerned. For it is on these that both pity and pardon depend, since *the person who is ignorant of any of these acts involuntarily*."[9]

So while we don't get ourselves off the ethical hook by denying knowledge of universal principles ("I didn't realize that murder is wrong—sorry about that"), ignorance of particulars *can* be a reasonable excuse. When he says that ignorance of particular objects and circumstances causes involuntariness, to what sorts of things is Aristotle referring? He lists as examples most of the "five Ws" you probably learned in grade school—who, what, when, where, and why—along with the "how" that often accompanies them; for instance, "one might give a man a drink to save him, and really kill him; or one might want to touch a man, as people do in sparring, and really wound him."[10] Or maybe you turn up your stereo and start dancing, not realizing that your roommate came home from work early and is napping in the next room; or you excitedly tell your friend all about your raise and promotion—just before she tells you that she lost her job.

We have seen that the virtues and vices for which we can be praised or

blamed are related to voluntary actions and passions: those actions we ourselves cause, with knowledge of the relevant features of the situation. Naturally, then, we might ask: Are virtues and vices themselves voluntary? Aristotle—and common sense, I think—answer "yes." The fact that we praise or
blame them, and encourage or discourage people to acquire them, indicates
that we already recognize their voluntariness; and they arise from voluntary
actions that have become habitual. But, as Aristotle points out, actions and
character traits are not voluntary in the same way: "We are masters of our
actions from the beginning right to the end, if we know the particular facts,
but though we control the beginning of our states of character the gradual
progress is not obvious any more than it is in illnesses; because it was in our
power, however, to act in this way or not in this way, therefore the states are
voluntary."[11]

So while it may not be within my power to be a courageous or temperate
person by tomorrow any more than it is within my power to gain a hundred pounds by tomorrow, by doing what *is* within my immediate control—
performing actions in accordance with courage or temperance (or weight
gain)—I can make some progress by next month and a lot of progress by next
year. Doing so, at least in the case of courage and (especially) temperance,
will at first require what Aristotle terms "continence"—the quality more
commonly known these days as "willpower."[12] We'll examine that topic in
more depth next.

Strength and Weakness of Will

As Aristotle notes, we typically speak of willpower primarily in the same
area to which temperance applies: physical pleasure. Where the person with
strength of will consistently resists strong temptations to do something
pleasant immediately rather than to delay gratification for the sake of higher
pursuits, the temperate person rarely experiences strong temptations of that
sort at all—she actually desires the higher pursuits (or their outcomes) more
than the immediate pleasure promised by the temptation.[13] For example, a
successful dieter may daily—even hourly—resist numerous strong desires
to consume sweets or fatty foods. That's good, but it's not as good as being
(mostly) free of such temptations, especially when we consider that, as psychologists have recently found, on average we spend eight hours a day desir-

ing things—and three hours a day trying to resist our desires.[14] We'll look more closely at the virtue of temperance in chapter 8. But since most of us are not yet entirely temperate—that is, we *do* experience strong temptations toward instant gratification, even against our better judgment—willpower is something we must work to increase. For instance, today as I write, three of my family members are happily enjoying what remains of the ice cream cake I made for my son's birthday. It sounds delicious to me too, but I'd better just keep writing.

Secondarily, as Aristotle also observed, we sometimes apply the notion of willpower to other areas of life such as avoiding procrastination and controlling our expressions of anger. In fact, as contemporary psychologists have discovered, apparently there really is just one reserve of willpower that is used in four broad categories: impulse control (resisting the sorts of temptations we were just describing), thought control (concentrating on the relevant topic and avoiding distractions), emotional regulation (warding off unwanted emotions such as sadness or anger, usually by *seeking* distractions), and performance control (focusing on the task at hand and persevering in it).[15] So my continuing to work on this book today instead of taking an ice cream break (and, likely, a nap shortly thereafter) is an exercise in both impulse control and performance control. Fortunately, I ate a reasonably healthy lunch not long ago, and researchers have found that keeping our blood sugar in steady supply supports willpower. (Unfortunately, dieting tends to decrease blood sugar—and thereby decrease the willpower needed to continue dieting. But all is not lost: lean proteins, vegetables, and whole grains tend to be compatible with both weight loss and continued strength of will.)[16]

In addition to recognizing these four areas in which willpower is necessary, we can see two main processes by which our willpower sometimes fails. Aristotle describes each process in terms of deliberation: the rational consideration of our options and their relative merits. Ideally, of course, we'd always deliberate well and choose the action that we determine to be the best overall. But sometimes that doesn't happen. First, we might be so overwhelmed by our own desires or emotions that we fail to deliberate at all, simply following our impulses—Aristotle calls this phenomenon "impetuosity." Second, we might exercise perfectly good deliberation but fail to abide by our own conclusions, instead letting our desires lead us into doing something we know we'll regret—a type of failure quite reasonably called "weakness."[17]

Impetuous people are less to blame than weak ones, he argues, because their failure is due to a stronger passion and because they don't abandon their own best judgment. He colorfully compares this phenomenon to tickling: "Some men (just as people who first tickle others are not tickled themselves), if they have first perceived and seen what is coming and have first roused themselves and their calculative faculty, are not defeated by their emotion."[18] Similarly to how some people can steel themselves against succumbing to retaliatory tickling because they anticipate it, if impetuous people can anticipate powerful temptations, they will be able to deliberate when confronted with them—and often come out victorious. As we'll see later in this chapter, contemporary psychologists confirm Aristotle's observations: among the most effective ways to prepare for temptation is to take a few slow, deep breaths—this technique "helps shift the brain and body from a state of stress to self-control mode,"[19] which allows for rational deliberation and decision making.

The second kind of failure—abandonment of our best judgment—is probably more common for most of us, and it is properly described as "weakness of will." It has always seemed a bit mysterious: Why would anyone voluntarily abandon a better idea for what she knew was a worse one? To answer that question, Aristotle appeals to the various senses of the word "know." First, actual knowledge currently in our conscious awareness is different from habitual knowledge not currently called to mind[20]—for example, you no doubt know that $2 + 5 = 7$, but you probably weren't thinking about it until just now. Failing to act on habitual knowledge is much less odd than failing to act on actual knowledge. Second, we might be said to have habitual knowledge and yet not have it (or at least not have ready access to it): Aristotle occasionally compares impetuosity and even weakness to being asleep, mad, or drunk.[21] In such a state, he suggests, one may even say something like "I know I shouldn't," but such words don't mean any more than they would mean coming from an actor reading a script.

For example, although she had previously overcome abuse, neglect, and her own teenage rebelliousness and was doing well in college, Lisa Nigro (an exemplar whose story can be found in chapter 9 of this book) relapsed into her earlier, unstable lifestyle in response to a family tragedy: "I just freaked out, and I left school, and I left everything. I went down a really bad path for two years. I moved to Tampa, Florida, and I started partying again. I was just totally out of control; I was just out of my mind."[22] Although at some level I'm sure Nigro was aware that she was making poor choices—certainly she was aware enough to communicate that fact to the friend who eventually drove from Minnesota to Florida to rescue her from herself—her access to that knowledge seemed sporadic at best.

To understand Aristotle's further analysis of knowledge and weakness of will, we'll need to take a brief look at the practical syllogism, which we'll discuss further in chapters 5 and 19 of this book. A practical syllogism begins with a universal premise—typically, one stating that all acts of a certain kind are to be avoided.[23] Next it has a more particular premise, stating that some act or group of acts fits within the scope of the universal. Finally, it concludes that the act(s) mentioned in the second premise are to be avoided. For example:

> All acts of deliberately harming innocent people are wrong.
>
> Trying out my new sword on a random traveler would be deliberately harming an innocent person.
>
> Therefore, trying out my new sword on a random traveler is wrong.

The problem with weakness of will isn't ignorance or a temporary forgetting of the general ethical principle stated in the first premise—that sort of problem is associated with vice (a bad habit that is the opposite of a virtue) or even outright wickedness. The problem is a lack of actual, currently exercised knowledge of the truth of the more specific second premise. Sometimes we fail to exercise such habitual knowledge as a result of rationalization—poor deliberation focused on less problematic aspects of the action. Other times, though, as we've observed in this chapter, weakness of will seems to act independently of rationalization: people deliberate well but yield to their strong appetites and thus fail to abide by their own reasoning. Either way, the effect is the same: the person acts badly even though at some level he knows better. For example, someone leaving a party may fail to act upon the soundness of this syllogism:

All acts of drunk driving are bad things to do.

Driving this car now that I've consumed six alcoholic beverages is an act of drunk driving.

Therefore, driving this car now that I've consumed six alcoholic beverages is a bad thing to do.

Perhaps that second premise occurs to him but he puts it out of his mind, telling himself that he's an exceptional driver or that he urgently needs to get home. Or perhaps he's having so much fun (or is just so drunk) that he doesn't even notice how impaired he is or remember how many beverages he consumed. In either case, someone with habitual knowledge of both premises fails to actualize his knowledge of the second one, with potentially disastrous results.

So how can we avert disaster? Fortunately, the topic of willpower has gained the attention of psychologists in the past decade; we'll now turn to their practical tips for getting more of it.

Improving Our Willpower: Fighting Temptation with Offense and Defense

Roy F. Baumeister, one of the leading researchers in the psychology of willpower, summarized the recent findings on the topic in his book (coauthored with journalist John Tierney) *Willpower: Rediscovering the Greatest Human Strength*. As I noted earlier in this chapter, according to Baumeister each of us has a single reserve of willpower upon which we draw for various tasks such as resisting temptation, concentrating our thoughts, and persevering in action. Baumeister and his colleagues have discovered several ways that we can increase our willpower; although some strategies might fall into both of the following categories, I think it makes sense to divide them into offensive and defensive types. The defensive techniques help us prepare for and resist temptations when we are confronted with them, and offensive strategies enable us to avoid encountering temptations in the first place. In this section we'll look at ways to prepare for temptation, strategies for facing it, and techniques that can help us reduce it—even or avoid it altogether.

Preparing for temptation. To prepare for temptation in a general way, we need to increase our general supply of self-control. There are many ways to do so, but their common theme is that they involve frequent small acts of perseverance or self-denial. For example, Baumeister and Tierney describe an experiment by one of Baumeister's students in which participants either wrote down what they ate or made a conscious effort to use good posture—after two weeks, they demonstrated significantly improved self-control.[24] Similarly, fasting periods such as the religious traditions of Ramadan and Lent can help believers to improve their willpower. McGonigal also recommends a few simple and effective ways to improve our general supply of willpower: exercise, meditation, and adequate sleep. And she reports that, to her students' relief, even five minutes a day of meditation (just sitting still and being attentive to your breathing will do) or a short walk (or any kind of physical activity, really) works remarkably well.[25]

Sometimes temptations are predictable and difficult to avoid. Holiday parties, for example, typically have large quantities of things like booze and sweets, but most of us can't avoid overindulging in those things simply by avoiding holiday parties altogether—at least not without seriously offending our relatives and closest friends. The good news, though, is that the predictability of these sorts of temptations allows us to plan in advance how we will face them—psychologists call this planning "implementation intention."[26] For example, during some of my healthiest days, when headed to my parents' house for a holiday visit I told myself, "When they serve food, I will eat only fruits, vegetables, lean proteins, and whole grains." It worked: there were enough things meeting those descriptions to form reasonable meals—and as psychologists have found, we tend to be more content (and deplete our willpower less)[27] with fewer options anyway. And by telling myself, "After helping clear the main meal I'll go for a walk with my (dieting) husband," I managed to find something else to do when dessert was being served—even though my sister is a professional dessert maker.

It's not just holidays that bring temptation, though: every day we encounter many opportunities for instant gratification at the expense of our long-term goals. With a little self-knowledge—usually of the sort that comes from experience giving in to such temptations—we can know which ones we'll have the most difficulty resisting. Then we can create "bright lines"—simple and unambiguous rules—around them. For example, if you are strongly tempted to continue doing things like smoking or drinking or eating junk food once you start, you probably won't do well with tolerant, nonspecific implementation intentions such as "I will smoke moderately" or "I will drink only on special occasions"—"just one more" is too easily labeled "moderate," and almost any occasion can be considered special. ("I finally washed those dishes today—let's celebrate!") For particularly strong and prevalent temptations, especially to consume things that are physically addictive, we may need instead to take a cue from effective twelve-step programs like Alcoholics Anonymous by adopting zero-tolerance policies for ourselves—policies that allow for no exceptions at any time.

Another strength of twelve-step programs is that they encourage monitoring. Keeping track of our own behaviors can be a useful tool for gaining the self-knowledge needed to determine whether it would be better to tell ourselves we'll have that beer "later" or "never"; and monitoring can also be a willpower strengthener in its own right. For example, I've heard from multiple health gurus the importance of writing down what we eat: "If you bite it, you must write it" is a common description of that implementation plan. Like some of the other willpower-enhancing strategies, monitoring may work in a few ways: maybe you forgo your afternoon candy fix because you don't want to have to look at your "eight juju fish" notation, or maybe the pleasure of eating them doesn't seem worth the effort of recording them, or maybe the thought of recording them just increases your awareness of the disproportion between their calories and their nutritional value. Monitoring can also act as proxy for—or, better yet, be used in service of—external accountability: it is more difficult to rationalize giving in to temptation when we are reporting our transgressions not just to ourselves, but also to a sponsor, friend, or significant other.[28]

Facing present temptations. For things that are readily available but should be resisted for the most part, psychologists have recently discovered that telling ourselves we will indulge "later" can be an effective strategy for facing present temptations. For example, in one study participants who were instructed to imagine they'd decided they'd indulge "later" ate fewer M&Ms (from a bowl placed right in front of them) while watching a movie than those instructed to imagine they'd decided either to eat freely or to avoid the candy altogether—they even ate fewer after they thought the experiment was over and no one was watching, and they craved M&Ms less the following day than did either of the other two groups.[29] And this strategy makes intuitive sense: by the time "later" arrives, perhaps you'll find you're no longer tempted, or perhaps you'll already have moved on to some other activity that precludes indulging.

A different sort of strategy for strengthening willpower in the face of unavoidable (or unavoidable now that we've put ourselves in their presence) temptations involves raising our minds to higher things. We might focus on transcendent thoughts or ideals—for example, we might focus on the noble reasons for which we are resisting temptations to gratify our desires or to quit an important task ("I promised my mom I wouldn't") or we might just distract ourselves by thinking about our ideal job or friend or vacation. Or, as it turns out, we can even increase willpower simply by turning to more abstract concepts generally (such as math problems, thoughts about what category various items fall into, or *why* rather than *how* some event occurs). All of these can be quite effective at dislodging us from the "here and now" mindset that wears down our resistance to the here-and-now temptation.[30]

Reducing the need for willpower. As we become familiar with the limits of our willpower defenses, we'll often find that an offensive approach to temptations is more effective. My husband likes to say, "Self-control begins at the grocery store." Of course, while it does take *some* self-control not to buy the ice cream that's on sale, resisting it at the store (especially if you shop on a full stomach!) takes a lot less self-control than resisting it once it's lurking in your own freezer. Psychologists call this strategy "precommitment"; as Baumeister and Tierney describe it, "the essence of this strategy is to lock yourself into a virtuous path. You recognize that you'll face terrible temptations and that your willpower will weaken. So you make it impossible—or somehow unthinkably disgraceful or sinful—to leave the path."[31] You make a public vow, or you flush your booze or cigarettes down the toilet, or you put yourself on a no-pay list at your local casino.

Finally, and not surprisingly to a reader of Aristotle, psychologists have recently confirmed that self-control is most effectively exercised in the context of a habit—with "automatic processing," as social scientists call it. Researchers analyzing many studies of people who scored high on self-control measures found that, contrary to what they had previously assumed, those with high self-control used it less (or at least less consciously) on the behaviors they controlled the most: that is, their impressive control was implemented mainly through automatic, habitual behaviors. Establishing good habits takes willpower up front, of course, but once virtuous habits are in place, acting on them is almost automatic.[32]

For example, as I have noticed, and you may have too, the second and third week of a new diet or exercise program tend to be the hardest: the novelty of the first week has worn off and the force of habit has not yet kicked in—until it does, and unless you can arrange for significant extrinsic incentives, you have to keep going on sheer strength of will. But if you can hang in there for those couple of weeks, the process of habit formation starts to generate its own momentum. Sticking to it becomes much easier—even (eventually) more or less automatic. And in even more encouraging news, a habit of self-control in one area of life can extend its reach into others. For example, as one study found, a clean workspace can cue us to stay on task, to take fewer risks, to eat healthier snacks, and even to donate more to charity.[33]

But what do we do if we're *really* far gone in the willpower department? How do we rebound from a situation like Lisa Nigro's—one characterized by *lack* of self-control? As she described herself during that difficult period, she was "totally out of control." How do we bounce back from something like that?

There are no quick and easy answers to that question, and I know that many people never do bounce back. But I can tell you how it worked for Nigro—and, in chapter 6, about the even more dramatic recovery of another exemplary woman. After dropping out of college and partying in Florida for two years, Nigro was fortunate to have a friend who cared enough to reach out—and she was smart enough or desperate enough to accept his help. She traveled with him back to her childhood city of Chicago and went to work in a group home for abused teens. As she recalls, "I wasn't going there to heal myself at all—I just took the job because I knew what these girls are feeling. And it was a really amazing job, and it taught me so much about forgiveness and the tenacity of people. No matter what, you're still going to get through."

Within a few years, Nigro's own tenacity seems to have been fully intact. She was bartending during this time, and, on a bet with one of her customers, she took the entrance exam for the Chicago Police Academy. After passing the exam, she was turned down at the interview stage. Undeterred, she appealed the decision: "So I went in front of this board, and they basically told me that the reason they turned me down as a cop was because I answered too honestly: 'You don't get along with your parents; you've used drugs.' But I said, 'It's been years since I used, and who else would you want to be on the drug team but me, because I know what's happening,' and on and on. And they finally said, 'OK,' and they let me in the Police Academy. And so I became a Chicago police officer. Yeah. [Laughs.] That was pretty awesome."

Nigro's rediscovered resilience was preceded and supported by honesty with herself and with others, and by willingness to face and overcome her flaws and failings. Those two broad topics are the subject of the next parts of this book. In part 2, we'll take a closer look at honesty: improvement of our lives and characters by examining ourselves, recognizing our (positive and negative) potential, refusing to rationalize away our faults, and ultimately developing the virtue of truthfulness. Then in part 3, we'll consider common flaws that we must overcome—and the virtues associated with overcoming them: obsession (the mental flaw of overly narrow focus) and how to overcome it with broad-mindedness, temptations of immediate gratification and how to overcome them with temperance, and, finally, the temptation to quit and the virtue of perseverance.

Part 2

KNOWING YOURSELF

*The Good, the Not-So-Good, and the
Potentially Good*

Chapter 4

EXAMINING YOUR LIFE

U PON GRADUATING with a bachelor's degree in engineering from UC Berkeley, Mauricio Lim Miller—a young immigrant who had been raised by a single mother—was faced with a difficult choice: Go on to a prestigious graduate program or accept a job in the nonprofit sector. Desiring to help low-income families like the one in which he had grown up, he chose the latter. Soon, however, he found himself disillusioned by his role in America's "War on Poverty":

I was hired to train an initial crew of twenty-five gang kids to get jobs in construction, for kids that wanted to leave the gang.... Two months into that job, and training these gang kids, I realized—because to be eligible to get into my program we had to go to those most in need—that I was sending a really backward message to a bunch of teenagers. I had two kids that were coming in to fill my last slot. One of them ["Andy"] had gone on a robbery and tried to talk his friend ["Bill"] into going on the robbery; Bill was trying to get out of the gang, so he said no. Bill brought Andy to apply for a slot to get out of the gang, and because I only had one slot, I told them that I had to give the slot to Andy. And they asked why, because Bill was the one that took the initiative to try and get his life together, and Andy didn't even want to be there. I said, "Well, because Andy has a permanent record and he's more in need." They looked at me, and then Andy looked at Bill, and I just remember him saying, "See, you should've gone on that robbery with me." So, I'm going, "What in the hell is this message that I sent those two teenagers?"[1]

This event was just the beginning of a pattern of frustrating experiences and periods of introspection that would last twenty years—until Miller decided he could no longer work in the traditional social service sector. In fact, when I asked about his greatest regret in life, Miller told me (with admirable honesty): "It took me twenty years to get out of doing something that I really didn't believe in. That was pretty stupid."

A bit later in this chapter we'll look at Miller's process of introspection a bit more closely. First, let's take a bigger-picture look at self-examination and its importance for all of us.

The Examined Life

You may have heard the saying that "the unexamined life is not worth living"—it's Socrates's most famous (reasonably authentic) quote. Its context, if you're not already familiar with it, may be more surprising: Socrates utters these words just after having gotten into considerable trouble—of the criminal conviction sort—for his attempts to help others examine their lives. The classic Greek dialogue *Apology* (the word "apology" in this case meaning "defense," not "expression of remorse") records Socrates's trial from the perspective of his most famous student, Plato.[2] More precisely, it records the defense's presentation—Socrates represented himself—and the sentencing; we don't hear the prosecution's case. Socrates stands accused of two crimes: atheism and corrupting the young people of Athens. He gives what appear to be air-tight arguments showing that he could not possibly be guilty of either crime; what has really brought him to trial, he suggests, is that he routinely annoys wealthy and powerful Athenian citizens with his (and his disciples') insistence upon thoroughly examining their claims to wisdom. Since such claims are usually discovered to be unfounded, and since no one—and particularly no one with a public reputation to uphold—likes to look foolish, Socrates isn't a very popular guy. In fact, people want him gone; hence the trumped-up charges.

Socrates, despite his convincing defense, is convicted by a narrow margin. Sentencing in ancient Athenian courts works like this: first the prosecution proposes a penalty, then the defense makes a counterproposal, and the jury chooses between the two. In this case, the prosecution proposes execution. Socrates at this point is expected to propose imprisonment or exile, and he probably could do so successfully. His fellow Athenians have no special reason to want him dead; they just want to be rid of him. Instead, he suggests that what he really deserves for his "crime" of helping people examine their wisdom and virtue is to be hosted in the Prytaneum—the public building in which foreign dignitaries and Olympic champions are entertained. As he sees it, the usual alternative penalties are not only unjust, but likely worse than death:

> When I do not know whether death is a good or an evil, why should I propose a penalty which would certainly be an evil? Shall I say imprisonment? And why should I live in prison, and be the slave of the magistrates? ... And if I say exile ... I am quite sure that into whatever place I go, as here so also there, the young men will come to me; and if I drive them away, their elders will drive me out at their desire: and if I let them come, their fathers and friends will drive me out for their sakes.
>
> Someone will say: Yes, Socrates, but cannot you hold your tongue, and then you may go into a foreign city, and no one will interfere with you? Now I have great difficulty in making you understand my answer to this. For if I tell you that this would be a disobedience to a divine command, and therefore that I cannot hold my tongue, you will not believe that I am serious; and if I say again that *the greatest good of man is daily to converse about virtue*, and all that concerning which you hear me examining myself and others, and that *the life which is unexamined is not worth living*—that you are still less likely to believe. And yet what I say is true.[3]

When my students (undergraduates at a liberal arts university) read this passage, a surprising number of them—almost all, really—say they agree with Socrates. Why? Maybe they think that's what I want to hear, or maybe they're especially philosophical for their age, or maybe they just don't realize how literally Socrates means what he says: he would rather be put to death than stop talking about virtue and how it applies to our lives. When I press them for reasons, their responses usually suggest the last hypothesis. While they may not (yet?) be so committed to self-examination and ethical virtue that they would rather die than give them up, they generally can give good reasons for pursuing these things. They don't want to go through the motions of life, and they see self-examination as essential to authentic living. They don't appreciate dishonesty from others, and they want to be honest with themselves too. And they—rightly, I think—see Socrates as a hero of sorts, standing up for truth and virtue. So while few of them are prepared to go as far has he did to defend his ideals, they see that such ideals are indeed worth defending.

So how do ordinary people like us go about becoming heroes—or at least practitioners—of self-examination? Socrates' own method was simple: Ask questions. Ask a lot of them, frequently, until you arrive at real answers.

As we saw in *Apology*, this examination method, when applied to others, isn't a good way to become popular. So if you want people to like you, you may want to apply it to them sparingly—at least until they show themselves to be open to this sort of interaction. As is frequently noted in the Confucian tradition, too much correction can strain relationships. For example, in Confucius's *Analects* we see: "Being overbearing in service to a lord will lead to disgrace, while in relating to friends and companions it will lead to estrangement."[4] And Confucian philosopher Mencius suggests that it's better for fathers not to teach their sons for similar reasons.[5] But the good news about *self*-correction is that estrangement isn't an option—you're stuck with yourself. And you'll like yourself much more in the long run if you're honest with yourself and know your own strengths and weaknesses—and work to overcome the weaknesses and build on the strengths.[6]

So what sorts of questions should we ask ourselves? If we follow Socrates's method—as philosophers and therapists have done to varying degrees for well over two millennia—we will ask challenging questions about our own knowledge and character. Such questions will arise at varying levels of specificity, from the very general (e.g., "Am I really as good a person as I like to think I am?") to the very particular (e.g., "Am I impartial enough regarding this coworker to provide a fair evaluation for his annual review?"). Answering honestly will require our calling to mind the relevant evidence from our own habits, actions, and motivations—repeatedly, without rationalization, and (because, as we'll soon discuss, we *do* tend to rationalize) paying special attention to evidence that points in an uncomfortable direction.

To help us develop a habit of honest self-examination, many traditions—both philosophical and religious—encourage a frequent pattern of structured self-questioning: either in conjunction with other events or practices or separately, on a weekly, daily, or even hourly basis. To take a religious example, Catholics are encouraged to examine themselves briefly at the beginning of every Mass and more thoroughly before going to Confession; following the advice of St. Ignatius Loyola, some Catholics also practice a daily *examen* in which they review the day's events—thanking God for their blessings, rejoicing over times they acted well, and resolving to improve upon times they didn't.[7]

The Confucian tradition also includes several concrete pieces of advice for daily and event-specific self-examination. Here is just one example of a Confucian daily self-examination: "Every day I examine myself on three counts: in my dealings with others, have I in any way failed to be dutiful? In my interactions with friends and associates, have I in any way failed to be trustworthy? Finally, have I in any way failed to repeatedly put into practice what I teach?"[8]

Confucius also advocates using particular events and observations as cues to look inward: "When you see someone who is worthy, concentrate on becoming their equal; when you see someone who is unworthy, use this as an opportunity to look within yourself."[9] His follower Xunzi elaborates: "When you see good, then diligently examine your own behavior; when you see evil, then with sorrow look into yourself. When you find good in yourself, steadfastly approve it; when you find evil in yourself, hate it as something loathsome."[10] Finally, Mencius reports, this saying about the appropriate impact of self-examination on one's behavior has been passed down from Confucius himself: "If I examine myself and am not upright, even if opposed by a man in baggy rags, I would not try to intimidate him. If I examine myself and am upright, even if it is thousands or tens of thousands of people who oppose me, I shall go forward."[11]

As one might expect, psychologists have a lot of concrete things to say about self-examination too—we'll turn to some of their recent findings in the next section. Because psychological research on self-examination and its impact on human wellbeing is vast and varied, my presentation will of necessity be quite selective. I'll briefly review a few of the ways in which the process is understood and studied, note fruitful comparisons with classical philosophical approaches, and suggest some practical ways in which we can apply the psychological findings to our own lives.

Self-Examination in Contemporary Psychology

When looking up the term "self-examination" in the psychology literature, as I did when doing research for this book, one won't readily find the sort of thing we're discussing here. The term is often used to refer to assessment questionnaires that can be self-administered, such as the Big Five personality inventory,[12] which measures traits such as extraversion and conscientiousness. In contrast, we're referring to the sort of self-examination we should do, preferably on a regular basis, *before* taking a personality test—at least if we want accurate results! Self-examination of the sort we're discussing comes with psychological labels such as "(self-)reflection" or "introspection"; the desired outcome of this process tends to be called "self-awareness" or even "insight." (As some psychologists note, personality questionnaires can also lead to self-awareness—particularly if they spark introspection.)

Although early discussions of self-awareness in the psychology literature tended to emphasize its evaluative aspects—when we focus on ourselves, we're pretty quick to judge whether or not we measure up to our own standards[13]—more recent work has tended to emphasize the value of non-evaluative awareness of our own preferences, strengths, and weaknesses.[14] Both aspects of self-awareness, it seems to me, are crucial for character development. We need an accurate understanding of our current traits to determine whether they have room for improvement (as most of them certainly do); and if they do, we need awareness of where we fall short of ethical excellence. (And, of course, we need motivation to improve ourselves; but that's not our current focus.) As we've seen, and as we'd expect, given that ethics is evaluative by nature, philosophical accounts and techniques of self-examination tend to focus on self-evaluation with an eye toward self-improvement, rather than on awareness of our traits for its own sake.

To take an interesting analogous example, psychologist James Bennett-Levy conducted a study on reflection involving therapists who were training to use cognitive therapy—a technique that involves encouraging and assisting clients' self-examination. Reflecting trainees reported gains in three areas related to what we might call "therapeutic virtues"—the excellences of a therapist: (1) better understanding of their roles as therapists, (2) better communication of the framework of cognitive therapy, which improved their bonds with their clients, and (3) greater confidence in the effectiveness of cognitive therapy as a practice and in themselves as therapists.[15] As Bennett-Levy notes, this gain of therapeutic wisdom isn't surprising given earlier research suggesting that reflection is key to developing wisdom more generally[16]—a virtue that both Confucians and Socratics recognize as essential to a flourishing human life.

Further, self-examination seems to be connected with an ethic of caring and leadership, at least among college students: In fact, self-reported measures of reflection, along with taking classes that required reflective writing, were among the strongest predictors of commitment to such an ethic.[17] Interestingly, however, self-examination among these students did *not* positively predict their psychological wellbeing—we'll say more on that finding in the next section.

Drawing again from the therapeutic side of psychology, and as we'll see exemplified in chapter 6, successful twelve-step programs like Alcoholics Anonymous emphasize evaluative self-examination via what they call a "searching moral inventory"—both as an intensive initial process (step four) and as a daily self-examination (step ten). Examples of such inventories abound and can easily be found online; many look like checklists of contrasting characteristics—often virtues and their opposing vices. For instance, a classic (perhaps even original) checklist dated 1939 lists "liabilities" on one side and the opposing "assets" on the other. Liabilities include resentment, selfishness, and false pride; their opposing assets are forgiveness, unselfishness, and humility.[18] Again, the similarities between this sort of moral inventory and the daily self-examination advocated by Socratics, Confucians, and religious thinkers is striking. In my own ethics classes, I ask my students to take one or two self-assessment measures (such as the VIA character strengths survey); I'm considering encouraging a daily inventory, similar to the ones from Alcoholics Anonymous, as well—as we saw in a more general way with willpower in chapter 3, and as we'll discuss in conjunction with the particular virtue of gratitude in chapter 15, daily mindfulness (or "monitoring") can be very effective in helping us establish new habits.

When researching versions of the daily moral inventory, I came across one that asked, "Did I demand to be in control? To be right? To be a victim?"[19] The list of questions intrigued me—it's eerily similar to a list I keep on my desk to help me snap out of my tendency to categorize myself as the "victim"

Things I tell myself:	Things I should ask myself instead:
I'm indignant.	Does justice require me to be offended by this?
I'm right.	Could an omniscient observer have a different interpretation?
Everyone would agree with me.	Would a saint react the way I am in this situation? (Have I exercised the legendary patience of a saint?)

Figure 4.1. My own self-examination tool

of routine disagreements. (Yes, sometimes even those of us who analyze and reflect for a living need a little help with self-awareness.) My own list is given in figure 4.1.

And you know what? I use it all the time, and it works. Actually, I usually don't get past the first question, because the answer is almost always "no"— and if I realize that I don't need to be offended, it's not a huge step to decide not to be.

When Self-Examination Isn't Such a Good Thing

As it turns out, though, too much self-evaluation—particularly if it's negative but does not lead to a plan for moving forward—can be counterproductive. Organizational psychologist Tasha Eurich vividly remembers her discovery of this surprising fact:

It was Tuesday evening around 11 pm. Holed up in my dark office, I sat staring at a set of freshly analyzed data. A few weeks earlier, my team and I had run a study looking at the relationship between self-reflection and outcomes like happiness, stress and job satisfaction. I was confident the results would show that people who spent time and energy examining themselves would have a clearer understanding of themselves and that this knowledge would have positive effects throughout their lives.

But to my astonishment, our data told the exact opposite story. The people who scored high on self-reflection were more stressed, depressed and anxious, less satisfied with their jobs and relationships, more self-absorbed, and they felt less in control of their lives. What's more, these negative consequences seemed to increase the more they reflected.[20]

As Eurich and a few other researchers eventually realized, *how* we reflect makes at least as much difference as *whether* we reflect.[21] If our self-examination quickly turns to rumination on what's wrong with our lives and why we (or those around us) are such miserable failures, it won't make us happier or more virtuous.[22] And, as Eurich and her fellow psychologists have also found, even our positive self-perceptions can be unhelpful if they're inaccurate—and unfortunately, that's fairly likely, given the biases to which we easily fall prey.[23] Among those participants she studied who *did* appear to benefit from introspection, Eurich noticed a striking difference: when reflecting on negative feelings or experiences, they tended to ask questions beginning with "What" rather than "Why." One of her interviewees explained the benefit of doing so: "If you ask *why*, [I think] you're putting yourself into a victim mentality.... When I feel anything other than peace, I say 'What's going on?'; 'What am I feeling?'; 'What is the dialogue inside my head?'; 'What's another way to see this situation?' or 'What can I do to respond better?'"[24]

Similarly, Eurich describes trying the "Ask What, Not Why" technique on a friend who was dissatisfied with his highly successful career. When she first asked *why* he wanted to change his career, her friend sighed hopelessly and began to rattle off a list of his personal shortcomings. When she changed course and asked *what* he disliked about his current work, he was able to identify two key aspects of his job that were unsatisfying; and when Eurich asked *what* he liked to do, her friend quickly identified aspects of his work that he found meaningful and fulfilling—and began to brainstorm ways to do more of those things and less of the things he disliked.[25]

Another way to guard against the dark side of introspection, Eurich suggests, is to pursue what she calls "external self-awareness": knowing how other people see us. While others can of course be mistaken, too, and don't have direct access to our thoughts and feelings, they do enjoy a lot more objectivity than we often have about ourselves. (She cites the common experience of meeting a friend's new significant other and knowing within minutes that the relationship is doomed.)[26] Realizing my limited insight into my own character traits, several years ago I asked my husband (who is highly observant and knows me better than anyone) to list my top three to five character flaws in priority order—that is, the order in which I should try to fix them. Apparently favoring marital harmony over his usual bluntness, he replied, "Um, no. I'm not going there." But months later, in a moment of exasperation, he revealed the truth: "You're petty, indulgent, prideful, and stingy!" I was so pleased to have this valuable information that I didn't even imagine myself to be the victim of that revelation—in fact, that week I gleefully announced my newly discovered vices to my unsuspecting colleagues, who were working with me on developing a moral self-concept assessment. And while I can't say I've fully eliminated my vices since then, awareness of my shortcomings certainly has helped me target my self-improvement efforts more effectively.

Several well-known moral leaders have also benefited from increased self-awareness through honest (and sometimes critical) feedback from others. We'll turn to their stories next.

Contemporary Heroes of Self-Examination

In *The Power of Ideals*, William Damon and Anne Colby carefully analyze the lives of six exemplary twentieth-century moral leaders to discover what patterns emerge in their lives, thinking, and character—and how we ordinary folk might apply lessons from the exemplars' lives to our own moral development. Strikingly, Damon and Colby note that "all six described regular practices of self-reflection through which they scrutinized their own behavior and motivations with a searching frankness. These practices included prayer, self-reflective diaries, honest discussions with friends and intimate partners, requests to colleagues and staff for candid feedback, and conscious efforts to take seriously criticism from opponents."[27] And for each of the exemplars, challenging circumstances triggered an increase in the intensity of their self-examination. For example, Nelson Mandela, who was sentenced to a lifetime of hard labor for his opposition to apartheid and spent decades in prison, wryly credited his long imprisonment with providing him plenty of opportunities for reflection.

In my own interviews with recognized moral exemplars—adults who have won national awards for long-term, voluntary service to others—I saw a similar pattern of honest self-examination. Of course, telling one's life story can itself be an opportunity for self-examination, as some of my interview-ees noted; but they also made clear, both in sharing overviews of their lives and in response to questions about specific events and values, that they were already in the habit of reflection. For some, this self-examination occurs in the context of prayer or other spiritual practices; for others, it takes place pri-marily through conversations with friends and family members. Most men-tioned a turning point at which, after a more intense period of introspection, they took a significant step in their outreach efforts. Mauricio Lim Miller, with whose unsatisfying early career in social services we began this chapter, had a more dramatic turning point than most.

As Miller continued with his work in the nonprofit sector, eventually be-coming the director of a social services agency with a staff of over a hundred people, he became increasingly disillusioned with his work. He saw his agen-cy's methods of "helping" low-income families as disrespectful of their abili-ties and potential, detrimental to their long-term wellbeing, and in blatant violation of common sense. First, access to assistance was limited, especially for those who were trying to improve themselves: "The more trouble you're in, the more eligible you are; and if you don't really do really bad things, you don't get anything. That was me: I really had to try and stay out of trouble, and because I did, I didn't get scholarships, I didn't get access to anything. You couldn't be an ordinary kid and get access. You either had to be in trou-ble or be really smart."

Second, there was an unsettling disconnect between "helpers" and their "beneficiaries." "Even though I was now in the world of 'helpers,' of people who wanted to help families like the one I was coming from, there was such a divergence between the two worlds. I and my colleagues in the social sec-tor would talk about 'us' and how we ran our families. When we would talk about 'them,' which [included] my sister's kids, it was like a different world. We talked about them as if common sense didn't apply, and so it was this huge split."

Finally, Miller observed marginalization of those to be "helped." As he was preparing to leave for a conference, he reflected, "A friend of mine asked me where I was going, and I said, 'I'm going to a conference around poverty issues that is being held at a Club Med in Mexico, where the walls are just high enough so that the people that we're talking about can't hear us talking about them.' And that was exactly right. I've gone to dozens of conferences.

Those of us that are in privileged positions and are very well intended—each is nice enough—totally exclude the people that we're talking about unless they're there to bolster us or the program." He concluded: "And so I was just like, 'This does not make sense. Essentially, what I'm doing makes no sense.'"

Still, Miller continued with his work in social service programming, eventually—to his dismay—serving the children of clients he'd served earlier in his career. Apparently, these families' situations had not improved as a result of the programs he offered. He continued to ask himself difficult questions of the sort Socrates would endorse: Is my program really helping anyone? Would I want this program for troubled and low-income members of my own family? If not, why am I offering it to other families? The answers he found were distressing: "Now that I was middle income and I could buy mentoring and I could buy drug rehab programs, I knew I could never send [members of my family] to a nonprofit program—because when *I* bought the service, the provider had to provide me with the service that I wanted. The families coming to my programs had to follow whatever my staff told them. We were not consumer-driven at all. We were driven by our funders. So by the late 1990s I was actually very depressed, even though we were considered really great."

Remarkably, the lowest point in Miller's self-examination came when he received a great honor extended to only ten or twelve community honorees per year: "Then I get a call from the White House—President Clinton was inviting me to the State of the Union address. And I turned him down, because to me it didn't make sense. Why would I be invited to anything important if what I was doing was insignificant?" With a little persuasion from his wife, Miller changed his mind and accepted the invitation, but he remained deeply troubled by the honor—and by his career more generally: "We did go, and we met the President, but you have to understand that this was at the very same time that I was the most disgusted with my own work. So it was just such a contradiction, and I'm thinking, 'Why am I being honored? If this is considered the best work in the country, then something is wrong with this country. Our standards are wrong.'"

As Eurich would certainly point out, Miller had been asking "Why" questions—and they weren't helping. His rumination was leading to anxiety and dissatisfaction rather than to positive change. But nine months after the State of the Union address, he had an unexpected opportunity to redirect his self-examination toward "What" questions—which led to a breakthrough in his thinking. The mayor of his city (Oakland, California) called him at home one evening, troubled by a ten-million-dollar grant proposal the city's Private Industry Council, of which Miller was a member, was preparing to send to the Department of Labor to fund youth development programming. Upon hearing that Miller hadn't actually seen the proposal, the mayor had an aide hand-deliver it to Miller's house with the instruction to read it immediately and then call him back. So Miller looked at the proposal's budget: it involved hiring 120 social workers, administrators, and employment specialists and starting three new youth development facilities. At first, he wondered why the mayor found the plan objectionable: "You would think that most mayors would be really happy to see ten million dollars' worth of youth programs coming to their city. But it was apparent to me that he wasn't happy about this. So then I go to what's going to be accomplished by hiring all of these social workers, and it says we're going to enroll eighty percent of the public school kids in Oakland, and we hope some get jobs, and we hope some get off of drugs, and we hope some stay in school."

When Miller returned the mayor's call, the mayor challenged him to devise a better plan—something that could be expected to have more significant outcomes. At first, he says, his reaction was typical for a director of a social service agency: Our programs would be more successful, he claimed, if we had more funding and fewer regulations. But the mayor pushed the challenge further:

He said, "So, if money and regulations were no problem, and you really wanted to bring about some fundamental change, think about what you would do and come to my office next month." Then he hung up. So, I'm like, "Whoa, that's interesting." When you're raised poor, there's always a box. Even running nonprofits, I had to please my funders, and so there's a box. And all of a sudden there's this guy who's pretty powerful saying, "What if there were no box and you could do anything that you wanted to do?" So that's pretty cool, except after two weeks, after a going through all of it and knowing social services for twenty years, I didn't know what I would do.

And it was that more structured, more focused, and more "what"-oriented round of self-questioning—under the pressure of the mayor's expectations, a deadline, and possibly even funding for his ideas if they were promising—that finally led Miller to start an organization with a mission and methods he believed in: the Family Independence Initiative.[28]

As we've seen in this chapter, examining ourselves regularly—and well—can have great benefits. By learning more about our traits, actions, and motives through careful, forward-looking introspection and with honest feedback from others, we can begin to identify our flaws. Acknowledging and addressing those flaws will require honesty and a refusal to rationalize: the topics of the next two chapters.

Chapter 5

REFUSING TO RATIONALIZE

JAMES McCORMICK, who was awarded the Citizen Honors Medal by the Congressional Medal of Honor Foundation for his exemplary work with wounded veterans, didn't always lead such an exemplary life. After an unhappy early childhood punctuated by frequent moves, with parents who often fought and eventually divorced, he was sent to live with his grandparents until he graduated from high school and joined the U.S. Army. By his mid-thirties, McCormick was himself twice divorced, having focused so heavily on his military career that he had little time to devote to his marriages and his four children. His grandmother admonished him to spend more time with his children, to no apparent avail. But a close brush with death while in combat overseas sparked a reconsideration of his priorities. As he describes the transition: "This is where James McCormick takes a look at himself in the mirror, and instead of blaming everything else or everyone else for the problems that occurred in my life—my divorces, my family relationships, the anger issues, losing the ability to connect with my children—I looked in the mirror and said, 'Well, maybe, it's me.'"[1]

That moment of reconsideration—of refusal to continue rationalizing away his share of the responsibility for the difficulties in his personal life— was the beginning of what McCormick calls the "redemption phase" of his life. He resolved to return from combat alive for the sake of his children— and he did in fact reconnect with them the following summer, raising them from that point on. Within just a few years, he was remarried (and remains happily married) to a widow he met at church, and he started Raising Cane Farms, a veteran-run bamboo farm in West Virginia whose mission is to "employ and help returning combat-wounded veterans by offering jobs and a place to work and relax with a team of other veterans, adjusting to a new phase in life after the war."[2]

As he looks to his future, McCormick's main goal is to do still more to assist his fellow veterans and to honor those—including his own children—who have sacrificed their personal interests for the sake of the country: "So the redemption phase still goes on, because I still feel like I owe a great debt to this country, and to God especially, and to my family, and to my children, for their sacrifice—and they made a sacrifice too, my kids did. And I want that sacrifice to have meant something, not just to get a chest full of medals and come home. But [I ask myself], 'What did you do with your life after the war? What did you do as a person? How did you help your fellow man?'" McCormick's answer to the questions he poses for himself comes in the form of reclaiming abandoned coal mines:

The Appalachian area, it's really been hit hard. The coal mines have shut down; they have ripped the mountains off of a lot of places in West Virginia, so we have hundreds of thousands of acres that are essentially sitting there, long void of life. I want to add bamboo and veterans to the reclamation process. And here's the beauty of how this project works: We're dealing with two scarred things—the person and the environment. I want to take you and teach you how to create life in an area that is void of life. And in the process, we're going to heal you, because you'll go there and plant this bamboo, and it's going to grow. And not only is it going to grow, but we're going to turn it into a product that is valuable and useful. So we can actually start to see an increase in jobs. This bamboo is also 35 percent more effective at cleaning the air than trees are. In twenty years, I can see some sort of an ecosystem there that sustains and supports life. Now, that's a beautiful thing, because I'm dealing with kids that are in their 20s, so in twenty years they'll be my age, and they'll be able to say, "I was part of that." We're not just healing the land, we're not just providing jobs, we're not just healing people, but we're giving hope and we're giving someone a reason to stay around as long as they can.

Refusing to Rationalize: An Older Exemplar

While McCormick's conscious decision to stop rationalizing resulted in externally observable positive outcomes, sometimes the only reward of refusal to rationalize is the internal satisfaction of living with integrity. For a dramatic example from classical philosophy, let's take another look at Socrates. Having been sentenced to death, he has been spending his final months in prison, awaiting his execution. And thanks to liberal rules regarding visitation, although he is not free to roam about Athens, he *is* able to continue performing his favorite activity: discussing philosophy—and ethics in particular—with his friends and disciples. Today his old friend Crito has once again broached a particularly thorny and acutely relevant philosophical topic: the ethical implications of escape.[3]

Crito knows this is his last chance to persuade Socrates—the execution will take place in a day or two—so he pulls out all the stops: Socrates, think of your children—how will they get along without you? Think of those who unjustly condemned you—how can you let them win? Think of us, your friends, who will miss you terribly and who will look like cowards if we don't help you get out of here. Don't worry about where you'll go if you escape—I have friends in other cities who will gladly take you in. And don't worry about the money we'll spend and the risks we'll take breaking you out: the informants are easily and cheaply bribed (and I've lined up a lot of benefactors), and we're happy to risk prosecution for such a noble deed—it's the manly thing to do.

It would be really easy for Socrates to go along with Crito's plan. He enjoys his life and would very much prefer that it continue. And of course he doesn't want to sadden his family and friends. But instead of rationalizing—persuading himself that the convenient position is the right one—Socrates takes a mental step back to remember the principles he has come to endorse through years of thoughtful reflection and experience. The real question, he realizes, is not how others will react to his death or his escape but how those principles—principles he has every reason to believe are true—apply to the decision he faces. What guidance can his carefully considered ethical beliefs provide in this difficult situation?

As it turns out, Socrates concludes that his principles compel him to decline Crito's offer. First, he concludes, Crito's arguments fail. It doesn't matter if ignorant people think his friends are cowards, for example; and he wouldn't be able to raise his children while spending his last few years in exile anyway. More importantly, as a voluntary member of the community of Athens—one who has remained there for seventy years, benefiting throughout his lifetime from the order and services its government provides—Socrates has implicitly agreed to obey its laws. In fact, Socrates points out, he likely could have "escaped" legally but chose not to: he declined to propose a penalty of exile at his sentencing, preferring death to leaving his homeland. It would be wrong, he reasons, to escape now through subversion of the system of laws that has protected and guided him all of these years.

My point isn't about the merits of Socrates's reasoning: Perhaps he overestimates the binding force of implicit agreements. Or maybe he underestimates his obligation to go on living for the sake of his family and friends. (If so, however, he's obviously correct to note that the occasion of his sentencing would have been a better time to attend to such considerations.) My point is about Socrates's refusal to rationalize. When presented with an easy opportunity to ignore his ethical ideals and try to justify doing what is expedient, he instead asks how he can act rightly.

Common Rationalization Strategies

We can easily imagine an alternate scenario in which someone in Socrates's position engaged in rationalization—justifying his abandonment of his ideals by redescribing his decision in more favorable terms. (Let's call this hypothetical character "Doliocrates," for the Greek *dolios* or "dishonest.") In fact, most of us have probably—consciously or not—used the following common rationalization strategies ourselves, but for purposes of illustration, I'll ascribe them primarily to Doliocrates rather than to us:[4]

Minimizing the act. Instead of rejecting the opportunity to escape from prison because it would violate his long-held ethical standards, Doliocrates might try to redescribe escape so that it appears to be no big deal: "Well, *maybe just this once* I can *bend* the rules *a little bit*," or *"All I'm doing* is assigning myself the penalty (exile) that the jury would have given me *anyway."* To those of us who are being honest (and who were not born moral exemplars), the italicized phrases should look familiar—they're used with alarming frequency in the stories we tell ourselves and others when trying not to own up to our ethical failures.

Using euphemisms. Closely related to minimizing is a second redescription strategy that Doliocrates might use to avoid taking ethical responsibility for his decision to escape: he could describe his prison break in more benign terms, such as "I'm *relocating* to Sparta," or "I'm *taking care of my health.*" And as with minimizing words, it's tempting for all of us (not just fictional characters whose lives are at stake) to view our actions in the best possible light—even if that means shining a very selective light that conceals more than it reveals.

Advantageous comparison. Another easy way to deflect responsibility—or any negative judgment—is to compare ourselves with someone even worse. We might use this strategy to make ourselves feel better about our nonmoral shortcomings ("At least my grades aren't as bad as Johnny's," or "At least I'm not as out of shape as Sally"); but of course Doliocrates, like the rest of us, could also use it to distract himself from his responsibility for escaping: "I'm nowhere near as culpable as that lawyer who falsely accused me," or "I'm not escaping in the hope of committing a crime spree like Kleftocrates did—*I just want to spend my last years in peace.*" (Notice how this last, italicized, clause also employs minimization and euphemism—rationalization strategies are frequently used together for increased rhetorical effect.)

Describing the act as commonplace. Rather than compare ourselves to those who are even worse, we (or Doliocrates) might welcome the distraction of appealing to *similar* behavior by actual or hypothetical others—we might tell ourselves (as though it justified our own misbehavior) "Everybody else is doing it," or "Anyone in my situation would do the same thing." So, for example, Doliocrates might say "Several recent inmates in this prison have escaped, so it's OK for me to do the same," or "No man my age could be expected to spend the rest of his life in a place like this."

Minimizing the consequences. Related to minimizing the act, another common rationalization strategy is minimizing our act's *consequences*—claiming that our actions didn't really hurt anyone (or at least didn't hurt anyone all that badly). This strategy is often used to dismiss people's ethical qualms about dishonesty generally: "Cheating on this exam won't harm my teacher or classmates—no one will even know," or "A little white lie never hurt anyone." In Doliocrates's case, it would be tempting to justify a decision to escape using similar reasoning: "I'll be out of my fellow Athenians' way whether I stay here or go into exile, so it makes no difference to them."

Blaming others. Another—often very effective—way to deny one's own responsibility is to shift blame onto someone or something else. We might do this sort of thing so routinely that we hardly notice it—especially if that person or situation really does bear *some* of the blame. For example, we might blame our lateness for work on traffic, conveniently ignoring the fact that we also overslept. Just this morning, in fact, I caught myself blaming my husband for my lack of time to go for a run even though I obviously could have made more effort to coordinate my schedule with his. Similarly, Doliocrates could easily find other people or situations to blame for his "need" to escape and conveniently forget that the decision to do so is ultimately his: "If Meletus hadn't drummed up those false charges, I wouldn't be in this situation in the first place," or "The guards aren't paying attention—they obviously don't care whether I stay or go," or even "The whole criminal justice system here in Athens is corrupt." As true as some of our blame statements might be (and I'm not suggesting that all of them *are* true!), none of them removes our responsibility for the part of the situation that's up to us.

Appealing to false moral justifications. Perhaps the most tempting form of rationalization is to convince ourselves that what we are doing is not wrong at all—in fact, we tell ourselves, it's actually morally *required*. We all want to think of ourselves as ethically good—certainly above average—and facing our transgressions interferes with our positive self-perception. For that reason, we seem to have an almost unlimited ability to justify our wrongdoing: Think of perpetrators of atrocious war crimes who describe themselves as dutifully "following orders." In Doliocrates's case, all he'd have to do is accept any of the questionable moral justifications Crito has already offered, for example, "I can't let my friends be thought cowardly," or "I have to escape for the sake of my children."

Moral licensing. As recent studies suggest, a particularly troubling way in which we might use false moral justifications is "moral licensing": using our recent good behavior as a justification for our current lack thereof—and possibly even for our *mis*behavior. Researchers suggest that this tendency comes from having met our need for positive self-perception: as long as our current lack of good behavior doesn't interfere too much with the self-image we've created (depleting our "moral capital"), we find it easier to take a break from our efforts to be virtuous.[5] So Doliocrates might justify his escape by telling himself, "I've spent most of my life serving the people of Athens; it's about time I *did something for myself.*" As before, notice that the italicized phrase employs an additional rationalization strategy: using euphemisms.

So the bad news is that rationalization strategies are plentiful and easy to use—sometimes without our even noticing. But avoiding rationalization is necessary for character development: after all, if we succeed in telling ourselves that there is nothing wrong with our behavior, we won't be motivated to improve. In their book *The Power of Ideals*, psychologists William Damon and Anne Colby helpfully sum up the importance of refusing to rationalize:

> It's hard to imagine that anyone fully avoids rationalization, but people do differ in the extent to which they try sincerely to live their beliefs, ideals, and principles. When individuals are described as persons of integrity, this generally means that moral values and goals are central to who they are and, at least as important, it means that they don't often rationalize their violations of those values in order to let themselves off the hook. The avoidance of rationalization (which we call inner truthfulness) is widely recognized as a central feature of strong moral character.[6]

We'll turn next to some specific strategies for developing this kind of integrity.

How to Avoid Rationalization

How does Socrates manage to avoid rationalization despite intense internal and external pressure to justify doing what is convenient? He himself reveals part of the answer: previous careful reflection and a long-standing habit of using his reason rather than blindly (or at least nearsightedly) following his desires and emotions. To work toward Socrates's level of inner truthfulness—and self-control—we can begin with the sort of self-examination we discussed in chapter 4. As we noted there, honest self-examination includes paying particularly close attention to unsettling information about ourselves.

A variation on this self-examination theme can help us to counter our rationalizing thoughts. When we find ourselves redescribing our actions and temptations in a way that makes them sound more favorable—perhaps with the rationalization strategies outlined above—it's time to stop and have an honest conversation with ourselves. We might ask ourselves questions like: "Might I be minimizing the consequences of this act?" or "Am I failing to accept my share of the blame for this problem?" In fact, if we're attentive enough to catch ourselves engaging in them (or if we habituate ourselves to be cautious about our own justifications), each of the rationalization strategies can be countered with a bit of well-directed reflection:

Connecting action and character. Instead of minimizing our actions, we can recognize how they reflect on our character. Socrates in fact seems to do this: he considers escape to be the act of an unjust and ungrateful man, one who disobeys the very laws that are responsible for his good upbringing and that he implicitly agreed to obey.

Using neutral—even negative—descriptors. Rather than use euphemisms to redescribe our actions, we can counter that rationalization by using accurate and neutral or (if applicable) negative descriptors to see whether the proposed action falls under a description of something we have no business doing. Socrates is especially good at this one. On behalf of the laws, he interrogates himself—describing escape as a breach of his agreement with them: "You, Socrates, are breaking the covenants and agreements which you made with us at your leisure, not in any haste or under any compulsion or deception, but having had seventy years to think of them, during which time you were at liberty to leave the city, if we were not to your mind, or if our covenants appeared to you to be unfair."[7]

Comparison with role models. While it's often tempting to try to boost our self-esteem by focusing on the more serious shortcomings of others, that's definitely not the way to improve—ethically or in any area of life. Instead, we should compare ourselves to role models and try to imitate them. Looking at the achievements of those who have done especially well in the area of ethical development can give us a realistic picture of what we're capable of—and of where we fall short and how we might do better in the future.[8] Socrates uses this strategy as well, at least in a general way. He insists that we should follow the advice and example only of good and wise people.

Discarding appeals to the commonplace. When you were young and wanted to do something your friends were doing, perhaps an older relative asked, "If your friends jumped off a cliff, would you do it too?" (My mother asked that, and so did my best friend's mother.) Socrates could have asked something similar of Crito: when arguing that we should follow only good and wise examples, he repeatedly contrasts that approach with following the crowd. For example, he says, if a gymnast ignored the advice of his physician or trainer and instead followed "the many who have no understanding," he would likely do serious damage to his body. Similarly, just doing what everyone else does is no way to excel ethically.

Extrapolating the consequences. Although minimizing the consequences of our action tends to involve a short-sighted focus on the immediate harm (or lack thereof), in truth, our actions aren't isolated—from each other or from the rest of the world. Each action we choose is potentially both part of a habit and an influence on the actions of others. By thinking about the further, longer-term, effects our actions could have, we may save ourselves from rationalizing some really bad decisions. In Socrates's case, he considers an escape's more negative potential effects on his children. If he brings them into exile with him, they'll lose their Athenian citizenship. (And if he doesn't, his friends' "escape for the sake of your children" justification becomes moot.) He also expresses concern regarding the impact of escape on his own afterlife.

Recognizing agency. Instead of blaming others for their part in our difficulties, we can more effectively move forward and develop our own character by recognizing and acknowledging our own contributions to the problem. Perhaps a coworker really *was* rude to me, but was I insensitive to the stress she was under? Maybe my teammate did drop the ball (literally or figuratively), but could I have thrown it better? In his own refusal to rationalize, Socrates notes that he could have proposed exile as a sentence; instead, he proposed a penalty he knew the jury wouldn't accept, effectively sealing his own fate.

Acknowledging incrimination. Rather than appeal to false moral justifications—reasons we "have to" engage in questionable behavior—we can acknowledge exactly what is wrong with the course of action we're considering. For example, despite being "helpful" or "necessary," is it also dishonest, selfish, or unfair? This sort of acknowledgment might be seen as Socrates's theme in the *Crito.* Along with his more specific objections to Crito's attempted justifications, Socrates consistently reminds Crito that simply deciding as an individual citizen to disregard the laws of his community would violate the principles of justice.

Moral commitment. In response to our temptations toward moral licensing—using previous good behavior as a "license" to lower our standards—we can choose instead to interpret our good behavior as a sign of our commitment to ethical excellence. This strategy is similar to Socrates's observation that he has chosen to remain under the laws of Athens all of his adult life; he concludes that he must accept these laws and find them better than the alternatives.

For reference, I list all of the rationalization strategies we've discussed, along with my proposed counter-rationalization techniques and some more contemporary examples, in figure 5.1.

As Socrates suggests with his imaginary interrogation by the laws and with references to God's will, a more general way to avoid rationalization is through accountability to someone with high ethical standards. Like some of the more specific strategies above, the use of accountability is effective in many areas of life. It comes recommended by fitness gurus,[9] leaders of twelve-step programs for overcoming addiction, religious traditions, and even experts on writing productivity.[10] And it works just as well for ethical development: as we have seen, all six of the twentieth-century moral leaders Damon and Colby studied employed counter-rationalization strategies involving accountability, including "honest discussions with friends and intimate partners, requests to colleagues and staff for candid feedback, and conscious efforts to take seriously criticism from opponents."[11] And this strategy certainly fits my more limited experience as well; in fact, when my students

Rationalization	Counter-rationalization
Minimizing the act: "I'm supposed to clean the grill before I leave work, but I'll just bend the rules a little bit."	*Connecting action and character:* "Do I want to be the sort of person who doesn't do the job s/he was hired to do? That's lazy, and it's unfair to my employer."
Using euphemisms: "I'm keeping more of my hard-earned money."	*Using neutral—even negative—descriptors:* "I'm committing tax fraud."
Advantageous comparison: "At least I'm not as cruel as those pranksters I saw on YouTube."	*Comparison with role models:* "I'm nowhere near as kind to my own family as Mother Teresa was to strangers."
Describing the act as commonplace: "I bet anybody who had the opportunity would look at the answer key."	*Discarding appeals to the commonplace:* "Even if most people would cheat, it's still dishonest and unjust."
Minimizing the consequences: "This bag of chips only weighs nine ounces, so it can't cause noticeable weight gain."	*Extrapolating the consequences:* "Do I really want to start a habit of consuming an extra 1,000 calories when I'm stressed?"
Blaming others: "My roommates were the ones who invited underage people to our party."	*Recognizing agency:* "I chose not to ask the underage guests to leave, or even not to drink."
Appealing to false moral justifications: "I need the extra commission money to pay for my kids' education."	*Acknowledging incrimination:* "I'd be getting the extra money by misrepresenting the condition of the car."
Moral licensing: "I already volunteered for a good cause this week, so there's no need to give my sister a ride to work."	*Moral commitment:* "I volunteered for a good cause this week because I value helpfulness—of course I'll help my own sister."

Figure 5.1. Counters to common rationalizations

ask for tips on ethical development, at the top of my list is, "Marry someone who is brutally honest."

Reconstructing Rationalization and Its Avoidance: The Practical Syllogism

Turning from Plato's *Crito* to the work of his star student Aristotle, we find a helpful philosophical analysis of what happens when we engage (either well or with rationalizations) in ethical reasoning: the practical syllogism.[12] To understand its function, we'll do well to take just a moment to consider logical syllogisms more generally. Also Aristotelian in origin, the syllogism is a deductive logical argument with three steps: a major premise, a minor premise, and a conclusion. ("Major" and "minor" are technical terms; they don't indicate importance—both premises are essential.) The major premise makes a universal claim about a category of things, for example, "All men are mortal," or "No cats are dogs." The minor premise states that some other thing or category of things fits within the scope of the major premise's subject, for example, "Socrates is a man," or "Orange tabbies are cats." Finally, then, we conclude that the description of the broader subject of the major premise also applies to the more specific subject of the minor premise: "Socrates is mortal," or "Orange tabbies are not dogs" (see figure 5.2).

Practical syllogisms, as the term suggests, are syllogisms regarding practical matters: what we should do or avoid. Those about what to avoid are particularly prevalent, first, because when we rationalize it's usually to justify *doing* something we actually should be *avoiding*; and second, because there are almost no categories of action that we should always do—so there are very few true major (universal) premises of the "do" sort available. (And the ones that *are* true usually are too general to be of much help in everyday ethical analysis—for example, "All acts of doing the right thing are acts that should be done." Perfectly true, of course, but it doesn't get us any closer to knowing what *is* the right thing.) On the "don't" or "avoid" side, though, practical syllogisms often can be quite useful: There are lots of categories of activities that are always a bad idea. Just to take a few examples, some more tempting than others: "Don't drink motor oil," "Don't seduce your best friend's significant other," and "Don't cheat on ethics exams."

Those few bits of advice sounded (I hope) like common sense. So you

Major premise	All men are mortal.	No cats are dogs.
Minor premise	Socrates is a man.	Orange tabbies are cats.
Conclusion	Therefore, Socrates is mortal.	Therefore, orange tabbies are not dogs.

Figure 5.2. Example categorical syllogisms

Major premise	Don't cheat on ethics exams.
Minor premise	This exam in front of you is an ethics exam.
Conclusion	Therefore, don't cheat on this exam in front of you.

Figure 5.3. Example practical syllogism: Ethics exam

might wonder: Why would we ever use practical syllogisms? After all, for any reasonably clever person, there's generally no need to spell out a syllogism like the one in figure 5.3.

But real life is more complicated than that, even for reasonably clever people—*especially*, in fact, for reasonably clever people, who possess an almost limitless ability to redescribe their actions. In fact, most of Aristotle's discussion of the practical syllogism revolves around rationalization and weakness of will rather than around sound moral reasoning.[13] So while it's true that we typically don't need or use practical syllogisms in an explicit way, now that we know how they work we can in fact use them to understand and avoid redescriptions of the rationalizing sort. For example, we might describe the same act as "moving a piece of metal," "trying out my new sword," or "killing an innocent passer-by"; the first two innocuous-sounding descriptions might be used to rationalize an act that also meets the third.[14] Or, to take a less sinister example, we might describe Mr. Smith's act as "mowing the lawn," "getting some exercise," or "avoiding his wife." Again, all three may be accurate; it is the mark of a rationalizer to fail to acknowledge the third.[15]

Because real life is complicated in this way, with an indefinite number of descriptions—even known, relevant descriptions—applying to a given act, the practical syllogism can come in handy when we're tempted to set our own actions in the most favorable light possible by employing any or all of the rationalization strategies we discussed above. Using the counter-rationalization techniques as a starting point, we can supplement our mini-

Major premise	Don't ever kill innocent passers-by.
Minor premise	That person is an innocent passer-by.
Conclusion	Therefore, don't kill that person.

Figure 5.4. Example practical syllogism: Innocent passers-by

mizing or euphemistic descriptions with as many relevant and accurate descriptions as our time and creativity allow; for example, in addition to the descriptions already listed, Mr. Smith might call his action "beautifying my yard," "keeping up property values," "breaking in my new shoes," or "annoying my napping neighbor." Or the samurai "trying out his new sword" could also describe his action as "lifting and lowering a three-pound object," "doing one rep of a tricep exercise," or "improving in the martial arts."

So here's the point: if even one accurate description falls into a category of universal "don'ts"—things we never have any business doing, such as "killing an innocent passer-by"—then the action is bad, no matter how many positive-sounding descriptions we can also apply. So we can list as many accurate descriptions as we can think of with the form, "This action is x"; each description is a potential minor premise in a practical syllogism. If, above one of those premises, we can accurately add a major premise of the form "Actions that are x are never to be done," or simply "Don't ever do x," then we know better than to do that action (see figure 5.4).

And even if none of the descriptions names something that is *always* bad, when one of them fits a category of actions that are *usually* bad, we should take the opportunity to consider carefully whether the present circumstances really justify going ahead with it anyway. For example, while it may not *always* be wrong to avoid one's spouse, it's not generally advisable and is probably a sign that something has gone wrong; does Mr. Smith have a good enough reason to avoid his wife on this particular occasion? Similarly, as we saw in the real-life example at the beginning of this chapter, James McCormick could accurately describe his volunteering for additional military deployments as "serving my country" and "advancing my career"; but it was only when he admitted that it was *also* accurately described as "avoiding my family" that he was able to turn his personal life around and to focus on improving the lives of fellow veterans.

Chapter 6

HONESTY

The Courage to Tell the Truth

SUSAN BURTON'S childhood was traumatic: to take just a few of the adverse events and patterns in her life, she was physically abused by her older brothers, molested by a neighbor, and raped at age fifteen—which resulted in the birth of her daughter. But her early adulthood was even more traumatic: her five-year-old son was accidentally run over by a police car and killed. After the death of her son, Burton turned to alcohol and drugs, for which she was repeatedly imprisoned—but was never offered treatment for her addiction.

Finally, after her sixth release from prison, someone reached out to Burton and she got the help she needed. She stayed in a recovery home and went through a twelve-step program—and has been alcohol- and drug-free ever since. Just a year after getting sober, she started reaching out to other women as they were released from prison, offering to put them up in her own home while they pursued treatment. Today, she is the founder and executive director of A New Way of Life, an organization dedicated to assisting formerly incarcerated women—helping them overcome their addictions and develop the stability and life skills necessary to keep them out of prison in the future.

Early in her recovery, Burton was very close to returning to prison herself; her story provides a vivid image of the virtue of truthfulness:

I was working through the steps of recovery, and the steps require you
to be honest and really to face your past—and I was on parole, and I had
absconded from parole. It seemed like my life was coming together, and
I reached this point where I exposed to my twelve-step sponsor in the recovery home that I was on parole and I had absconded. And they told me
I had to face the parole department. And I prepared myself to go back to
prison in order to move forward on what we call, "Clear up the wreckage
of your past."

And I went to the parole department, and the lady was just livid. She
was so angry with me, as they say, you could've fried an egg on her head.
[Laughs.] And I said to her, "I'm sorry I didn't show up for my appointment." My appointment had been months earlier. I said, "But I was under
the control of drugs and alcohol. I'm in a program now, and I'm no longer
under the control of drugs and alcohol. The program requires you to be
honest, so I came to you to tell you I'm sorry, and I'm here to turn myself
in." And she didn't arrest me. She said she was going to give me a pass, and
it would be the last pass she ever gave me, but she didn't arrest me.

And I felt like that was just one of the biggest things that ever happened in my life: that I had gotten a break, I had gotten a pass, and I could
go forward with my recovery. And I felt like the universe had wrapped
this sort of invisible shield around me to help protect me as I go forward.
And I never lost that feeling—that I'm in the zone of protection, and all I
have needed to do is continue to do the right thing, by myself and by the
people, for myself and for the people.[1]

Closely related to the more general ethical virtue of honesty, truthfulness
focuses especially on self-representation: the degree to which our image of
ourselves—as presented to ourselves and to others—reflects who we really
are. In Burton's case, it was crucial to her recovery that she make an accurate
representation of herself and her behavior—first to herself, then to her sponsor, and finally to her parole officer. Disclosure of her misdeed required two
of the life skills we've seen thus far in this book: self-examination and refusal
to rationalize. And her willingness to do so for the sake of progressing in her
recovery required recognition of her potential to become a fully recovered
person. As we saw with the stories of Socrates, Mauricio Lim Miller, and

James McCormick, these practices are personally and interpersonally valuable in their own right; they also contribute to the development and exercise of truthfulness.

As we also see from Burton's story, exemplary truthfulness (and honesty more generally) often requires courage. It takes no special virtue to be honest when nothing of importance is at stake, but even for those of us not threatened with dire consequences for our truthful disclosures, facing the truth frequently means acknowledging our shortcomings and fears. In the rest of this chapter we'll take a closer look at truthfulness and honesty, and at how we might develop and exercise them in our own (usually more ordinary) circumstances.

Truthfulness (and Lack Thereof) in Contemporary Life

In *The Power of Ideals*, William Damon and Anne Colby note that truthfulness seems to have fallen out of fashion in contemporary society. Although it traditionally has been promoted as an essential virtue (for example, think of the Roman goddess Veritas or of famous stories about U.S. presidents George Washington and Abraham Lincoln), today popular media and even educational institutions often minimize the importance of truthfulness—promoting favorable self-deception and self-esteem at all costs. But, as Damon and Colby point out, such strategies not only undermine interpersonal trust; they also are detrimental in the long term for those who exercise them: a false confidence in one's own abilities leads to a lack of openness to constructive feedback or even private recognition of one's own limitations—which in turn leads to a lack of growth and improvement.[2]

Why, then, do most of us occasionally struggle with honesty? If being truthful is ultimately in our own interest and in the interest of those around us, shouldn't a decision in favor of honesty with ourselves and others be easy? I think much of our self-deception stems from fear of seeing ourselves as we really are—a form of cowardice. To combat this tendency, understanding the long-term benefits of truthfulness is indeed a good first step. As we've all experienced, however, the short-term attractions of self-deception (or deception of others) can be difficult to resist. Sometimes we recognize such temptations for what they are—temptations—but still act against our better judgment; sometimes we are so carried away by desire or anxiety that we simply don't give the decision adequate thought.[3] And of course once self-deception begins, it has a way of perpetuating itself by denying its own existence. As we have seen, we can simply rationalize our not-so-good behavior in an alarmingly wide variety of ways: by describing it with euphemisms, by comparing ourselves with those whose behavior is even worse, or by denying our responsibility for (or the consequences of) our action or inaction.

The ease with which we can rationalize is, in part, why it is so important to have formed a habit—or virtue—of truthfulness *before* encountering the situational pressures that tempt us to think or act dishonestly. For example, the twelve-step program with which Susan Burton was involved encouraged honesty and truthfulness: in addition to beginning with the admission of one's addiction, such programs emphasize performing "a searching and fearless moral inventory" of oneself and confessing the findings of the inventory to one's sponsor.[4] That blossoming habit of admitting painful truths about herself, along with a genuine desire for recovery regardless of the cost, gave Burton the courage to be truthful even with her parole officer. We, too, can start by forming habits of acknowledging unpleasant truths to ourselves and to a trusted confidante, which will make it easier to be honest, even at considerable cost. Toward the end of this chapter we'll consider some practical ways to exercise truthfulness in the more mundane situations we typically face; first, though, we'll work to better understand the nature of the virtue itself.

The Virtue of Truthfulness

In book 4 of his *Nicomachean Ethics*, Aristotle examines truthfulness as a virtue. Like Damon and Colby, he focuses on inner truthfulness: acknowledgement of one's own strengths and weaknesses. He begins by describing the more common opposing trait of boastfulness: claiming more than is really true about oneself—that is, claiming through words or deeds to have valued attributes that one doesn't really have, or claiming to have them to a greater degree than is really accurate. As Aristotle points out, boasters come in three main kinds: those who boast for no obvious reason, those who boast in the hope of impressing others and being praised or honored, and those who boast for material gain. The first kind Aristotle describes as contempt-ible in a futile sort of way rather than morally bad, the second as bad but not *that* bad, and the third as "an uglier character."[5] Cicero, who was also influ-enced by Socrates, condemns even more strongly than did Aristotle those who boast for the sake of gain: "While wrong may be done in two ways, either by force or by fraud, ... of the two, fraud is the most detestable. But of all forms of injustice, none is more heinous than that of the men who, while they practice fraud to the utmost of their ability, do it in such a way that they appear to be good men."[6] Of course, one could boast for multiple reasons and fall into both of the last two categories. To take a fictional example, Shawn Spencer from the TV comedy *Psych* claimed to be a psychic both to impress people and to secure employment with the police department as a "psychic detective." (Spencer also used his boastful deception to solve crimes, which does complicate matters somewhat—Aristotle doesn't specifically ad-dress people who boast in order to do something worthwhile. But he does say that falsehood is blameworthy in itself.)[7]

Like the more general virtue of honesty, Cicero is suggesting, truthful-ness is closely related to justice: it is unjust to deceive fellow members of our community. Aristotle also links honesty closely with justice, but he seems to consider truthfulness and justice to be related more by causation than by def-inition; he says that in discussing the truthful person "we are not speaking of the man who keeps faith in his agreements, i.e. in the things that pertain to justice ... but the man who in the matters in which nothing of this sort is at stake is true both in word and in life because his character is such"—but, he adds, "such a man would seem to be as a matter of fact equitable [i.e., just]. For the man who loves truth, and is truthful where nothing is at stake, will still more be truthful where something is at stake; he will avoid falsehood as something base, seeing that he avoided it even for its own sake; and such a man is worthy of praise."[8]

Aristotle also discusses a less-bad vice opposed to truthfulness: mock-modesty—disclaiming or belittling one's own good qualities. Although a mock-modest person is generally pleasant to be around, especially when using understatement subtly and not too excessively, it's not virtuous to ap-ply falsehood as a social lubricant. (And, as Aristotle also notes, sometimes mock-modesty is actually a thinly disguised form of boasting: it's an invita-tion to the listener to "reassure" the speaker of the obvious strengths he or she is disclaiming.) Better, Aristotle argues, to be someone "who calls a thing by its own name, being truthful both in life and in word, owning to what he has, and neither more nor less ... [because] falsehood is in itself mean and culpable, and truth noble and worthy of praise. Thus the truthful man is another case of a man who, being in the mean, is worthy of praise."[9] I saw this sort of truthfulness in most of my interviewees. While they tended not to brag about their virtues and accomplishments, they generally did acknowledge their strengths—and how they had used those strengths to do the sorts of things that resulted in recognition.[10]

As we saw in chapter 1, excellences of character (moral virtues) are formed by habituation: repeatedly acting in a virtuous way leads to a habit—a character trait—of the corresponding virtue. And truthfulness is no exception to this rule. We develop the virtue by performing actions in accordance with truthfulness, by representing the facts, especially about ourselves, honestly—both to ourselves and to others. That brings me back to my previous point: as Susan Burton did, we need to develop the habits of honesty and truthfulness *before* facing situations that will strongly tempt us toward dishonesty.

Interestingly, in his dialogue *Gorgias*, Plato speaks in favor of making truthful confessions much like Burton's—in fact, he argues that we should immediately and unhesitatingly confess any wrongdoing to the authorities. Like Aristotle, Plato (or Socrates in Plato's story) is primarily concerned with improving the offender's character; unlike Aristotle, though, he doesn't suppose that this improvement will occur solely through habituation. He also doesn't suppose that penalties will be waived (as happened with Burton) or lightened (as, for example, with student athletes at some high schools) when policy violations are self-disclosed. Rather, he argues that *punishment itself* will help the offender to improve in character: "The one who avoids paying what's due always [is] more miserable than the one who does pay it.... And if he or anyone else he cares about acts unjustly, he should voluntarily go to the place where he'll pay his due as soon as possible; he should go to the judge as though he were going to a doctor."[11]

As becomes clear elsewhere in *Gorgias*, Socrates takes quite seriously the analogy between judge and doctor. In much the same way that an unpleasant medication or surgery cures a bodily ailment, he argues, just punishment "cures" the offender's psyche of injustice.[12] And while that claim may be a bit overstated, it does seem to fit well with recovery programs' encouragement, as Burton recalled, to "clear up the wreckage of your past"—including health problems, damaged relationships, and legal issues. As addiction recovery experts point out, failing to deal with these fears and problems will increase anxiety—and it is often anxiety that leads people to fall back into self-destructive behaviors.[13] So while punishment itself may not cure the self-destruction, accepting punishment for past misdeeds may well put one in a better mental position than will attempting to avoid detection.

Now that we've considered Plato's and Aristotle's philosophical accounts of the virtue of truthfulness and its opposing vices, we'll next examine the psychological aspects of the most obvious truthfulness-related failure: deception of ourselves and others. Then we'll look at some features and dramatic examples of truthfulness in the lives of several exemplary leaders before discussing ways in which we can apply the philosophical and psychological accounts, and emulate the exemplars, in our own (presumably more ordinary) lives.

Self-Deception: The Enemy of Inner Truthfulness

Not all that long ago, I caught my (then) four-year-old son smashing his toy car into his two-year-old sister. Although he clearly did so on purpose, he insisted it had been an accident. Naturally, I asked how he possibly could have "accidentally" crashed into her when she was readily visible and there was plenty of room to drive elsewhere. Making his best attempt at an angelic expression, he replied, "Because I didn't know that forward wasn't backward."

We might lie about ourselves—even *to* ourselves—for all sorts of reasons: as Aristotle mentioned earlier, perhaps we are trying to impress others or to get ahead—like people who inflate their qualifications when applying for jobs. Maybe we think our dishonesty will benefit someone else, as in the common lie people tell to spare their friends' feelings: "No, those pants don't make you look fat."[14] Or maybe, like my young son, we want to avoid something scary or unpleasant such as punishment, disapproval, or guilt.

Actually, according to psychologists who study self-deception, the desire to appear angelic is among the most common reasons that people deceive themselves. To at least some degree, many of us have a "moralistic bias," that is, a tendency to overinflate our own perceptions of our morally good qualities and actions, conveniently ignoring our ethical failures and telling ourselves how saintly we are for doing (or enduring) things that really aren't that big a deal. As psychologists Delroy Paulhus and Oliver John tell us, moralistic bias is "a self-deceptive tendency to deny socially deviant impulses and to claim sanctimonious 'saint-like' attributes. This tendency is played out in overly positive self-perceptions on such traits as agreeableness, dutifulness, and restraint."[15] So while perhaps we adults seldom attempt deception (of ourselves or anyone else) as obvious as that of a sibling-smashing preschooler, we tend to use our more developed intellectual abilities for, among many other things, more subtle lies—sometimes even subtle enough to fool ourselves into thinking we're much better people than we really are.

In addition to moralistic bias, Paulhus and John note, another common human tendency provides ample motivation for self-deception: "egoistic bias"—the propensity many of us have to believe that we are better than others in nonmoral dimensions such as intelligence, attractiveness, or social influence. And self-deceptive bias seems to be related to deliberate deception of others: as Paulhus and Reid showed in another article, there appears to be a close relationship between deception of others for "impression management"—the psychological term for attempts to make others think better (or at least not think worse) of us—and self-deceptive denial of negative traits.[16] And as with moralistic bias, egoistic bias likely has fear of acknowledging our negative traits as its underlying motivation. (Interestingly, at least one negative trait—narcissism—has been found to be associated with self-deception. So a narcissist could be expected to deny, among other things, that he or she is a narcissist.)[17]

To avoid self-deception, we might begin with the techniques we discussed earlier for self-examination and (especially) avoidance of rationalization, which, if successful enough, amounts to a form of self-deceit. We might also take a bit of additional advice from classical philosophy and from contemporary psychology: to seek accountability and surround ourselves with good influences.

Seek accountability. As with anything that requires self-control, accountability to others can reinforce our commitment to avoid deceiving ourselves. We can and should, of course, directly ask those we trust to help us avoid self-deception when we are making important decisions or judgments. In addition, psychologists have recently suggested that two more specific types of accountability may be helpful in improving our truthfulness: verbalizing our commitments and receiving feedback about ourselves publicly rather than privately. In one study, participants who verbalized their commitments were significantly more likely to honor them than were those who agreed with a simple "okay" or who merely received instructions with which to comply.[18] Although the participants in this particular study were children, the technique seems likely to be effective with adults too: it is natural that we would most fully "own" those commitments that we verbalize most explicitly.

In another study, participants who tended to repress negative information about themselves—and hence ignore negative feedback from others—spent much more time reading negative feedback when it was given to them publicly than when it was given privately; they also showed superior ability to recall the negative information they had received.[19] We can learn a more general lesson here, too: when we anticipate receiving negative feedback or information, we can arrange to do so in a manner that holds us accountable to take it seriously. For example, we might ask to receive our performance evaluation in person—or, if that isn't practical, we might arrange to meet later with our supervisors or coworkers to discuss the written feedback they provide. (This technique might work even if the feedback is given anonymously. For example, perhaps I could invite some of my former students to form a focus group of sorts to discuss the anonymous student course evaluations I have received in recent years and make suggestions.)

Surround yourself with good influences. As with seeking accountability, the advice to surround ourselves with good influences is not specific to developing truthfulness: we need good influences in all areas of our lives. Although (as we saw in chapter 2) Confucian philosophers Mencius and Xunzi disagree regarding the moral quality of our human nature, they have eerily similar advice regarding how to improve our characters. We need good environments and good teachers. In fact, Xunzi concludes his famous essay "Man's Nature is Evil" by exclaiming, "Environment is the important thing! Environment is the important thing!"[20] And Mencius, as we have seen, compares companions who are negative influences to frost and weeds that threaten the growth of our "sprouts" of virtue.[21]

Psychologists have recently confirmed in an interesting way the importance of avoiding negative influence in the area of truthfulness. In a variation on a classic study in which children of various ages were told not to peek at an object while the experimenter left the room and were asked afterward whether they had in fact peeked, the researchers told some of the participants a lie before beginning this test of self-control and honesty. As one might expect, among school-age children, those to whom lies had been told were more likely to "cheat" (peek) and, if they did cheat, were more likely to lie about having done so[22]—the researchers rightly note that their findings have important implications for parents and educators. And as with the study regarding verbalizing our commitments, these findings also seem to have implications for adults: it's easier to justify being not-quite-honest with ourselves or with others if we surround ourselves with people who behave in the same way. But if we make a point of selecting honest companions—in business, educational, and social environments—our truthfulness will likely improve.

Virtual accountability and influences. Unfortunately, some of us—including Susan Burton when she was growing up—lack obvious candidates for the roles of good influence and accountability partner. What can we do when selecting virtuous companions and accountability partners isn't a realistic option? While adverse circumstances no doubt bring some disadvantage in ethical development, when overcome they can provide profound opportunities for learning and personal growth. (Although I was blessed with a happy childhood, many of the best people I know—including several of my award-winning interviewees—were not so fortunate. But they have come out of their negative experiences better people than I likely ever will be.) In addition to their amazing resilience, those who grow up to be exceptionally virtuous despite lacking obvious examples of good behavior often have something else in common: they turn to someone outside their immediate social circle—sometimes even someone whom they have never met in person—to provide the positive influence and accountability they need. This practice is similar to Mencius's recommendation that the most virtuous people in one region (for whom there is no obvious local role model or accountability partner) befriend the most virtuous people in other regions—and, if they don't find suitable companions in other regions, that they "make friends in history" through stories of well-known exemplars.[23] For example, as we'll explore at more length in chapter 11, one of my interviewees took Mother

Teresa (whom he eventually did meet in person) as a role model. Another focused on her relationship with God (whom she might be said to have "met," but not in the ordinary sense of the word) for both guidance and companionship. And any of us who want to become virtuous, even if we lack good role models in our lives, can learn from stories of great moral leaders—next we'll consider a few of those leaders and how they exercised the virtue of inner truthfulness.

Two Marks of Exemplary Truthfulness

In contrast to the distressingly typical indifference (or worse) toward truthfulness in contemporary popular culture, Damon and Colby found in their examination of the lives of several twentieth-century moral exemplars that the virtue was alive and well in them, and that, as classical Confucian and Socratic philosophers would have expected, truthfulness was in many ways key to their effective exercise of virtue and leadership. In fact, in these moral leaders Damon and Colby encountered five main themes or forms of truthfulness; in this section we'll examine two of these themes: discernment and resolve. We'll also look at their applications in the lives of Damon and Colby's exemplars and in the lives of those I interviewed—including Susan Burton, with whose high-stakes truthfulness we began this chapter.[24]

Discernment. The process of discernment, closely related to the self-examination we discussed earlier in this book, involves considering our options in light of our espoused values and principles. Sometimes the right path is fairly obvious once we consider the ethical truths we profess to believe; sometimes discernment is more difficult, especially when the outcomes—or our own motives—aren't entirely clear. As an example of discernment, Damon and Colby point to Lutheran pastor and theologian Dietrich Bonhoeffer's decision to return to Nazi Germany and face probable persecution for his opposition to Hitler's regime. The decision was quite difficult for Bonhoeffer—he wasn't normally a risk-taker and wasn't confident in his own motives. But as his diary shows, he had developed a habit of self-examination in light of his principles—of honest discernment—that continued to guide him through his most difficult choices.[25] As with Burton's decision to return to her parole officer, Bonhoeffer's decision to return to Germany had high stakes and thus required significant courage. (Unfortunately, unlike Burton's parole officer, the Nazis didn't give Bonhoeffer a pass.)

Mauricio Lim Miller also faced a difficult decision: whether to continue or abandon his career in the traditional social service sector. Through years of self-examination, Miller determined that his position was not in line with his values or his common sense. Still, he did not take the step of leaving until he'd discerned a better alternative. He founded a new organization, the Family Independence Initiative, which emphasizes respect and trust for low-income families and for their ability to rely upon themselves and each other to escape poverty.[26]

We also saw Susan Burton's use of discernment in light of her newfound commitment to honesty and recovery. Since starting A New Way of Life to assist women facing struggles similar to her own, Burton has had to discern several important decisions for her organization. Here is just one example of a difficult choice she made:

I had a contract with the Department of Probation to provide housing for women who were coming into our home. And the contract provided a couple of hundred thousand dollars a year in resources for housing the women, but the contract also made me feel like I was extending law enforcement tactics into our housing services. I felt exposing the women to the oversight, to harassment, and to the tactics that didn't allow us to build trust, was damaging to the building of our relationships and to people building their own character and self-esteem and integrity.

And I terminated the contract, and it was a wise decision in hindsight. But it was a scary decision, because people had to be paid and the organization had to survive, and this was one of our primary contracts—our primary sources of income for the housing scene. But I terminated the contract, trusting that our mission and the way I treated people was more important than the dollars they were giving us. And what happened is the next month, somebody gave us $275,000. That was very reinforcing and reassuring that if I do the right thing, the right thing will come.

Burton's careful consideration of, and willingness to act on, the principles she had come to endorse, even at the risk of great cost to herself and her organization, showed remarkable discernment. That decision also showed great resolve—the next quality we'll discuss.

Resolve. Of course, it is one thing to discern our obligations in light of the truths we profess; it is often quite another to muster the courage to act on them—especially in the face of significant opposition. Like other aspects of truthfulness, the resolve to tell and act upon the truth regardless of the personal costs is a habit best developed before dire consequences become a threat—it's much easier and generally much more effective to "practice" in less-threatening situations and work our way up than to suddenly decide to be truthful just when the stakes are highest.

To take a striking example, for Nelson Mandela "getting the truth about apartheid out to the world was worth the price of his own life." When being tried for conspiracy, "Mandela was more determined to use the trial as a showcase of the evils of apartheid than to gain release or leniency. With this in mind, he delivered an address that was sure to seal his conviction but that vividly drew the world's attention to the extreme injustice of South Africa's policies."[27] As a result, he was sentenced to life in prison—and served twenty-seven years of that sentence before being released and, eventually, being elected president of his country. Mandela believed that acknowledging the truth about its history was the only way for South Africa and its citizens to move forward. To that end, during his presidency he and Bishop Desmond Tutu formed the Truth and Reconciliation Commission to investigate and acknowledge—but not primarily to prosecute—the injustices committed under apartheid. To the surprise of many around the world, thanks in large part to Mandela's ongoing resolve to expose the truth, the Commission's work was successful in helping to bring healing and unity to a deeply wounded and divided nation.[28]

Like Mandela, Susan Burton has had to use both resolve and courage in her efforts to assist formerly incarcerated women—and, more recently, to raise awareness of and work to eliminate the problem of mass incarceration. Inspired by the book *The New Jim Crow*,[29] Burton believes that the high rates of incarceration among African-Americans, especially for drug-related offenses, represents an ongoing problem with racial injustice. Although she was sixty-five years old at the time of our interview, when I asked what might be coming next in her life Burton made no mention of retirement. Instead she replied, "The next chapter of my story is to use my book that's coming out as a tool to educate and bring women into the conversation of mass incarceration, to bring visibility and solution to the problem of the growth of women inside prisons and jails. I'm going on a book tour, and on each stop, I want to stop at a prison in the area and talk to women in prison, and educate the broader community about alternatives to incarceration, and supports for women after incarceration." Like Mandela, she sees important truths about grave injustices—and she is willing to make significant personal sacrifices to address them, and to help others to see and act upon those truths.

Truthfulness for the Rest of Us

While you and I likely won't be called upon to sacrifice life and liberty for the sake of the truth, we should—like Mandela and Burton—be willing to accept the sacrifices necessary to grow in truthfulness. As I suggested earlier in this chapter, among the most typical—and often the most painful—sacrifices we more "ordinary" folks may have to make is of our inflated egos: a "searching moral inventory" of ourselves, as the twelve-step programs call it, is bound to be unpleasant for anyone but the greatest of saints. For example, common instructions for the inventory include close attention to one's resentments, harm of others, and sexual transgressions—and to the selfish motives and undesirable character traits (also known as ethical vices!) that tend to underlie such problems. As we saw earlier, all of us—not just those of us suffering from addiction—can benefit from honest assessment of our own actions, motives, and character.

I found a striking example of this kind of truthfulness in another of my interviewees, "Connie"—who, like Burton, is a veteran of a twelve-step program. Also like Burton, Connie confronted and overcame her addiction and began a thriving nonprofit for which she has received national recognition. While facing the truth about her own addiction certainly required a significant amount of inner truthfulness, what struck me even more in our interview was Connie's more recent confrontation of a difficult truth regarding her relationship with her disabled sister, "Anna":

My sister Anna has always been a little bit developmentally delayed, and so it was always just kind of understood that Anna was a little bit special and we all needed to take care of her. When her husband died, and my mother was also a widow, they moved in together. And it continued to be my job to take care of them, which involved financial support as well as driving them when my mother couldn't drive anymore. When my mother died, one of the things that she asked me to do was continue to take care of Anna. By then I was pretty resentful and angry and tired of that role, but I did it for my mother.

So Anna moved into an assisted living place, which was pretty nice, and I still had to do her medications and things like that. And I did what I felt like I had to do out of responsibility but wasn't always very nice about it. Because her health eventually deteriorated, for the last four years she's been in a long-term nursing facility, and it's primarily Medicaid and just not a good place. But I sort of checked it off as "Well, she's getting some level of care, and I'm doing the minimum," so I haven't really seen her very much. I hate going to that place—it just appalls me, and I just find it awful, so I've really ignored her except for the basics for the last couple of years.

So I regret that I've not done right by her, that I should have gotten a better place. Over the last couple of weeks, I've spent a lot more time with her, and I've realized that the level of care she was receiving was substandard, and that probably was causing a lot of her illnesses. And so it all came to a head last week, and I got her—she was admitted to the hospital, which is a wonderful facility with wonderful nurses. She's cognitively very confused and having some dementia and hallucinations, but every once in a while she's lucid. And so I've really made amends to her, and now I'm trying not to dwell and feel guilty about what I haven't done and just focus on what I *can* do. But if there's anyone in my life that I have not done right by, it would be her. And so I'm really trying to—well, I'm not trying, I *am* doing it differently.[30]

As we see in this quote, Connie has developed a habit of inner truthfulness that has enabled her to confront the painful truth about her resentment and neglect of her sister, and (as the twelve steps also require) to apologize and attempt to make amends. She provides an excellent role model for those of us who also occasionally struggle with resentment and poor treatment of our closest family members and friends—and that's likely all of us.

Just as we all can benefit from a truthful moral inventory of our resentments and misdeeds, we would do well to examine and acknowledge our weaknesses more generally. That acknowledgement, even of very minor shortcomings, can be quite unsettling. The modern world often encourages us to be—or at least pretend to be—independent and supremely competent, so an admission of weakness or a request for assistance is often experienced as though it were humiliation or defeat. We need to remind ourselves and those we care about that this perception is simply inaccurate. All of us have strengths and weaknesses; there's no shame in that fact. And together we can pool our collective strengths to help overcome our individual weaknesses— but only if we have the honesty to admit our weaknesses and the courage to accept help.

I need to remind myself of these truths quite frequently. Like many academics, I like to think of myself as more intelligent, competent, and independent than most people—that is, I struggle with pride. (We'll discuss pride and humility in more depth in chapter 12.) But at some point, now several years ago, I had to admit that (also like many academics, it turns out) I absolutely stink at managing my own schedule. My standard for prioritizing my workload naturally tends toward, "Will something bad happen to me tomorrow if I don't do this today?"—which is not a good way to meet long-term goals like earning tenure or writing books. Fortunately, my husband is a natural-born manager; so I was able to pool my competence in teaching and writing with his competence (and accountability!) in time management, resulting in my mostly thriving at work—and being able to pay my bills.

Ironically, another difficulty of everyday truthfulness can be acknowledging our strengths. Many of us, especially women, have been socialized to avoid speaking too highly of ourselves—so it can be socially awkward to acknowledge our talents and skills, even for a good purpose. And speaking of good purposes, admitting that one has abilities in a particular area can bring requests for favors—so hesitation to take on additional commitments can also lead to denial of one's strengths. Cathy Heying, a social worker turned mechanic, remarked that she'd always enjoyed having a career without obvious practical relevance—her friends never asked her to facilitate group therapy, for example, on her days off. Now that she knows how to repair cars, however, friends ask her for help all the time.[31] To a lesser extent, I've experienced the same thing now that I help edit a quarterly philosophy journal: colleagues ask me to edit everything from short conference papers to three-hundred-page books. But while denying one's strengths can limit this sort of effect, a more honest and effective solution to overcommitment is self-restraint in taking on extra work—learning to politely decline when appropriate rather than denying our abilities.

Finally, I think some of us struggle with honesty because in much of contemporary society the truth itself—not just inner truthfulness—has fallen out of fashion. Public discussions of important issues have an alarming tendency to dissolve into polarized shouting (or sarcasm) matches or stubborn relativism—or, worse yet, toward an incoherent mix of both. As we'll see in the next chapter, Xunzi offers an insightful analysis of our tendency to miss the truth's big picture—and he (along with contemporary psychologists and an exceptionally virtuous interviewee) gives advice that can help us grow in respect for the truth and for each other.

Part 3

FIXING YOUR FLAWS

*Broadening Your View and Taming
Your Inner Beast*

~

Chapter 7

BROADENING YOUR VIEW

A FEW YEARS AGO, while on a treadmill in the university gym, I found myself watching an episode of a reality TV show surrounding a certain family that seems to enjoy fame and fortune for no particular reason. In this episode, the oldest sister (whose name I've happily forgotten) was suffering some angst: her long-time boyfriend had once again done something stupid and irresponsible, this time ending up in the hospital. She was struggling to discern whether to stick with him—and even whether to pick him up when he was discharged. Understandably concerned about his well being, she was inclined to do both; but her sisters made a valiant effort to persuade her otherwise. She was too close to him and too emotionally wrapped up in the situation, they argued, to see the big picture. As they pointed out with numerous examples, their sister's boyfriend had demonstrated a pattern of irresponsibility and lack of consideration for years. It was time to face the harsh reality that things weren't likely to change—and to move on.

That afternoon, despite some embarrassment, I confessed my reality-TV watching to my students. Why? The episode I had just seen gave a perfect example of the very concept we were studying: obsession. In his essay "Dispelling Obsession," Confucian philosopher Xunzi begins by warning us of its danger: "The thing that all men should fear is that they will become obsessed by a small corner of truth and fail to comprehend its overall principles."[1] Xunzi goes on to caution us about how easily and subtly obsession can arise in our minds, how difficult it is to recognize and overcome without help, and how—with the help of good philosophy and good friends—we can in fact overcome it.

The Risks of Obsession

The main danger of obsession—narrow-minded focus on one part of a truth or situation to the exclusion of the big picture—is that we almost certainly won't know when we're afflicted: when we are in an obsessed mindset, it will seem to us that we are thinking clearly and seeing all there is to see. Like the forms of self-deception we considered in chapter 6, obsession is self-concealing and self-perpetuating. That's why it is a possibility for any-one—even high-ranking world leaders, and even otherwise-great philoso-phers. As Xunzi puts it, "Even the ruler of a chaotic state or the follower of a pernicious doctrine will undoubtedly in all sincerity seek what is proper and try to better his condition."[2] In fact, Xunzi is able to cite several real-life examples of rulers who became obsessed and of the disasters that en-sued. These rulers became obsessed with their favorite concubines or with crafty advisors and ignored the wiser advice of their more-qualified and less self-serving ministers—and lost their kingdoms to others who heeded more sound principles and advice. He also notes several well-known subjects who became obsessed with attaining power illegitimately, which resulted in their execution; those who avoided obsession and supported just rulers enjoyed much better life outcomes.

More surprisingly given their dedication to wisdom, education, and care-ful reflection, many philosophers have also been obsessed—generally with their own teachings rather than with wealth and power. Here are a few philosophical examples Xunzi mentions: obsession with consequences leads to ignoring the ways in which they're brought about; obsession with lessen-ing desires leads to neglecting the legitimate and wholesome ways in which desires can be satisfied; and obsession with the power of circumstances leads to underestimating the power of human intelligence and freedom. "These various doctrines comprehend only one small corner of the Way, but the true Way must embody constant principles and be capable of embracing all changes. A single corner of it will not suffice."[3] By focusing on a small corner of truth as though it were the whole picture, the philosophers who advocated these teachings led themselves and many others into distorted ways of thinking.

And of course, obsession is not limited to reality-TV stars, politicians, and philosophers; it afflicts ordinary people of all ages and walks of life. Although I'm not aware of comprehensive research on such things, I have enough anecdotal evidence to be fairly confident that obsession is among the leading causes of relationship drama.[4] In fact, when my students asked whether I'd ever helped anyone overcome obsession, all I had to do was remind them that I'm a parent of teenagers: "Do any of you remember what it was like to be a thirteen-year-old girl? I help people overcome obsession every week!" Like the politicians and philosophers who become obsessed with their advisors or teachings, adolescents and others experiencing relationship drama can easily let it fill their mental screens, zooming in so closely on their negative (or positive) emotions that they are unable to see how these things fit into the big picture of their lives.

In addition to its self-disguising nature, the other main reason that we are all at risk of obsession is that its sources can be so diverse. Any time we—even rightly—recognize distinctions among things in our lives, the distinctions can become sources of obsession. As Xunzi says, we can become obsessed "by desires or by hates, by the beginning of an affair or by the end, by those far away or those close by, by breadth of knowledge or by shallowness, by the past or by the present."[5] For example, we can be obsessed with fitting in or standing out, with the guy next door or our celebrity crush, by an urge to scan our social media feeds or by a desire to know every last detail about our roommate's latest dating misadventure.

With potential sources of obsession turning up literally everywhere, we can't avoid becoming obsessed simply by avoiding things that might cause it: we can't stop distinguishing among things, and neither Xunzi nor any other Confucian or Socratic philosopher suggests that it would even be reasonable to try—things really *are* distinct, and there's no good reason to pretend otherwise. Further, as Plato argues, *failure* to distinguish things that are relevantly different can also be a source of obsession: having limited experience with something can lead to a failure to distinguish its varieties, which in turn can lead to an assumption that our limited experience encompasses the whole realm of possibility. Plato shows how detrimental such limited focus can be in the case of pleasure: someone who has experienced only the pleasure of satisfying physical desires and assumes that there are no other pleasures will lack incentive to seek higher—more uniquely human and fulfilling—pleasures such as those that come with mastering a difficult task or skill, achieving a long-term goal, having a meaningful conversation, or even winning a baseball game or reading a good book. Such a limited view of pleasure can easily lead to an obsession with instant gratification—and to all the negative outcomes that tend to come with it.[6]

So the bad news is that sources of obsession are everywhere, we likely won't realize that we've fallen into obsessed ways of thinking and acting, and the results can be disastrous. Fortunately, there is good news too: obsession is to a great extent avoidable, and when it does occur it can be overcome.

Avoiding and Overcoming Obsession

In "Dispelling Obsession," Xunzi outlines three main ways that the sage avoids becoming obsessed—and that we learners can do likewise. Since obsession is essentially a problem with our thinking, it is not surprising that Xunzi's proposed safeguards are primarily cognitive. The sages, he explains, have developed three mental qualities that dispel obsession: their minds are empty, unified, and still. These qualities allow them to understand the Way (path) of virtue, which provides the bigger-picture clarity that is the true antidote to obsession:

> How does a man understand the Way? Through the mind. And how can the mind understand it? Because it is empty, unified, and still. The mind is constantly storing up things, and yet it is said to be empty. The mind is constantly marked by diversity, and yet it is said to be unified. The mind is constantly moving, and yet it is said to be still.[7]

Since none of these three qualities is self-explanatory to contemporary readers (and striving for an "empty" mind sounds especially odd!), let's take a closer look at the meaning and practice of each.

By "empty," Xunzi means something like "having room for more." As he points out, with intellect comes memory, and with memory comes a wealth of stored information—no human being of normal mental capacity has a mind that is literally empty. "Yet the mind is said to be empty," Xunzi explains, "because what has already been stored up in it does not hinder the reception of new impressions."[8] A mind that is able to learn more is empty in the relevant sense.

At first glance, then, the condition of an empty mind may seem easily met: after all, even young school children are expected to learn new things every day while remembering at least some of the information they learned before. But when we recall Xunzi's examples of sources of obsession (desires and hates, beginnings and endings, the past or the present), we realize that in some areas of our lives we may not be leaving room for new impressions. New information—especially information that seems to conflict with our desires or opinions—can easily be ignored or squeezed out, leaving room only for our distorted or biased ways of thinking: for our obsessions.

Some of the rulers Xunzi discussed seemed to suffer from lack of emptiness: their excessive attention to their concubines or their unscrupulous advisors led them to dismiss information that could have led to a more objective assessment of these people and their advice. Lack of emptiness seems to be the main problem in the teen angst sort of obsession as well—an intense focus on the present relationship and the emotions that accompany it leaves little room for a rational assessment of the relationship in terms of its healthiness, stability, and proper place among one's other relationships and interests. It also rears its ugly head when we—at any age—allow ourselves to overindulge in a bad mood: instead of seeing the positive aspects of our life or day for what they are, we instead can go on a sort of mental hunting expedition for things to resent, calling to mind a litany of minor, often irrelevant, gripes.

Similarly, the need for—and difficulty of achieving—"unity" in our minds arises from our intellectual capacity. Intellect brings an awareness of differences, which means that we understand various facts at the same time; there is diversity in our minds. "And yet the mind is said to be unified because it does not allow the understanding of one fact to impinge upon that of another."[9] So just as an empty mind has room for additional information and impressions, a unified mind has room for understanding of diverse truths—and of how these truths relate to each other without contradiction. And just as education in general requires and cultivates a certain degree of emptiness in one's mind, a good liberal arts education requires and cultivates at least some unity: For example, it can help us see how philosophy, biology, and psychology all contribute in complementary rather than competing ways to our understanding of human life.

Even for people with well-rounded educations, though, the need to guard against disunity in the mind is real. As with emptiness, unity can easily be restricted to convenient areas, and in other areas, especially emotionally sensitive ones, we can develop a sort of mental tunnel vision and become blinded to information and impressions that threaten to disrupt our safe, narrow views. As we saw with Xunzi's examples, even apparently very wise philosophers can become too attached to their own teachings and miss the value that others' insights could add, seeing such insights as threats to their own views rather than considering whether at least some aspects of the new teachings might be compatible with theirs. In medieval Europe, this kind of intellectual disunity happened in a pretty dramatic way with the rediscovery of Aristotle's texts. At first, many philosophers and theologians viewed his work as a threat to their worldview; overcoming this initial resistance required centuries of vigorous debate.[10] More commonly—and more intensely—we see mental disunity in divisive political campaigns: often for blatantly self-serving reasons, candidates will ignore, distort, or attempt to discredit any positive information regarding opposing candidates and their positions.

A lack of true mental unity can emerge more subtly in a common form of false unity known as "confirmation bias": our tendency to interpret new information as confirming our preconceived ideas—and to ignore information that doesn't fit with our preexisting mental picture.[11] For example, if I form an initial impression of a new colleague as unreliable—say, because she is late, perhaps with good reason, to our first meeting—I may tend to discount evidence in favor of her reliability. Even if she consistently does her share of work on joint projects and shows up on time for our next ten meetings, I may focus on her being three minutes late to the eleventh meeting as further evidence that she is unreliable. (This false unity also interferes with emptiness: I don't have room for further information about my colleague's reliability, because my first impression is taking up too much mental space.)

Finally, to understand the Way of virtue and thereby avoid obsession, the mind must be "still." The meaning of this last essential quality is a little more intuitive than the others; Xunzi explains it as follows: "When the mind is asleep, it produces dreams; when it is unoccupied, it wanders off in idle fancy; and if allowed to do so, it will produce from these all manner of plots and schemes. Hence the mind is constantly moving. And yet it is said to be still, because it does not allow such dreams and noisy fancies to disorder its understanding."[12] So a still mind is an ordered, peaceful mind: one that does not allow itself to become distracted or led astray by the random, sometimes irrational, thoughts that arise in all of us when our minds wander.

The power-hungry, ill-fated subjects Xunzi described probably came to be obsessed primarily through a lack of mental stillness. They allowed their mental wanderings to develop into plots and schemes—and, ultimately, unsuccessful attempts to seize control of their governments. This mental restlessness is another phenomenon that most of us have probably experienced to some degree. Thankfully, those of us still alive to read or write this book have had less-disastrous results—at least we haven't been executed!—but acting on our irrational whims and fancies almost never turns out well. (If such fancies are especially bad, acting on them *can* in fact lead to execution—unfortunately, news reports are full of stories of people acting out fantasies of kidnapping, rape, murder, or even cannibalism—but acting on our fancies typically affects us in more mundane ways.) Just to take one example that my students sometimes report in their reflections on obsession, acting on an impulse to stay out late enjoying beverages with friends instead of studying can lead to a poor grade on an exam the next morning.

The Psychology of (Some) Obsession

There may be many different types of obsession—ranging from the (almost) purely intellectual obsession of the philosophers Xunzi mentions to the (almost) purely emotional obsession associated with teen heartbreak. Psychologists have recently devoted significant effort to the study of a very common, mostly emotional variety they term "rumination": roughly, the practice of dwelling excessively on a problem or negative emotional experience without moving forward.[13] (This is the sort of obsession I tend to find, among other places, in my teenage daughters.) As psychologists explain, rumination involves revisiting emotionally charged, negative experiences by seeing them again from a "self-immersed perspective"—through one's own eyes, as though reliving the experience. In fact, researchers have found that rumination reactivates the same networks in the brain that were activated by the original event—retriggering the same thoughts, emotions, and even fight-or-flight response.[14] So despite the conventional wisdom that reflecting on one's feelings will bring peace, those who reflect by ruminating tend to remain just as upset as before. (We saw this phenomenon in chapter 4 as well: not all introspection, it turns out, is productive.) Why? As Xunzi would point out, rumination makes it impossible to develop emptiness, unity, and stillness. Focus on one's own perception of the experience prevents the intake of information about others' perspectives; fear that those perspectives might make it more difficult to maintain our views of ourselves as the "good guy" or the "innocent victim" in the story block any motivation to unify others' understandings with our own; and our angst about the situation and focus on our negative feelings disallows any progress toward mental stillness.

To move toward emptiness, unity, and stillness, the research suggests, we need to reflect on our experiences from a "self-distanced" perspective. For example, we might replay the scene as though viewing it from the perspective of an external observer or a fly on the wall—or, some have suggested, as a friend: someone who knows you well but is not immediately and emotionally involved in the situation. Another effective way to promote distance in our own reflections is by using third-person pronouns or our own names—for example, asking in the third person about our distant selves, not "Why did I feel that way?" or "Why did I react like that?" but "Why did she feel that way?" or "Why did Mary react like that?" (Or, taking a cue from Tasha Eurich's research, which we discussed in chapter 4, instead of "why" questions we could ask "what" questions, such as "What was she feeling?" or "What could Mary have done differently?")[15]

In a clever series of experiments, Kross and colleagues found that this latter method of attaining distance reduced the social anxiety associated with making first impressions and also—more importantly for our purposes—significantly reduced participants' tendency to ruminate on their performance after giving a speech for which they were not given adequate time to prepare.[16] Self-distancing, this time using an external visualization or "fly on the wall" reflection method, even reduced aggression against rude experimenters and fake participants, who were subtly trying to provoke the real participants' anger.[17] Notably, self-distancing is like distraction in that it tends to result in reduced negative feelings in the short term; unlike distraction, however, it also leads to reduced rumination and thus to reduced negative feelings in the long term. As Kross and Ayduk put it, "When people go to the movies to stop thinking about a problem they feel better during the film. However, when they are reminded of their problem after the movie ends, the distress returns.... In contrast, people who self-distance while reflecting receive both immediate and delayed benefits."[18]

Self-distancing, then, allows people to understand what they are feeling and perhaps even why they are feeling it—without triggering the rumination that otherwise tends to set in when we reflect on our own emotions. It also encourages us to understand the perspective of others: in fact, the "fly on the wall" method is itself a form of perspective-taking. Thus, self-distancing seems to promote emptiness (having room for new understanding) and perhaps even unity (the ability to see other points of view without falsifying one's own). And it obviously fosters stillness as well, via reduced anxiety and aggression. Further, I can personally attest that it's at least moderately effective even with middle-school-aged kids: after learning about self-distancing techniques, I've encouraged my own children (while on time-out for excessive bickering with siblings) to replay the perceived offense from a fly-on-the-wall perspective, which has at least helped them calm down. (Perhaps the success of the technique can be explained partly by the novelty of pretending to be a fly—or an angel, as one of them prefers to imagine himself!)[19]

Less Rumination, Less Regret

While I was interviewing people who have won national awards for doing good, one of the patterns that struck me most was the difficulty at least half of these exemplars had in answering one of the standard questions: "What is your greatest regret?" Some, like Estella Pyfrom (whose story appears in chapter 3), couldn't think of any regrets at all. Others could come up only with either a fairly trivial failing (e.g., buying too much clothing) or someone else's action (e.g., a high school boyfriend killing the interviewee's dog) rather than a serious failing on his or her own part. With many people, this difficulty might signify excessive pride or a lack of reflection; but in general, my interviewees displayed both humility and self-knowledge—so there had to be a better explanation. As it turned out, a few of my exemplars had to think about the question for a while but then *did* describe a significant regret; it was this last group that gave insight into why other exemplars may not have had significant regrets—and into how we can reduce our own regrets in life.

In short, what was striking about the exemplars' regrets (or lack thereof) is that it seemed *they didn't ruminate*. They saw their failings as opportunities for learning and personal growth, and many could easily name positive outcomes that had arisen from them. For example, as we saw earlier in this book, Mauricio Miller's disillusionment with his social services career (chapter 4) gave rise to his innovative work with the Family Independence Initiative; and James McCormick's regret about volunteering for military deployments at the expense of time with his children (chapter 5) led him to retire from active duty and become their primary caretaker. And Judy Berry (see chapter 14), overcoming the neglect and verbal abuse she had suffered as a child, went on to become her elderly mother's primary caregiver and strongest advocate—and to found an organization dedicated to helping other patients with dementia.

The most striking story of refusal to ruminate on past injustices and failings, though, came from Gloria Lewis, founder and director of a small organization called Care in Action USA. Born and raised in Barbados, Lewis enjoyed a close-knit family and community life but dreamed of moving some day to the United States, where (so she inferred from stories and TV shows) everyone lived in mansions and had plenty of leisure time. Surprisingly, she had an opportunity to do just that: As a young single mother, she became engaged to a tourist—a horse jockey who was a U.S. citizen—and left Barbados to join him in Maryland. Leaving her son with her parents, Lewis expected to send for him as soon as she got settled into her dream home. Instead, she soon found herself stuck in a tiny apartment, waiting alone all day for the return of a husband who was physically abusive, unfaithful, and addicted to drugs. When her second son, conceived in the hope of saving her marriage, was still quite young, Lewis left her husband and started over—moving to Fort Lauderdale, Florida, and working multiple low-paying jobs just to meet her and her sons' basic needs. She was eventually remarried, to a man who had just served a nine-year prison sentence and had serious anger issues.

Despite all of her struggles, Lewis exudes compassion—or, as the name of her organization puts it, care in action. After a long and difficult path helping her husband work through his anger (she describes his recovery as the high point of her life) while raising her younger son and continuing to work low-paying jobs, she led her family to dedicate much of their time to serving the homeless in their community:

I looked at all of my missteps, all that I've been through, at so many people around me in the same situation, and there was always this calling on my life that I had to do something to make a difference. I would stay up until two or three in the morning writing letters. I didn't know what I was supposed to do, but I had to do something. I wrote over one hundred letters to the media, to churches, to politicians, to public figures. Nobody would answer. I kept looking to people to make that move. I kept looking for the circumstances to line up in order for me to get to the next step. It still wasn't lining up.

And then I told my husband, "We've got to go feed the homeless," and my husband kept saying, "We can't feed us; why do you want to feed the homeless?" I said, "You don't understand. I have to do this—this is not me. What is in me is stronger than me, and I can't get it to go away. I have to do this." And so he said, "Okay, let's go."[20]

With the help of her husband and her teenage son, Lewis started with twenty meals every Sunday, then forty, then sixty, and now two hundred dinners—plus one hundred breakfasts. As of this writing, she and her family have just begun serving meals on Mondays as well—while continuing to hold full-time, working-class jobs.

Soon Lewis and her husband discovered—and felt called to meet—many other needs among the people they served: help finding jobs, transportation, and clothing, and, most of all, encouragement and a listening ear. They even freely share their personal phone numbers: "Now we've got people calling my husband whenever they're down and depressed. Now we've got people calling us just to give them hope."

Those of us who tend to ruminate often play the victim, dwelling on how (we think) others have wronged us. As I confessed in chapter 4, I have to resort to systematically questioning my own perceptions because I'm guilty of embracing the victim mindset far too often. Lewis, it seems, does the opposite: in addition to reaching out and helping strangers, she makes a point of seeing the good in all people—even those who have harmed her—and of forgiving them. She is convinced that "there are no bad people in the world.

There are only good people who made bad choices in bad situations." And apparently, she has always been disposed toward compassion and forgiveness rather than rumination on past or even current injustices. When I asked her to tell me about any vivid adult memory, she shared this striking story:

About twenty-five years ago I caught my ex-husband in the house with a young girl about eighteen years old, and the girl was pregnant by my husband. And at that time, I could've been angry at the girl. I could've lost it on her. But I said to the girl, "You know what? I could be mad at you, but I'm not mad at you. You're young, and just like he snowballed you, he snowballed me. Call your mom, because you're going to need her. My husband is not going to be there for you, just like he's not there for anyone. Here's my number, and you know where I live. If you need anything, you can call me."

True to form, she has forgiven her ex-husband as well: she attributes his behavior to his addiction and is grateful to him for warning her to stay away from drugs. She encourages her son to forgive him as well, telling him, "The only thing your father did wrong was not to be there for you and support you. But he gave you life, and he's still your father. The wrong that he did to me, that's not your fight. Don't hold it against him."

Considering her amazing propensities toward forgiveness and compassion, I almost thought Lewis was never tempted to ruminate. But there is one topic on which she has to fight rumination head-on: her children. Her greatest regret, she told me, was the problems her sons have faced—which she attributes, at least in part, to her failure to provide a stable home and a good father figure for them when they were young. Lewis's older son, who was raised primarily by his grandparents, got into some trouble as a teenager and young adult, even spending several months in jail. Her younger son, whom she primarily raised herself, won't stop drinking. Lewis describes her regret—and her temptation to ruminate on it—like this: "If our kids don't turn out the way we assume they're supposed to turn out, then we label it as a failure on our part. And it beats us up, day in and day out, and we question ourselves. 'What did I do wrong? How did I make those mistakes? What could I have done for this not to happen?' And so it beats you up." Lewis sees her younger son's alcoholism as stemming from a similar sense of failure and self-condemnation, which has led her to encourage him—and herself in the process:

> I constantly tell him, "I don't need a professor for a son. I don't need a doctor. I would rather have a garbage collector who has love and compassion in his heart. I would rather have a kid that will come visit his mom than a kid who will just write a check and not even come to see his mom or pick up the phone. You might have your issues, but when I see you help people, the way you give away the last dollar in your pocket, the way you take the shoes off of your feet and the shirt off of your back and give it to another person, then I've done my job. It means that I taught you what you needed to be taught in life, which is to have compassion for others."

In fact, like several of the exemplary people I interviewed, Lewis has learned to see a positive side to her struggles and regrets. She's no longer ashamed of her failures as a parent, she says, because she can use her experiences to encourage other families and to understand the addictions and struggles she encounters among the homeless people she serves.

As Lewis made clear throughout our conversation, she is motivated by a deep religious faith, and she credits God both with the inspiration for her work with the homeless and with the turnaround in her own and her husband's lives. Her belief that God can use her missteps for a greater purpose also keeps her from ruminating upon negative aspects of her experiences. And her hope and positivity can provide inspiration for all of us:

> I know that the call God had on my life was to use my struggles and all of my mess to help people to come to Him in their mess. Between my sons, my husband, and me, I don't think that there is one thing that society feels is wrong—my husband, being an ex-convict, being a felon on drugs, my son drinking, my other son in jail, the abuse that I went through in my marriage—I don't think there's anything that we haven't touched. But yet, through all that mess, we still find the strength, the encouragement to go help somebody.

If Lewis, who has endured so much and who still struggles to make ends meet, can reach out to help and encourage others, what excuse do the rest of us have?

As we have seen in this chapter, obsession—dwelling on a small part of the truth and losing the bigger picture—is an easy mental trap for all of us to fall into. And rumination—dwelling on negative emotional aspects of an experience like committing or suffering a wrong—is a common but avoidable type of obsession. To become more like Gloria Lewis and the other exemplars I interviewed, and to enjoy better psychological health, we should work to reduce (or, ideally, eliminate) rumination in our lives. Following Lewis, we can focus on the positive and avoid blaming people. Following Xunzi, we can also cultivate dispositions of emptiness (open-mindedness), unity (recognition of other truths and perspectives), and stillness or mental peace. And, as recent psychological research on the related notion of self-distancing indicates, we can begin to cultivate these dispositions by taking an external view of ourselves—for example, by replaying a negative experience in our mind's eye from the perspective of a fly on the wall or by retelling our story in the third person.

As it turns out, Xunzi's uncanny psychological insights don't end there. Next we will look at additional empirically supported ways in which both he and Plato recommend attaining mental peace and harmony—or, Xunzi might say, "obsession-proofing" our minds—through the virtue of temperance.

Chapter 8

TEMPERANCE

Taming Your Inner Beast

IMAGINE you're four years old, and someone sets a delicious-looking marshmallow on the table in front of you. She offers to give you a second marshmallow if you wait to eat this one until after she comes back from a fifteen-minute errand; if you can't wait until then, you only get this one—but of course, you can have it *right now*. Walter Mischel and his colleagues at Stanford University did that very thing in a series of experiments beginning in the 1960s. Surprisingly (to me, anyway, as someone who has considerable experience with preschoolers), under some conditions, up to two-thirds of the young children tested managed to wait to eat their treats until the experimenter returned. Even more surprising was the correlation between the children's self-control as four-year-olds and their emotional, social, and academic competence as adolescents. To take just one dramatic result, years later the SAT scores of those who waited for the second marshmallow exceeded those of kids who succumbed to the sweet, fluffy temptation by an average of 210 points.[1] And by age twenty-five to thirty, those who had greater ability to delay gratification as preschoolers "were more able to pursue and reach long-term goals, used risky drugs less, had reached higher educational levels, and had a significantly lower body mass index."[2]

When extended to various areas of life, used for good purposes, and practiced until it becomes a habit, this quality of self-restraint can grow into the virtue of temperance: the character trait associated with pursuing appropriate types and amounts of physical pleasure. Despite the surprising trends just described, it's hard to find good stories about temperance: moderation tends not to make for high drama. (In fact, one reason it's such a valuable quality is that it helps us *avoid* drama.) But it's woven into the everyday lives of good people everywhere: the mother who is "not hungry" when there isn't quite enough dessert to go around, the father who patiently endures the lack of intimacy with his wife for weeks or months following childbirth, and—in its beginning form—maybe even the child who resists the marshmallow (or his siblings' desserts) sitting on the table.

Confucius proposes further simple signs of temperance—and suggestions for acquiring it. For example, he describes a virtuous person as "not motivated by the desire for a full belly or a comfortable abode" but instead as content with simple provisions—and motivated by a desire to do right and follow the lead of good teachers and role models;[3] and he advises us that "very few go astray who comport themselves with restraint."[4] And Confucius's *Analects* records a story of a wise teacher who was reputed never to speak, laugh, or take anything. As his disciple explained, the truth was perhaps even more surprising: "Whoever told you that was exaggerating. My master only spoke when the time was right, and so people never grew impatient listening to him. He only laughed when he was genuinely full of joy, and so people never tired of hearing him laugh. He only took what was rightfully his, and so people never resented his taking of things." Amazed, Confucius replied, "Was he really that good? Could he really have been that good?"[5]

My favorite story of temperance is simple enough to be told in one sentence: as a young seminarian, Maximilian Kolbe would give away his fruit (his favorite part of the school meals) to his classmates. That little act of self-denial has always struck me as a great way to grow in both temperance and generosity. After all, it wouldn't take much kindness or self-discipline to give away things you don't enjoy much anyway, and as a habitual practice, denying yourself bigger, more essential things is not sustainable, so sacrificing an everyday favorite food or activity for the sake of others is much more realistic and habit-forming. And after building that foundation of virtue, Kolbe went on to share his food with fellow prisoners in a Nazi concentration camp and ultimately died after volunteering to take the place of another man in a starvation bunker.[6]

Of course, as Kristjánsson reminds us, willpower is not equivalent to temperance: "Temperate agents do not need to force themselves to eat their broccoli; they eat it because they like it!"[7] But it is a large step in that direction: as with any virtue, temperance forms gradually as we develop the habit of doing the actions it prescribes. And, of course, its opposing vice—self-indulgence—is characterized by an obvious lack of self-restraint.

Self-Indulgence: The Nemesis of Temperance

Unlike temperance, self-indulgence (its commonsense opposite) *does* tend to make for some drama. We need not look very far to find stories of celebrities, politicians, or perhaps even our own wayward relatives who have over-indulged in things like intoxicating beverages and romantic liaisons. To take just one recent example, U.S. congressman Anthony Weiner resigned in 2011 after a lewd photo (which he initially denied posting) appeared on his Twitter page and he was subsequently found to have exchanged sexually explicit texts with several women. More material of a similar nature emerged when he was running for mayor of New York City in 2013; and in 2017 he was sentenced to twenty-one months in prison for repeatedly exchanging explicit photos and video with a fifteen-year-old over social media.[8]

As we see from cases like these, and as Aristotle also observes, temperance and the opposed vice of self-indulgence "are concerned with the kind of pleasures that the other animals share in"—touch and taste—and thus "self-indulgence would seem to be justly a matter of reproach, because it attaches to us not as men but as animals. To delight in such things, then, and to love them above all others, is brutish."[9] Interestingly, we tend not to describe as self-indulgent people who take unusual delight in intellectual pleasures, or even in the pleasures of beautiful sights and sounds. Self-indulgent people, Aristotle explains, go to excess in their desires for the pleasures of taste and touch in three ways: (a) they delight in some things they ought not delight in at all; and among those they *should* enjoy, they delight in them (b) more than they ought and (c) more than most people do.[10] So a self-indulgent person might (a) delight in other people's significant others or food (for example, to motivate myself to keep working today after a long day of teaching, I "stole" some of the chocolate my daughter had left sitting in my office); and even with regard to pleasant things that are rightfully one's own (like the less-

tasty snacks in my drawer), a self-indulgent person might eat more than is
(b) reasonable or (c) normal.

As you may have noticed, the third sense in which Aristotle says self-indulgent people overshoot the mean of temperance—delighting more than
most people in the pleasures of taste and touch—is relative. Rather than use
objective standards, it compares one's behavior to the statistical norm. That
would be a problem if taken alone—anyone who lived in an especially indulgent society (such as most of the United States, some might say) could simply
point out that "everyone else is doing it" as a justification for the "moderate" nature of her own indulgence. As we saw in chapter 5, that's actually a
common way that people rationalize all sorts of misbehavior. But since this
comparison is only one of three ways to spot self-indulgence, when combined
with the others it actually makes for a fairly useful test. When considering,
for example, that third serving of wine or cheesecake, we can ask ourselves,
(a) "Is this the sort of thing I shouldn't consume at all?"; and if it's not, then
(b) "Is this more of a good thing than is reasonable or healthy?"; and (c) "Am
I eating or drinking more than everyone else?" A "yes" answer to any of the
three questions gives a strong reason to suspect self-indulgence.

Another way to know that you tend toward self-indulgence—as many of
us unfortunately do—is to observe your response to a lack of pleasure. Does
it pain you not to receive the pleasant things you'd like or were expecting?
For example, does giving up sweets sound almost unimaginably difficult? Do
you want to yell or cry when you find out that your roommate ate the left-
over pizza you were hoping to have for supper? Once again, if you answered
"yes," you're probably at least a little bit self-indulgent.

Stoic philosopher Seneca associates this overindulgence in culinary pleasures with a lazy approach to life. He criticizes those who "count it pleasure
to surrender your miserable body to sluggish ease, to court a repose that differs not much from sleep, to lurk in a cover of thick shade and beguile the
lethargy of a languid mind with the most delicate thoughts, which you call
tranquility, and in the secret retreats of your gardens to stuff with food and
drink your bodies that are pallid from inaction."[11] Even more generally, Cicero argues that overvaluing pleasure and ease raises obstacles to the development of any virtue: "He who so interprets the supreme good ... by his own
convenience, and not by the standard of right—he, I say, if he be consistent
with himself, and be not sometimes overcome by natural goodness, can cul-

tivate neither friendship, nor justice, nor generosity; nor can he possibly be brave while he esteems pain as the greatest of evils, or temperate while he regards pleasure as the supreme good."[12]

As we saw in chapter 2, classical Confucian philosophers Mencius and Xunzi have different—sometimes competing—metaphors for character development: Mencius compares it to cultivating plants, while Xunzi uses craft metaphors like straightening warped wood or sharpening dull metal. Plato has his own moral development metaphor: it involves a man, a lion, and an enormous many-headed beast. Before exploring that metaphor and its relationship to temperance and self-indulgence, let's take a brief look at its context in Plato's *Republic*.

The State and the Psyche

In the opening book of the *Republic*, Socrates (who, as usual, is the hero of Plato's story) discusses the nature and effects of justice with several interlocutors—including aggressive rhetorician Thrasymachus, who argues that if one can get away with it, it is smarter and more beneficial to be unjust. Although Socrates scores a "win" in that debate (Thrasymachus concedes defeat), Socrates's friends don't find his arguments compelling. They want to hear more. In fact, they are so interested in hearing more that they play devil's advocate, picking up Thrasymachus's argument where he left off. Isn't it true, they ask, that justice is just a social convention—a sort of compromise we all make between committing injustice against others for our personal gain and suffering others' injustice at our own loss? And if so, isn't it prudent to go ahead and commit injustice whenever we know we can get away with it? To illustrate this point, Socrates's friend Glaucon (who happens to be Plato's brother) tells a now-famous story that you may recognize in more recent book and movie plotlines:

A shepherd named Gyges was tending sheep in the king's pastures when an earthquake opened up the ground—revealing, among other strange sights, a dead man wearing nothing but a gold ring. After taking the ring from the corpse and putting it on his own finger, Gyges discovered that he became invisible when he turned the setting inward toward his palm but reappeared when he turned it outward. He soon took advantage of his good fortune: he arranged to be a messenger to the royal court, and once he arrived there he snuck into the palace and managed to seduce the queen, con-spire with her to kill the king, and subsequently take over the kingdom. Socrates's friend asks:

> Suppose now that there were two such magic rings, and the just [person] put on one of them and the unjust the other; no man can be imagined to be of such an iron nature that he would stand fast in justice. No man would keep his hands off what was not his own when he could safely take what he liked out of the market, or go into houses and lie with any one at his pleasure, or kill or release from prison whom he would, and in all re-spects be like a God among men. Then the actions of the just would be as the actions of the unjust; they would both come at last to the same point. And this we may truly affirm to be a great proof that a man is just, not willingly or because he thinks that justice is any good to him individually, but of necessity, for wherever anyone thinks that he can safely be unjust, there he is unjust.[13]

Sure enough, when I ask my students what they would do with the Ring of Gyges, almost no one says "perform random acts of kindness"; far more common answers include mildly unjust actions like "sneak into concerts" and "eavesdrop on my friends' conversations." As they point out, we usually aren't motivated to conceal our good behavior—invisibility is naturally seen as an opportunity to behave badly. So in attempting to convince his friends of the intrinsic value of justice—that the virtue is worth having even when no one is looking—Socrates really has his work cut out for him.

Socrates's more thorough defense of justice takes the form of an extended analogy between the state and the human psyche. He describes each in terms of three parts: The state is composed of a large group of artisans (e.g., doc-tors, shepherds, and merchants), a much smaller militia, and an even smaller group of wise rulers. Similarly, the psyche is composed largely of our desires, along with a much smaller "spirited" or "passionate" part and an even small-er rational part. In a just state we find harmonious order, with the few wise rulers guiding the many artisans and the militia, and being defended by the latter against internal and external threats; and in the just psyche also we find harmonious order, with our reason guiding our many desires and our spirited emotions—again, with the latter (when guided by reason) being our best defense against internal and external sources of disorder (i.e., temptations) that threaten our mental wellbeing.

To show the superiority of justice over injustice, Socrates must contrast the just state and psyche he has described with unjust (disordered) variations. As it turns out, there are four different varieties of unjust state and psyche, which Socrates presents as progressive deteriorations from the ideal or just variety. For simplicity, I'll only describe the types of psyche; the corresponding state is ruled by the corresponding class of citizens. Whereas the just (or aristocratic, a word that means literally "rule of the best") psyche is guided by reason, the timarchic ("rule of honor") is led by the spirited part; the oligarchic ("rule of the few") is ruled by necessary desires—that is, desires for things we actually need; the democratic ("rule of the people") is governed by all desires indiscriminately—desires for things necessary and unnecessary, good and bad; and the tyrannical psyche has been taken over entirely by unnecessary, harmful desires. As you can see from the following excerpts, the life of the tyrannical man looks a lot like that of a person suffering the consequences of severe addiction:

> He is drawn into a perfectly lawless life, which by his seducers is termed perfect liberty.... Every day and every night desires grow up many and formidable, and their demands are many.... His revenues, if he has any, are soon spent.... Then comes debt and the cutting down of his property.... And if his parents will not give way [to his demands for money], then he will try first of all to cheat and deceive them.... And if he fails, then he will use force and plunder them.... Meanwhile the old opinions which he had when a child, and which gave judgment about good and evil, are overthrown....
>
> [Tyrannical people] are always either the masters or servants and never the friends of anybody; the tyrant never tastes of true freedom or friendship.... The best elements in him [i.e., his reason and spirit] are enslaved.... He becomes and is of necessity more jealous, more faithless, more unjust, more friendless, more impious, than he was at first; he is the purveyor and cherisher of every sort of vice, and the consequence is that he is supremely miserable, and that he makes everybody else as miserable as himself.[14]

The other day while standing in line at the auto parts store, my husband and a fellow customer were discussing the unlikely topic of methamphetamine addicts. The young man working behind the counter spoke up: "I was a meth addict." Never one to feel awkward (as I would) in such situations, my husband said, "That's really interesting. How long can you go without craving it?" The young man immediately snapped his fingers and replied, "About that long." And, I'm told, the every-second-of-every-day craving can last a decade or more—it closely matches Socrates's description of desires that "grow up many and formidable." In the public service announcements I occasionally hear on the radio regarding the dangers of methamphetamine addiction, it sounds just like that description we saw above. Recovering addicts confess to being enslaved to their desires, losing their friends and their jobs, and stealing from their families—making life miserable for themselves and everyone who cares about them.

Why Doing What We Want Makes Us Miserable

Socrates's most memorable argument for the futility of injustice is a colorful analogy or "model" of the human psyche as strange three-part creature. The first and largest part is "a multitudinous, many-headed monster, having a ring of heads of all manner of beasts, tame and wild, which he is able to generate and metamorphose at will ... a second form as of a lion, and a third of a man, the second smaller than the first, and the third smaller than the second." The three are joined as one being, with the outside fashioned "into a single image, as of a man, so that he who is not able to look within, and sees only the outer hull, may believe the beast to be a single human creature."[15]

Now suppose that creature is you. What will your life be like, Socrates asks, if you choose injustice? He argues that injustice won't—indeed, *can't*— be to your benefit, even if (actually, *especially* if) you can get away with it: "To him who maintains that it is profitable for the human creature to be unjust, and unprofitable to be just, let us reply that, if he be right, it is profitable for this creature to feast the multitudinous monster and strengthen the lion and the lion-like qualities, but to starve and weaken the man, who is consequently liable to be dragged about at the mercy of either of the other two; and he is not to attempt to familiarize or harmonize them with one another—he ought rather to suffer them to fight and bite and devour one another."[16] Whether in the community or in the psyche, injustice is a civil war: when indulged without the guidance of reason, desires battle with each other and with our emotions, ultimately leaving every part of us the loser.

But just in case we're still tempted to think that choosing to follow the stirrings of desire rather than the wisdom of reason might be a good way for us to live, Socrates asks us some pointed rhetorical questions:

> How would a man profit if he received gold and silver on the condition that he was to enslave the noblest part of him to the worst? Who can imagine that a man who sold his son or daughter into slavery for money, especially if he sold them into the hands of fierce and evil men, would be the gainer, however large might be the sum which he received? And will anyone say that he is not a miserable caitiff [i.e., coward] who remorselessly sells his own divine being to that which is most godless and detestable? … From what point of view, then, and on what ground can we say that a man is profited by injustice or intemperance or other baseness, which will make him a worse man, even though he acquire money or power by his wickedness?[17]

As Socrates goes on to point out, we all grasp this point intuitively, even if we sometimes fail to apply it to ourselves. We routinely criticize people—whether they're celebrities or our own friends or family members—whose indulgence of their desires is obviously out of control, whose spirited qualities are allowed to overdevelop into bad temper or excessive pride, or whose spirit is underused and atrophies, leading to a cowardly pursuit of luxury and ease—or a listless default to the path of least resistance.

So how can we avoid the fate of a "miserable caitiff"? The answer, as in so many matters of integrity, is both surprisingly simple and often difficult: to succeed at mental and moral harmony where the various types of unjust psyches fail, we must empower the smallest part of the psyche, reason/man, to rule over the two larger parts: spirit/lion and desire/beast. Reason's guidance of our spirited part is courage; when reason with the help of spirit tames desire, we have temperance; and the harmony of the reason-ruled psyche as a whole is called justice. Next we'll take a brief look at these aspects of inner harmony—particularly temperance—and how they can be acquired.

Training the Lion, Taming the Beast

To better understand the roles of courage and temperance in Socrates's analogy—and in the good human life it represents—it may be helpful to recall from chapter 1 of this book how virtue in general improves our lives. As we saw there, an ethical virtue is a human excellence: *arete*, the Greek word we translate "virtue," actually means "excellence." And excellent traits of character such as generosity, patience, and justice—and, yes, temperance and courage—are major components of an excellent human life. These virtues of character represent a "mean" or right amount of the action or feeling they concern: for example, generosity involves giving the right amount to the right recipients and in the right way. And because virtuous people enjoy doing good things, virtue makes our lives not only objectively excellent but also meaningful, enjoyable, and pleasant.[18]

We have ample evidence of the intrinsic rewards of ethical excellence. To take just one well-known example, those who respond generously to others' needs tend to be rewarded with a "helper's high," a sense of personal well-being.[19] And, more generally, we tend to be satisfied with ourselves and our decisions when we do the right thing—even (maybe especially) when it isn't easy—and to be plagued by guilt and regret when we don't. For instance, as I noted in chapter 6, one of my interviewees said her greatest regret in life was her failure to devote time and effort to her disabled sister; similarly, James McCormick regretted not spending enough time with his children when they were young. Other exemplars most regretted conflicts with friends and family members; one even admitted an affair. As one would likely infer from their having won national awards for meaningful service to their communities, all have done their best to make amends, learn from their missteps, and become better people—and are much happier as a result. These internal responses to our own behavior correspond quite well with Plato's theory: the satisfaction that comes with ethical behavior could just as easily be called "the harmony of justice," and the regret that results from choosing to do wrong can reasonably be described as "the inner conflict of injustice."

A man striving to avoid that inner conflict, Socrates says, "should ever so speak and act as to give the man within him in some way or other the most complete mastery over the entire human creature. He should watch over the many-headed monster like a good husbandman, fostering and cultivating the gentle qualities, and preventing the wild ones from growing; he should be making the lion-heart his ally, and in common care of them all should be uniting the several parts with one another and with himself."[20] Extending the three-part creature analogy, I like to think of attaining this just inner harmony as a process of equipping the noble man (reason) with the right tools for the job of running the psyche: the whip of courage and the pruning shears of temperance.

Interestingly, in his analogy for the harmonious tripartite psyche, Socrates uses rather different terms to describe the inner man's relationships with each of the two other creatures—which suggests differences between the two corresponding virtues. With regard to courage, he speaks of making the lion (spirit) the man's (reason's) ally and their working together to subdue the much-larger beast. Although I don't think Plato intended his three-part creature analogy to extend to anything like the modern circus, the inner man's relationship with the lion has interesting parallels with contemporary lion training practices. (Trainers, I'm told, bristle at the term "lion tamer": they emphasize that, although a lion can indeed be *trained*, it is a mistake to suppose that it will ever be *tame* like a dog or a housecat.) Out of concern for humaneness as well as effectiveness, today's lion trainers tend to focus on gradually earning the animal's trust and then, like the man in Plato's analogy, working with it cooperatively—in contrast to the trainers of the last century, whose methods depended on gaining control of the lion through pain and fear.[21] (So the stereotypical whip I always picture has fallen out of fashion; anyway, as I prefer to imagine, the trainer uses it solely for pointing and noisemaking.)

Like the lion, our spirited part cannot be "tamed"—emotions like fear and anger are by nature intense feelings suited to conquering challenges or avoiding harm. But this part of our nature can be "trained" to follow the guidance of reason—which directs us to pursue the noble and, in doing so, to fight or flee those things (and only those things) that present significant threats to our and others' wellbeing. Recognizing those threats, knowing when to evade them and when to take them on directly, and *not* adopting a fight-or-flight response to non-threats, are all hallmarks of training our spirited part to follow reason—and thus of the virtue of courage.

Temperance is a different story: The beast has heads with various natures—some noble or "tame" and some wild. Rather than attempt to be-friend or control them all, the man (with the lion's help) must nurture the tame ones and eliminate those that threaten to harm the rest of the psyche. The development of courage is a process of allying reason and spirit—it is not a process of weakening or eliminating spirit or of changing its nature. And although temperance doesn't exactly alter the nature of desire either, it alters the *configuration* of desires in our individual psyche by eliminating those that are naturally ignoble or "wild" and thus unsuited to cooperate with reason and spirit.

The Beasts of Contemporary Psychology

Clocky—an alarm clock with wheels that was invented by an MIT stu-dent—rolls off your nightstand and around your room beeping at the ap-pointed time, forcing you to get out of bed and chase it down. Despite mini-mal marketing, in the first two years of production about thirty-five thou-sand Clockies were sold at fifty dollars each. Why would people pay twice as much for this kind of annoyance as they would for a less-annoying alarm clock? You probably know already: if you don't get out of bed, you just might hit the snooze button, and hit it again, until you're late for work. But why would you do *that* instead of sticking with your perfectly rational decision from the night before about what time you should get up? Because your rea-son—your "inner man"—is not always in control of your "beast." Borrow-ing a bit of terminology from psychologist Jonathan Haidt,[22] authors Chip and Dan Heath describe this inner conflict in terms reminiscent of Plato's *Republic*: Your rational mind, they say, is like a man riding on top of—and attempting to steer—a huge elephant. While the Rider can succeed by force of will for a short while, he soon becomes exhausted. To succeed in the long term, we have to motivate the Elephant to follow the Rider's chosen path willingly. Sometimes—as with Clocky—we do well to resort to "tricking" the Elephant into going along with the Rider's plan.[23]

If you're observant, you probably noticed that there are only two elements to the psyche in this description: the Rider and the Elephant. Perhaps the Heath brothers didn't see an important distinction between spirited emo-tions and desires. (Plato defended the distinction at length, reminding his friends that there are situations in which we become angry with ourselves for giving in to our desires—sometimes even at the same time that we're giving in.) But I think something much like Plato's tripartite model of the psyche is implicit in their descriptions. They speak of getting the Rider (reason) and the Elephant ("our emotional side") working together as a means to overcoming something else in us: usually our desire for comfort, ease, or pleasure—or, as Plato would say, our many-headed beast.

Contemporary psychologists, including some of those whose work we discussed in chapter 3, have discovered a few effective ways to help us point our inner elephant (or lion) in the direction that reason knows we should go. For example, like those who purchase a Clocky, we can precommit; or we can tell ourselves that we'll indulge "later." As the Heaths and McGonigal both noted, we can also start to move our emotions toward reason's side by appealing to our (current or ideal) identity.

In a classic study, Stanford psychologists Jonathan Freedman and Scott Fraser sent researchers door-to-door in upscale Palo Alto neighborhoods posing as volunteers for Citizens for Safe Driving. The researchers asked homeowners to permit huge, ugly billboards reading "Drive Carefully" to be installed on their front lawns; not surprisingly, fewer than 17 percent agreed. The surprise came in when, in a similar neighborhood, they preceded the same request with another request: that the homeowners display a less-than-postcard-sized sign saying "Be a Safe Driver" in their car or home windows. Almost all agreed to the tiny sign—and, two weeks later, a whopping 76 percent agreed to the huge eyesore billboard![24] The homeowners had come to identify themselves, the researchers concluded, as people who care about safe driving.

The same sort of appeal to identity was remarkably effective in a Texas anti-littering campaign in the 1980s. As a *Smithsonian* article tells the story, "In the late 1980s, the Texas Department of Transportation had a mess on its hands. It was spending $20 million annually on trash pick-up, and that number was increasing by about 17 percent year over year. Trash littered the highways and it only seemed to be getting worse—everything is bigger in Texas, after all. So the department put out a request for a marketing campaign to address the rubbish."[25] Because the most-guilty demographic was sixteen- to twenty-four-year-old males, an appeal to their identity as Texan men was especially in order: hence the now-famous slogan "Don't Mess With Texas." Clever advertisers stocked truck stops and fast-food restaurants with bumper stickers displaying the new slogan—but not its anti-littering purpose—

months ahead of the launch of their new ads, which featured famous Texans including country music stars and NFL football players. And litter along Texas roads declined by 54 percent within two years; within four years it was down by an impressive 72 percent.

What do driver safety billboards and anti-littering campaigns have to do with temperance? As McGonigal suggests, we can draw on the power of our own identities to enlist our emotions on reason's side and tame our inner beasts. Willpower, as she describes it, comes in three varieties. There's the "I will power" associated with persevering when we're tempted to quit, and the "I won't power" associated with developing temperance—resisting temptations of instant gratification. And there is a third aspect of willpower supporting the other two: "I want power"—"the ability to remember what you really want. I know, you think that what you really want *is* the brownie, the third martini, or the day off. But when you're facing temptation, or flirting with procrastination, you need to remember that what you *really* want is to fit into your skinny jeans, get the promotion, get out of credit card debt, stay in your marriage, or stay out of jail. Otherwise, what's going to stop you from following your immediate desires? To exert self-control, you need to find your motivation when it matters."[26] When we're tempted, in the heat of the moment, to think that our rational decisions are just "rules" trying to stop us from having what we want, the best strategy may be to remind ourselves that we identify more strongly with our longer-term goals: the person who wants health, success, good relationships, and, ultimately, *eudaimonia* is the real you—not just some oppressor bent on making sure you have no fun.

To further facilitate our development of temperance, we can also run our own internal "public awareness campaigns," not on safe driving or littering, but on the effects of dopamine. This neurotransmitter, released when the brain perceives an opportunity for reward—that is, anything we think will make us feel good—directs the rest of the brain to focus on obtaining that thing. As McGonigal explains, the effect of dopamine is variously described as desire, wanting, seeking, or craving. Dopamine isn't all bad, of course; it has its evolutionary advantages. "The promise of happiness—not the direct experience of happiness—is the brain's strategy to keep you hunting, gathering, working, and wooing."[27] And, as McGonigal suggests, even today we can harness its power by promising ourselves rewards for persevering in tasks we'd rather avoid.

But, especially in post-hunter-gatherer society, it can draw us toward not-so-ideal "rewards": for example, it fuels addictions to everything from junk food to pornography to social media. (Many video games, advertisements, social media, and even grocery store layouts are actually designed to exploit our weakness in the face of dopamine.)[28] McGonigal says students in her class on the science of willpower report a sense of empowerment when they become aware of dopamine triggers—both natural and intentionally placed—in their everyday environments. And that makes them more able to resist—either directly, by declining what they now see is an empty promise of reward, or indirectly, by avoiding trigger-rich things like catalogs and casinos.[29]

The Joys of Inner Harmony

As we saw in chapter 2 of this book, although he wasn't aware of the effects of dopamine, Xunzi pointed out many respects in which our natural, untrained desires and emotions can lead us astray. He emphasized that point in his discussion of *lǐ*, a word that, depending on context, can refer to "ritual"—behavioral norms associated with the legendary sage kings—or to "principle"—the virtue that arises from internalizing the personal and interpersonal ethical norms embodied in the endorsed behaviors. Xunzi's latter sense of *lǐ* is remarkably similar to Plato's description of temperance: "What is the origin of *lǐ*? I reply: man is born with desires. If his desires are not satisfied for him, he cannot but seek some means to satisfy them himself. If there are no limits and degrees to his seeking, then he will inevitably fall to wrangling with other men. From wrangling comes disorder and from disorder comes exhaustion. The ancient kings hated such disorder, and therefore they established *lǐ* in order to curb it, to train men's desires and to provide for their satisfaction."[30] While Xunzi acknowledges that there is something paradoxical about satisfying desires and emotions by training them, he insists that, as in other areas of life, the paradox makes the point no less true:

Let [the king's officials] understand clearly that to advance in the face of death and to value honor is the way to satisfy their desire for life; to spend and to supply what goods are needed is the way to satisfy their desire for wealth; to conduct themselves with respect and humility is the way to satisfy their desire for safety; and to obey *lǐ* and good order in all things is the way to satisfy their emotions. He who seeks only to preserve his life at all cost will surely suffer death. He who strives only for profit at all cost will surely suffer loss. He who thinks that safety lies in indolence and idleness alone will surely face danger. He who thinks that happiness lies only in gratifying the emotions will surely face destruction. Therefore, if a man concentrates upon fulfilling *lǐ*, then he may satisfy both his human desires and the demands of *lǐ*; but if he concentrates only upon fulfilling his desires, then he will end by satisfying neither.[31]

Why, according to Plato and Xunzi, is training our desires the best way to satisfy them? A couple of aspects of the answer are obvious: If we train our desires to seek what is readily available rather than what is scarce, we won't find ourselves faced with disappointment when we can't obtain the desired good—or with conflict when our having as much of it as we'd like is not compatible with leaving some for our neighbors. And if we train our desires to seek what is healthy rather than what is destructive or addictive, the satisfaction of one desire won't lead to other, unsatisfied, desires.[32] But according to Xunzi, training our desires to adhere to *lǐ*—embodying the personal and interpersonal norms of wise moral leaders—is also *objectively* good: it amounts to wanting what is both intrinsically just and beneficial for others. And once our desires are properly directed, ritual provides the means by which they, along with our emotions, are elicited, expressed, and ultimately satisfied. Since our desires in their unrefined state tend to disregard virtue and to favor what is immediately beneficial for ourselves, we need models—the sages—to show how our desires can and should be redirected toward better and more fulfilling targets.

So while wholesale elimination of particular desires might at first sound unnecessarily harsh, it actually makes a good deal of sense. Just as piranhas and hyenas are not the sorts of animal that make good house pets, urges to consume Windex and firecrackers are not the sorts of desire we should encourage or indulge at all. And more mundanely but just as truly, neither are desires we might more realistically have for things that aren't good for us or anyone else, such as seducing our roommate's significant other, punching our annoying sibling, or eating that tempting piece of pecan pie despite our nut allergy. Probably almost all of us have had desires for things we've recognized as bad for us. At the very least we shouldn't act on those desires; ideally, we wouldn't have them at all.

Similarly and even more commonly (and perhaps more challengingly), we shouldn't indulge—and, ideally, should entirely get rid of—desires for excessive amounts of things that are not so bad in moderation: for example, eating chocolate cake, using social media, and socializing at dance clubs.[33] While the process of eliminating unhealthy desires may not itself be pleasant, at least at first, life without them—that is, a life with the fully developed virtue of temperance—is more pleasant in the long run than the alternatives. Indulging unhealthy desires leads to problems, as unhealthy things inevitably do; and constantly denying them is obviously not fun either.

And once our desires are healthy and "tame," we can satisfy them without guilt or fear of negative consequences—a much more pleasant way to live. As Confucius cautions us, fully attaining this state will likely take significant time. He describes himself as setting his mind upon learning at fifteen years old and taking until he was seventy to be able to "follow my heart's desires without overstepping the bounds of propriety."[34] While we should not be surprised if ethical self-improvement is life-long for us too, we should also expect that the process, like the fifty-five (!) years between Confucius's beginning in learning and his full achievement of success, will be characterized by increasingly closer approximations of the excellence for which we are striving. And that is good news indeed.

Chapter 9

PERSEVERANCE

The Strength to Keep Going

JUST TWENTY-FIVE years old and fresh out of the police academy, Lisa Nigro was assigned to an area she describes as Chicago's "worst district ever" as part of an undercover team focused on drug busts. It was a striking experience, in which she saw the best and the worst—especially the worst, unfortunately—in humanity. She also came into contact with, and developed a deep compassion and respect for, many homeless people in her community. Five years later, she decided to take a leave of absence from the police force and consider other career options. A self-described possibilities thinker by nature, Nigro had a habit of cutting out and saving inspirational stories she found in the newspaper. One such story sparked her dream of the Inspiration Café, a restaurant she started for the homeless members of her community: "I had read a story about a café in Atlanta, Georgia, that served the homeless with dignity and respect, and I was super curious about it. And [my husband] Perry said, 'Let's go down there and see it,' and so we drove down there, and we got to work at the Café 458 in Atlanta. And by the end of that trip I was like, 'That's what I want to do. I want to go back to Chicago, and that's what I want to do.'"[1]

Of course, a lot of us hear inspiring stories every day. But it is one thing to find an idea inspiring; it's another thing entirely to make it a reality as Nigro did—even though in the beginning she had neither the financial resources nor the community support she would need. How? She started small, with what she *could* do—and she worked her way up, persisting in her efforts until she achieved her dream. The details are really quite charming:

> I come back to Chicago and I want to start The Inspiration Café, but no one believes I can do it because I don't have a college degree or anything, and they don't believe in me and just say that I'm a dreamer. I wanted to show people that I was super serious. So I just took my nephew's red Radio Flyer wagon, I made sandwiches, and I got catering equipment to put hot coffee in so it would stay hot, and I just hit the streets where all the homeless people were. And I started serving sandwiches and coffee. And eventually that turned into doing it out in my car, because I had more and more people that wanted that. And then … my friend got me a school bus, and we drove it out and had a mobile café. And the news reporters realized, "Oh, this girl is not going away—this girl is for real," and they put me on the news. And then someone that saw me on the news, who I actually had asked for space from a long time ago, called me up and said, "Hey, I saw you on the news; I'm one of the landlords that you asked for space. I totally believe in your vision. I'll give you space for a dollar a month for six months, and see what you can do." And so I started the Inspiration Café, serving the homeless with all donations from my friends: tables and chairs, and a Mr. Coffee coffee maker, a toaster, and a wok.

In founding the café, and (as we'll soon see) in her current work with challenges related to disability, Nigro stands out in her display of a very important virtue: perseverance.

A Foundational Virtue

Perseverance—the tendency to "keep on keeping on" in the face of obstacles—is needed to achieve any challenging goal. If we quit as soon as things get hard, we'll never get there. Similarly, perseverance is needed to establish almost any habit (except maybe a habit of laziness!), because habit formation requires us to repeat similar actions dozens or even hundreds of times. And as we saw in chapter 1, virtues of character are formed by habituation—specifically, habituating our appetites (our desires and emotions) to follow the guidance of our reason. Medieval Aristotelian philosopher Thomas Aquinas handily explains the need for multiple deliberate actions to form habits: Our appetites incline us to a wide variety of things—for example, the appetite for sweets inclines us to chocolate, cheesecake, and gummi candy. But our practical reasoning judges the particulars of one situation at a time—for example, "I shouldn't buy those delicious-looking gourmet gummi bears right now." So it takes a while to accumulate enough rational decisions to form an effective guide for the appetites.[2] So to develop any virtue—any habit of acting, feeling, and desiring in excellent ways—we need something a lot like the virtue of perseverance.

Confucius expresses the necessity of perseverance in character development as follows: "The task of self-cultivation might be compared to the task of building up a mountain: if I stop even one basketful of earth short of completion, then I have stopped completely. It might also be compared to the task of leveling ground: even if I have only dumped a single basketful of earth, at least I am moving forward."[3] The important thing for improving ourselves is to continue in our efforts—whether we are just beginning or near the end of our journey, forward progress is the key to reaching our destination.

Confucian philosopher Xunzi also clearly recognizes the importance of perseverance for moral development. He emphasizes the need for this virtue repeatedly in the first two essays of his collected works: "Encouraging Learning" and "Improving Yourself." For example, here is one of his more interesting descriptions of perseverance, laced with colorful analogies:

> Pile up earth to make a mountain and wind and rain will rise up from it. Pile up water to make a deep pool and dragons will appear. Pile up good deeds to create virtue and godlike understanding will come of itself; there the mind of the sage will find completion. But unless you pile up little steps, you can never journey a thousand *li*; unless you pile up tiny streams, you can never make a river or a sea. The finest thoroughbred cannot travel ten paces in one leap, but the sorriest nag can go a ten days' journey. Achievement consists in never giving up. If you start carving and then give up, you cannot even cut through a piece of rotten wood; but if you persist without stopping, you can carve and inlay metal or stone. Earthworms have no sharp claws or teeth, no strong muscles or bones, yet

above ground they feast on the mud, and below they drink at the yellow springs. This is because they keep their minds on one thing. Crabs have six legs and two pincers, but unless they can find an empty hole dug by a snake or a water serpent, they have no place to lodge. This is because they allow their minds to go off in all directions. Thus if there is no dark and dogged will, there will be no brilliant achievement.[4]

Although Aristotle doesn't discuss perseverance as a virtue separate from other virtues such as courage or temperance, like Xunzi, he sees it as essential to the acquisition of these other virtues. He argues that the way to acquire any virtuous disposition is by repeatedly performing virtuous actions for as long as it takes to develop a habit. Aquinas, however, acknowledges perseverance as a virtue in its own right. He explains his reasoning in this way:

According to [Aristotle], "virtue is about the difficult and the good"; and so where there is a special kind of difficulty or goodness, there is a special virtue. Now a virtuous deed may involve goodness or difficulty on two counts. First, from the act's very [nature]; secondly, from the length of time, since to persist long in something difficult involves a special difficulty. Hence to persist long in something good until it is accomplished belongs to a special virtue.[5]

Because of its relationship to difficulty, Aquinas classifies perseverance under the cardinal virtue of courage; interestingly, so do psychologists Christopher Peterson and Martin Seligman. In their *Character Strengths and Virtues*, Peterson and Seligman classify twenty-four character strengths under the headings of six "core virtues" that they found present among many ethical traditions. Also like Aquinas, the authors characterize courage in terms of "emotional strengths that involve the exercise of will to accomplish goals in the face of opposition, external or internal."[6] Under this heading of courage, in addition to perseverance (which they often call "persistence," although they acknowledge that "perseverance" has a more positive connotation), they include bravery, integrity, and vitality; they define perseverance as "voluntary continuation of goal-directed action in spite of obstacles, difficulties or discouragement."[7]

Perseverance as a Psychological Trait

Like the classical philosophers, Peterson and Seligman recognize that there is a right amount of persisting: There is such a thing as persisting too long in pursuing something impossible, imprudent, or just plain wrong. But, they argue, the character strength of perseverance is closer to this extreme than it is to being a habitual quitter.[8] In Aristotle's terms, then, the virtue of perseverance lies closer to the excess of persisting than to the deficiency. Reviewing the psychology literature surrounding perseverance, Peterson and Seligman found that it is related to a variety of factors, such as self-efficacy (belief that one can succeed), intrinsic motivation, and self-control. We'll return to some of these traits later, in our discussion of how we can develop the virtue of perseverance. If we do develop it, Peterson and Seligman argue, we can expect four types of reward: (1) increased chance of success, (2) increased enjoyment of future successes, (3) improvement in related skills and resourcefulness, and (4) increased belief in ourselves.[9]

As we noticed in chapter 3, perseverance (like temperance) is closely related to willpower—which, not surprisingly, is associated with success in various areas of life. Baumeister and his colleagues have identified four aspects of willpower, including what they call "performance control": focusing on and persevering in the task at hand.[10]

Further, Angela Duckworth and her colleagues (including Peterson) have studied perseverance in conjunction with a trait they call "grit": a combination of perseverance, persistence, and work ethic.[11] As they describe it, "Grit entails working strenuously toward challenges, maintaining effort and interest over years despite failure, adversity, and plateaus in progress. The gritty individual approaches achievement as a marathon; his or her advantage is stamina. Whereas disappointment or boredom signals to others that it is time to change trajectory and cut losses, the gritty individual stays the course."[12] Duckworth and colleagues conducted six studies linking grit to achievement in various spheres: educational level and career stability (among adults over twenty-five), retention in a difficult training program (among West Point students), grade point average (among both West Point and University of Pennsylvania students), and ranking in a national spelling bee (among children). They consistently found that grit predicted achievement—often more accurately than other obvious predictors such as IQ, SAT scores, or the Big Five trait of conscientiousness.

Developing Perseverance

As Peterson and Seligman point out, perseverance can be self-reinforcing "insofar as people will stay with a course of action because they have already invested some time, energy, money or other resources in it."[13] And interestingly, Duckworth and her colleagues found that, although the related trait of grit is relatively stable, it does tend to increase over time: even among those with similar educational achievement, older adults tend to score higher in grit than younger ones. That finding is encouraging for those of us who want to grow in perseverance—it suggests that such growth is possible and even normal. What are the best ways to increase our perseverance? In addition to Baumeister and Tierney's advice for improving our willpower more generally (which you can find in chapter 3 of this book), we can identify several techniques that are helpful for increasing our perseverance. We'll begin with some bigger-picture advice that has withstood the test of time: Xunzi's suggestions for learning and self-improvement. Then we'll look at some techniques recently studied by psychologists—these are more specific and hence more limited in scope.

Philosophical Wisdom for Improving Our Perseverance

As we have seen, Confucian philosopher Xunzi recognizes the importance of perseverance as a foundational virtue for developing other good character traits. He describes the process of increasing our perseverance as an instance of building on our natural capacity—similar to waving from a high mountain or shouting downwind.[14] To grow in perseverance (and in virtue more generally), Xunzi recommends that we begin by finding good environments and companions, for until we have established our character firmly, our tendency will be to adopt the habits of those around us. As Xunzi colorfully phrases it: "The root of a certain orchid is the source of the perfume called *zhi*, but if the root were to be soaked in urine, then no gentleman would go near it and no commoner would consent to wear it. It is not that the root itself is of an unpleasant quality; it is the fault of the thing it has been soaked in. Therefore a gentleman will take care in selecting the community he intends to live in, and will choose men of breeding for his companions."[15] Xunzi encourages us to associate only with those who are respectful, reasonable, and gentle—these are the qualities that we will want to "soak" in.

In addition to associating with worthy companions generally, Xunzi advises us to be especially careful about the teachers and role models we follow. We need teachers, he explains, because "to be without a guide ... and attempt to do everything your own way is to be like a blind man trying to distinguish colors or a deaf man, tones. Nothing will come of it but confusion."[16] Since in the case of formal instruction we are presumably striving to develop the understanding and skills that our teacher displays, it is crucial that we find one whose knowledge and skillset is valuable enough to merit our emulation. Xunzi recognizes, however, that not all education is formal: other role models (and, as we saw just above, companions more generally) can also be a strong influence on our development. Part of perseverance in moral development, then, is being open to correction from those around us. As Xunzi, following his own role model Confucius, puts it: "He who comes to you with censure [i.e., rightful criticism] is your teacher; he who comes with approbation [i.e., rightful praise] is your friend; but he who flatters you is your enemy."[17]

At first it may seem that Xunzi advocates persisting indefinitely when trying to reach our goals. Take, for example, the following passage:

If he keeps putting one foot in front of the other without stopping, even a lame turtle can go a thousand *li*; if you keep piling up one handful of earth on top of another without ceasing, you will end up with a high mountain. But if you block the source of a river and break down its banks, even the Yangzi and the Yellow River can be made to run dry; if they take one step forward and one step back, pull now to the left and now to the right, even a team of six thoroughbreds will never reach their destination. Men are certainly not as widely separated in their capacities as a lame turtle and a team of six thoroughbreds; yet the lame turtle reaches the goal where the team of thoroughbreds fails. There is only one reason: one keeps on going, the other does not.[18]

However, he recognizes that this trait, like other ethical virtues, lies in a mean—that although perseverance is closer to not knowing when to quit than to giving up too easily, there are situations in which persistence is foolish. In fact, a final piece of advice from Xunzi regarding increasing our perseverance is to set reasonable goals: no one can or should keep going indefinitely, especially when the costs of doing so clearly outweigh the hoped-for benefits of success. For example, his advice to aspiring scholars is not to waste mental energy trying to solve paradoxes of logic—an intellectual should devote her brainpower to more pressing (and solvable!) issues rather than "be an unwitting plodder who tries to exhaust the inexhaustible, to pursue to the end that which has no end."[19]

Psychological Advice for Increasing Perseverance.

For those things that *are* worthy of pursuit, though, the virtue of perseverance generally requires us to develop more—not less—persistence toward our goals. Fortunately, over the past few decades psychologists have confirmed the effectiveness of several different methods of improving our perseverance.

In the more specific area of perseverance following failure, it turns out that many of us can increase our perseverance by adjusting the way we explain that failure. Our "explanatory style," as psychologists call it, encompasses three aspects of how we attribute bad events: (1) to factors internal or external to ourselves (2) to global or more local (specific) causes, and (3) to stable or unstable characteristics. In a classic study, Dweck and her colleagues found that children who persevered after failure differed from those who did not in that they tended to attribute their failure to lack of effort: an internal but not global or stable characteristic—in other words, something about themselves and within their control. By contrast, those who attributed failure to a lack of ability (an internal, stable cause) or to adverse circumstances (an external factor) tended not to persevere—they stopped trying. Focusing on twelve children who suffered from learned helplessness (despair in the face of failure), Dweck and colleagues found that Attribution Retraining Treatment—training the children to attribute their failure to lack of effort—was effective in fostering perseverance; the standard Success Only Treatment was not: "The subjects in the Success Only Treatment continued to evidence a severe deterioration in performance after failure, while subjects in the Attribution Retraining Treatment maintained or improved their performance."[20] So if we can similarly retrain ourselves to attribute more of our successes and failures to effort, we too can probably expect an increase in our perseverance.

On a related note, expecting a particular task to be difficult can increase our willingness to persevere in it. For example, among groups of students matched for sex and internal versus external explanatory style, those who were told that the problems they were trying to solve would be difficult persevered longer than those who were told they would be easy. (The problems, which involved rearranging plastic shapes to form patterns, were actually impossible.) The researchers attributed this finding to the threat to self-esteem that we can experience when failing at something we expect to master. Failing at a more difficult task, they suggest, is less a blow to our egos and thus safer; whereas we're disinclined to risk further failure at something that should be easy.[21] Perhaps simple awareness of this result can help remind us to persevere—and not to invest so much of our egos in succeeding the first time we try.

Robert Eisenberger has extensively studied a perseverance-related characteristic opposite of learned helplessness: He calls willingness to exert significant effort toward one's goals "learned industriousness." He has found that the amount of effort people are willing to put forth is affected to some degree by external rewards: if high effort is rewarded, people (and rats and pigeons, as it turns out) are willing to exert higher effort on future tasks. Eisenberger explains this result by appeal to classical conditioning: we come to associate the reward with the exertion of effort. If low effort is subsequently rewarded, though, our willingness to put forth high effort decreases: "There is considerable evidence that rewarded high effort does produce a generalized increase in industriousness. Increasing the degree of required performance involving one or more tasks raised the subsequent vigor and persistence of various other activities, including rats' lever pressing and runway traversal; depressed mental health patients' card sorting; learning-disabled and typical preadolescent students' handwriting, drawing, and mathematics performance; and college students' manipulatory behavior, perceptual identifications, essay writing, anagram solving, and resistance to cheating. Extended effort training produced long-term effects with both rats and humans."[22] Those of us with students or children may want to make particular note of those results: an easy quiz toward the beginning of the semester or a raise in allowance without an increase in responsibilities may discourage future effort.

Another apparent opposite of learned helplessness, a psychological trait called "self-efficacy," also seems to be related to perseverance. As Albert Bandura defines it, an expectation of self-efficacy in striving toward a goal is "the conviction that one can successfully execute the behavior required to produce the outcomes."[23] In other words, self-efficacy is confidence in our own competence. Bandura explains the connection between self-efficacy and perseverance like this: "Expectations of personal mastery affect both initiation and persistence of coping behavior. The strength of people's convictions in their own effectiveness is likely to affect whether they will even try to cope with given situations.... People fear and tend to avoid threatening situations they believe exceed their coping skills, whereas they get involved in activities and behave assuredly when they judge themselves capable of handling situations.... Efficacy expectations are a major determinant of people's choice of activities, how much effort they will expend, and of how long they will sustain effort in dealing with stressful situations."[24]

So if we can increase our sense of self-efficacy, at least in certain domains of activities, we may be able to increase our perseverance in those same areas. In fact, Bandura cites several studies to that effect. When given bogus feedback on their problem-solving performance, designating it as above or below average, students with the positive feedback—whose self-efficacy had been arbitrarily increased—performed better on subsequent intellectual tasks. As Bandura summarizes the research, "Among students equated for ability but differing in self-efficacy, those with a higher sense of efficacy manage their time better, are more persistent, are less likely to reject good solutions prematurely, and are more successful in their problem solving."[25] So those of us trying not to decrease our children's or students' efforts by making initial tasks too easy will want to be sure not to make them too difficult either—the idea is to make success within reach for those who put forth appropriate effort. We may also want to heed Bandura's general suggestions for improving self-efficacy: (1) viewing failure as "informative rather than demoralizing"; (2) social modeling or "seeing people similar to oneself succeed by perseverant effort"; (3) being persuaded to believe in oneself; and (4) understanding and improving one's general physical and emotional states: e.g., by exercising and reducing anxiety.[26]

Regarding exercise of perseverance in particular projects, an interesting recent study (again of university students, the easiest folks for psychology professors to study) of project perseverance found that people tend to be more perseverant in projects that they find more personally meaningful.[27] This result isn't terribly surprising: the meaningfulness of our projects is related to our intrinsic motivation to pursue them, and it is quite reasonable to expect that when we are more motivated to pursue a project we will work harder and persist longer in doing so. In fact, as Peterson and Seligman note, we are more likely to persist in tasks that we connect with our identities or that we find pleasant—that is, tasks that are intrinsically motivating. And they refer to studies finding that people who learn how to *make* tasks more enjoyable or more meaningful are able to persist longer in them.[28] One caution, as we noted in chapter 1, is that extrinsic motivation—external rewards such as money or prizes or even good grades—can interfere with intrinsic motivation. Especially in the case of anticipated and salient rewards (such as performing the task for payment), we can too easily come to see ourselves as performing the task *only* for the reward.[29] That's one reason that I like to tell myself (and my students) that I get paid only for grading and going to meetings—I do the teaching, reading, and writing for fun. (Socrates actually thought it was unethical to accept payment for teaching philosophy; I wonder whether he'd have objected to being paid for grading and committee work.) My young adult son takes a different, but thus far also effective, approach to preserving intrinsic motivation: because he really enjoys carpentry and car repair, he made a point of not going into those professions—he didn't want doing those things for a paycheck to ruin his enjoyment of them.

Finally, Rachel White and her colleagues have an intriguing suggestion for improving perseverance in tedious but important tasks—especially for young children: role playing. In their fascinating study, 180 four- and six-year-olds were instructed to be "good helpers" and perform a tedious task—but were permitted to take breaks at will with a tempting video game. As one might expect, on average the children managed to stay on task only 37 percent of the time. But those who were instructed to think of themselves as a fictional hard-working role model like Batman or Dora the Explorer (for instance, asking themselves "Is Batman working hard?") persevered with the task significantly longer than those who merely thought of themselves in the third person or—least perseverant—in the first person. As a parent, I found this result pretty exciting: I wonder whether I can get my kids to weed the garden a little longer next summer by encouraging them to pretend they're superheroes. And while that specific technique isn't likely to be as effective with adults (I have no plans to dress up as Supermom, for example), imitating role models is a great way for all of us to grow in virtuous character traits—including perseverance.[30]

A Role Model of Perseverance

As we began to see at the beginning of this chapter, Lisa Nigro is one such inspiring role model for the virtue of perseverance. Although she was not given the educational, social, or financial advantages many successful people enjoy, she managed to land a job on the Chicago police force and to start the Inspiration Café. Shortly after the café was established, she gave birth to her two children: twins Emily and Nick. In the decades that followed, Nigro stepped back from café's day-to-day operations but continued to have a role in it and in several other nonprofit projects; she looked forward to retiring and traveling with her husband. But her life took an abrupt turn when her son, Nick, contracted the West Nile virus: he went into cardiac arrest, and, though Nigro and her husband successfully resuscitated him, he suffered serious brain injury from lack of oxygen. That event, Nigro says, "landed me in the place where I'm at right now: full-time caregiver for my son, Nick. And at the hospital, no one thought that he was going to survive, and it was one of those times again where my faith and my inner vision knew that something bigger is in store in this situation. And so, and it's been a really unbelievable, remarkable journey."

We saw that Nigro had already developed a remarkable habit of perseverance, overcoming significant previous challenges. She also obviously finds her son's life and wellbeing personally meaningful, and that clearly contributes to her motivation to persevere on his behalf. But as she has found both through research and through her own work with Nick, this new life path calls for even more perseverance than she displayed on the police force and in the nonprofit sector—in fact, she describes it as her life's biggest challenge. "There are two different kinds of brain injuries: There are traumatic brain injuries like car crashes, boat accidents, and things like that. And those people have one giant mountain to climb to heal, and it's a huge, huge path. But for anoxic brain injuries—for people who survived a drowning, a hanging, a suicide attempt, an asthma attack, or a cardiac arrest where they're dead and brought back to life—they have five mountains to climb." So this journey with her son is a long-term one, and it's sometimes a hard-fought battle: physicians (and insurance companies) are skeptical about claims of progress and about the possible benefits of starting or continuing treatment. So in addition to being Nick's primary caregiver, Nigro is his most strenuous advocate: she regularly video records her interaction with her son and documents his progress. As she puts it, "You have to document every piece of the journey with the person that you're working with, because insurance companies, hospitals, doctors, no one believes you. You have to really plead your case like you're in court."[31]

In addition to helping Nick as his caregiver and advocate, Nigro has found that she can use her experience to give hope to other families going through similar struggles. Her outreach began with a blog for her son:

I started writing this blog to Nick; I was writing it so I wouldn't forget what was going down. And it has been remarkable—people from around the country have reached out to me and have said, "Your words on the page have changed my day." ... So I'm actually at the point now where I'm just going to be real: in this blog that I'm writing for Nick, about Nick, I didn't put in any filters. And I think it's because I'm doing it just straight from my heart, and occasionally I'm swearing or occasionally I'm just saying stuff that is just raw and real—people have come to love it because I'm sure they feel that.

Where many people would have seen this situation as an occasion for despair, Nigro—again, she's a "possibilities thinker"—not only has hope for herself and her family but sees her struggles as an opportunity to share that hope with others. So in addition to persevering with Nick's recovery, she is encouraging other families to persevere in their own caregiving and advocacy: "I just really want to be the person that, when someone is in the hospital, going through anoxic brain injury, they find our story. And I want them to see these stories of hope; I just want to be that little drop of water that they need in the desert—because it's a giant desert in this journey." In fact, she describes that project—"being a beacon of hope for those families"—as her next calling in life.

And Nigro doesn't want to stop there: Ultimately, her goal is to change things at a system and policy level—to help ensure that the potential of other people who suffer brain injury is not overlooked: "Neurologists and doctors and insurance companies don't have the patience or the wherewithal to wait it out or see where the person can go. So they get housed in nursing homes and things like that, and people don't see their potential. And so that's what I want to change." If anyone can bring policy change with only her tenacity and grit as resources, surely that person is Lisa Nigro. And if we take inspiration from the challenges she has overcome and continues to face, perhaps each of us can grow in perseverance and bring positive change to our own situations as well.

Part 4

GOOD THING IT'S NOT ALL ABOUT YOU

Understanding, Humility, and
Learning by Example

~

Chapter 10

UNDERSTANDING OTHERS

ANDY WELLS grew up on a small farm on Minnesota's Red Lake Indian Reservation—an area with few obvious opportunities for success. Through hard work, intelligence, and a bit of charm, he managed to overcome his situational obstacles and thrive as an engineer, a college professor, and, eventually, the owner of Wells Technology, a successful manufacturing business. Wells made a conscious decision to locate his business in his hometown—he wanted to help improve the local economy and provide more employment opportunities for the next generation of young adults in his community. As he soon found, many young adults in his area faced another obstacle in addition to the limited economic and educational opportunities he'd overcome: they also had criminal records. He tells the story of one who stands out in his mind: "One young man came here, and he's a big fellow, very polite, and he asked for a job. And he filled out the application; like most applications it said: 'Are you a felon?' He checked 'Yes,' and I saw that and said, 'I'm sorry, but we don't hire felons.' And he said, 'Yeah, I hear that every place I go.' So as he walked back to his car, I could see a lady in there and two kids."[1]

To his credit, Wells realized that the check mark in the "Yes" box didn't define this man's character. He asked himself, "How would I feel going back to my family when nobody would give me a second chance?" The young man, he reasoned, had made one stupid mistake when he was as a bored, inadequately supervised teenager. "And now he's paying for that his whole life. And I just don't think that's right." So he called the man back and hired him—an act he considers to be an important turning point in his career and his community outreach:

> I realized that everybody makes mistakes. And maybe sometimes they're not really serious, or maybe they're not against the law, so we don't call it a legal issue; there may be just a mistake financially—we bought a bad car, or we went to school and it wasn't the right course, and we had to drop it. We all make mistakes. We don't know sometimes; you have to try. But it's like riding a bicycle: just because you fall down doesn't mean you can't get up again. And these guys and gals have made mistakes and they need a second chance—and I realized when I saw him walking back that this was my chance. I could see failure, but I could see success at the same time. I could see his past failure, I could see his future success, and it was kind of like being out on a satellite: you can see the Earth, but you can see outer space. You know, you're kind of right in the middle. But I knew it would take something like me or somebody doing something to help him. It wouldn't happen by itself. And so it was a point in my life where I had to make a decision to do something good. And we did, and it's been very satisfactory.

It would have been easier for Wells to mentally justify the no-felons policy he shared with most other employers and just let the young man walk away—to see only the man's felony and not his potential, or to ignore his own mistakes and flaws. As Socratic philosopher Cicero, in a letter on ethical development addressed to his son, astutely observed, "We perceive any delinquency more readily in others than in ourselves."[2] Even without handing your acquaintances a form with check boxes to confess their mistakes, you also probably find it easier to spot their character flaws than to see your own. Maybe you have a friend or coworker or significant other with a habit of interrupting, or hogging the spotlight, or leaving things half-finished, or inconveniencing you by showing up late for events she doesn't think are important. You wonder how she can stand being that way—until you realize (maybe even because she points it out in response to your complaints) that you do the same thing. For me, anyway, this phenomenon has been among the most humbling aspects of parenthood: I have no choice but to observe my own character flaws as they're reflected in my children's behavior. Their petty grievances against each other, the impatience in their voices when having to re-explain a seemingly simple process to a beginner, their half-hearted way of pursuing routine tasks of clear benefit to the family—there's no denying that they get those from me.

As with most of the bad news in this book, though, the ease with which we spot others' flaws comes with good news too. Actually, it comes with three pieces of good news: First, if we try just a bit harder, we—like Andy Wells—also can easily spot others' character strengths. Second, understanding others' strengths and weaknesses is a good thing: good for instrumental purposes such as assigning work, good for discerning relationships such as whom to marry, and good in itself, because people matter. Third, returning to a prevalent Confucian theme,[3] we can turn both the positive and negative observations inward—we can reflect on the extent to which we possess the same strengths and weaknesses, which is a good early step toward self-improvement. In fact, Cicero's observation that we spot others' delinquencies more easily than our own is immediately followed by this: "Therefore those pupils whose faults their masters mimic in order to cure them are most easily corrected."[4]

An Objection

"Wait a minute," you might reasonably object. "Are you trying to tell me that you can know other people's personal characters—their inner states and traits—just by external observation? How can that be true? And even if it *is* true, isn't that sort of thing judgmental?" The short answer here is "yes and no." Yes, we can learn a lot about others through careful observation—we do that sort of thing all the time. As Confucius puts it, "Look at the means a man employs, observe the basis from which he acts, and discover where it is that he feels at ease. Where can he hide?"[5] Mencius described learning about people's flaws and limitations by listening to the principles they espoused and by observing the career paths they chose.[6] Or, similarly, we can observe people's characters indirectly by observing their mistakes: "People are true to type with regard to what sort of mistakes they make. Observe closely the sort of mistakes a person makes—then you will know his character."[7] And no, we needn't observe people in a judgmental way (although, of course, we may be tempted to do so)—knowing others can be a means toward showing them compassion, befriending them, and even helping them build on their strengths. Let me explain.

Back in the days of the classical Confucians and Socratics, higher education was much less systematized than it is today. Rather than go to a university for about four years and study with dozens of teachers for a few months each, as my students do, an aspiring student would identify a particular teacher he admired; assuming he was accepted as a disciple, he'd study with that same teacher for several years or even decades. (I use the male pronoun here because at the time, teachers and students were almost exclusively men.) As you can imagine, then, Confucius got to know his students quite well, both through conversation and through direct observation. And as he colorfully explained, with reference to his notoriously lazy disciple Zai Wo, Confucius had learned along the way that conversation alone was not sufficient. Upon discovering him sleeping during the day, Confucius commented, "Rotten wood cannot be carved, and a wall of dung cannot be plastered. As for Zai Wo, what would be the use of reprimanding him? ... At first, when evaluating people, I would listen to their words and then simply trust that the corresponding conduct would follow. Now when I evaluate people I listen to their words but then closely observe their conduct. It is my experience with Zai Wo that has brought about this change."[8]

Interestingly, though, Confucius learned the same lesson through his more positive experience with his star pupil, Yan Hui: "I can talk all day long with Yan Hui without him once disagreeing with me. In that way, he seems a bit stupid. And yet when we retire and I observe his private behavior, I see that it is in fact worthy to serve as an illustration of what I have taught. Hui is not stupid at all."[9] And with the disciples who fell somewhere in between Zai Wo's incorrigibility and Yan Hui's virtue, Confucius used his knowledge of their strengths and weaknesses to tailor his replies regarding inquiries on a given topic to the individual student's needs: for example, book 2 of the *Analects* recounts Confucius's explaining filial piety (devotion to parents) to four disciples in four different ways, ranging from outward obedience to respectful demeanor to more general moral uprightness.[10]

While we can have the most confidence in the assessments we make based on repeated interaction over a long period of time, as Confucius does of his students, sometimes a briefer but particularly vivid interaction can give us significant insight into someone's inner characteristics. To take an example that was especially striking in my own life, my husband, Jerry, once brought a new coworker—a young man in his mid-twenties—to our house for a visit. The three of us chatted in our kitchen for about half an hour before the two of them decided to go outside and hang out. Later, after the visitor had left, Jerry asked me about my impression. I said something like, "Interesting guy. Seems basically decent, but too bad about the paranoid schizophrenia." Naturally, Jerry wondered why I'd say that: I'm no psychiatrist, I'm not even very observant, and I'd just met the guy. But he made it easy to guess: his mannerisms were nervous to the point of being distracting, and most of his stories were about people (e.g., the Illuminati) being out to get him. And sure enough, a year or so later he was in prison—still, sadly, not getting the treatment he needed—for having killed someone in the hope of releasing the person from demonic possession.[11]

We also observe others' traits via their behavior in less dramatic, more everyday contexts, for example, to decide whether to pursue a romance with a coworker or limit our interaction to a good working relationship, to seek competent teammates for a project, to determine whether we can trust our sibling to keep a secret from the rest of the family, or to estimate the likelihood that we can eat French fries in front of our dieting friend without presenting an irresistible temptation. (My husband, for instance, can't seem to resist fresh baked goods—so I don't bake unless it's someone's birthday.) And while the conclusions we draw in these everyday cases are *judgments*— for instance, of compatibility, trustworthiness, or self-control—in the sense that they are beliefs we've formed about the way things are based on the evidence available, they need not be drawn in a *judgmental* (condemning or overly critical) way.

Fortunately, avoiding the temptation to be judgmental is fairly simple— at least in theory. To avoid condemning or excessively criticizing others, all we really need is humility: the virtue that enables us to recognize our own flaws and the fallibility of our judgments. Unfortunately, though, the virtue of humility can take considerable time and effort to cultivate. And, like other character excellences, it's cultivated by repeated performance of the relevant acts—like recognizing and reflecting on our own limitations. So, until we form a firm habit of humility (which we'll discuss chapter 12), we'll have to rely on willpower (see chapter 3), reminders, and accountability to help us perform those relevant acts. We can also arm ourselves with evidence about the limitations of our ability to form accurate judgments—we'll turn to that sort of evidence next.

Some Surprises from Social Psychology

On the one hand, human beings have a surprising ability to form accurate beliefs about each other even from very brief observations and interactions. Beginning at around age four, we can generally infer others' beliefs, desires, and intentions from their behavior and predict their future behavior based on evidence of their mental states—at least in simple and straightforward situations. For example, in a classic study design, young children predict whether the experimenter will look for a key where she left it or where they know it to have been moved in her absence—although three-year-olds generally predict the new location, assuming the experimenter's knowledge matches their own, four- and five-year-olds tend to predict the old location, inferring that the experimenter lacks access to the new information.[12]

By adulthood, we have the capacity to form reasonably accurate judgments about *some* traits in others by observing their nonverbal behavior for a shockingly brief time—with no interaction and without hearing them speak. For instance, an analysis of several studies found that the average observer of nonverbal behavior will, in less than a minute, have a decent guess regarding a stranger's extraversion, sexual orientation, racial bias, status within a company, and even intelligence.[13] In fact, some researchers have speculated that such judgments were the adaptive purpose of humans' large brains: we need the increased cognitive capacity to help us quickly form the interpersonal assessments necessary for complex social interactions—for example, to "affiliate and connect with desirable others."[14]

Given our surprisingly good track record with inferring some mental states and personal characteristics, it's also surprising how poorly we fare at guessing others. With states, for example, we tend to be terrible at guessing whether others are lying. (Lying, I take it, involves the mental state of having a belief that contradicts one's own explicit claims.) In fact, average human judgment regarding deception is only 54 percent accurate—barely better than a coin toss—and rises to only 56 percent in "experts" such as police officers, detectives, and secret service agents.[15] And we seem to form beliefs about people's character traits at least as quickly as about traits like extraversion and sexual orientation—but with much less accuracy. For example, we apparently form impressions about people's likeability, trustworthiness, and competence based on exposure to their photographs for a tenth of a second.[16]

Further, just as Cicero observed thousands of years ago, psychologists have confirmed that we tend to give ourselves—but not necessarily others— the benefit of the doubt when it comes to attributing character traits. For example, we tend to give ourselves moral credit for *intending* to perform good behaviors, while we withhold such credit from others until they actually perform them.[17] We attribute character traits to people based on irrelevant information such as their attractiveness or physical resemblance to a friend or celebrity. Further, we have a strong tendency to make assumptions about people's characters based on stereotypes about their race, gender, or age.[18] And as we've noted elsewhere in this book, we're all subject to confirmation bias—the tendency to be attentive to information in favor of our preexisting views and to ignore information that counts against them—so our impressions can be difficult to change, whether or not they're rational.

To guard against our natural tendency to seek confirmation of our negative impressions of others, an obvious first step is to look for their strengths. And as we did in the beginning of this chapter, we can take a cue from Andy Wells.

Spotting Others' Strengths

As I soon found out, Wells's decision to give his applicant with a felony conviction a second chance was in keeping with his long-standing habit of seeing potential in people. A story from his days as a professor at Bemidji State University illustrates this quality: When he was teaching Entrepreneuring, Wells would break his class of thirty into six companies of five students each, and they'd pool money for stock instead of buying a textbook. They would create and manufacture a product, sell it, and use the proceeds to hold a banquet for which they learned how to do proper introductions and toasts. One term, Wells had a student, "Curtis," who was doing poorly—he had to get at least a C so that he could stay on the basketball team, but he wasn't very scholarly:

Because everybody knew Curtis wasn't very good in school, his team-mates didn't want him to be president or have any high level job. So the last job was salesman, and that's what he got. I said, "I'll tell you a little secret, Curtis. The salesman always becomes the hero in the end—because they've got to sell these products, and that's very difficult to do. So you just think now, already, how are you going to sell these products? And you'll do fine."

So weeks went on, and they made a cutout shape of Minnesota with a clock in it; and they decorated it with some loons [the state bird] and stuff. They made hundreds of them. And they each were supposed to go out and sell a certain number. And they came back after the first couple days and hardly anyone sold any, because they had to sell wholesale, not retail. They couldn't just sell to their friends or their parents; they had to sell to a furniture store or something like that.

So Curtis comes back and says, "I've got an idea. I'm going to do it like the Fuller Brush Company does: I'm going to get ladies together, and I'm going to sell to them at wholesale. And then they're going to have parties and sell them for me." And so he arranged it, and he sold all of his right away. And then the rest of them said, "Oh man, I can't sell mine!" And he said, "Well, I'll sell yours for you." And so pretty soon he'd sold every-body's clocks. He became the big hero.

Fifteen years later, Curtis called Wells at home one evening with an update. Because Wells had told him—and helped him to demonstrate—that he had great potential in sales, he started selling cars; he became so successful that he was now the owner of a BMW dealership. That phone call, Wells says, taught him how important it was that he'd believed in the young man—that he could see his potential.

Wells's choice to see strengths and potential where others saw only weak-nesses and flaws reminds me of a passage regarding young people from Con-fucius's *Analects*: "We should look upon the younger generation with awe because how are we to know that those who come after us will not prove our equals?"[19] At least until someone reaches age forty or fifty without learning anything, he says, we should assume that he has the potential for greatness.

When we look at others, especially those about whom our impressions are not so good, can we see their potential and their strengths? Simply reminding ourselves to do so may be effective—other people's strengths and potential are often as obvious as those flaws we've already spotted. In case they're not, however, here are a couple of more systematic ways we can guide our reflection: First, we can try looking at a list of possible strengths, such as the one on which the VIA strengths survey is based, with someone else in mind. Surely, everyone we know reasonably well exhibits at least a couple of the strengths listed.[20]

Second, we can use a variation on a technique that business leaders sometimes use to combat overconfidence in their decision making: imagine that we find out we were completely wrong—then try to explain why.[21] For example, after a week at a new job or taking a new class, you think you're going to hate it. Imagine that three months from now you absolutely love it. Now imagine why that might be true. Rather than leading us to seek evidence of possible strengths directly, when applied to people this strategy invites us to notice evidence *against* our impressions about their apparent weaknesses or lack of potential. In this way, it's a bit less open-ended: instead of browsing a list of twenty-four possible strengths, for example, you look for evidence against two or three flaws—or, perhaps, at least for evidence that those flaws aren't as serious as you initially thought. (And if, on further reflection, they really *are* that bad, maybe we can return to that list of character strengths: is it possible that the person's strengths can compensate in some way for her weaknesses?)

Understanding others—with their strengths as well as their weaknesses—is a good first step toward the other main benefits of understanding. In the next section we'll look at three main types of benefits: instrumental, interpersonal, and intrinsic.

Three Good Things about Understanding Others

There are at least three ways in which understanding others' positive and negative characteristics is good: First, as it often turns out, such understanding is sometimes also instrumental to other goals—as Confucius points out, for example, a good leader knows how to delegate tasks to those best suited to perform them. Second, it's good to discern others' characters for the purpose of knowing whom to trust and whom to regard more cautiously. Finally, and more intrinsically, it's good simply to be able to get to know people on a personal level and to learn to see things from their perspectives. Understanding others—especially others who initially puzzle or irritate us—can help us become better people: more empathetic and more appreciative.

Instrumental Understanding

A first set of reasons for understanding others might be called "instrumental reasons"—as long as we keep in mind that "instrumental" doesn't necessarily mean "selfish." (There could, of course, be selfish reasons for seeking to understand people, for example, in order to deceive or manipulate them. But since we're interested in positive moral development, we'll set such motivations aside and concentrate on those that are more ethically acceptable.) As I mentioned earlier, a leader must understand those she is leading in order to guide them effectively. Confucius brings up understanding of others several times in book 12 of the *Analects*, in which he discusses virtuous leadership: for example, "Fan Chi asked about wisdom. The Master replied, 'Know others.' Fan Chi still did not understand, so the Master elaborated, 'Raise up the straight and apply them to the crooked, and the crooked will be made straight.'"[22] Similarly, "A gentleman helps others to realize their good qualities, rather than their bad."[23] To succeed in bringing out others' good qualities and not their bad ones, or to assign important roles to those who will be positive role models, the gentleman (virtuous leader) must first recognize others' positive and negative characteristics. Clearly, then, understanding others is essential for effective leadership—again, in an instrumental but not necessarily self-centered way. In fact, early in the *Analects* Confucius encourages us *not* to be self-centered in our concerns about understanding: "Do not be concerned about whether or not others know you; be concerned about whether or not you know others."[24]

Confucius also points out that understanding other people is a key to interpersonal success more generally: "Someone who is accomplished is upright in his native substance and fond of rightness. He examines other people's words and observes their demeanor, and always takes the interests of his inferiors into account when considering something—no matter whether serving the state or a noble family."[25] As is clear from the surrounding context, there are some who wish to define "accomplishment" as something like "reputation" or "fame." Confucius will have none of that shallow definition:

No one can rightly be considered accomplished merely because he is known by others. After all, one could be known for all sorts of reasons, good or bad. Like the wise leader we discussed in the previous paragraph, one who seeks to be truly accomplished must be concerned with whether he understands others—not just whether he is known by them. Further, someone who is accomplished "always takes the interests of his inferiors into account." Apparently, merely understanding others isn't sufficient for accomplishment—one must also consider their needs and interests when making decisions. And this sort of consideration of others is crucial for close relationships, which we'll discuss next.

Interpersonal Understanding

In addition to aiding interpersonal skills generally, understanding others helps us to discern whether and how to develop our ties to particular people. As I noted earlier, understanding others' personal characteristics helps us make both momentous decisions such as whom to date or even marry, and more everyday ones such as with whom to share a secret or how to avoid creating excessive temptation for a dieting friend.

As we'd expect, given the importance of the topic and the universal human need for companionship, both the Socratics and the Confucians give substantial advice regarding the discernment of relationships. Most of Aristotle's advice comes in the context of developing close friendships—a topic we'll examine in depth in chapter 16. For insights regarding the discernment of relationships more generally, we'll turn primarily to Confucius and Cicero.

Confucius (perhaps again because of his experience with Zai Wo) describes his discernment process for educating students: "I will not open the door for a mind that is not already striving to understand, nor will I provide words to a tongue that is not already struggling to speak. If I hold up one corner of a problem, and the student cannot come back to me with the other three, I will not attempt to instruct him again."[26] As Slingerland notes in his commentary following this passage, the educational method Confucius suggests in this passage closely resembles that of Socrates: developing the student's potential and helping him express his implicit ideas through a series of challenging questions. An advantage of this educational method, from the perspective of a teacher striving to understand students' characteristics, is that it can also be useful in discerning *whether* to educate: it can be applied both before and after the teacher is certain about the student's commitment and potential. A student uncommitted to learning—unwilling to do his part—will of course derive little benefit from such instruction; and Confucius thinks that's as it should be.

Confucius also advocates similar discernment regarding less formal relationships with conversation partners: "If someone is open to what you have to say, but you do not speak to them, this is letting the person go to waste; if, however, someone is not open to what you have to say, but you speak to them anyway, this is letting your words go to waste. The wise person does not let people go to waste, but he also does not waste his words."[27]

This advice may be especially timely for our current cultural environment: We seem to err on the side of maximal self-expression, with many of us freely detailing our activities and opinions (e.g., on social media or in team meetings) regardless of whether they are likely to be of benefit to others—indeed, regardless of whether others are even listening. We routinely let our words—and the time and energy we put into them—go to waste.

On the other hand, many of us let people go to waste, too, by holding back from having important conversations that could enrich our lives and our relationships with others. How frequently do we—the same people who often over-express our more trivial thoughts—neglect to have meaningful conversations with people who are open to them? How often do we "waste" those relationships and people? As Confucius sums it up: "People who can spend an entire day together indulging their predilection for petty cleverness, without their conversation ever once touching upon rightness—these are hard cases indeed!"[28] With a little more discernment regarding what we really want to express and who is (and isn't) open to hearing it, we could enjoy much more productive and fulfilling dialogue, both with our families and friends and in our educational and professional relationships.

While Cicero certainly agrees with Confucius's general point regarding discerning relationships, he emphasizes that, given the imperfections of the human condition, we should err on the side of developing relationships with anyone whose character traits seem even somewhat promising: "Since we pass our lives, not among perfect and faultlessly wise men, but among those in whom it is well if there be found the semblance of virtue, it ought, as I think, to be our purpose to leave none unbefriended in whom there is any trace of virtue."[29] Immediately, however, he adds this qualifying statement: "But at the same time those have the highest claim to our kind offices who are most richly endowed with the gentler virtues, moderation, self-control, and ... justice." So while we would do well, Cicero thinks, to befriend anyone with some semblance of virtue—especially given the shortage of virtuous people in the world—those who are most virtuous are those most deserving of our overtures of friendship.

Later in the same passage, Cicero discusses two more factors for discerning with whom to pursue relationships—in particular, upon whom to bestow favors: "As to the good will borne to us, our first duty is to bestow the most on those who hold us in the dearest regard. We ought, however, to judge of their good will not, as young people often do, by ardent expressions of love, but rather by the firmness and constancy of their attachment." But, he adds, "in bestowing benefit and in returning kindness, other things being equal, it is in the highest degree incumbent upon us to do the most for those who need the most."[30]

According to Cicero, then, understanding others—again, their backgrounds, traits, needs, and goals—can help us discern whether and how to pursue relationships with them in at least four ways:

1. we should be friendly toward anyone who shows some semblance of virtue;
2. we should make a special effort to befriend those who are most virtuous;
3. we should be especially kind toward those who show themselves to value us the most highly; and
4. we should be particularly sure to be kind toward (and to return the kindness of) those with the most need.

By employing Cicero's advice, we may also succeed in avoiding the twin dangers of pride and flattery: "In the extreme of prosperity, especially, resort is to be had to the counsel of friends, and even greater authority to be given to them than under ordinary circumstances. In such a condition we must also take heed lest we open our ears to flatterers, and suffer ourselves to be cajoled.... We are always liable to be deceived, thinking that we deserve the praise bestowed upon us, whence proceed numberless mistakes." But trustworthy friends can help us avoid the influence of those by whom we might otherwise be manipulated.

Intrinsically Good Understanding

A third way in which understanding others is valuable is simply for its own sake: knowing others is just plain good. Other people matter, and relating to them requires that we have some understanding of their background, traits, values, and goals. So in addition to being essential for discerning whether and how to pursue relationships and being instrumental to our other goals, understanding others can be virtuous. In fact, *shu*, the name of an important Confucian virtue closely related to what Westerners call the Golden Rule, is often translated "understanding." Confucius himself describes the virtue of understanding as central to his teaching. He says all he teaches "can be strung together on a single thread"—"dutifulness tempered with understanding";[31] and when asked to choose just one word that can serve as a guide for one's whole life he replies, "Is it not 'understanding'? Do not impose on others what you yourself do not desire."[32]

Further, the ability to show sympathy (or empathy) by putting oneself in another's place is a key aspect of the chief Confucian virtue *ren*—especially as the definition of this virtue developed in later passages of *Analects* and in the work of Confucius's successor Mencius. Variously translated "goodness," "humaneness," or "benevolence," *ren* (in classical Chinese, a cognate of, and partly composed of, the character for "human being") was initially understood to indicate complete human virtue; later, it came to refer more specifically to kindness or benevolence between people. We can already see benevolence—and understanding—as a crucial component of this general virtue fairly early in *Analects*: "Desiring to take his stand, one who is Good [*ren*] helps others to take their stand; wanting to realize himself, he helps others to realize themselves."[33]

Mencius, the most famous of Confucius's ancient successors, also considers *ren* or benevolence to be a chief ethical virtue—perhaps *the* chief virtue, with righteousness (a virtue a lot like Confucius's dutifulness) being a close second. As we saw in chapter 2, Mencius argues that all human beings are born with an innate feeling of compassion, which is activated upon witnessing the (potential) distress of others. This feeling of compassion, while not itself a virtue, is the beginning or "sprout" of benevolence.[34] Insofar as un-

Understand others → empathize → activate compassion →

act compassionately → develop benevolence

Figure 10.1. Causal chain from understanding to benevolence

derstanding others helps us to activate and act upon our compassion in appropriate ways, then, it helps us to cultivate this chief Confucian virtue. So the causal chain from understanding others to benevolence should look like figure 10.1.

I say that the chain *should* look like the simplified one in the figure because, although the theoretical link between understanding and benevolence might appear to be fairly straightforward, the process of virtue development can of course go awry at various points. In particular, as Christian Miller notes, activation of empathy—and even of compassionate motivation to relieve others' distress—can occur outside of virtue development; in fact, some of us tend to avoid situations that activate our empathy precisely *because* we don't want to be motivated to act on it.[35] We'll discuss the virtue of benevolence, its Western counterpart of mercy, and their relation to empathy and compassion in more depth in chapter 18. For now, we'll turn to a final main reason for understanding others: we can use our observations of others to learn about—and, ultimately, improve—ourselves.

Others' Flaws, Our Flaws

As we have seen, we have an alarming tendency to perceive flaws and failings in other people—a tendency that, with a bit of conscious reflection, we can work to counteract in ourselves. The Confucians propose a powerful way to give others the benefit of the doubt in our social interactions: we can find in their apparent flaws, particularly as manifested in their behavior and demeanor toward us, an opportunity to reflect upon whether their negative actions and attitudes might be caused (at least in part) by *our own* flaws. In this way, we can add a fourth "i-" benefit to the instrumental, interpersonal, and intrinsic goods we discussed in the last section: understanding others promotes productive *introspection*.

Adopting the strategy of looking within ourselves upon perceiving others' faults can be helpful in a few ways: First, if we really are partly to blame, it presents an occasion for apology and self-improvement—and, if we do become better people, for eventual improvement of our relationships. As a bonus, Confucius suggests, holding ourselves to a higher standard than we expect of other people is conducive to more pleasant social interaction in the short term as well: "Demand much of yourself, but ask little of others, and you will keep resentment at a distance."[36] Second, if upon careful reflection (and perhaps seeking counsel from an objective and honest friend) we determine that we are not to blame, the reflection can bring peace of mind: it can put to rest nagging questions like "What's wrong with me?" and "What did I do to offend this person?" Third, whether we are to blame or not, taking time to reflect on our own possible contribution to the negative situation at least forces us to pause, take a deep breath, and try to assess the matter charitably before resorting to blaming the other person. Confucian philosopher Mencius eloquently describes the strategy as follows:

The benevolent love others, and those who have propriety revere others. Those who love others are generally loved by others. Those who revere others are generally revered by others. Here is a person who is harsh to me. A gentleman in this situation will invariably examine himself, saying, "I must not be benevolent. I must be lacking in propriety. How else could this situation have come upon me?" If he examines himself and *is* benevolent, and if he examines himself and *has* propriety, yet the other person is still harsh, a gentleman will invariably examine himself, saying, "I must not be devoted." If he examines himself and *is* devoted, yet the other person is still harsh, a gentleman says, "This person is completely lost.... What point is there in rebuking [him or her]?"[37]

So, according to Mencius, the gentleman (virtuous person) starts with a thorough examination of himself—on three counts, in the example in this passage—before concluding that he is not to blame for the other person's harshness. However, the gentleman appears not to blame the other person, either. His conclusion in this passage sounds much more like pity, and sometimes that's appropriate. For example, when reflecting on the abuse and neglect they suffered as children, Lisa Nigro and Judy Berry (whose stories appear in chapters 9 and 14, respectively) tried not to blame their parents for their failings, focusing instead on the adverse circumstances and mental health problems the parents themselves had faced.

As Mencius himself would likely recognize, though—like other Confucians, he has a strong tendency to emphasize the importance of attention to the particulars of a situation—pity and blame can, to varying extents, *both* be appropriate responses to others' unacceptable treatment of us. While reacting exclusively with pity may *seem* the kindest response to maltreatment, it indicates that one has given up on the person—that the other is written off as "completely lost." Where there is hope for the other's development of virtue, better to hold him or her accountable, as Mencius often does and advocates with the kings and disciples he advises. As we saw in chapter 2 of this book, he even describes setting a low standard, when someone (whether oneself or another) is capable of achieving more, as "stealing" from that person.[38] So just as we can steal from our own virtue by failing to examine ourselves and look for ways to improve, we can steal from our misbehaving friends and family members by making no attempt to help them become better people.

On the other hand, though, that same attentiveness to the particulars of the situation—and the person—will tell us that there also must be a limit to our efforts at holding others accountable for their flaws, a limit determined not only by their ethical potential, but also by their receptivity to our well-intentioned correction and the strength of our relationship with them. With all virtuous activity, as the Confucians and many of the Socratics, including Aristotle, recognize (and as we discussed in chapter 1), there are many ways to stray from the right path—wrong time, place, motive, and manner, among others—but vices fall into two main categories: excess and deficiency. And correction of others' flaws is no exception. When asked about correcting friends, for example, Confucius advocated a middle path, replying, "Reprove your friend when dutifulness requires, but do so gently. If your words are not accepted then desist, lest you incur insult."[39] Like the ancient sages, then, we too must carefully discern whether and how to correct our companions' behavior—including their mistreatment of us—and when it's time to stop. And while there is no substitute for attention to the particulars of the situation and of the person, we find in the words of Mencius and Confucius some helpful step-by-step guidance:

1. First, thoroughly examine your own behavior and character—you may be partly responsible for your companion's negative demeanor toward you. If so, strive diligently to improve yourself.

2. If, after honest self-examination (see chapter 4), you determine that the problem really is with the other person, try to discern whether he or she might be able and willing to improve.

3. If there is a reasonable chance that he or she is open to improvement—and, specifically, to correction from you—then offer such correction as gently as you can while communicating clearly and honestly.

4. Cease attempts at correction when (a) they're no longer needed thanks to the person's improvement, (b) they're no longer effective because of a lack of receptivity, or (c) they're beginning to strain your relationship. If (b) or (c), proceed to step 5.

5. Repeat steps 1–4 (yes, start again with step 1 in case the problem was with your method or demeanor in offering correction) until it becomes apparent that no further progress is likely.

6. If after you follow steps 1–5 the person seems incapable of treating you decently, you may need to distance yourself from her or him; but continue to be civil when interaction is necessary or desirable. (This is where negative role modeling comes in—someone treating you poorly is showing you how *not* to behave.) Try not to hold a grudge—pity rather than blame is appropriate insofar as people are incapable of improvement.

7. As always, use this experience as an opportunity for continued learning and reflection: Was there anything you could have done better in this situation? Are there other friends toward whom *you* have behaved badly?

Andy Wells, with whose story we began this chapter, appears to have adopted a practice similar to the one I just outlined: when some of his employees with criminal records started to fall back into their old, self-destructive habits, he first asked himself what *he* could have done differently. As we'll see next, the results have been remarkable.

Exemplary Understanding

As we have already seen, Andy Wells likes to find and build upon people's strengths. He hires people with criminal records, believing they deserve a second chance; and as a professor he changed students' lives by believing in them. Wells continues that pattern today, believing in the potential of his employees—even those with troubled pasts. He's not naïvely optimistic, however; he's seen his share of failure, too, and he's developed ways to improve his employees' chances of success:

> When we first started training people [with troubled pasts], we had a lot of failures. But we learned every time. We learned what went wrong. And a lot of times we realized it was stuff *we* were doing that we could have done better. And now, for example, they have to have a support person. We can help them here, but they're only here eight hours, and they're gone sixteen. A lot of times their old friends show up and want to party and do stuff, so I tell them, "You need to have a support person outside of here. Maybe it's a clergy member, or it's a grandparent, or somebody of significance to you who is successful, that you can go to, or who's watching what you're doing. So if they know you're starting to party with some guys, they can get you straightened out again." And so that helps a lot too.

When Wells saw that some of his employees returned to self-destructive paths, he easily could have laid all of the blame on them ("I give them a second chance when no one else will, and *this* is the thanks I get?") or written them off entirely and become apathetic about their long-term employment prospects. Instead, as Mencius recommends, he first took the opportunity to consider whether his own approach could be improved—and he found that it could. Wells's acknowledgment of mistakes in dealing with employees, and his willingness to learn from those mistakes, have been instrumental in helping many young people to move beyond their troubled backgrounds and establish secure lives.

As Confucius recommended, Wells also makes a point of understanding his employees through meaningful conversations: they talk about success, or about their hopes and fears. Once, he says, when he asked about fears, instead of the usual responses such as heights or spiders, one young man said, "I'm afraid I can't live up to what you expect of us. You expect so much." Wells replied, "Well, I see your capability. I know you can do it. I see other people do it; you're very capable of doing it too." And he sees potential in all of his employees—not just the generic "You're a good person" or "I'm sure you have some sort of talent" kind of potential, but concrete, individual potential. He speaks fondly of the Native American women who make beautiful jewelry and who use their eye for detail to develop great skill at assembly. He proudly shows off photos of graduates of Wells Academy—his nonprofit educational program teaching manufacturing and life skills to young Native Americans—who have gone on to attain four-year engineering degrees. And he happily provides references for skilled trainees whom he'd love to hire himself but who decide to pursue jobs elsewhere. As Wells sums it up, "I like believing in people, and seeing them discover themselves." If we follow his lead, we may be surprised to learn that those we are initially tempted to label as "unlikeable" or "untrustworthy" have a lot of good qualities too.

Chapter 11

IDENTIFYING ROLE MODELS

Positive and Negative

AMONG the earliest ways we learn about the ethical life is through positive and negative role models. American folklore, for example, tells us of the honesty of beloved early presidents: George Washington confessed to chopping down his father's cherry tree, and Abraham Lincoln walked for hours to return a penny to a customer he'd accidentally shortchanged. Classical children's stories and fairy tales are often littered with characters presented for our aversion: "The Boy Who Cried Wolf" and "Pinocchio" teach us about honesty through the disastrous results of their main characters' *dis*honesty, "The Fisherman and His Wife" teaches about gratitude through the wife's chronic *in*gratitude, and the emperor in "The Emperor's New Clothes" warns us of the dangers of pride and flattery. "The Three Pigs," a perennial favorite, teaches patience and diligence (and a bit of cleverness) through both the negative examples of the first two brothers, who quickly build flimsy houses to maximize playtime, and the positive example of conscientiousness in their brick-using brother; similarly, "The Hare and the Tortoise," through the positive and negative examples of its two main characters, teaches the value of perseverance—and the dangers of overconfidence.

As we saw in chapter 9, Confucian philosopher Xunzi also uses a turtle (a lame one!) as an illustration of perseverance: "If they take one step forward and one step back, pull now to the left and now to the right, even a team of six thoroughbreds will never reach their destination. Men are certainly not as widely separated in their capacities as a lame turtle and a team of six thoroughbreds; yet the lame turtle reaches the goal where the team of thoroughbreds fails. There is only one reason: one keeps on going, the other does not."[1] In this chapter we'll take a closer look at role models—direct and indirect, positive and negative—and at their influence on our ethical development.

Direct Role Modeling

As in literature, in our own lives, too, we seem to learn earliest and best from role models. Many of the exemplary people I interviewed credited their best traits to parents or mentors; and stories of people who make messes of their lives are often striking in their *lack* of positive role models. To a more limited extent, as the Confucians repeatedly pointed out, anyone with whom we come into contact can serve as either a positive role model or a negative one: "When walking with two other people, I will always find a teacher among them. I focus on those who are good and seek to emulate them, and focus on those who are bad in order to be reminded of what needs to be changed in myself."[2] For example, a friend of mine recently recounted a vivid childhood memory of a stranger who has served for him as a negative model of (in)temperance:

> We were sitting on the train and a man sat across from us, facing us. He then got out a ham biscuit (just thick-cut ham on a biscuit), slathered it in ketchup, and ate it, sweaty and red-faced, with labored breathing. Just as I thought the scene was over, he pulled another ham biscuit out of his bag and did it all again. There was something about the combination of smells, sounds, and sights that really made it an image of intemperance— probably as motivating for me to be temperate as any exemplars of moderation regarding food.[3]

Margaret Martin, founder of the Harmony Project—an organization providing cost-free musical instruments, lessons, mentoring, and performance opportunities to children from low-income neighborhoods—has also experienced negative role modeling. In fact, she says the greatest challenge she has faced in life has been "to live with integrity in a world that doesn't value it—in a world that takes casually things that matter deeply."[4] Despite—or, perhaps, partly because of—the lack of integrity she observed growing up (for example, from a father "who was always a womanizer," teachers who mocked their students, and a relative who habitually blamed her misdeeds on others), Martin came to value being a person of integrity above all else. When I asked how she has coped with the significant challenges she has faced, Martin said, "The only way I can cope with that is to try to be the best person I can be, and to demonstrate living with integrity myself. I can't be those other people. I just try to demonstrate living with integrity and encourage my kids to do the same."

As we would hope, several of my interviewees did have stories of positive childhood role models as well. For example, Gloria Lewis, founder of Care in Action USA, an organization focused on outreach to the homeless, speaks fondly of her parents' modeling of generosity while she was growing up in Barbados—even though she didn't always appreciate it at the time:

My parents had next to nothing, and there were even times when we had to give away what we didn't have—because if we were hungry, but there was some person that was hungrier, we had to give up what we had, because we knew that we would be able to sustain but we didn't know if they would be able to sustain. If we had crackers and we were getting ready to eat [a meal], and a kid showed up at the door that we knew that was going home to nothing, then we had to give up our food, because we can go eat crackers, but this kid is going to go home to nothing. You know, my Dad came home to six lemons, two or three potatoes, and six bananas—we never were taught to keep it for tomorrow. We were always taught to share it, give two to this neighbor, two to that neighbor, and share it; tomorrow will take care of itself. And that's the way we were always taught.[5]

Of course, when we are very young, we may not yet be able to sort good influences from bad ones—which helps us see why Aristotle emphasized the importance of a good upbringing as a prerequisite to ethical and political instruction: "We must begin with things known to us. Hence anyone who is to listen intelligently to lectures about what is noble and just ... must have been brought up in good habits."[6] Once we have matured enough to distinguish positive role models from negative ones, we can benefit from both—and, judging from the target audiences of fairy tales, such discernment (perhaps with a bit of help) has long been thought possible at least to some extent while we are still quite young.[7] But as psychologist Albert Bandura and his colleagues showed over fifty years ago, such discernment is far from perfect: children frequently imitate the inappropriate and even violent behaviors they witness, whether in person or through the media.[8]

According to the Confucians, learning from role models of both the positive and negative varieties is a life skill whose importance does not diminish when we reach adulthood. On the contrary, the more we expand our spheres of action, the more roles we take on; and of course the more roles we take on, the more we have need of role models. So, for example, Confucius discusses with one of his disciples the need for an aspiring public servant to identify positive role models for help in honing his skills and character: "Any craftsman who wishes to do his job well must first sharpen his tools. In the same way, when living in a given state, one must serve those ministers who are worthy and befriend those scholar-officials who are Good."[9]

Given the relative rarity of Goodness, though (which, as we recall, means something like "complete virtue"), sometimes one must settle for companions who teach us through their weaknesses as well as their strengths: "If you cannot manage to find a person of perfectly balanced conduct to associate with, I suppose you must settle for the wild or the fastidious. In their pursuit of the Way [of virtue], the wild plunge right in, while the fastidious are always careful not to get their hands dirty."[10] Another option when suitable (positive) role models aren't available—probably in addition to, rather than instead of, Confucius's advice to be less particular—is to "befriend" historical role models by examining their lives and writings,[11] as the later Confucians and Socratics did with the founders of their traditions, or even to "befriend" fictional role models from literary works.

An Example of (Mostly) Positive Role Modeling

Noah Levinson, founder of the nonprofit medical aid organization Calcutta Kids, presents a particularly striking example of ethical growth through affinity with a famous—one might even say "legendary"—role model: Mother

Teresa. His affiliation with her began from a conversation he had with a classmate and ultimately led him to devote a significant part of his own life to assisting the destitute people of Calcutta:

[My classmate] talked about how, when he was getting into a little bit of trouble in school, his father had said, "Things are a little too easy for you, and you're going to get a dose of reality. So I'm sending you to work at Mother Teresa's Home for the Dying Destitutes, and you don't have a choice." This was a pretty transformative experience for my friend, and I was really inspired, and I was ready for something that had a spiritual component to it but was also an opportunity for an international experience. So I said to him, "How can I go and do this? How can I go to Mother Teresa's?" He said, "If you go, then I'll go back too."

So we decided to go. We did a combination of working at two of Mother Teresa's homes. It was extraordinary. We spent mornings working at an orphanage specifically for mentally challenged and physically handicapped children, and we spent the afternoons at Mother Teresa's Home for the Dying Destitutes. At the Home for the Dying Destitutes, we would basically do whatever of the sisters of The Missionaries of Charity wanted us to do. It could be washing dishes after a meal. It could be washing soiled clothes by hand. It could be hanging the laundry in the sun to dry. It could be sitting with somebody as they were dying, holding their hands. It could be giving a massage to someone who had terrible back pain. It could be tending to an open wound that was infested with maggots—we would use tweezers to individually remove the maggots. It could be spoon feeding those people too weak to feed themselves.

I had never in my life felt such a sense of purpose; I'd never felt such drive. It didn't matter if I was washing dishes or holding the hand of somebody as they were dying. I felt like I needed to get out of bed every morning because if I wasn't going to do those dishes, if I wasn't going to hold the hand of this person, then who was going to do it? It was really a very, very special feeling and it was intoxicating. Ultimately it came down to a sense of profound purpose.[12]

While Mother Teresa and the Sisters of Charity were clearly positive role models of love and compassion—so much so that Levinson spent a second summer in Calcutta with her organization—his motivation to start his own charitable organization in Calcutta was drawn from the limitations of Mother Teresa's work: in this way, she also functioned in some sense as a negative role model for the way in which his compassion was exercised. His impetus to approach poverty in a way different from Mother Teresa came from a personal encounter with a dying young man—an encounter he considers too unlikely to be mere coincidence:

Sudip was a beggar on the other side of the Ganges River. Every Sunday, street children from that side of the river were invited to the headquarters of a local organization to receive a meal, have a clean place to bathe, and get bandages for their sores and cuts—all of this plus an afternoon of games and songs. I had gone one day the previous summer to volunteer with this program and was put in charge of distributing bandages and dressing wounds. On that day there were over 150 children, many of whom needed medical attention. For over three hours I dressed small wounds and distributed basic medicines. But after seeing fewer than half of the children, we'd run out of supplies, and the remaining children were told to come back the following week.

Sudip was one of the kids still in line when the medicine and bandages ran out. I remember watching him and feeling particularly bad about his unattended injury—a small wound on his forehead. Much later, I learned that he had bumped his forehead against the head of a rusty nail. Now, a year later, here was Sudip, dying of that head injury and lying on a cot at the Home for Dying Destitutes. I was with Sudip constantly until the following day when he died in my arms....

In a city with more than 12 million people, it was difficult to consider it mere happenstance that Sudip and I had met again.... This to me was a message telling me that I needed to do more.[13]

Levinson and his friend soon decided what that "more" was, and they began the daunting task of establishing a mobile medical clinic for children like Sudip. And when Levinson and his colleagues found, based on analysis of extensive research, that preventive care for pregnant women and young children was the most effective way to keep people from ending up among the dying destitutes, they shifted the focus of their work. Today Calcutta Kids serves hundreds of women and children in Calcutta's slums, taking effective measures to raise birthweights, prevent malnutrition, and cure early childhood diseases.

Role Modeling in Philosophy, Psychology, and Education

Just as Levinson developed and exercised his compassion by working with—and in contrast to—Mother Teresa and her Home for Dying Destitutes, we all can become better people through our association with companions of various sorts. As we saw earlier in a famous passage from the *Analects*, Confucius had a highly useful ability to learn from anyone: "I focus on those who are good and seek to emulate them, and focus on those who are bad in order to be reminded of what needs to be changed in myself."[14] We would all do well to cultivate the Confucian habit of consciously looking for ways to improve our own character upon observing others' conduct, whether good or bad. Rather than dwell on how annoying it is that our significant other interrupts our great stories with irrelevant questions, could we reflect instead upon whether we are also prone to interruption or other forms of conversational rudeness? Similarly, rather than simply admire our friend's generosity with her time, could we consider how to emulate it in our own interactions with others? As Confucius summarizes the strategy in another passage: "When you see someone who is worthy, concentrate upon becoming their equal; when you see someone who is unworthy, use this as an opportunity to look within yourself."[15] And notice that the term "worthy" or "unworthy" needn't be a judgment regarding the other person's overall character: as we discussed in chapter 10, particular strengths and flaws are much easier to observe—they're also much more manageable targets for imitation or avoidance.

Philosopher and education expert Kristján Kristjánsson, in his discussion of role modeling and moral education, emphasizes the importance of understanding and emulating particular virtues. Too often, he observes, contemporary character education emphasizes emulation of particular exemplars *as persons* rather than of their understood and admired virtues—an approach that sells students' cognitive abilities short and can lead to uncritical hero worship. Drawing on Aristotelian philosophy, he proposes a more theoretically informed approach to encouraging emulation of role models in secondary education. Emulation, he argues, is a beginner's virtue consisting of four elements:

> (1) the emotion of distress at the relative absence amongst ourselves of desired, honoured goods which someone else possesses; (2) the zeal to make efforts to deservingly acquire similar goods without taking them away from the emulated other; (3) true self-understanding and rational self-persuasion, which directs us towards goods that are attainable for us and, thus, towards future honours of which we can realistically become worthy; and (4) a striving for goods that are "appropriate attributes of the good"—that is, goods that are morally worthy or, at least, not morally unworthy.[16]

The methodological problem with character education's typical approach to role modeling, Kristjánsson argues, is that it focuses on the second and fourth elements—motivation and behavior—to the exclusion of the first (affective) and third (cognitive) components.

In an intriguing article, philosopher Vanessa Carbonell has proposed a more detailed account of just how the affective and cognitive aspects of our response to moral exemplars might motivate us to strive to be like them. Our knowledge about exemplars, Carbonell argues, can have a "ratcheting-up effect" on our moral aspirations by dispelling our preconceived ideas about what counts as "unrealistically virtuous" or "too much sacrifice." That is, learning about how much some exemplars have willingly sacrificed (she highlights Paul Farmer, a humanitarian physician, and Susan Tom, who adopted a dozen children with special needs), and about how they have lived satisfying lives despite—and sometimes because of—the sacrifices they have made, should prompt us to reconsider where we have drawn the line in our own willingness to sacrifice for the greater good.[17]

In a fascinating series of empirical studies conducted at Stanford University, we see a glimpse of the Confucian advice to take care *not* to emulate those we don't admire. Marketing professor Jonah Berger and psychology student Lindsay Rand cleverly influenced undergraduate students to make healthier eating and alcohol consumption choices by subtly associating heavy drinking and junk food with "avoidance groups" or "out-groups": groups of people that, as researchers determined in a preliminary study, the students didn't dislike but in which they didn't want to be seen as members. For example, in studies that were supposedly about responses to news media, students read a fake newspaper article associating junk food with either their in-group (undergraduates) or an out-group (graduate students or online gamers); students who read the articles associating junk food consumption with an out-group went on to make significantly healthier eating choices.

In my favorite of Berger and Rand's studies, graduate students were again the chosen out-group. At the beginning of the academic year, two similar freshman dorms displayed anti-alcoholism posters in their halls: One had the usual statistics about the dangers of binge drinking and concluded, "Think when you drink. Your health is important." Good message, right? Students bright enough to be admitted to Stanford should be rational enough to take it seriously—and should be motivated to keep their brain cells. The other dorm's posters depicted a graduate student with a bottle of alcohol. It said, "Lots of grad students drink, and lots of them are sketchy. So think when you drink. No one wants to be mistaken for this guy." Guess which posters were more effective? Sure enough, it was the negative role modeling ones. Amazingly, according to their anonymous self-reports, the students in the dorm with the grad student poster drank over 50 percent less alcohol over the following week.[18]

But Who Wants the Life of a Moral Exemplar?

Of course, it is one thing to describe *how* emulation works, under the assumption that people want to be like highly ethical exemplars and not like out-group members; it is quite another to show that people really *do* want to emulate them—after all, the exemplars are generally not in-group members either. For the most part in this book, I have assumed that my readers want to be better people—that seems the most obvious motive for reading. And, of course, we considered the connection between virtue and the excellent life in some depth in chapter 1. But I'm painfully aware that not everyone immediately sees the desirability of heroic virtue, especially compared to competing pursuits. For example, last year a guest speaker at my university surveyed the student audience regarding which kind of life they would choose for themselves or their children: (a) a life of heroic virtue along the lines of Mary Jo Copeland, who devotes her life to caring for the homeless and is known as "Minnesota's Mother Teresa,"[19] or (b) a life of fame and fortune with a side of philanthropy along the lines of Taylor Swift.[20] About 80 percent chose (b). So it's worth pausing occasionally to consider why moral excellence— and, in this case, emulation of moral exemplars—is worthwhile, even when compared to other, not-obviously-immoral options.

In a famous 1982 article, philosopher Susan Wolf argued that striving to be a moral exemplar (or "moral saint," to use her term) *isn't* worthwhile. The moral saint would have to devote her entire life to making sure every one of her actions was as morally good as possible; thus, Wolf argues, she would be bland, humorless, devoid of hobbies, and unattractive as a potential friend or mate.[21] Perhaps the students at my university who voted in favor of pursuing Taylor Swift's lifestyle rather than that of Mary Jo Copeland shared Wolf's worries. Since that time, though, several philosophers and a few psychologists have explicitly worked to refute her argument; many others have provided evidence that can be used against it. As the most popular line of critique goes, Wolf has moral sainthood all wrong: there have been (and still are) real-life moral saints, and their lives aren't at all what she describes. Despite the long hours (she gets up at 4:00 a.m.) that Mary Jo Copeland devotes to caring for the homeless, she is perhaps the most joyful person I have had the honor of meeting: Even in her mid-seventies (as she was when I met her), she was full of zest for life and simply exuded love, meaning, and purpose. And while Swift's life of fame and fortune undeniably has its perks, it also comes with a lot of work and stress as well as constant public scrutiny and very little room for privacy—and although she may indeed be well-adjusted for someone in her situation, she has also acknowledged suffering from anxiety and obsessive-compulsive disorder.

Carbonell, as I mentioned earlier, also uses case studies to counter Wolf's theory about the desirability of being a moral saint: as we saw, she proposes Paul Farmer and Susan Tom as counterexamples. In another article,[22] she goes into further depth in her description of Paul Farmer's life, with its joys and meaning as well as its sacrifices. Farmer, Carbonell argues, is almost the opposite of what Wolf would expect such a saintly person to be: although he spends most of his time treating the very poor in developing countries for no salary and subsists on minimal food and sleep, he is charismatic and funny and enjoys life. Rather than obsess about whether each of his actions is a moral as possible, he concerns himself with the *content* of his ethical commitments: that the poor and marginalized should have access to medical care. This concern, rather than dragging him down, provides a strong sense of direction and purpose in his life. In short, despite—or, again, because of—his personal sacrifices, he is flourishing.

Similarly, Robert Merrihew Adams cites examples such as Mother Teresa and St. Francis of Assisi to show that saints can be joyful and diverse, with interests and pursuits other than making every action as moral as possible. While agreeing with Wolf that moral principles aren't suited for "maximal devotion," Adams emphasizes the traditional religious notion of a "saint" as "holy"—and he suggests that an adequate conception of sainthood places God (rather than morality) as devotion's central object. This religious notion of a saint, Adams argues, is actually wider than Wolf's: saints need not focus exclusively on being as moral as possible, but instead are people who "submit themselves, in faith, to God, not only loving Him but letting His love possess them, so that it works through them and shines through them to other people."[23] Under this definition, he suggests, there are many types of saints with varying interests, abilities, and activities—and we should all aspire to sainthood.

Although not all of the exemplars I interviewed were religious, they as a group largely embodied Adams's wider notion of sainthood: in addition to being obviously very good, they were interesting, friendly, and sometimes funny, with varying backgrounds, interests, and goals. They were happy with their lives. Above all, they were *interesting*—there was not a single one whose life was, as Wolf suspected a saint's life must be, "strangely barren," or whose personality was "dull-witted or humorless or bland."[24]

Perhaps one could object that there are also other, less saintly or exemplary, ways to flourish as a human being. However, even if these other ways of flourishing exist, (1) their existence does nothing to show that exemplary flourishing is *not* worthy of emulation; (2) they can't diverge *that* much from ethical exemplarity—as we saw in chapter 1, being an excellent human being is closely tied to living an excellent, meaningful, and deeply satisfying human life; (3) the ethically exemplary life is preferable to any variety of personal flourishing that doesn't also promote others' wellbeing—given that human flourishing is good and more human flourishing is better, my flourishing by helping you flourish is better than is my flourishing alone; and (4) being ethically excellent (like being excellent in other ways) is good in itself—it's a good way to be, even if no one else notices.

What Can We Model in Exemplary Role Models?

As we saw Kristjánsson argue earlier, there are wrong ways to go about role modeling—especially in education. Trying to copy the persona of an ethical exemplar without understanding what it is that makes him or her exemplary quickly devolves into hero worship, and, in some cases, to copying the exemplar's inevitable flaws as much as her virtues. So the most obvious answer to the question regarding what we can emulate in role models seems to be their virtues: Mary Jo Copeland's compassion and generosity or Nelson Mandela's commitment to truth and justice. Noah Levinson, as we also saw earlier, took this more reasoned approach to Mother Teresa as a role model—emulating her compassion and dedication even while critiquing some of her organization's methods. And since cultivating particular virtues is the main topic of this book, we've seen several stories of role models' virtues along with philosophical and psychological insights on how to cultivate them.

In this final section on role models, however, I'd like to suggest that we can emulate, in addition to their particular virtues, some more general aspects of exemplars' approach to life: moral centrality, a redemptive outlook, and awareness of our influence on others. First, consider the personal trait that psychologists tend to call "moral centrality." This big-picture characteristic, despite its name, is not the one Wolf held in suspicion: that of focus on making every action as moral as possible or of "morality itself, or moral goodness, serving as the object of a dominant passion."[25] But it *does* partly resemble her initial characterization of what she calls a Loving Saint, whose happiness "would truly lie in the happiness of others, and so he would devote himself to others gladly, with a whole and open heart."[26]

In their in-depth studies of living moral exemplars, psychologists Anne Colby and William Damon were struck by the degree to which these role models' personal identities and goals were united with their ethical concerns. As they observed about the exemplary people they interviewed, "these men and women have vigorously pursued their individual and moral goals simultaneously, viewing them in fact as one and the same. Rather than denying the self, they define it with a moral center.... They seamlessly integrate their commitments with their personal concerns, so that the fulfillment of the one implies the fulfillment of the other."[27]

In a series of careful studies, psychologists Lawrence Walker and Jeremy Frimer have worked to analyze and better understand these sorts of observations. Using both interviews and surveys of exemplars as well as of "ordinary" people, they propose that, as our agency-related interests (such as desires for power and achievement) develop, they tend to conflict with our also-developing communal interests (like benevolence and universal concern for others). This conflict can be resolved in a few ways: we can endorse our agency at the expense of communion, promote communion at the expense of our agency, or integrate the two interests so that they can be furthered together. While it probably seems obvious that the third option is preferable, it is also difficult; so more often, we choose either agency or communion (typically agency, at least in the West) at the expense of the other.[28] Ordinary people whose interviews indicated integration of agency and communion (by combining them in the same thought, as moral exemplars often do) tended to engage in more virtuous behavior. And, as we'd expect by this point, in their earlier study comparing exemplars to ordinary folks, the exemplars tended to be happier with their lives.[29]

While we may not (yet) be ethical exemplars, we may be able to become more like them by consciously striving to unite our agency drives with our communion concerns—associating benevolence with achievement, for example, by setting goals to promote others' wellbeing. Perhaps we're not yet ready, as Noah Levinson already was in his early twenties, to move to a foreign country and devote our lives and careers to serving the very poor; but in smaller ways, we can also set service-related goals. For example, can you take some ownership in an important event or fundraiser for your family's school? Put some of your professional skills or personal strengths to work serving others through your religious or community organization? Or, if those sound daunting, can you set some specific goals aimed at becoming a better spouse, parent, or friend? To give you a concrete example, here is one of my own modest goals: because I'm by nature unobservant and mildly negative, I'm trying to make a conscious effort to notice and remember the nice things my husband does for me. Taking a cue from cognitive behavior therapy's founder Aaron Beck, I've recently started a "marriage diary," in which I write down his little kindnesses.[30] (Just an hour ago, for example, he helped me free up a little more time for writing—and kissed me goodbye when he sent me off to my home office.)

Another difference that Walker and Frimer (influenced by McAdams, who developed the interview questions they used)[31] noticed in the exemplars was the strong presence in their life narratives of redemptive themes—stories of good coming out of a bad situation. In fact, in the exemplars (but not in the comparison participants), there were over twice as many stories of this sort as of contamination—bad coming out of something good.[32] These sorts of retelling of our life narratives, which McAdams terms "the redemptive self," are typical of exemplary individuals both historically and today. As McAdams and his colleagues summarize their view, "The redemptive self is a story about how a gifted protagonist encounters suffering in the world and, equipped with a sense of moral steadfastness, manages to overcome adversity to establish a long-term personal legacy toward aiding others in their community."[33] Importantly, they have also found that among the rest of us, those "whose autobiographical narrative accounts more closely approximate the redemptive self exhibit higher levels of positive societal engagement and enjoy better psychological wellbeing."[34]

Along with uniting our motives of agency and communion, then, a good approach for those of us who want to emulate moral exemplars as role models might be to look for redemption sequences—instances of something positive coming out of something negative—in our own lives. Was there a time that you didn't get the house or the job or the mate you wanted, only to end up with something (or someone) better? Did you ever make a stupid mistake that taught you a valuable lesson? Did an illness or loss in your life lead to greater emotional or spiritual development? Notice that redemption sequences don't necessarily end with a good so fabulous that you're *glad* the bad thing happened (although sometimes they do); it's enough that we recognize and appreciate the good. To emulate an exemplar's overall outlook on life, we'll do well to focus much more on the redemption in our stories than on the occasional contamination.

Finally, drawing from Noah Levinson's story as well as from the common life experience of parenting, I'd like to suggest we can better emulate our role models by recognizing that other people are looking up to *us*. For Levinson, the transition from being a student to starting a nonprofit was difficult—it brought intense pressure and even a period of depression. But, in true re-demptive fashion, he looked for meaning and purpose in that experience and went on to rise to the challenges he faced and to do great things for the people of Calcutta. More recently, he has had another profound experience of being a role model—this time for college students working with him as interns. He spoke very highly of the abilities and aspirations of his student interns before adding:

> But what I realized was how much I enjoy working with people of that age—that period of exploring what we want to do with our lives, figur-ing out our values. And the mentorship that I was providing felt like the responsible thing to do considering these young peoples' added value to Calcutta Kids. But it was also something that I actually really loved to do. I've found myself thinking a lot about that this year: in my current clinical social work internship providing psychotherapy to college and graduate students, I support students of similar age to our Calcutta Kids interns as they wrestle with existential questions of how to meaningfully engage with the world.

Being in a position of role model for his young interns led Levinson to seek actively to be a good mentor to them—and, later, to other students. Some-thing similar happens with many of us when we become parents: we can't help but be aware that our children are watching and imitating us, and if we love our children and want them to turn out well, that means we'd bet-ter become (or at least act like) people who are worth emulating. (And, as I noted in chapter 4, our children have a handy way of letting us know when we're failing in that task: they mirror our vices.) Similarly, our success (or lack thereof) at role modeling tends to be reflected back to us in the culture and habits we create in our organizations, classrooms, and sports teams—or anywhere that people are looking up to us. That extra motivation and feed-back may be just what we need to take the next step toward emulating our own role models by becoming worthy role models ourselves.

Chapter 12

HUMILITY

Living with Your Limits

THANKS to his dedication and hard work and his openness to expert advice, Noah Levinson, still in his twenties, was now the proud leader of a successful nonprofit organization—too proud, as he later came to see. As a foreign founder of the India-based public health organization, he wanted to be sensitive to the cultural environment in which he worked—and, ultimately, to ensure Calcutta Kids' long-term stability by empowering a team of local professionals to be its leaders. But like many founders, he was attached to his own ways of doing things—ways that seemed to be working well—and wasn't very interested in hearing suggestions for change.

To Levinson's credit, he did recognize that his organization had some "HR concerns," so he again sought expert advice: he brought in a local expert in education, public health, and development. This expert, who later became the organization's co-director and Levinson's wife, gradually helped him to see that the way forward was to set aside his ego—and to be open to new, more culturally appropriate, ways of running the organization:

Calcutta Kids was a very successful public health organization, which I think in many ways had a value structure based on my understanding of how successful organizations in the United States worked. She challenged a lot of those ideas, and using her background in psychology and under-

192

standing cultural nuance, she was able to communicate more holistically with our management team and our health workers. And she was able to see and learn that there were things the team might have done differently, but they didn't really feel like they had a voice to be able to share that. In our conversations we often returned to the fact that the ultimate goal of this organization was for it to be a locally owned, locally sustainable organization, and if the people there were feeling like they couldn't really challenge me, then I was doing exactly what I had promised myself that I wasn't going to do.

It was hard for me to hear those things, and there was some internal work I clearly had to do in addressing an ego that was working against the larger values of the organization. But I remembered how strongly I felt about how I really wanted this organization to not fall into the trap of so many NGOs that are started by foreigners. I asked her to help me, because I wasn't sure about how to proceed. She had done work in HR before, so she did some revolutionary work with the team. She was able to help them, so that they could share their voice in a way that they hadn't before; and out of this came new ideas, new solutions, really fantastic conversations, and a new vision for the organization which was going to be based much more on values than on rules. It's a very different organization than it was when I was running it the way that I thought it should be run, and I think it's a much healthier organization, one which really is run by people who live in that community, and who are deeply committed to the work, and who spend time doing what's going to be best for the organization and what is ultimately going to be best for ensuring a healthy community.[1]

Levinson also shared a concrete example of this new, grassroots approach and its success:

There was a meeting of a group of pregnant women and mothers-in-law—in India mothers-in-law are often awfully hard on their daughters-in-law. Basically, there was one pregnant woman whose mother-in-law didn't attend, and at the meeting, this pregnant woman, she spoke about how unsupportive her mother-in-law was, how the health workers were constantly telling her that she needed to eat more during pregnancy, she needed to get more rest, and she needed to not carry the heavy buckets of water from the tube-well to the house—and that the more she told her mother-in-law this, the more her mother-in-law made her do just the opposite.

There were some mothers-in-law that heard this in the meeting, and they decided that as soon as the meeting was over they themselves were going to go and talk to this woman's mother-in-law. So four or five strong mothers-in-law went to this other mother-in-law's house and said, "This is totally unacceptable." And they had a whole narrative of exactly what this mother-in-law would need to hear, they used the narrative that had worked to convince them to support their daughters-in-law. *They* were the ones that were making the changes that needed to happen. This never would have happened under the health program that I was running.

————————

Levinson's willingness to accept correction and advice—even as the leader of a successful organization—actually showed impressive humility. In fact, his humility was what struck me most throughout his interview: he always seemed to be reflecting on how much he had learned from others—and on how much he still had to learn. His humble approach to leadership also reminds me of Mencius's descriptions of wise teachers and sagely ancient rulers: "Zilu was pleased if someone informed him of his faults. When King Yu heard good teachings he bowed down in thanks. The Great [Sage Emperor] Shun was even greater than they. He was good at unifying himself with others. He put himself aside and joined with others. He delighted in copying from others in order to do good.... To copy others when they do good is to do good with others. Hence, for a gentleman [i.e., virtuous person] nothing is greater than to do good with others."[2]

The last two sections of this book have shared a theme that we began to see with the honest self-reflection emphasized in chapter 4: the importance of humility. Along with understanding ourselves, knowing others—valuable fellow human beings with their own strengths and weaknesses—should remind us of our limitations and dependence. In this chapter we'll take a closer look at the virtue of humility in the Socratic and Confucian ethical traditions, contemporary psychology, and everyday life. As we'll see, despite its historically mixed reviews, humility is an essential characteristic that, like truthfulness, lays a foundation for further ethical development.

Although it is a frequent theme in the recorded interactions of both Confucius and Socrates, humility doesn't often appear explicitly in the theories and texts of the traditions they inspired—and when it does appear, it is not universally extolled as a central virtue. Later Western philosophers like Hume and Nietzsche even had negative things to say about this quality, with Hume seeing no use for it outside the monastery and Nietzsche going so far as to accuse the weak of inventing the "virtue" in order to prevent the strong from reaching their potential.

Why has humility been neglected or even disparaged despite its role in Confucius's and Socrates's lives and teachings? While the historical causes may be complex, it is apparent that a large part of the shift, at least in the West, has been definitional—leading to perhaps more merely verbal disagreement than substantive debate. This definitional evolution began quite early and continued during the medieval period with the not-always-smooth integration of Christian and Greek thought. The result has been a mixed perception—and unclear definition—of humility both in post-medieval philosophy and in the words and aspirations we encounter in everyday life. So in this chapter we'll first look at Socratic humility, both in its original state and as it evolved in Aristotle's work and in the medieval period; then we'll examine the more stable but less explicit Confucian notion of humility as it appears both in ancient texts and contemporary culture. Then we'll draw from each tradition and from contemporary authors and exemplars to develop a general account of humility and examine ways in which we can develop and apply it in our own lives.

Socratic Humility

Perhaps Socrates's most famous speech, recorded in Plato's *Apology*, is his defense against the charges of irreligion and corrupting the youth. As Socrates points out early in his speech, he is on trial not because there is any plausibility to such charges, but because he and his followers have annoyed prominent citizens by revealing their ignorance. Why did he insist on engaging in such seemingly arrogant behavior despite others' obvious displeasure? Socrates explains that an oracle of Apollo revealed him to be the wisest of men—a claim Socrates could not, despite his reluctance to contradict a deity, accept in any straightforward way: He knew himself not to possess any special wisdom.

In order to understand what Apollo might have meant, Socrates conversed with the reputedly wise, finding to his dismay that they only pretended to wisdom; he thus concluded each time that he was at least wiser insofar as he knew what he *didn't* know. Unfortunately, many people misunderstood Socrates's efforts to understand the oracle's words as an arrogant claim that he himself was wise; in fact, he humbly expressed doubt even regarding Apollo's apparently singling him out as wisest in this limited way: "The truth is, O men of Athens, that God only is wise; and in this oracle he means to say that the wisdom of men is little or nothing; he is not speaking of Socrates, he is only using my name as an illustration, as if he said, 'He, O men, is the wisest, who, like Socrates, knows that his wisdom is in truth worth nothing.'"[3] So in the hope of helping other people seek and acquire this limited wisdom, Socrates helpfully shows them that they aren't wise yet—after all, people are unmotivated to search for what they think they already possess.

Sometimes people grew to appreciate Socrates's efforts. For example, Xenophon tells the story of Euthydemus, a pretentious young man who thought himself learned because he owned a lot of books. Although at first he avoided talking with Socrates, he came to appreciate being shown the error of his ways and eventually sought true wisdom by becoming Socrates's disciple.[4] And Socrates himself appreciated being shown when he was in error, as we see in his words to a well-known rhetorician:

> I am one of those who are very willing to be refuted if I say anything which is not true, and very willing to refute any one else who says what is not true, and quite as ready to be refuted as to refute—for I hold that this is the greater gain of the two, just as the gain is greater of being cured of a very great evil than of curing another.[5]

Unfortunately, though, Socrates and those like him are a small minority—as we noted above, Socrates found himself facing (and, eventually, convicted of) criminal charges thanks to the majority of the Athenians' lack of appreciation for his brand of humility.[6]

Aristotle, a fellow Athenian philosopher just two generations younger than Socrates, tended to begin his investigations from the starting point of received opinion—which, given Athenians' response to Socrates, may partly explain why he discussed "undue humility" as a vice opposed to optimal self-assessment. He also had different goals. In his *Nicomachean Ethics*, Aristotle primarily discusses character traits and their development; so when he considers undue humility, he sees it as related to an assessment of one's character as a whole rather than of one's wisdom or knowledge. We quickly see, then, why Aristotle finds no room for undue humility in the character of a virtuous person: if one is virtuous, an accurate self-assessment requires her to recognize the goodness of her character—it requires a positive outlook on the self that Aristotle calls greatness of soul, often (somewhat misleadingly) translated "pride."[7] A more modest assessment of one's own character, an undue humility, would entail a lack of self-knowledge—a problem that Socrates himself reported as a chief concern of the gods and a source of numerous personal and political calamities.[8] However, Aristotle doesn't appear to endorse pride in the usual, egotistical sense: he names vanity—an overinflated self-assessment that we might more naturally term "pride"—as a vice opposing greatness of soul. Further, his description of truthfulness (as we discussed in chapter 6) includes a significant degree of modesty in self-representation.

Cicero, perhaps more directly influenced by Socrates, includes in his ethical advice a realistic intellectual modesty and an openness to correction akin to Socratic humility:

Nor yet is it out of place, before forming our judgment in doubtful cases, to consult men of superior natural intelligence or those who have become wise by experience, and to ask them what they think as to any matters in which the question of duty is involved.... As painters, and sculptors, and poets, too, like to have their work pass under review by the people, that if any fault is found by a considerable number of persons it may be corrected, and as they earnestly inquire both of themselves and of others wherein the fault consists, so for us there are many things to be done and left undone, and changed and corrected by the opinion of others.[9]

Cicero also extols other aspects of what we (and the Confucians, as we'll soon see) might reasonably call humility: for example, concentration on doing great deeds rather than on receiving recognition for them, lack of arrogance in dealings with those of lower social status, avoidance of obsession with power and reputation, recognition of our frailty and limitations, and reverence for the wisdom and authority of elders.[10]

Despite the emphasis placed on various aspects of humility by Cicero and other classical Western writers, philosophers did not list it among essential ethical virtues until the beginning of the medieval period, in which the integration of Christian, Jewish, and Islamic religious thought with classical philosophy was a central intellectual task. While a full account of medieval theories of humility is well beyond the scope of this book, a few representative examples will serve to demonstrate some of the main developmental trends.

Because of their religious beliefs and interests, the medievals tended to situate human virtue in the context of one's relationship with the God of traditional theism: an eternal, all-powerful, entirely perfect being. Thus it is not surprising that they saw humility, which involves acknowledgment of our limitations and imperfections, as central to the ethical life. Augustine, whose writing in many ways set the tone for medieval Christian thought, frequently emphasizes the importance of humility—and warns against the dangers of pride—in his *Confessions*, *The City of God*, and in his letters. For example, in a letter giving advice regarding progress in Christian virtue, he says:

I wish you to prepare for yourself no other way of seizing and holding the truth than that which has been prepared by Him who, as God, saw the weakness of our goings. In that way the first part is humility; the second, humility; the third, humility: and this I would continue to repeat as often as you might ask direction, not that there are no other instructions which may be given, but because, unless humility precede, accompany, and follow every good action which we perform, being at once the object which we keep before our eyes, the support to which we cling, and the monitor by which we are restrained, pride wrests wholly from our hand any good work on which we are congratulating ourselves. All other vices are to be apprehended when we are doing wrong; but pride is to be feared even when we do right actions, lest those things which are done in a praiseworthy manner be spoiled by the desire for praise itself.[11]

Maimonides, a Jewish thinker, also emphasizes humility in his *Laws Concerning Character Traits*. And Thomas Aquinas, who was among the most systematic of medieval philosophers, provides a thorough account of humil-

ity—explaining its essential nature, how it relates to temperance, and why it
is compatible with Aristotelian greatness of soul. Humility moderates self-
confidence, keeps us from aiming for glory against right reason, and leads
us to acknowledge both our dependence on God and the good we find in
others.[12]

From even this very short summary we see that, despite the shift in emphasis in the medieval period toward a more explicit and prominent role for
humility and an integration of religious considerations into its definition,
the humility-related qualities admired by these later philosophers mirrored
those mentioned in the accounts of Socrates and in the writings of Cicero
and even Aristotle. These qualities can be divided into two main categories,
one primarily internal and the other external:

1. *Accurate (not overinflated) self-assessment.* This self-assessment
   includes recognition of our ignorance, limitations, and frailty while
   not excluding recognition of our strengths; it results in openness to
   correction and respect for others' wisdom and authority.
2. *Modesty in behavior.* Such modesty includes a lack (or at least a
   relative lack) of striving for power, reputation, or reward for our
   good qualities and actions: a focus on doing the right thing rather
   than on being recognized or rewarded for doing so. Like accurate
   self-assessment, this modesty may lead to expressions of openness
   to correction and deference to others' wisdom and authority.

The Confucians also discussed both of these main aspects of humility, adding some features paralleled in contemporary psychological accounts. We'll
turn next to Confucian descriptions and illustrations of humility.

Confucian Humility

Unlike the medieval Western thinkers—but like their classical predecessors—the Confucians did not explicitly name humility as a key virtue for
character development. Like both classical and medieval Western philosophers, they clearly saw it as a necessary and integral component of the ethical
life—both as a worthy quality in its own right and as instrumental for moral
(and general) education. Also like the medievals and like Cicero, Confucius
and his followers embraced several different but related aspects of the virtue

of humility. So while the development and focus of an account of humility progressed somewhat differently in the Confucian tradition than in the tradition inspired by Socrates, the endpoints of these accounts are surprisingly compatible.

As Sara Rushing notes, there is no word in *Analects*—or, indeed, in classical Chinese—that is straightforwardly equivalent to the English word "humility"; the term sometimes rendered "humility" also reasonably can be translated "modesty," "respect," "deference," or "reverence."[13] So the Confucian notion of humility (like Cicero's) includes a cluster of related concepts. Rushing helpfully identifies three main themes in this cluster: learning and reflecting, realistic self-assessment, and human limitations.[14] We can also relate many of the themes we have identified in Socratic philosophy to those three: Cicero explicitly addresses several aspects of realistic self-assessment; both Socratic humility and Aristotelian greatness of soul might be interpreted as relating primarily to realistic self-assessment and secondarily to learning and reflecting; and Socratic humility also addresses human limitations, as does Cicero's discussion of our frailty.

In *Analects*, as we have seen, there is also a strong emphasis on realistic self-assessment, often expressed in contrast not only to unrealistic self-assessment but also to assessment of others or to concern about receiving recognition for one's accomplishments. To take just a few of the many good examples, Confucius instructs his followers, "Do not be concerned that no one has heard of you, but rather strive to become a person worthy of being known."[15] In response to a question regarding accumulating virtue and reforming vice, he says, "Put service first and reward last—is this not the way to accumulate Virtue? Attack the bad qualities in yourself rather than the badness in others—is this not the way to remedy vice?"[16] And he warns against overestimating one's abilities: "If you are shameless in what you propose, you may then find it difficult to put your words into practice."[17]

We have already noted the importance of reflection upon seeing the good or bad qualities of others; this is another important aspect of Confucian humility. And as Rushing points out, in addition to reflection on specific qualities and events, Confucius emphasizes the importance of acknowledging the need for learning more generally—we noted earlier his advice to learn as much as possible before acting, and he warns that other apparent virtues, when practiced without love of learning, result in vice:

Loving Goodness without balancing it with a love for learning will result in the vice of foolishness. Loving wisdom without balancing it with a love for learning will result in the vice of deviance. Loving trustworthiness without balancing it with a love for learning will result in the vice of harmful rigidity. Loving uprightness without balancing it with a love for learning will result in the vice of intolerance. Loving courage without balancing it with a love for learning will result in the vice of unruliness. Loving resoluteness without balancing it with a love for learning will result in the vice of willfulness.[18]

While the link between humility and love of learning isn't as obvious as that between humility and reflection on one's own qualities, recognition of the need for learning in ethical development relates to humility in at least three ways: First, it represents acknowledgment that we don't yet have all the answers. Second, it shows willing deference to the truth, even truth that doesn't suit our preferences. Third, many interpreters of the Confucian tradition, including Xunzi, understand "learning" itself to be directed primarily to ethical development. For example, in his essay "Encouraging Learning," Xunzi says that the objective of learning "begins with learning to be a man of breeding, and ends with learning to be a sage."[19] He further elaborates, "He who does not comprehend moral relationships and categories and who does not make himself one with benevolence and righteousness cannot be called a good scholar. Learning basically means learning to achieve this oneness."[20]

Regarding the theme of acknowledging the limits of our knowledge, the Confucian account emphasizes modesty in self-representation and lack of arrogance in our dealings with others—especially those of lower social status. For example, Confucius gives this approving description of a modest military hero: "Meng Zhifan is not given to boasting. When his forces were retreating he stayed behind to defend the rear, but as they were about to enter the city gates he spurred his horses ahead, saying, 'It was not my courage that kept me back, but merely that my horses would not advance.'"[21] And regarding a successor to the throne who declined it in order to allow his more worthy nephew to rule, Confucius remarked, "Surely we can say that the Great Uncle possessed ultimate Virtue! He declined rulership of the world three times, and yet remained unpraised because the common people never learned of his actions."[22] And Confucius is pleased when his disciple Zengxi, in contrast to his compatriots, expresses modest but virtuous ambitions.[23] And Confucius himself speaks modestly but not unrealistically regarding his own virtue, describing himself as culturally refined but unable to become a virtuous leader in practice and as neither sagely nor even Good, although he perseveres in his efforts.[24]

A related quality, also occasionally praised in the *Analects*, is a different sort of modesty: contentment with simplicity in material things, as opposed to a desire to acquire and show off luxuries or tokens of status. We see hints of this quality in Confucius's approval of the Great Uncle's declining the throne and even of Zengxi's modest desires; it is even more apparent in his description of the legendary sage king Yu: "I can find no fault with Yu. He subsisted on meager rations, and yet was lavishly filial in his offerings to the ancestral spirits. His everyday clothes were shabby, but his ceremonial head-dress and cap were exceedingly fine. He lived in a mean hovel, expending all of his energies on the construction of drainage ditches and canals. I can find no fault with Yu."[25] Mencius praises the sage emperor Shu for similar reasons: for example, even as heir to the throne he continued to cultivate his parents' fields.[26] And Confucius is continually impressed by his star pupil Yan Hui's simplicity: "What a worthy man was Yan Hui! Living in a narrow alley, subsisting on a basket of grain and gourdful of water—other people could not have borne such hardship, yet it never spoiled Hui's joy. What a worthy man was Hui!"[27]

Confucius also illustrates and approves another aspect of humility: lack of arrogance in social interactions. For example, he instructs a disciple on how to behave toward those under his authority: "When in public, comport yourself as if you were receiving an important guest, and in your management of the common people, behave as if you were overseeing a great sacrifice."[28] Arrogance, according to Confucius, can overshadow even the greatest of abilities: "If a person has talents as fine as the [legendarily talented and virtuous] Duke of Zhou, but is arrogant and mean-spirited, the rest of his qualities are not worth notice."[29] On the other hand, we see Yan Hui praised for his lack of arrogance: "Able, and yet asking questions about abilities that one does not possess; using what one has much of in order to ask about what one lacks; having, yet seeming to lack; full, yet seeming empty; offended against, and yet feeling no need to retaliate. I once had a friend who was like this."[30] And Confucius's followers marvel at the effectiveness of their teacher's own unassuming manner: when one disciple wonders how Confucius finds out so much information about the government of each state he visits, a more knowledgeable disciple explains, "Our Master obtains it through being courteous, refined, respectful, restrained, and deferential. The Master's way of seeking it is entirely different from other people's way of seeking it, is it not?"[31]

Humility Today in Theory and Practice

As philosopher Iris Murdoch astutely observed, "humility is a rare virtue, and an unfashionable one, and one which is often hard to discern. Only rarely does one meet somebody in whom it positively shines, in whom one apprehends with amazement the absence of the anxious avaricious tentacles of the self."[32] And despite the beauty and harmony of the Confucian and Socratic approaches to humility and the virtue's prominence in medieval accounts, it has been relatively neglected in the recent Western revival of theoretical interest in virtue as well—as several philosophers, theologians, and social scientists have noted, their own efforts notwithstanding.

Comparative educational researcher Jin Li suggests two main reasons for the humble status of humility: Westerners tend to see it in more cognitive terms (e.g., as centrally concerned with open-mindedness and fallibility), perhaps leading them to consider it less essential for moral goodness; and modern Western emphasis on qualities like self-confidence and recognition of personal rights may cause ambivalence toward humility. By contrast, Li proposes, in countries with Confucian heritage, where ethical self-cultivation is seen as the primary and life-long human project, humility is valued as essential for moral development. The value placed on humility is demonstrated in the way it is emphasized and taught to young children. For example, rather than boast about or hide their high (or low) achievement in school, the norm for Chinese children is simply to disclose their achievement level to their peers—with the understanding that disclosure to a higher (or lower) achiever indicates a request for (or offer of) help. Further, caregivers and teachers routinely follow praise for achievement with reminders of the need to remain humble; they also admonish displays of arrogance, and they praise—and are expected to model—humble behavior.[33]

Perhaps philosophers' relative neglect of humility is to some extent compensated by the recent attention of several psychologists. In fact, recent empirical work suggests that humility may be a more central personality trait than psychologists originally thought. Based on their research regarding personality trait descriptions in various cultures (and twelve different languages!), Michael Ashton and Kibeom Lee go so far as to advocate modifying the standard "Big Five" personality inventory to include a sixth factor: Honesty-Humility. This group of traits, which they theorize is linked to social reciprocity—in particular, to potential cooperators' trust that one is not exploiting them—includes honesty-related descriptions such as "sincere," "faithful," and "honest" as well as humility-related words like "modest," "unassuming," and "unpretentious." As one might expect, then, traits showing *lack* of honesty-humility include "pretentiousness," "greed," and "slyness"— the two last of which are described in terms of tendencies to take advantage of others.[34]

Psychologists have also been inquiring into the benefits of humility. For example, Christopher Peterson and Martin Seligman, pioneers of the positive psychology movement, count humility as an important character strength linked to temperance and spirituality—a stance strikingly similar to that of Aquinas. They suggest that humility (like temperance) is valuable for self-regulation: humble people are less likely to take foolish risks or make poor decisions in order to impress others and more likely to make efforts to overcome their flaws.[35] And in a recent series of studies, some of their colleagues in that movement found that humble people consistently tend to be more helpful than less-humble ones.[36]

Psychologist June Price Tangney, upon surveying several theoretical accounts and empirical findings, proposes a synthesis of various philosophical and psychological accounts of humility. The result is a definition consisting in several qualities quite harmonious with the descriptions we saw in Confucian and Socratic philosophy; these include accurate assessment of one's abilities and achievements, ability to acknowledge mistakes, low self-focus, and appreciation of others' contributions. As Tangney quite plausibly argues, given this definition, we should expect true humility to be rare: the typical human being has a strong tendency to "self-enhance," to emphasize and remember positive information about herself while downplaying or ignoring the negative. And many of us tend to be overly self-focused as well. But, as

Tangney also observes, humility is conducive to our wellbeing: "moderate" modesty (i.e., a lack of boastfulness) in our self-presentation makes us more likeable to others, and the "self-forgetting" (focus on values and on other people rather than on oneself) can help us avoid the anxiety, depression, and social phobias that can be associated with excessive self-focus.[37]

Given the relative rarity of true humility and its role in both altruism and human wellbeing, it makes sense that this virtue would be an important mark of an exemplary person. As we close this chapter, we'll consider the role of humility in the lives of several well-known twentieth-century exemplars and in that of Noah Levinson, with whose story we began.

Humility in the Excellent Life: Case Studies

In their seminal study of living moral exemplars, psychologists Colby and Damon began with a nomination procedure for exemplars that included interviews of a diverse set of philosophers, historians, social scientists, and theologians to arrive at five selection criteria—one of which was "a sense of realistic humility about one's own importance relative to the world at large, implying a relative lack of concern for one's own ego."[38] In that study, they used the humility primarily as an exclusionary criterion: they eliminated from consideration potential participants who were notably *lacking* in humility. (For the most part I did the same in my own selection process.) Intrigued by the conflicting attitudes toward, and definitions of, humility in the contemporary literature, they sought in a more recent work to examine more closely the role of humility in the lives of six twentieth-century moral leaders.

After in-depth study of the writings and lives of these leaders, they identified six main themes, themes that are quite consistent with both Tangney's findings and the accounts of the classical Confucians and Socratics: (1) a relatively low self-focus accompanied by honest self-reflection and caution regarding the "moral risks posed by the ego," (2) a "sense of perspective" in which they saw themselves as just part of a larger story, (3) acknowledgment of the dignity and contributions of people across the social scale, (4) lack of focus on honors and accomplishments and refusal to accept special privileges, (5) recognition of the fallibility of their judgments and the need for advice and criticism from other people, and (6) open-mindedness toward opposing viewpoints despite certainty regarding their essential moral convictions. For example, Damon and Colby demonstrate, Nelson Mandela showed a sense of perspective through his use of self-deprecating humor in public speeches; Eleanor Roosevelt was known for her solidarity with ordinary laborers; and Jane Addams, despite her opposition to World War I, deferred to the judgment of her fellow Hull House residents regarding making the house a draft registration site.[39]

To sum up what we have found so far in this chapter, then, Socratic and Confucian accounts of humility are surprisingly compatible—especially given the very different cultural contexts in which they were developed and the lack of an explicit name and role for the virtue in either account until well after the classical period. When we combine the two accounts, we see several internal (self-assessment) and external (modesty) features of humility, several of which are also emphasized by contemporary psychology. Because I'm such a nerd, I find it helpful to outline them like this:

1. Accurate self-assessment, including:
   a. Recognition of our own limitations, especially:
      i. Ignorance—we don't yet know all there is to know.
      ii. Ethical development—we are not yet as virtuous as we could be.
      iii. Human frailty—not everything is within our control.
   b. Appropriate responses to those limitations:
      i. Learning—we don't invent truth but need to *learn* it to remedy our ignorance; and we often need to acknowledge others' wisdom and accept their teaching, advice, and even correction in order to do so.
      ii. Role modeling—others are not only wiser than we are but also more virtuous in various ways, and imitating them can help us grow in virtue.
      iii. Acceptance of "givens"—we need to recognize what is beyond our control in order to do what we can with (or despite) the reality we are given.

2. Modesty in behavior, including:
   a. Focus on doing good/right rather than on external recognition, such as:

    i. Material rewards,

    ii. Power or influence, and

    iii. Public acknowledgment.

b. Lack of arrogance in social interactions, including:

    i. Respectful treatment of those with lower social status,

    ii. Not boasting about one's accomplishments,

    iii. Actively seeking knowledge, advice, and correction from others, and

    iv. Willingness to admit and remedy errors.

c. Material simplicity, including:

    i. Contentment with what is sufficient rather than constant desire for more, and

    ii. Avoidance of public display of luxuries or other signs of wealth or status.

Regarding open-mindedness in particular, as Damon and Colby noticed, all of the exemplars they studied (both in *The Power of Ideals* and in their earlier *Some Do Care*) demonstrated a remarkable combination of certainty about their moral principles and open-mindedness toward others' perspectives. Exposure to others' points of view, they demonstrate, need not lead to clashing of wills: respectful listening is an important step toward understanding, discovering truths to which one was previously not exposed, and sometimes even building consensus. Damon and Colby were especially struck by this characteristic in Eleanor Roosevelt. Because she was known as a fair and open-minded listener, she was often asked to mediate disputes between employers and laborers. It was this reputation for open-mindedness that ultimately led to Roosevelt's successful leadership in drafting and passing the *Universal Declaration of Human Rights*—with overwhelming consensus despite initial opposition and deep cultural differences among represented nations. Her modeling of respectful listening led to a recognition by leaders of diverse nations that (1) there are universal human rights that nations are duty-bound to uphold (e.g., to liberty, family, and education), and (2) many such rights can be upheld by a variety of legitimate means and in a variety of social and economic contexts. And as the successful drafting and lasting influence of the *Declaration* demonstrates, it is indeed possible to avoid naïve ethical relativism while upholding respect for cultural diversity.[40]

As I mentioned earlier, when interviewing Noah Levinson of Calcutta Kids I was especially impressed by his humility. As I look at the outline the Socratic and Confucian philosophers just helped me construct, I can think of examples from our three-hour interview of each of the virtue's features; and I didn't ask any questions about humility—these features came out naturally in his responses to questions about other topics. As we saw in chapter 11, even though he came to approach India's needs differently, he deeply admired and was profoundly influenced by the virtuous example of Mother Teresa and her Missionaries of Charity. To take an example of another aspect of humility, when giving an overview of his life story, he told me about how his upbringing helped him to embrace material simplicity: his parents had grown up wealthy but grew to value spirituality and service above material goods. When Levinson was still a toddler, they inherited a large sum of money, gave it away, and moved their family into a Catholic Worker house with a soup kitchen and helped feed the homeless; later, they lived until Levinson was in high school on the farm that supplied the soup kitchen with produce—and provided some homeless people with short-term housing. Levinson sums up the influence of these years fondly: "That sort of instilled in me a different idea of what success was—the idea that being selfless and helping others was the way that you could be successful. Material goods were overrated, and the mystery of God and spirituality was something that could be wrestled with, challenged, and could also be a huge driving force in my life."

As we saw in the story of his organization's transformation, Levinson was also willing to seek advice and admit error; he also showed by doing so that—although it did take external help to recognize the implications of the way he was running Calcutta Kids—he valued the wellbeing of those he served and the sustainability of the organization above any desire for power or influence. In fact, when I asked him what he thought that memory said about him, his reply sounded almost like a textbook definition of the first modesty-related component of humility: "If I truly believe that something is right, no matter how much it pains me personally, that's okay if it's for that greater good, or for that greater truth."

Even Levinson's description of his guiding ethical principles shows deep humility. Here is how he describes his ethical approach:

I think that it is centered around "do no harm"; but it's more complicated than that, because I think that there is so much harm that we potentially do by promising to do no harm. So, with the idea that "do no harm" is the guiding principle, an understanding that we *will* do harm is essential, as is our responsibility to work through that. In my work in India, although I really believe that I've always had the best interest of others at heart, I'm sure that there have been things that we've done that have not truly been for the best of the community, and there are people that could be very upset about that. So, while thinking about the idea of the intention of doing no harm, I think about that with an understanding of my inherent fallibility.

Finally, when I followed up with a question regarding what he considered to be the single most important value in human life, he chose acceptance—and, in particular, acceptance in the context of the Serenity Prayer, which makes for a nice closing reflection on humility for all of us:

> God, grant me the serenity to accept the things I cannot change,
> Courage to change the things I can,
> And wisdom to know the difference.[41]

Part 5

GIVING PEOPLE
WHAT THEY DESERVE

What You Owe Your Parents, Your Benefactors,
and People in General

❧

Chapter 13

JUSTICE

Treating People Rightly

G ROWING UP with an alcoholic and abusive father, and worried about her mother's wellbeing, Cathey Brown made a conscious choice at eight years old to be the perfect child: "I made straight As, I had perfect attendance, and I never broke a rule."[1] She graduated from high school with honors, earned excellent grades in college, and became a teacher—which, she says, had been her career goal since about age ten. Despite loving her job, when her daughter was born Brown left teaching to become a stay-at-home mom—conforming to strong social and familial expectations. As she describes the situation, "it was a combination of post-partum depression and now having nothing as far as work or school or anything—I got extremely depressed." Brown went to see her doctor, who prescribed Valium—the standard treatment at the time—which diminished her appetite. So, at her doctor's recommendation, she began drinking wine (an appetite stimulant) as well.

Brown didn't realize she had become an alcoholic herself until several years later: "My mother became quite ill, and the doctor asked me about her drinking. And by that time my mother had also become an alcoholic, so he asked me about *my* drinking—which I thought was a strange question, but he really did help me begin to look honestly at my drinking and drug use. True to my pattern, I just started researching it." After encountering a woman at the Council on Alcohol and Drug Abuse who read Brown and her situation with unsettling accuracy, Brown entered a twelve-step program—which, she says, "really began the journey not only of my own recovery but what was to become my life's work." She explains:

> In my research, I found that alcoholism and drug abuse tend to run in families, and I was really concerned about my daughter. Her father was also a drug addict and alcoholic, and I was, as well as her grandparents, and so I knew she was at extremely high risk. So I started looking around for things that I could do to keep that from happening, and there just really weren't any programs in our area. So I went to some training and started Rainbow Days with the idea that I would do it part-time for a little while—and we're now in our thirty-fifth year.

Instead of simply working one-on-one with her daughter or sending her to a program elsewhere, Brown started an organization aimed at helping local children in situations similar to her daughter's. Perhaps you can already see Brown's commitment to justice: in addition to natural motherly concern for her daughter, she was motivated to make sure other children with alcoholic parents had a fair chance at avoiding alcoholism and leading healthy, successful lives. Brown also showed a strong commitment to pursuing justice in a more obvious way, through political channels, when the ability of her organization to help those children was threatened:

> The state of Texas had a group that oversaw all the grant dollars for treatment and prevention services, including services like we do at Rainbow Days. And they were talking about a pilot program that would put all the money into a behavioral health managed care system, and so we were all going to lose our funding and it was going to be a really bad thing. And it appeared that there was no recourse. So several community representatives went to meet the director of this agency and tried to talk her into keeping prevention out of this pilot, and she absolutely wouldn't do that. So we had to take it to their board.
>
> I don't like injustice, and I don't like things that don't make sense and don't seem fair. And none of these things seemed fair or made sense or

were just. And so I mobilized all the prevention service providers in our area to go in to give testimony on the day of the meeting. And so probably twenty-five to thirty of us showed up to this meeting. They have open testimony before they start the business part of the meeting, so we took well over an hour giving testimonies. And then the executive director stood up and gave all the reasons that she and her staff had decided that what we were asking for wasn't doable and shouldn't be done. So it really looked like it was a lost cause, but at least we had put up a good fight.

The head of the commission was a very thoughtful and wise man, and he just sat there for a few minutes and he talked about how much he appreciated our comments, and he said, "You know, it's hard to know exactly what we should do." And then he paused and he said, "No, I *do* know what we should do. I'll entertain a motion to take prevention out of this pilot project." And so they did, and it literally saved prevention as we knew it in our area. And it was such a high because we had made it happen—and I used to teach government, and so it was like sometimes democracy really can work. [Laughs.]

Susan Burton, whose story we saw in chapter 6, is similarly passionate about justice; unfortunately, her experience with promoting (and receiving) it through government channels has been much less positive. Here is a brief recap of her story: growing up in south Los Angeles in the 1950s and '60s, Burton endured abuse and racial discrimination; in her twenties she suffered from severe depression following the death of her son. Turning to drugs to ease her pain, she soon found herself addicted—and repeatedly incarcerated (but not treated) for her drug abuse. Finally, after her sixth release from prison, someone reached out and offered help: "I got sober in Santa Monica. I saw people being treated differently there than people in south L.A., which was a predominantly black and poor neighborhood. Santa Monica was more of a white upper-class neighborhood, and people were treated totally differently for possession of drugs or their addiction—there were more resources [for treatment] there. So, that caused me to think that if women in south L.A. had a place to go when they left prison, if they had support, then perhaps they wouldn't return to prison."[2] And that, as we saw, was the beginning of Burton's organization, A New Way of Life, which provides support for formerly incarcerated women and their families.

Burton notes another turning point in her life and work: one in which she shifted her focus toward advocacy for social justice. Upon reading the bestselling book *The New Jim Crow*,[3] Burton was convinced by the author's argument that the high rates of incarceration among African-Americans, especially for drug-related offenses, represents an ongoing problem with racial injustice. This new perspective, Burton says, led her to increased self-forgiveness and "to make a deeper commitment to the work I was doing; and that helped me to build the organizing, advocacy arm of the organization, to fight the discrimination and to educate our community more about how they needed to come together and stand up for themselves or for others."

Although she tried at first to address social injustices through focus on legislative reform, Burton soon became disillusioned with the formal political process. She tells the story of her change in perspective:

I used to be very optimistic, and then I started going to our state capitol. And I was watching as the laws were being made. And I understood what kind of effect those laws were going to have in our community. There were just so many new ways being passed to criminalize people, and harsher sentencing. And then we were told about certain bills, and by the time they were passed through the legislature they would be changed so radically that we had no way of correcting it. You know, they will start off like a little kitten and then they come out like a wolf. And then, a lot of times, there would be bills that were created and passed without you ever even knowing about them until after they were passed. Like they will come up with it through the night and pass it in the morning.

My political and social commitment has changed: from being an incarcerated person, and then a person who's actually worked with the legislative process, I've come to the conclusion that things aren't going to change through that process radically enough to make any big difference for people in communities like my community. And so my commitment to improve social conditions just gets deeper and deeper, with each turning day. I just don't believe that our social struggles will be addressed through any legislative process. I think that legislative stuff is the problem. I believe that it's going to be by the people, for the people, to create a remedy for the social ills within their community. It's not going to happen through government—I think they made this mess.

Brown's and Burton's differing perspectives regarding political avenues for pursuit of justice obviously stem, at least in part, from their differing personal experience: Brown's voice was heard, and she successfully accomplished her objective; Burton was often denied a political voice, and she has experienced too many unpleasant legislative surprises. But let's dig a little deeper: Is there anything more to say about those experiences and their relationship to justice? As it turns out, there's quite a bit to say: Aristotle's analysis, now thousands of years old, clearly applies to the two women's experiences and perspectives—and to so much else in life.

Aristotle on Justice

As Aristotle explains in book 5 of his *Nicomachean Ethics*, we tend to use the word "justice" in two main senses: a wider sense in which "just" acts include any good or virtuous actions affecting others, and a more specific sense focused on fairness in social and economic interactions. This specific sense, which is the main topic of his discussion, itself admits of two main divisions: distributive justice, focused on equitable distribution of benefits and burdens, and corrective justice, which attempts to restore the balance when this fair distribution is violated.

Distributive justice, as Aristotle describes it, does not always (or even typically) require an equal distribution in an absolute sense: people can reasonably and fairly have differing amounts of a benefit such as money or a burden such as household chores. What it *does* require is an equal proportion or ratio of the amount of the benefit or burden distributed to the merit of each person to whom it is allotted.[4] For example, suppose you and I work as dishwashers at the same restaurant. Assuming we are equal in ability, conscientiousness, and whatever else might be relevant, if you work twice as long as I do, you should be paid twice as much. Now suppose that, thanks to your willingness to work twice as long as I do, you are promoted to Head Dishwasher and become responsible for supervising my work as well as doing your own. Now our boss would act unjustly if she continued to pay you at the same hourly rate I am earning—and I'd be the first to campaign for your raise.

Corrective justice does just what its name suggests: it attempts to correct for prior breaches of justice.[5] So imagine that, even after campaigning for your raise, I become envious of your higher income and steal cash from your wallet while you're diligently working. When my crime is discovered, the first order of business should be to correct the financial aspect of my injustice by returning the stolen money to you. That's the easy part. Less straight-forwardly but just as importantly, you have been harmed by my breach of your trust and my intrusion into your private business. (After all, who knows what else you might keep in your wallet?) A judge might justly assign me a significant penalty: perhaps a jail sentence or a hefty fine. It will be more difficult to restore your peace of mind. Seeing my being justly punished may help; an apology from me might go a long way too. But if my transgression causes you significant ongoing distress, fairness may also require financial compensation and therapy—funded by me.

As we can already see even with this simple case of theft, it can be difficult to restore the balance of justice—in some cases, such as murder, it's down-right impossible. In those situations, we simply have to do the best we can. The virtue of justice, then, is the trait of correctly discerning equitable distri-butions and the best methods of rectifying breaches of that equity—and of acting on this discernment in the right way, under the right circumstances, and for the right reasons. So we can see why Aristotle says that developing justice is more difficult than many people seem to think:

Men think that acting unjustly is in their power, and therefore that being just is [also] easy. But it is not; to lie with one's neighbour's wife, to wound another, to deliver a bribe, is easy and in our power, but to do [or not to do] these things as a result of a certain state of character is neither easy nor in our [immediate] power. Similarly, to know what is just and what is unjust requires, men think, no great wisdom, because it is not hard to understand the matters dealt with by the laws.... But *how* actions must be done and distributions effected in order to be just, to know this is a greater achievement than knowing what is good for the health; though even there, while it is easy to know that honey, wine, hellebore, cautery, and the use of the knife are so, to know how, to whom, and when these should be applied with a view to producing health, is no less an achieve-ment than that of being a physician.[6]

In the story above regarding Brown's campaign to restore funding to programs aimed at preventing alcoholism, distributive justice (as Brown argued) required that at least some state funding be set aside for prevention—and particularly for the sort of prevention programs that her group and other nonprofits provided—rather than all funding being directed toward state-run treatment. Because she and the other nonprofit leaders were successful in restoring distributive justice via the established political process before any harm was done, Brown was satisfied with the democratic process and its outcome.

In contrast, Susan Burton's life story is littered with incidents that she (quite reasonably, it seems to me) understands to be tragic failures of distributive and corrective justice. Her race and socioeconomic status left her with disproportionately heavy burdens and few benefits in early life. When her son was run over by a police car while crossing the street, she received no compensation, no apology, and no consideration of her and her neighbors' request for a traffic light at the intersection. When she turned to drugs and alcohol, corrective justice was not on her side either—she was repeatedly imprisoned and not offered treatment. And when she finally recovered and tried to work with the legislative process to restore justice, she encountered too many disappointing—even deceptive—legislative twists. But as we saw above, although she has given up the belief that it will be achieved through legislation, Burton has not given up on justice for communities like her own. She hopes that justice can be achieved through grassroots efforts of committed people like her.

Justice, Rightness, and Integrity

Although their experiences with governmental efforts at justice have been quite different, Burton and Brown share, in addition to their commitment to distributive fairness, a commitment to justice in the wider sense of living by ethical principles and willingness to sacrifice personal comfort in order to do right by others. As we saw in chapter 6, Burton terminated one of her organization's largest funding contracts because it required what she considered to be excessive monitoring of her clients, putting A New Way of Life in an oversight (and potentially adversarial) role that was inconsistent with its mission. And Brown describes her approach to decision making with Rainbow Days in a similar way:

We can't fix all the problems, but we often say that we're just going to do the next right thing—and that may or may not be the financially smart thing, and it may not be what other people would think is the way it should go. But if we believe it's the right thing, then that's how we'll ultimately make a decision. And even in our own agency, some people will say, "That's going to be so much more extra work," or, "You don't have to do that," but if it feels like the next right thing to do, we'll do it.

This commitment to following one's ethical convictions, even at considerable cost to oneself, fits well not only with Aristotle's description of the virtue of justice, but also with both Confucian philosopher Mencius's virtue of rightness and psychological accounts of integrity.

In Confucian ethics, the virtue of rightness is among the most important character traits one can possess—second, perhaps, only to benevolence.[7] Although it encompasses behavior that might reasonably be described as relating to fairness in distributing things to (or accepting things from) others, Confucian rightness is focused primarily on the goodness and dignity of the person acting: it is beneath a good person to violate her ethical values and principles. In fact, Mencius describes as "the sprout of rightness" that feeling of disdain we might have at the thought of doing something shameful.[8] Many unethical decisions, as described by Mencius, stem from failure to hold fast to our principles in the face of incentives to abandon them—for example, by accepting a job with a corrupt leader because it comes with a high salary. To grow in rightness, we must apply our feeling of disdain at doing unethical things to those situations in which we have not yet dared to apply it: "People all have things that they will not do. To extend this reaction to that which they will do is rightness."[9] No doubt there are some things you would refuse to do no matter how much someone offered to pay you—for example (I hope), kill an innocent person or betray a close friend. To grow in rightness, we need to draw the "do not cross" line not just barely above the level of especially awful actions like those, but much higher: at the violation of any of our considered ethical values or principles.

We often describe someone with Mencius's virtue of rightness—someone committed to his or her ethical principles, even when such commitment seems disadvantageous—as having integrity. As psychologist Barry Schlenker notes, in addition to steadfast ethical commitment, the term "integrity" suggests wholeness: an undivided character. It is also related to several other positive qualities: "Integrity involves honesty, trustworthiness, fidelity in keeping one's word and obligations, and incorruptibility, or an unwillingness to violate principles regardless of the temptations, costs, and preferences of others."[10] Schlenker developed a questionnaire assessing integrity as opposed to expediency as a guiding principle; participants rate the extent to which they agree or disagree with integrity-related statements such as "The true test of character is willingness to stand by one's principles, no matter what price one has to pay," as well as expediency-related ones like "Regardless of concerns about principles, in this world you have to be practical, adapt to opportunities, and do what is most advantageous for you."[11]

As Schlenker correctly hypothesized, favoring expediency over integrity—or the second of the two statements just quoted over the first one—predicts "a wide variety of unethical and illegal activities, including reported lying, stealing, cheating, infidelity, broken promises, and drug use"—even after statistically controlling for other traits like moral disengagement.[12] And integrity is positively connected with helping and volunteering—especially for principled and altruistic (as opposed to self-serving) motives. It is also positively related to empathy and self-esteem—but, importantly, *not* to dogmatism or narcissism.[13] In fact, Schlenker concludes by listing seven main features of integrity—all of them positive: (1) commitment to ethical principles, without closed-mindedness; (2) positive outlook toward life (e.g., greater sense of purpose and meaning); (3) more beneficial beliefs about oneself (e.g., greater desire to be respected than liked); (4) greater authenticity and inner orientation (e.g., more satisfaction with one's roles and identity); (5) more positive orientation toward others (e.g., greater empathy and trust); (6) a more spiritual and less materialistic outlook; and (7) less rationalization of unethical or illegal behavior.[14]

In addition to being similar to Mencius's virtue of rightness, Schlenker's account of integrity—both as commitment to ethical principle and as undivided wholeness of character—also sounds a lot like Plato's virtue of justice as described in the *Republic*.[15] As we saw in chapter 8, unlike Aristotle's more typical account of justice as focused on equity in interpersonal relations, Plato defines justice more broadly and internally: as harmony among our reason, desires, and emotions. More specifically, this harmony in the psyche is achieved when our reason calls the shots: our less-reliable desires and emotions, if left in charge of our actions, can easily lead us astray—into the realm of impulsive, ill-advised actions and their sometimes-disastrous aftermath.

For example, depending on your personality and how you do the counting, you may have had dozens or even hundreds of desires before breakfast this morning: to hit the snooze button one more time, for an intravenous connection to your coffee pot, to find something better to wear today, for Eggs Benedict instead of bran flakes and skim milk. In fact, willpower experts estimate that we spend about eight hours a day desiring things.[16] Some of these desires may be perfectly harmless and easily satisfied—maybe a better outfit already lurks in the back of your closet—but some (like intravenous coffee!) are not; I suppose that is why (as we saw when discussing willpower) we spend about three hours a day resisting our desires.

If we don't have a good way to distinguish good desires from not-so-good ones, we'll be at the mercy of whatever desires pop into our heads. And those desires won't always be compatible even with each other, let alone with our reason. For example, your desire to hit the snooze button may conflict with your desire to get to work on time; and satisfying your craving for Eggs Benedict may be incompatible with satisfying your desire to fit into your favorite jeans. This inner conflict—both among desires and between desires and reason or emotion—is unpleasant for you and for everyone around you. By contrast, when our reason successfully enlists the help of our spirited emotions like fear and anger to "rule" our appetites—satisfying the healthy desires and subduing or eliminating the harmful ones—our mental lives have the harmony that Plato calls "justice" and Schlenker calls "integrity": a much more pleasant state of being than the alternatives.

Also like Schlenker's notion of integrity, justice in Plato's sense of the term involves adherence to our ethical standards and principles even when doing so seems disadvantageous—at least in the short term. In Plato's *Republic*, Socrates is tasked with explaining why it would be a bad idea to use an invisibility ring to gain unfair financial and interpersonal advantages. The reason it would be so tempting, of course, is that in the short term it sounds like it's *not* such a bad idea—the advantages are glaringly obvious. A just person must resist temptations to satisfy desires through unfair means; and in doing so, Plato argues, he or she will satisfy deeper, longer-term desires for inner peace and wellbeing.[17]

The interesting thing about stories of getting away with injustice—whether through superpowers and invisibility rings or through more ordinary ways of imposing our will or escaping detection—is that we all recognize the temptation to behave unjustly *as a temptation*. That is, we all seem to have a natural sense of justice that, as we immediately recognize, would prick our consciences if we went ahead and pursued the unfair advantage. In the next section we'll consider that sense of justice, its origins, and its limitations.

Our Sense of Justice—and Injustice

A couple of years ago, I was summoned to the local middle school to meet with my eighth-grade son and his guidance counselor. Fortunately, my son was not in trouble—I was there to help plan his illustrious high school career. To that end, I'd dutifully filled out a form giving my perspective on his interests and strengths. The counselor, with whom I'd become acquainted thanks to attending similar planning conferences for my son's two older siblings, led off our conversation by remarking that I was the only parent who had ever listed "strong sense of justice" among her child's strengths. (As we learned a bit later, I was also the only parent ever to list "contribute to the common good" among her goals for her child—I think by that point my son wished he had a "normal" mom!) In this section we'll take a brief look at how the sense of justice tends to develop in normal(ish) people like my kids.

In my experience, most school-aged children—not just those with ethicists for parents—have a fairly powerful sense of justice. In its early stages, this intuitive sense of justice is often misdirected. Sometimes young children seem to equate "justice" with self-interest: For example, when my son was in fourth grade he repeatedly complained that it was "no fair" that he had to wash dishes once a week—even though his siblings had the same chore and had been doing it since they were the same age. (I asked whether he really thought it would be more fair if everyone but him took a turn doing dishes, to which he replied, "No, Mom—I think *you* should do them every day.") Other times, somewhat less problematically, children's sense of justice tends toward strict equality rather than equity (fairness): when dividing candy, for example, my children have typically favored an equal distribution, regardless of whether the recipient is a toddler or a teenager. (I've occasionally had to step in to prevent sugar overdoses in three-year-olds.) And when one of them earns a reward that can be shared without depletion, such as extra screen time, the other children are usually invited to join—unless they have been especially antagonistic.

Psychologists have observed similar behavior among children in laboratory settings. For example, when distributing wooden "treats" to two puppets, four-year-olds tend to distribute equally unless there is an odd number of treats—in that case, they give more treats to the more helpful puppet;[18] and even twelve- to eighteen-month-old infants have been observed to react negatively to unequal distributions of goods.[19] Although they show some attention to proportional equity as early as age five (e.g., in assessing how "nice" a benefactor is[20]), children tend not to focus primarily on equity or merit until much later.

With a sense of justice comes a corresponding sense of *in*justice—not just the self-interested cry of "no fair!" at the prospect of chores, but concern that others are also treated fairly. Psychologist Martin Hoffman has suggested that this sense of injustice has its roots in empathy: specifically, in empathic distress—our sharing of the suffering we observe in others. As Hoffman explains, when we witness another's suffering and believe that it is undeserved—not "reciprocal" with the person's actions, character, or other form of merit—our empathic distress becomes an "empathic feeling of injustice, including a motive to right the wrong."[21] Hoffman gives a helpful example, borrowed from Robert Coles,[22] regarding the change in a young Southern boy's perception regarding racial integration after encountering a new African-American classmate: upon observing how his classmate remained calm and polite, not retaliating in the face of insults and threats, he went on to defend and befriend him—and came to the conclusion that racial discrimination is unjust.

Even very young children seem to have the beginnings of a sense of injustice. Recent laboratory studies have found that toddlers will actively intervene in transgressions against third parties,[23] and even infants tend to prefer a smaller gift from a do-gooder to a larger gift from a wrongdoer.[24] And in real life (as opposed to just in the lab), I've observed the same sort of thing almost every day while raising kids: they will actively try to stop each other from "stealing" another sibling's unused clothing or toys, and a baby will tend to prefer other family members to her usually antagonistic older brother even if he's offering better treats.

Although our empathic tendencies are helpful for cultivating a sense of injustice, they can also interfere with justice. As Hoffman explains, empathic overarousal—"an involuntary process that occurs when an observer's empathic distress becomes so painful and intolerable that it is transformed into an intense feeling of personal distress"[25]—can interfere with our ability to make fair and unbiased judgments. In fact, we share common empathic biases: tendencies to empathize more strongly with our families and friends, those who are similar to us, or the people whose suffering we see here and now. Those biases, Hofmann suggests, are precisely why we need objective principles of justice.[26]

Justice for Hidden Others

Because of our here-and-now bias—and because they're most likely to hold us accountable!—it is probably easiest to behave (mostly) justly toward those with whom we interact every day. For example, perhaps you have no difficulty dividing household chores with your family members or roommates, and maybe you're not often tempted to cheat on your significant other or to shoplift from your local convenience store. Good. But because our obligations of justice toward those with whom we regularly interact can be so straightforward and even mundane, it's easy to think we have met our justice-related obligations—to check our mental boxes and think about something more interesting. And when more difficult questions of justice do arise in our lives—for example, whether to curve our students' exam grades or how to divide our time and attention among our needy children or friends—the answer depends heavily on the particular details of the situation. But when it comes to those we don't often (or ever) see, most of us are much less just than we'd like to think. The numbers and types of people in this general "other" category are overwhelming if we try to think of them all—literally billions of people that we could group in millions of ways. For the sake of space and our sanity, let's consider just two areas in which our empathic biases can interfere with our exercise of justice toward those we might call "hidden others": (un)fair trade and the American system of criminal law.

If you take a look at the labels on your clothing, chances are you'll see that it was made in far-away countries that allow unjust labor practices. For the sake of the clothing manufacturer's profit margin and your cost savings, women—and perhaps even children—likely toiled in sweatshops for excessively long hours in exchange for extremely low wages and substandard living conditions. And if you think of the source of some of the foods you consume, the story may get worse still: throughout the world even today, millions of people are quite literally enslaved for the sake of providing us with affordable luxuries such as coffee and chocolate.[27] As I expect you'd agree, it would be unjust of you to personally exploit any of the dozens, hundreds, or maybe even thousands of people who contribute to feeding and clothing you and providing you with various consumer products on a daily basis. But you likely aren't in the habit of giving much thought to whether you are doing the same people an injustice by buying a pair of jeans, a calculator, or a cup of coffee.

The fact that we tend to worry less about injustice via ordinary shopping than via direct exploitation is natural for obvious psychological reasons: we don't experience the kind of interaction that would call the injustice vividly and continually to mind. To some extent, it *may* also be reasonable ethically: while it is never acceptable to exploit people directly and intentionally, it may be practically impossible to avoid *any* participation in others' exploitative practices. So where—and how—do we draw the line? Like so many matters, the details of a good answer will require attention to the specifics of your situation and a lot of prudence; but to get you started, I can offer a philosophical distinction and a bit of personal experience.

First, many philosophers have proposed a distinction between formal co-operation and material cooperation in another's injustice. Formal cooperation involves intending the injustice along with the perpetrator: participating in and endorsing the injustice itself. So it's never ethically acceptable. For example, if you tell me that you intend to rob the local bank and I offer to drive your getaway car, I'm formally cooperating in your act of robbery. By contrast, material cooperation need not involve intending or endorsing the other's injustice; but it does involve contributing in some way to the other's action. For example, I teach all of my students basic logical skills, including fallacies. Suppose I learn that one of my students intends to use his new knowledge of fallacious reasoning to trick his parents into giving their extra cash to him instead of to a worthy charity or to his more honest sister. By continuing to teach my usual logic lessons, I'd be cooperating with my student's planned injustice materially—but not formally: Indeed, I'd do my best to persuade him not to go through with it!

Material cooperation, it is traditionally argued, is sometimes justifiable, particularly when the cooperator has a good reason for the action she or he performs—good enough to justify knowingly (but not intentionally) contributing to the bad action of another. In my case, knowledge of logic is (I think) a significant good—and teaching it is my job. So I'd be justified in continuing to teach it. But in the absence of good reasons, even material cooperation is unjustifiable. For example, to alter the first case above, suppose you ask me for a ride to the local ice cream shop—the one right next to the bank. Unless there are truly exceptional circumstances (maybe you suffer from severe ice cream deficit disorder?), my driving you there even though I know you're in the habit of robbing banks is not justifiable material cooperation—and I could rightly be held accountable as your accomplice. More generally, the worse the injustice and the closer its connection to my contribution, the more difficult it is to have a good enough reason to engage in material cooperation.

My point in bringing up the distinction, of course, is that for most of us the situation is more like dropping you off at the ice cream shop than like teaching my student logic. We know (or reasonably should know) that our consumer habits contribute to exploitation, we could do a lot more to reduce our contributions to this injustice, and instead we simply take the path of less resistance—the chocolate or jeans or office supplies that are cheapest or most attractive or most convenient.

On the other hand, many of us can't reasonably avoid *any* cooperation with the injustices found throughout our economic environment. We have only so much time and money—we can't devote it all to researching and purchasing ethically sourced products—but that's no excuse for not making a reasonable effort. Here is how I started: because I didn't have enough time to research all of the foods in the supermarket, nor the money to shop only at my local health food store (which is committed to ethical sourcing), I did just enough research to learn which of the foods I regularly bought were most likely to be produced using slavery and other unjust labor practices: coffee, tea, bananas, and chocolate. I decided I would buy only certified fair-trade versions of those products; the rest of my groceries would just get my usual (pretty low) level of scrutiny, which aspires toward reasonably healthy and local. Clothing was easier: for financial reasons as well as ethical ones, most of my family's clothes come from thrift stores—even though many of those articles were probably produced with unjust labor practices, I'm not contributing to those practices, because I'm buying the clothing second hand. When buying new big-ticket clothing items like work boots or winter coats, I look for versions made here in the United States—where there are stricter laws protecting workers.[28] With smaller "consumable" items like socks, though, I confess I don't yet have a good approach—I just buy what's on sale.

Although U.S. labor laws may be ethically ahead of those in many developing countries, its legal system allows for a distressing amount of injustice. As we saw in chapter 10, Andy Wells was bothered by the lack of opportunity that people with felony convictions faced—and he began to hire them himself. Susan Burton, as we have seen, knows about the difficulty firsthand—and she too has worked to address it, through personal outreach and community activism.

While issues surrounding exploitation and fair trade have been bothering me for a decade or more, criminal law issues have started to haunt me more recently. Although I am free of legal trouble myself, several folks I know have repeatedly seen employment and even housing doors closed due to their past (nonviolent) missteps—missteps for which they have already been punished. That, I take it, is unjust. Further, upon hearing Burton's story and (at her recommendation) reading *The New Jim Crow*, I've become persuaded that—intentionally or not—the burdens of these closed doors fall disproportionately upon people with low income and of minority races. That's a further injustice.

Despite my certainty that these injustices exist, I'm still not quite sure what my role is in addressing them. As far as I can tell, I could avoid material cooperation in the injustices only by refusing to pay my taxes—and that, of course, would be another injustice (freeloading off my fellow citizens) and would accomplish nothing other than to put me in the same position as my legally troubled acquaintances and community members. Clearly, I can (and regularly do) discuss injustices like these with the students in my ethics classes and vote for policies and representatives I expect to promote justice.[29] I can (and occasionally do) also offer my limited skill set (teaching philosophy) to inmates at my local county jail in the hope that it will be of some benefit. But I'm still discerning whether and how I'm called to a more significant role in addressing systemic injustice.

Interestingly, Susan Burton's work in learning about and addressing issues of justice and incarceration led not only to community outreach but also to "a deeper layer of forgiveness for [herself] and for [her] community members, understanding the larger context in which they were held back and harmed." As we'll see next, forgiveness is often a virtuous response to injustice—mercy and justice are complementary virtues. And with the prevalence of injustice on both large and small scales, both are essential to an ethically excellent life.

Injustice and Forgiveness

As we have seen, family life, from early on, offers daily opportunities to develop and refine our senses of justice and injustice—especially if we grow up with siblings or with a close-knit extended family. Because injustices do occur among normal human beings who frequently interact with each other, family also provides many opportunities to respond to others' injustices with forgiveness—and forgiveness is often necessary if we want to continue interacting with each other in a functional way.

Of course, those outside our families can do us serious injustices as well—and it's often to our benefit as well as theirs if we forgive them too. One of the most dramatic stories I've heard regarding injustice and forgiveness came from one of my interviewees. Patty Webster is the founder and director of Amazon Promise—an organization she started after spending some time in the Amazon as a tour guide. Despite her lack of medical training, tribespeople often sought her help with first aid and treatment of illnesses; seeing a need for more assistance than she could provide, she gathered supplies and a team of medical professionals for a small clinic and mobile outreach. The dramatic injustice occurred during one of the group's trips to provide medical care to several remote villages in the Peruvian rain forest: "The native people thought that we going to peel their faces off and steal their fat as airplane fuel, and they were threatening to kidnap the women in our group and kill people. And it was all a misunderstanding, but it was frightening—it was very devastating and eye-opening at the same time. We had to be rescued by helicopter."[30]

Naturally, I wondered how the native people had such a mistaken impression of the medical group's purpose. Webster explained: "We were trying to work with the government, and they were supposed to let these villages know; they had asked us to go to these villages. There were probably fifteen villages or more on this river, and with these tribespeople, you have to stop in every single village to let them know who you are and why you're there, but the government never even told them we were coming. Well, one rumor led to another, and all of a sudden the whole river's frightened, and it was just a bad scene."

Fortunately, the group had a short-wave radio and GPS, so they were able to call for help. Webster attributes her group's survival until rescuers arrived to a couple of lucky coincidences: most of the villages' men were gone hunting in preparation for an upcoming celebration, and it was raining the night before they were rescued. "The last night we were stranded out on the river, and they came by that night and shot out guns at the boat. It was raining, and the rain helped us, because if it hadn't been raining—pouring—who knows what they would have done. But because it was raining so hard, they stayed back. And in the morning, we got the word, 'OK, helicopters are coming,' and so we got out."

Eighteen years later—the year before I interviewed Webster—she and her group went back to the same area:

———————

The new mayor of that zone asked us if we would go back to that river. And I've been back to that river a few times, but on the lower part—not up near where the issue was. We were all pretty excited—the staff and the volunteers—but everybody had been very traumatized. Even though it's been a long time, you don't forget that threat on your life and how surreal and spooky it is out there because it's the jungle. And so my fantasy was, "Some day these villagers are going to realize what they did and ask for forgiveness"—but I didn't think that would ever happen, because these are stoic, fierce warrior natives.

And so we went out there. The mayor had set up his base of operation in this village, and everything went very well. They held an historic meeting there, and they brought together eighty-five different chiefs; there were four or five different indigenous languages being spoken. And we held the clinic for two days—it was fabulous. At end of the second day, when we were leaving, several of them came up to me and wanted to sit down. They said, "We want to apologize for what happened to you, and we want to ask for forgiveness." And I was like, "What?!" [Laughs.] They asked for forgiveness and they wanted us to come back to the villages where the incident happened, and they promised that nothing bad will happen. It was just a really cool moment in my life to hear this from some of these people. So, anyway, we're going back in May if we can get the Air Force to help us. And that's our plan: to go back to where the situation happened.

———————

When the tribespeople asked Webster to forgive them, exactly what were they requesting that she do? While it's clear that forgiveness involves both a past injustice and some sort of change on the part of the victim, the details are more complex. For example, does forgiveness require goodwill or positive emotions (or at least a lack of negative emotions) toward the offender? Does it necessarily involve reconciliation? An apology on the offender's part? In the next section we'll take a look at what forgiveness is—and isn't—and how we can better achieve it.

Forgiveness in Theory and Practice

The sort of injustice that Patty Webster and her volunteers (nearly) suffered is exceeded, perhaps, only by cases in which serious harm is perpetrated out of malice rather than ignorance. For example, for a hundred days in 1994, members of the Hutu tribe in Rwanda brutally murdered their Tutsi neighbors. Immaculee Ilibagiza, a survivor of the Rwandan genocide, is an amazing model of forgiveness. Her parents and brother were killed; she survived only by remaining hidden—along with seven other women—in the tiny interior bathroom of a local pastor's home. Despite the trauma she suffered, she found the inner strength to forgive those who so deeply and deliberately harmed her.

When reading *Left to Tell*,[31] Ilibagiza's striking memoir, I was puzzled at first by her apparent belief that forgiveness of the perpetrators required her not to be angry with them. Anger seemed to me to be exactly the right response to an injustice as severe as the systematic killing of innocent people, including one's own family. (When we describe this sort of thing as "an outrage," I take it that's because outrage seems perfectly justified.) It would be sufficient forgiveness, I reasoned, to resolve not to retaliate—an act of the will rather than of the heart. But Ilibagiza went much further, renouncing not only vengeful behavior but even negative emotions—clearly, I thought, going well beyond the requirements of forgiveness. Yet even the "sufficient forgiveness" of non-retaliation, as I came to see on further reflection, is itself a gift that goes well beyond what the offender is "owed."

Something like this "sufficient forgiveness," sometimes accompanied by the more emotionally involved forgiveness Ilibagiza endorses, seems to be at work in recent movements in communities worldwide toward restorative justice. An alternative to harsh prison sentences, which are often ineffective in reforming offenders as well as in providing peace of mind to victims, restorative justice focuses on bringing victims, offenders, and community stakeholders together to speak openly about the offense and its impact. The goal of these "victim-offender circles" is to guide the offender toward understanding the harm he or she has caused, making amends, and reconciling with the community and (if possible) the victim: or, in Aristotle's terms, toward bringing about true corrective justice.[32] And studies suggest that the restorative justice approach tends to be far more effective than the traditional legal system: both victims and offenders are more satisfied with the process, offender compliance with the sentence is higher, and recidivism is reduced.[33]

Ilibagiza practiced something similar to the victim-offender circle of restorative justice in her own process of forgiveness: years after surviving the genocide and moving to the United States, she returned to Rwanda to meet with the man who had killed her family. (Unlike in restorative justice, though, she had no say regarding the offender's punishment: he was already serving a prison sentence for his crimes.) As Ilibagiza seemed to suggest in a later interview, in addition to being a possible component of forgiveness, a lack of anger and hatred can be an easily recognized sign that one's effort to forgive has been successful:

I went to [the] prison because I was scared that my anger would come back and that my forgiveness wasn't real. The head of the jail was a friend of my father's. He brought the man out. I broke down in tears out of compassion for him. This was a man who used to have children, a beautiful family, and a great job. I would go with his family to eat. He was a friend of our family's, never an enemy....

He came in, his hair was upside down, he was in a bad state, and I just cried. I'm so glad I never saw my father this way. And I felt that Jesus said, "This is what I told you. They don't know what they do." How can anyone want to be here? If you knew what you did, you wouldn't have ended up here. But in the same way all of us don't know what we do when we hurt people, when we are being unfair—it will come back. I told him I forgive him. My heart was yearning to tell him that. I wanted to free him from thinking that I was angry with him.[34]

Because she felt compassion rather than anger toward her family's murderer, Ilibagiza knew that her forgiveness of him was genuine. (She also, it seems, chose to attribute the man's injustice to ignorance rather than to malice. Although the available evidence doesn't seem to offer much support for that interpretation, Ilibagiza is in good company: Socrates, for example, attributed to ignorance the apparently intentional wrongdoing of his accusers.)

Further, setting aside negative emotions can be good for us—and in fact, Aristotle associates the virtue of good temper with a disposition to forgive.[35] And as several recent studies have shown, a forgiveness-focused program that includes letting go of anger and resentment and embracing compassion can lead to increased hope and self-esteem, decreased anxiety and depression, and a more positive attitude toward the offender—both compared to a control group and compared to an alternate forgiveness program focusing on simply making a commitment (i.e., act of will) to forgive.[36] The authors of the study embrace a definition of forgiveness quite similar to the one Ilibagiza seems to endorse implicitly: "Forgiveness is one's merciful response to someone who has unjustly hurt. In forgiving, the person overcomes negative affect (such as resentment), cognition (such as harsh judgements) and behaviour (such as revenge seeking) toward the injurer, and substitutes more positive affect, cognition and behaviour toward him or her. Although the forgiver has a moral right to such negatives as resentment and condemnation, he or she foreswears these nonetheless."[37]

How can we become more forgiving of the injustices we suffer? Perhaps we can begin by recognizing, in addition to what forgiveness is, what it *isn't*: Forgiveness is not justifying, excusing, condoning, or ignoring the harm or wrongdoing. Pretending that the act wasn't wrong eliminates the reason for forgiveness, and declining to seek revenge for selfish or purely pragmatic reasons (such as belief that one would not be successful in retaliating or that offering "forgiveness" will impress a potential date) does not count as for-giveness—one must intend to extend genuine mercy to the offender.[38]

To extend this mercy, Robert Enright proposes that forgiveness is accom-plished via a process that can be broken into four main stages:

1. Uncovering: One comes to understand the nature of the injury and its emotional effects.

2. Decision: One recognizes forgiveness as a strategy for healing and commits to forgive.

3. Work: This active phase of forgiveness can include increased understanding of—and, sometimes, compassion for—the offender, acceptance of the pain one has suffered and refusal to inflict it on others, goodwill toward the offender, and even reconciliation.

4. Outcome/deepening: One experiences emotional relief from forgiving the offender and may also find meaning in his or her suffering or a new purpose in life and in the community.[39]

We see each of these stages in Immaculee Ilibagiza's story. In her book, she elaborates on the suffering she underwent, her decision to forgive, and how she came to view the offenders with understanding and compassion. And the meaning and purpose she has found continue to bear fruit in her writings and outreach efforts. Similarly, the participants in the studies I de-scribed above went through these stages in their forgiveness of, for example, parents who had (in the participants' perception) deprived them of love, or relationship partners who had hurt them.

For serious injustices that each of us will probably suffer at some point, Enright's stages of forgiveness can be of great help with our own healing as well as with possible reconciliation and healing for those who wrong us. For more minor, everyday injustices, we may not need to go through such an elaborate process. In these everyday cases, at least for me, the first stage is to consider the possibility that there hasn't been a significant injustice at all: perhaps the perceived injustice resulted from ignorance or miscommunica-tion. (As I mentioned in chapter 4, I often have to ask, "Does justice require me to be offended by this?"—and usually the answer is "no.")

If there really has been a significant (though relatively minor) injustice, we might next, as Enright suggests for stage three, attempt to understand the offender's perspective and extend goodwill—which normally will allow us to reconcile with the other person and move forward. Like me, you probably experienced this sort of thing with your friends as a teen—when relationship drama can run high, but (at least sometimes) the core of friendship persists. With more effort than it should have required, I also took this approach as a new faculty member when treated unjustly by a more senior colleague. Sure enough, we soon reconciled—not surprisingly, my gesture of goodwill prompted him to apologize, which made reconciliation quite easy[40]—and were able to maintain a good working relationship thereafter.

Finally, let's keep in mind a lesson from social-worker-turned-mechanic Cathy Heying. When we face everyday minor injustices, forgiveness leaves us feeling so much better in the long run than even the most tempting retaliation:

I can be sarcastic and have a temper, and when I lose that I can kind of say something snarky to a customer. A guy one time told me I didn't care about poor people, and I kind of lost it on him, and he was quiet; and I felt so good in the moment—it felt good to just kind of tell him off. And then I felt sick afterward, and it sort of felt like being drunk and then having a hangover. Like it felt so good, so much fun, so satisfying, and then I just felt sick the rest of the day.

And I try not to lose track of that sick feeling. I mean sometimes, just like being drunk and having a hangover, it takes several times before you realize like, "Yeah, this is fun, but it's going to result in that, remember?" And so to just be ever mindful of that, and take deep breaths; or if I find myself going there, I try to say, "You know what, I am not bringing my best self to this conversation right now. I'm just going to step away for five minutes," or "Can I call you back in five minutes? Then we can talk about this some more."

And to just try to name it to them and to myself because, although it still doesn't mean it feels any less hard, I feel better at the end of the day about how it went. And that should not be rocket science, but it seems like it's a lesson I have to keep learning: that love and kindness always does better than snark in the long run.[41]

Love and kindness do indeed make our lives better—whether we are interacting with the public or with our own families. In the next chapter, we'll explore the family-focused virtue of filial piety—and hear the story of someone who went to heroic lengths to extend forgiveness and kindness to a family member.

Chapter 14

PIETY

Revering Your Roots

ALTHOUGH several of my interviewees—winners of national awards for exemplary long-term community service—experienced trauma as children, Judy Berry's childhood was among the worst. When she was ten years old, her father died of a cerebral hemorrhage related to his alcoholism; her mother, who suffered a psychological breakdown upon her husband's death, uprooted Judy and her older sister, relocating with them from New York to California. There they moved in with Judy's aunt, a strict woman with no children of her own, who insisted that for the sake of the mother's mental health no mention must ever be made of her deceased husband. The living arrangement (and ban upon mention of her father) continued through Berry's teen years, which were similarly traumatic:

My emotions were bouncing all over the place as a teen; I got into trouble. I guess now that I'm older and I've gone through a lot, I understand that it was just the trauma and my need to find a place of acceptance, because my mom wasn't able to provide that. And my aunt was very judgmental and just was concerned that we didn't do anything to disturb my mother. So I went through a portion of my life where I was doing things like running away from home; I wound up spending a month in juvenile hall. I had a lot of issues with my mother, because her way to try to control me and my behavior was to threaten me all the time with going back to juvenile hall if I didn't behave myself. She made me a ward of the court. And so that meant that all she had to do was pick up the phone, and I would be back in jail.[1]

———————

Partly to escape her home life, Berry married two weeks after her eighteenth birthday; twenty-five years and two divorces later, she began counseling therapy, which she credits with helping her to understand the dysfunctional patterns in her adult relationships as well as to understand and forgive her mother: "I went through discovering about alcoholism and how it affects families, and my mother's breakdown, and how you don't get your emotional needs met because nobody's there. But I also learned that they did the best they could with what they had." Berry went on to care for and honor her mother in rather amazing ways that I'll describe in this chapter; for now, though, let's just take a moment to appreciate what a big step forgiveness must have been for someone who had been treated so poorly by the very people who should have been the most loving and supportive toward her, and who had been suffering from the residual effects of that poor treatment for decades.

Chances are, someone you know had a pretty lousy childhood too. According to a recent article published by the *Journal of the American Medical Association*, about 18 percent of U.S. children aged fourteen to seventeen report having been physically abused at some point; 22 percent report having been neglected; and 27 percent report having been emotionally abused.[2] As saddening—even infuriating—as these stories of childhood trauma can be, most of them aren't shocking. We're all flawed in various ways, and some flaws (and degrees of flaws) are more compatible with decent parenting than others. And there's nothing stopping people who will make lousy parents from having children. The question is this: What should our attitude be, as adults, toward our flawed parents and other caregivers? And how much should the answer to that question change when their caregiving or influence was not so good or even downright horrible? In this chapter we'll consider Confucian and Socratic answers to those questions, which tend to take the form of reflections on filial piety: the virtue related to honoring parents and elders. While filial piety has been especially prominent in Confucianism, it was also acknowledged by classical Socratic philosophers and their medieval successors. At the end of the chapter I'll advocate a "moderately Confucian" approach and suggest a few ways in which it can be applied in a contemporary Western context.

Why Filial Piety?

In today's Western culture, we tend to emphasize autonomy, independence, and personal fulfillment—so a virtue based on reverence for our parents and elders may seem at best a nice but old-fashioned idea and at worst a recipe for harmful codependence. Further, long-distance moves in connection with career, marriage, or just personal preference are fairly common, resulting in decreased time with our families of origin—so even if filial piety seems like a nice idea in theory, it comes with significant practical difficulties. Given those complications, we first need to consider whether this trait is worth having; and then, if so, how we can go about cultivating it without sacrificing other important pursuits. Interestingly, three primary arguments in favor of filiality are found in both the Confucians' and Cicero's writings: it is natural, it is necessary, and it is conducive to virtue. We'll explore those three arguments next.

First, filial piety is *natural*. Like religious piety, it is a proper understanding of, and relationship in feeling and action to, what is sacred or worthy of reverence—especially the sources of our existence.[3] As Mencius puts it, "That which people are capable of without learning is their genuine capability. That which they know without pondering is their genuine knowledge. Among babes in arms there are none that do not know to love their parents. When they grow older, there are none that do not know to revere their elder brothers."[4] As contemporary Confucian scholar P. J. Ivanhoe summarizes the point, "our experiences in the earliest periods of life offer us the first opportunities to develop a sense of ourselves as related to others, our first experiences of being loved for who we are, and our first dim understanding of our mutual interdependence, which can give rise to a sense of having obligations to others and a desire to live in harmony with other human beings, and, by extension, the rest of the world."[5] Mencius briefly describes how this innate knowledge of familial respect and affection extends outward toward those outside one's family but differs in its intensity and manifestation: "Gentlemen, in relation to animals, are sparing of them but are not benevolent toward them. In relation to the people, they are benevolent toward them but do not treat them as kin. They treat their kin as kin, and then are benevolent toward the people. They are benevolent toward the people, and then are sparing of animals."[6]

Although writing from half a world and several centuries away, Cicero sees much the same set of phenomena:

> From the tie of common humanity ... there is a nearer relation of race, nation, and language, which brings men into very close community of feeling. It is a still more intimate bond to belong to the same city.... Closer still is the tie of kindred; for by this from the vast society of the human race one is shut up into a small and narrow circle. Since the desire of producing offspring is common by nature to all living creatures, the nearest association consists in the union of the sexes; the next, in the relation with children; ... the union of brothers comes next in order, then that of cousins less or more remote.[7]

So in both traditions, we might envision human relationships as forming concentric circles, similar to an archer's target board, with the innermost circles containing spousal and parent-child relationships, then relationships between siblings, followed by other relatives; wider circles include friendships, communities, nations, all of humanity, and even the non-human world. To be fulfilled as human beings, we do well to be especially nurturing of our closest and earliest natural bonds.

A second argument we see in favor of filial piety is that it is *necessary*. The order and wellbeing of a society, according to both the Confucians and the Socratics, reflects the order and wellbeing of its members—particularly its families, the fundamental and natural societies of which the larger civil society is composed. As Cicero says, "The home is the germ of the city, and, so to speak, the nursery of the state"; and "human society and fellowship will be best maintained, if where there is the most intimate relation, the greatest amount of kindness be bestowed."[8]

And, the Confucians argue, the wellbeing of a society depends in two ways upon filial piety. First, indirectly, because the people's relationships with their parents and elders influence their attitudes toward their government. For example, as Confucius observes early in *Analects*, "A young person who is filial and respectful of his elders rarely becomes the kind of person who is inclined to defy his superiors, and there has never been a case of one who is disinclined to defy his superiors stirring up rebellion."[9] Second, there is a more direct connection between filiality and a society's health: people's attitude toward their state or its leaders can itself be described as filial or unfilial. In fact, Confucians often describe good rulers as being "father and mother" to their people. Like a parent, a ruler or government should ensure that subjects' material needs are met, enable them to fulfill their roles and obligations, and help them to grow in virtue—primarily through example.[10]

Finally, in addition to being natural and necessary, the Confucians and Socratics argue, filial piety is *conducive to virtue*. Of course, since both the Confucians and at least some of the Socratics consider filiality itself to be a virtue, they will not consider anyone to be fully virtuous without it. Less obviously, though, they argue that filial piety is conducive to *other* virtues, and to good character more generally. For example, Confucius associates filial piety with respectfulness more generally, with conscientiousness and trustworthiness, and even with Goodness or complete virtue.[11] Cicero advises us that imitating our parents is appropriate except in the cases of their faults (which we should of course try to avoid) and of following career paths for which we're not suited. Even if he can't imitate his parents in their (admirable) particular pursuits, though, Cicero urges that a good son "ought at least to exhibit the qualities which are at his own command, justice, good faith, generosity, moderation, temperance.... But the best inheritance that fathers can give their children, more precious than any patrimony however large, is reputation for virtue and for worthy deeds, which if the child disgraces, his conduct should be branded as infamous and impious."[12] Going even further, he adds in another work, "In my opinion filial affection is the foundation of all the virtues."[13] As Cicero might ask, if we can't even respect our parents—the sources of our existence—whom *can* we respect?

We see that according to Cicero, filial piety can lead to a host of other virtues; and failing to exercise them is disgraceful impiety—at least in the case of parents who have admirable traits. Not only are the Confucians very much in agreement with that assessment of filial piety, but they elaborate and illustrate the point much more fully than do the Socratics. So focusing primarily on classical Confucian texts, we'll next examine the nature and obligations of filial piety more closely—both in the case of good (or at least good-enough) parents and in the case of not-so-good ones.

Filial Piety and the Good (Enough) Parent

As P. J. Ivanhoe explains, the virtue of filial piety is best understood as "a special form of gratitude, reverence, and love"; it is "a cultivated disposition to attend to the needs and desires of one's parents and to work to satisfy and please them."[14] The Confucians—and the cultures they have influenced through the centuries—are known for their emphasis on this kind of reverence for one's parents: reverence not just in actions but even in thoughts, while parents are alive and even after they pass away. To take just a few of the many examples in Confucius's *Analects*:

1. When your parents are alive, you should not travel far, and when you do travel you must keep to a fixed itinerary.[15]
2. Nowadays "filial" means simply being able to provide one's parents with nourishment. But even dogs and horses are provided with nourishment. If you are not respectful, wherein lies the difference?[16]
3. When someone's father is still alive, observe his intentions; after his father has passed away, observe his conduct. If for three years he does not alter the ways of his father, he may be called a filial son.[17]

To most contemporary Western readers, even those now persuaded that filial piety is good, the conduct advocated in these passages probably sounds unnecessary and unrealistic—how many of us really feel obligated, as adults, to continue following the ways of our parents (even after they die!), to refrain from traveling much while they are alive, or even to provide them with food?

It is tempting to dismiss these and similar passages as simply outdated; and current technology and social conditions do handily fulfill some of the functions that used to require physical proximity. For example, if our parents are tempted to worry about us while we travel, they can contact us by phone or social media—as long as we respond in a timely fashion, any anxiety should be relieved much more effectively than could be accomplished by leaving an itinerary. And thanks to things like private retirement accounts and public social security programs, most of our parents won't need to depend on us for nourishment in their old age.

But like any good philosophical account, the Confucian account of filial piety brings a lesson without an expiration date—even if the way in which that lesson is expressed has legitimate cultural and situational variations. And the main lesson we derive from the Confucians is the importance of an attitude of loving respect for our parents in addition to outward expressions of that respect. To apply this lesson to our own lives, we need to consider each passage carefully and determine how its more concrete but seemingly outdated aspects might be adapted to our own situation. One caution, though: as we saw in chapter 5 of this book, rationalization is a constant temptation. In this case, we might want to rationalize by interpreting away any challenging aspects of a passage so that they seem to instruct us to do something easy—maybe even something we already do. That way, we can check our filial piety obligations off our mental list, congratulate ourselves, and think about something more self-serving. Let's try hard not to do that. Since I'm writing this book I'll go first, giving updated yet challenging personal applications of each of the passages above.

1a. When you haven't seen your parents for a while, check in with them: call just to see how they're doing; email photos of the kids; mail a few of the younger ones' drawings. (Every time I read the *Analects*, I have to ask myself, "How long has it been since you've called your mom?" Usually the answer is, "Too long.")

2a. Nowadays "filial" seems to mean showing up on holidays and avoiding confrontation. We extend this minimal civility of non-confrontation every day even to strangers. If you don't love and respect your parents enough to genuinely care about their—and, by extension, other family members'—thoughts, feelings, and needs, are you treating them any better than strangers? Can you take time the next holiday to help your parents with a project (maybe hosting the gathering?), or just to sit and talk with them for a while without distractions? Or, for a more literal and more challenging interpretation of the original text: if your parents' need for companionship or physical assistance increased (e.g., if one of them died, or if your parents needed assisted living arrangements but couldn't afford to pay for them), would you be willing—even happy—to have one or both of them nearby, maybe even in your house?

3a. While your parents are alive, treat them with genuine respect and appreciation for all they have done for you—after all, without them you wouldn't even exist.[18] After they have died, further their legacy: tell your children or grandchildren stories about them; try to exhibit (and give them credit for) their good qualities; donate to charitable causes that were important to them. And if your cultural and faith traditions include prayers or activities meant to honor or benefit the deceased, participate in those too.

Feel free to use my updated interpretations as a starting point, but you'll likely have to adapt them to your own life circumstances. The point, though, is to capture the spirit of the Confucian lessons to express love and respect for our parents in concrete, situationally appropriate ways. Maybe you live with your parents and can just tell them tonight in person how much you appreciate them; or maybe they need more space rather than more interaction. But if they have been especially bad parents, perhaps you don't have anything appreciative to say about them and are hesitant to interact with them at all. We'll talk about that situation next.

Filial Piety and the Not-So-Good Parent

If filial piety is an important virtue, and our psychological health is important too, what are those with bad parents to do? How, if at all, should they interact as adults with parents who have consistently treated them poorly? Although up to this point in the book contemporary psychology has confirmed much of the advice we've received from the Socratics and Confucians, on this point there appears to be some tension. While these days victims of abuse and neglect (and even "victims" of minor offenses and disagreements) are advised to distance themselves from "toxic" people and environments, the classical Confucians advocate a version of filial piety that looks unconditional and very nearly unlimited. In fact, some of the most well-known passages in both *Analects* and *Mencius* (at least among Westerners, who tend to find them shocking) are those advocating strong expressions of piety for outstandingly awful parents. Here are a few striking examples regarding the legendary sage emperor Shun—a former peasant who was so virtuous that the preceding emperor, Yao, gave him his two daughters in marriage and chose him over his own sons as his successor. Even as heir to the throne, Shun continued to work in his unloving parents' fields in the hope of winning their affection:

> Shun thought, "In exerting my strength to the utmost in plowing the fields, I have merely done my duty as a son. What have I done that my parents do not love me?!" The Emperor Yao directed his children, nine sons and two daughters, the various officials, the sacrificial oxen and sheep, the full storehouses and granaries, to serve Shun even while he toiled amid the plowed fields. Many of the nobles of the world went to him. The Emperor planned to oversee the world with him and eventually transfer it to him. But because he was not reconciled with his parents, Shun felt like a poor homeless person.... Others delighting in him, taking pleasure in beauty, wealth, esteem—none of these was sufficient to relieve his concern.... People of great filiality, to the end of their lives, have affection for their parents.[19]

Shun's filiality becomes even more amazing when we hear more about how his family treated him:

> Shun's parents ordered him to go up into the granary to finish building it. Then they took away the ladder, and his father set fire to the granary. They ordered him to dig a well. He had left the well, but (not knowing this) they covered the well over. Shun's brother, Xiang, said, "The plan to bury this ruler of the capital was all my achievement! His oxen and sheep—those can go to our parents. His grain storehouses—those can go to our parents. But his shields and spears—mine. His zither—mine. His bow—mine. And his two wives shall service me in my bed!" Xiang then went into Shun's home. Shun was on his couch, playing his zither. His face flushed with embarrassment, Xiang said, "I was wracked with concern, worrying about you, my lord!" Shun said, "My numerous ministers, rule them with me."[20]

And when asked to speculate regarding what Shun would have done had his father committed murder, Mencius responds that although he would not have prevented the Minister of Crime from arresting his father, he would have renounced the throne and helped him escape: "Shun looked at casting aside the whole world like casting aside a worn sandal. He would have secretly carried him on his back and fled, to live in the coastland, happy to the end of his days, joyfully forgetting the world."[21]

Similarly, in a famous *Analects* passage, Confucius claims that a good son will assist his misbehaving father in evading the law:

> The Duke of She said to Confucius, "Among my people there is one we call 'Upright Gong.' When his father stole a sheep, he reported him to the authorities."
>
> Confucius replied, "Among my people those whom we consider 'upright' are different from this: fathers cover up for their sons, and sons cover up for their fathers. 'Uprightness' is to be found in this."[22]

The actions condoned in these passages—and the behavior they have occasionally been used to justify in Confucian-influenced governments—have rightly been criticized as being extreme. While they admirably seek to encourage adult children to give their parents the respect they are due, these acts do so at the expense of justice. And justice is the very virtue in which filial piety—like all virtues involving giving and receiving what is due—is based.[23] So by defying justice, an unlimited and unconditional version of filiality undermines its own foundations. A workable and defensible account of filial piety, one that portrays it as a virtue among other important virtues, must give guidance for honoring our families *virtuously*—by directing us to do so in accordance with (or, at the very least, *not* by violating) other virtues. So what *is* the child of a not-so-good parent to do? Now that we have laid the theoretical foundations, I'll briefly propose my "moderately Confucian," answer to that question.

A Moderately Confucian Approach to Filiality

As it turns out, the classical Confucians themselves, in other passages, give us some direction regarding how to harmonize filial piety with other virtues. So I'll start with their more moderate discussions of the topic, taking those—along with some reasonably successful real-life examples—as inspiration for my own account.

An early Confucian passage that is reasonably interpreted to advocate harmony between piety and virtue more generally gives an account of Confucius's conversation with Meng Yizi, a local tyrant whose family (the *de facto* rulers of Confucius's state) was known for its excesses:

> 4. Meng Yizi asked about filial piety. The Master replied, "Do not disobey." Later, Fan Chi was driving the Master's chariot. The Master said to him, "Just now Meng Yizi asked me about filial piety, and I answered, 'Do not disobey.'" Fan Chi said, "What did you mean by that?" The Master replied, "When your parents are alive, serve them in accordance with the rites; when they pass away, bury them in accordance with the rites and sacrifice to them in accordance with the rites."[24]

Perhaps the harmonizing of virtues in this passage is not as clear to contemporary Western eyes as it was in its original context: Rituals or rites (symbolic actions)[25] were used to express, and give guidance for following, ethical principles; and ritual propriety was itself considered an important virtue. So, as Slingerland explains in his commentary on the passage, by instructing the would-be-filial son to honor his parents by obeying the rites—rather than obeying the parents themselves—Confucius is here prioritizing ethical considerations over the parents' own wishes and customs. So a more contemporary expression of Confucius's advice at the end of the passage might look something like this:

> 4a. When your parents are alive, express love and respect for them in a way consistent with virtue and ethical principle. When you can ethically honor their wishes, do so; when you can't, respectfully explain why not and find an alternative, ethical way to honor them. After they pass away, continue to honor them ethically: emphasize their good qualities and memories without covering up their flaws. (For more concrete ideas, see my passage 3a above or Judy Berry's story below.)

One particular instance in which we see some moderation of the Confucian approach toward not-so-virtuous parents—though not as much moderation as we might have expected given the passage just quoted—is that of remonstration: raising objections to others' decisions or behavior. Although the Confucians do not advocate publicly opposing one's parents in their unethical practices, they do at least encourage us to attempt privately to change their minds:

> 5. In serving your parents you may gently remonstrate with them. However, once it becomes apparent that they have not taken your criticism to heart you should be respectful and not oppose them, and follow their lead diligently without resentment.[26]

So this passage, while acknowledging that challenging a parent's unethical decision may be appropriate, does not go so far as to advocate refusal to go along with it—in fact, quite the opposite. To further moderate the instruction of this passage, we need to find a way to express genuine love and respect for parents without compromising our own virtue and ethical principles. As we noted above, sacrificing justice for the sake of filial piety undermines piety's very foundations. So a version of the passage that more fully harmonizes filial piety with other virtues might read as follows:

> 5a. Remonstrate with your parents if their behavior or decisions are unethical. Be as gentle and respectful as you can while clearly conveying your objection. When it becomes apparent that they have not taken (and probably will not take) your criticism to heart, you should remain respectful, both in your treatment of them and in how you speak about them to others; but do not assist or support them in their unethical behavior.[27]

The Confucian-based advice I gave in chapter 4 for responding when other people treat us badly (or do bad things more generally) applies to the bad-parent situation as well, so I'll adapt it briefly here:

> 1. Examine your own behavior and character in case your own faults are partly responsible for your parent's negative attitude toward you. If so, try to improve yourself.
> 2. If the problem really is with your parent, try to discern whether he or she might be able and willing to improve.
> 3. If he or she may be open to correction from you, then offer such correction as gently as you can while communicating clearly and honestly.

4. Stop attempts at correction when (a) they're no longer needed thanks to improvement, (b) your parent is no longer receptive, or (c) the correction is straining your relationship. If (b) or (c), proceed to step 5.
5. Repeat steps 1–4 until no further progress is likely.
6. If your parent seems incapable of treating you decently, you may need to distance yourself from her or him; but continue to be civil when interaction is necessary or desirable, and try not to hold a grudge.
7. Use this experience as an opportunity for continued learning and reflection—if only about how *not* to treat your children.

Contrary to what Confucius advocated, then, I think we can safely conclude that filial piety does *not* require us to cover up our parents' wrongdoing—but, if that wrongdoing wasn't directed toward us, we may be obligated to visit them in prison.[28] And even if it *was* directed toward us, if we have enough strength to handle it, forgiveness and even a closer relationship may be a beautiful thing, as we'll see below.

A Contemporary Exemplar of Filial Piety

We began this chapter with a brief account of Judy Berry's lousy childhood: by the time she was in high school, she experienced (and was required to repress) the death of her father, moved across the country to a difficult home and school environment, and suffered emotional neglect, verbal abuse, and imprisonment. We also saw that she eventually achieved some understanding of—and forgiveness for—her mother's terrible parenting. While that achievement in itself represents an impressive exercise of filial piety, Berry went on to do much more to care for and honor her not-so-virtuous mother. After her mother retired, still suffering from mental illness, Berry invited her mother to move into her home. After a few years, when her mother developed dementia, Berry was no longer able to care for her at home; she spent years seeking adequate professional long-term care:

My mother progressed really bad [with her dementia], and I had seven years of her being in long-term care. And she was kicked out of twelve places because of her aggressive behavior. And it was unbelievable, how she was treated. I was constantly getting calls from places saying they were sending her back to the hospital, or that they were kicking her out. So I saw her go from living in an assisted living apartment to a nursing home, and she was on the dementia unit. They'd use all these psychotropic drugs, and every time I tried to complain about it, they told me I knew nothing about health care, and that her behavior was a function of her brain damage.

And I didn't buy it, because I could see that most of the time she acted out, it was because they weren't paying any attention to her emotional needs. She wanted somebody to sit with her, validate her, talk to her, hold her hand. And when they didn't, and they would ignore her, they'd walk by and she'd stick her foot out and trip them. [Laughs.] But then she became a "behavior person," and no place wanted her unless they would drug her so much that she wouldn't even get out of the chair. And the last two years of her life, she lived in a cherry chair, in a nursing home. A really dingy one, because that was all that would take her. And she was torn apart; I was torn apart.

Although she was not able to provide the kind of long-term care she wanted her mother to have, Berry continued after her mother's death to work toward providing that sort of care for other dementia patients as a way of honoring her mother's memory: "I'd been kicked out of many, many nursing homes, just because I would try to just see if they paid attention to her. They'd always say to me, 'You don't know what you're talking about. We've fed her, and toileted her, and done all these physical things.' But nobody even mentioned emotional needs. And so I tried to get the money to build a house [for dementia care], couldn't find anybody that would support that, and then she passed away."

Not willing to give up, Berry persisted even after her mother's death. Eventually, she found funding to build a house for dementia patients, in which the care, while obviously meeting residents' physical needs, would focus on their emotional and spiritual needs. "It took me eight months to fill it," she said, "because I had no proof that any of this was going to work." They took their residents off of the psychotropic drugs that they, like Berry's mother, had been required to take to control their behavior. "And then it was really a fantastic experience to see their personalities come back after the drugs were taken away. And we just got to know them like the inside of our hand. We knew who they were, what they did, where they went, their life history. And we used that to meet their emotional needs—individual, emotional needs. I've always felt it wasn't rocket science; we just treated them like a human being."

As Mencius would have recommended, when patients would become frustrated, the staff would look to their own behavior to discern whether there was a need they were failing to meet—and, Berry says, there always was. Over seventeen years, her house took in over three hundred people—"all people whose families had gone through what I had gone through," Berry says—and because their approach to care was so effective in meeting needs, they never had to hospitalize a single patient due to mental or behavioral issues.

In addition to honoring her mother through the quality of care she provided dementia patients, Berry was determined to make that care accessible regardless of families' financial situations:

Because of the pain I went through with my mother when I didn't have money to get anything better, part of my mission was that I would make it available to low-income people. And when I couldn't make ends meet, I started a foundation in memory of my mom that raised money over the fifteen years, and so we made the bottom line work. We won national awards; it was just amazing what the staff were able to do with these people. And it was probably the one time in my life when I was the closest to self-actualization, where you follow a dream and you go through all the barriers.

Like most of the exemplars I interviewed, Berry was happiest when serving others; unlike most of them, though, this service (both the concrete caregiving and the fundraising) was motivated by forgiveness and filial piety for a not-so-good parent. Berry's story provides hope for those of us who suffered (or even still suffer) from neglect or mistreatment by caregivers.

For the rest of us (including myself) who were fortunate enough to have been raised by loving parents, filial piety is rooted not only in respect for our parents as the sources of our existence but also in profound gratitude for the time, love, and sacrifice they invested in us. Gratitude is a virtue in its own right; we'll more thoroughly consider that virtue and its cultivation next.

Chapter 15

GRATITUDE

Acknowledging Goodness

SISTER TONI TEMPORITI—social worker, Catholic nun, and founder of Micro-Financing Partners in Africa—exudes gratitude: I bet if
she took the VIA character strengths survey, gratitude would be among
her signature strengths.[1] During our interview, she often—literally dozens
of times—described her life as "wonderful" and "exciting," her family and
friends as "amazing" and "inspiring," and herself as "blessed."[2]

With those sorts of descriptions, it would be tempting to think that Temporiti's life must have been unusually good in some obvious way, that she
must be especially wealthy or talented or popular. But when I simply remove
those ultra-positive adjectives she habitually uses, her descriptions of the
"chapters" in her life story (that was the first question I asked everyone) tend
to be fairly ordinary. For example: "I was born in Saint Louis, Missouri, in
a community called the Italian Hill, where my mom and dad settled after
their parents came from Italy. Very much a neighborhood, very connected to
the Church and to their neighbors. I grew up with a mom and dad, extended family. I have one brother who is older, and that would be chapter one.
Chapter two would be grade school in the neighborhood: a chance to have
some mentor teachers, and they are continued reference points for me as I go
on in my life. Chapter three is high school: a lot of friends that are lifelong

and still friends now. Chapter four is college." (And lest you think she must have had abnormally great teachers in elementary school, when I asked her to elaborate on her experience, the teacher who most stood out was one who was mentally ill and verbally abusive—the mentor teachers were those who later did their best to help rebuild the kids' self-esteem.)

Perhaps Temporiti *did* enjoy a happier-than-average family life growing up—with parents and extended family who loved her—but many of us have enjoyed early advantages of that sort as well. Where Temporiti *really* exceeds the norm is in her appreciation of her relationships—her gratitude. You'll see that gratitude shine through when I reinsert her positive adjectives: "I was born in Saint Louis, Missouri, in a wonderful community called the Italian Hill.... I grew up with a wonderful mom and dad, extended family.... a very wonderful chance to have some mentor teachers through grade school.... a wonderful high school experience. A lot of good friends: friends that are lifelong and still friends now. Chapter four is exciting, with college." And, truth be told, the college chapter was where it became too difficult to edit out the positive adjectives and still keep a coherent story line:

> College was an amazing time. I had two mentors who were life-changing for me. These two wonderful priests introduced me to theology and the study of scripture and of liturgy, and I was on fire with their inspiration and their knowledge and their willingness to mentor me. So I went on to get a Master's in theology. At that same time, I was dating an amazing fellow. I had very much been interested in religious life [i.e., becoming a nun], and he encouraged me to try it, or I would always wonder if that was what I was supposed to do. And so I entered the religious community that I'm now a part of, Sisters of the Most Precious Blood, and felt at home. And I was very lucky to have someone who loved me enough to let me go; and it was a very difficult, wonderful, growing time for both of us. So it was a wonderful chapter.

As Temporiti so clearly demonstrates, and as we have already begun to see, appreciating our roots and role models naturally should lead to gratitude. As P. J. Ivanhoe explains the Confucian understanding of this connection, "The true basis for filial piety is the sense of gratitude, reverence, and love that children naturally feel when they are nurtured, supported, and cared for by people who do so out of loving concern for the child's well being."[3] The virtue of gratitude, though discussed more explicitly in some classical Confucian and Socratic works than others, is universally recognized as indispensable in good moral character and good relationships.[4] As Cicero says, "There is no more essential duty than that of returning kindness received."[5] He elaborates elsewhere, connecting other virtues—including filial piety— with gratitude in words that Toni Temporiti seems to embody:

> While I wish to be adorned with every virtue, yet there is nothing which I can esteem more highly than being and appearing grateful. For this one virtue is not only the greatest, but is also the parent of all the other virtues. What is filial affection, but a grateful inclination towards one's parents? ... What friendship can exist between ungrateful people? Who of us has been liberally educated, by whom his bringers up, and his teachers, and his governors, and even the very mute place itself in which he has been brought up and taught, are not preserved in his mind with a grateful recollection?[6]

Further, gratitude is connected to several other virtues featured in this book, including truthfulness, justice, and humility. If we are honest with ourselves, we'll recognize and acknowledge that our material and personal successes depend at least as much on other people's kindness and on favorable circumstances as they do on our own worthiness: so inner truthfulness will bring both gratitude and humility—and justice will require us to express it.

Stoic philosopher Seneca argues that the reverse is true of ingratitude— it is the worst of vices and is at least suspected of begetting the rest: "Homicides, tyrants, thieves, adulterers, robbers, sacrilegious men, and traitors there always will be; but worse than all these is the crime of ingratitude, unless it be that all these spring from ingratitude, without which hardly any sin has grown to great size."[7] He helpfully identifies three chief causes of ingratitude: pride, greed, and jealousy.[8] Over the next few pages, we'll take a closer look at philosophical and psychological insights into the virtue of gratitude and the vice of ingratitude; their nature, origin, and effects; and how we can develop the former and avoid the latter.

What Is Gratitude?

Leading gratitude researcher Robert Emmons describes gratitude in terms of two stages: (1) acknowledgment of the good things in one's life, and (2) recognition that those good things come at least partly from other people—gratitude is essentially other-directed. For example, I may be *glad* that I buckled down and got some work done today, and I may be *relieved* that those storm clouds just missed my picnic, but I can't be *grateful* to myself or to the clouds: true gratitude (as opposed to mere gladness) requires a benefactor. More specifically, Emmons explains, gratitude "requires a willingness to recognize (a) that one has been the beneficiary of someone's kindness, (b) that the benefactor has intentionally provided a benefit, often incurring some personal cost, and (c) that the benefit has value in the eyes of the beneficiary."[9] So gratitude is by nature a three-term relationship: I (the beneficiary) am grateful to someone (the benefactor) for some kindness (the benefit).[10] For example, this afternoon I am grateful to my husband for taking our sons to get much-needed haircuts and to my daughter for starting supper: my husband and daughter have removed two time-consuming tasks from my to-do list, freeing me up to write for another couple of hours.

In his essay "The Blessings of Gratitude," contemporary philosopher Robert C. Roberts notes that resentment mirrors gratitude in having this three-term relation—only in this case, a negative one: if I am resentful, I (the "maleficiary") resent someone (the malefactor) for some offense or harm (the malefice). Among the blessings of gratitude, then, is its opposition to resentment; Roberts argues that gratitude is also, to a somewhat lesser extent, opposed to the negative states of regret and envy.[11]

Among the classical philosophers who wrote the most about the virtue of gratitude was Seneca, whose book-length essay *De Beneficiis* [On benefits] deals primarily with the exercise and cultivation of generosity in giving benefits and gratitude in receiving them. Like Emmons, he describes gratitude as a joyful response to another's intentional provision of a benefit. Here is one representative example: "When a man bestows a benefit, what does he aim at? To be of service and to give pleasure to the one to whom he gives. If he accomplishes what he wished, if his intention is conveyed to me and stirs in me a joyful response, he gets what he sought."[12]

As we'll later see empirically confirmed by contemporary psychologists, Seneca recognized that gratitude is itself a joy—it extends our delight in a benefit by recalling it to mind: "He who is happy in having received a benefit tastes a constant and unfailing pleasure, and rejoices in viewing, not the gift, but the intention of him from whom he received it. The grateful man delights in a benefit over and over, the ungrateful man but once."[13]

Although Seneca emphasizes the voluntary, no-strings-attached nature of a true benefit or gift (as opposed to a trade or a bribe), he also encourages us to look for opportunities to return the benefactor's favor:

> Although we say that he who receives a benefit gladly has repaid it, we, nevertheless, also bid him return some gift similar to the one he received.... What, then, shall you do? There is no need for you to take up arms—perhaps some day there will be. There is no need for you to traverse the seas—perhaps some day you will set sail even when storm-winds are threatening. Do you wish to return a benefit? Accept it with pleasure; you have repaid it by gratitude—not so fully that you may feel that you have freed yourself from debt, yet so that you may be less concerned about what you still owe![14]

I'm not sure whether the phrase or notion of a "debt of gratitude" originated with the Stoics, but we can see that it was certainly alive and well among them. And according to Seneca, although, at least initially, gratitude is sufficient payment, when we are beneficiaries of gifts, we need to keep in mind not only that (a) there may be an obligation to reciprocate the gift more concretely in the future, but also that (b) gratitude itself is a duty not to be taken lightly. Far more than just mumbling "thanks" and moving on, true gratitude expresses itself publicly when appropriate (and when the benefactor is comfortable with public thanks)—that is one reason for the close tie between gratitude and humility. Just as we readily share the good news of our blessings with our friends and acquaintances, we should be eager to share the good news of the generosity of our benefactors:

> When we have decided that we ought to accept, let us accept cheerfully, professing our pleasure and letting the giver have proof of it in order that he may reap instant reward; for, as it is a legitimate source of happiness to

see a friend happy, it is a more legitimate one to have made him so. Let us show how grateful we are for the blessing that has come to us by pouring forth our feelings, and let us bear witness to them, not merely in the hearing of the giver, but everywhere. He who receives a benefit with gratitude repays the first instalment on his debt.[15]

Here the notion of gratitude, publicly expressed if appropriate, as a "first instalment" on a debt handily captures points (a) and (b) above. The opening clause of the quoted passage—"when we have decided that we ought to accept"—also hints at a further reason that gratitude is not to be taken lightly.

Since real gratitude involves extending the memory of our benefits—repeatedly calling to mind and reflecting on the ways in which we've been blessed—that memory includes fondly calling to mind those who have blessed us. One complication of this robust notion of gratitude, in addition to its requiring some humility, is that it ties us more closely to our benefactors than might be comfortable—or even advisable—in some circumstances. For this reason, Seneca notes that it is sometimes reasonable to turn down a gift. Obviously that decision—like gratitude itself—is not something to be taken lightly: we shouldn't belittle others' generosity or insult those who are reaching out to us in kindness. Still, there are situations in which graciously declining the offer of a benefit is in order; although discerning the particulars requires prudence (a virtue we'll discuss toward the end of this book), here are a few general examples:

1. The potential benefactor is someone we can't safely befriend—or, perhaps, even call fondly to mind—e.g., because of serious relationship problems.
2. The potential gift is something we can't reasonably accept—for instance, because we can't or shouldn't use it, it is inappropriately extravagant, or the benefactor needs it more than we do.
3. The potential "gift" is not a true benefit—for instance, because we have reason to believe that it comes with hidden strings or because the manner in which it is offered creates burdens that outweigh any benefits it might bring.[16]

Similarly, Seneca notes, there are circumstances in which we should not return favors to our benefactors. The most obvious of these, as he has already acknowledged, is when we are unable to repay the benefit because of our own lack of resources; and even if we are, strictly speaking, able to repay it, we should not if doing so would cause us significant hardship without being a similarly significant blessing to the benefactor. Confucius briefly suggests an alternate standard for repayment in such circumstances: responding with a similar intent or virtue rather than a gift of similar monetary value.[17] For example, if a friend gives us a generous birthday gift that we can't afford to reciprocate, perhaps on her next birthday we can be generous with our time by helping her clean her car or redecorate her house.

Also, as Seneca points out, we are unable to repay benefits to those who refuse to accept repayment—and we should not try to insist that they do accept: "It is not displaying gratitude to repay something that you have willingly accepted to someone who is unwilling to accept it. Some people, when a trifling gift has been sent to them, forthwith, quite unseasonably, send back another, and then declare that they are under no obligation; but to send something back at once, and to wipe out a gift with a gift is almost a repulse.... He who is too eager to pay his debt is unwilling to be indebted, and he who is unwilling to be indebted is ungrateful."[18] Somewhat less obviously, we are effectively unable to return benefits to benefactors whose resources are so great (e.g., kings or God) that we are unable to effect a noticeable increase—in such cases, it is best to express our gratitude toward them directly but to "pay it forward": that is, to repay the favor indirectly by benefiting others.

In short, then, gratitude is a joyful response to a benefactor's gift. While it is (almost) always appropriate to acknowledge that gift with sincere thanks and to repeatedly call the benefactor's generosity to mind, the extent to which gratitude obligates us to return his or her favor varies with the circumstances—including our own resources, the benefactor's resources, and the benefactor's receptivity to repayment. Insistence on immediate repayment, especially when the benefactor resists, raises the possibility of false gratitude masking ingratitude—we'll take a closer look at that vice next.

The Vice of Ingratitude

There was once a valiant soldier whose successes in battle drew the attention of his king, who tended to reward him lavishly. During one of his missions, the soldier was shipwrecked and cast ashore, half-dead. A fellow citizen found him, carried him to his own home nearby, and for thirty days tended him at his own expense. When he was well enough to travel, the soldier departed, promising to tell the king of the citizen's generosity and to return to show his gratitude. But the soldier secretly thought to himself, "What a beautiful estate this is! I'd like to have it for my own." When he returned to the king, he recounted the story of the shipwreck but conveniently neglected to mention the help he'd received; instead, he asked for his benefactor's estate as a reward for his bravery. Without giving the matter much thought, the king granted his request. When the dispossessed benefactor appealed to the king, telling him the whole story, the king quickly changed course: he restored the estate to its owner, seized the soldier's other property, and had his forehead branded with the words "Ungrateful Guest."[19]

Although our ingratitude isn't always as flagrant as the soldier's in this classic folktale, it's a pervasive problem in societies of abundance: humans' amazing adaptability to their circumstances has the unfortunate side effect of desensitizing us to our blessings.[20] Without conscious thought and effort, we are less likely to develop the virtue of gratitude than its opposing vice of ingratitude.[21] By taking a brief look at this common vice and its causes, we'll be in a better position to avoid it and to cultivate gratitude in ourselves.

As we noted earlier, drawing from psychologist Robert Emmons' definition, gratitude involves acknowledgement that I've been the beneficiary of someone's kindness, that the benefactor has intentionally provided this benefit, and that the benefit is valuable to me. Ingratitude, then, can be expected to involve failure in one or more of these areas: denial or insufficient acknowledgment of what I've received from another, of its value, or of the benefactor's kind intentions. These failures, as it turns out, are closely related to the three vices Seneca identifies as the chief causes of ingratitude: pride, greed, and envy.

Pride may incline me to believe that any benefit I've received is my due— payment of sorts for my worthiness—rather than the free gift of a benefactor. For example, to my shame, as an undergraduate student I neglected to write a thank-you letter, as suggested by my college's financial aid office, to the family who had funded my scholarship; I justified my negligence by telling myself that I deserved the scholarship for being such a good student. (I'm presently trying to remedy that omission, but I'm not sure my benefactors are still alive.) Similarly, in the story above, the soldier's pride may have led him to convince himself that he really did deserve his benefactor's estate as a reward for all he had done for the king. Pride also seems to be at work in the false gratitude that Seneca described: the insistence on immediately repaying any benefits received so as not to acknowledge indebtedness. So pride is a chief cause of the first failure I mentioned: failure to acknowledge what I've received from another.[22]

"Nor does greed suffer any man to be grateful," Seneca adds, "for incontinent hope is never satisfied with what is given and, the more we get, the more we covet."[23] If I'm continually focused on what more I can get from my benefactors, I'm unable to appreciate what they have already given me—as I put it above, I deny the value of what I've received. For example, if I sit at my dying grandmother's bedside, not in an expression of filial love and devotion—gratitude for her positive influence in my life—but in hope of finding a prominent place in her will, I'm both supremely greedy and profoundly ungrateful. Seneca has a harsh assessment of one who would do that, saying that despite his apparent devotion he "is only a fisher for legacies and is just dropping his hook. As birds of prey that feed upon carcasses keep watch near by the flocks that are spent with disease and are ready to drop, so such a man gloats over a death-bed and hovers about the corpse."[24] And the ungrateful soldier's greed is similarly obvious: rather than show appreciation to his benefactor for restoring his life and health, he fails even to mention this kindness to the king, aiming instead to acquire his generous host's estate.

Finally, I may deny or dismiss the good intentions of my benefactor through envy: "It is possible for no man to show envy and gratitude at the same time, for envy goes with complaint and unhappiness, gratitude with rejoicing."[25] We often see envious ingratitude in children: for example, "Johnny got a bigger piece of cake than I got!" or "Why didn't I get to go first?" Unfortunately, this childish sort of ingratitude is a character flaw that many of us have trouble outgrowing—and constantly comparing the benefits we've received to those of others can seriously dampen our appreciation for many of the good things in our lives and relationships. As adult siblings, coworkers, and friends, we often have trouble resisting comparisons of our benefits with others'; and when our own benefits seem to come up short—as they inevitably do sometimes, especially since some gifts are impossible to distribute equally—we can easily forget about the good things we have been given and focus on the seemingly better things given to others.[26] At this point pride may further contribute to our envy-fueled ingratitude, convincing us that we are *more* deserving than those who have received more advantages. And envy of his benefactor was perhaps second only to greed in causing the soldier's ingratitude: by focusing on the beauty of the estate that the king had not yet given him (i.e., his benefactor's property), he failed to appreciate both his host's kindness and that of the king, who had already been very generous with his rewards.

Fortunately, ingratitude can be overcome through the development of opposing habits of thought and action. We have discussed humility, the virtuous habit that combats pride, in chapter 12; we will take a closer look at generosity, the antidote to greed, later in this book. But gratitude is of course the most obvious opposite of ingratitude in all of its forms and causes; and the appreciation of existing blessings that it involves also directly opposes envy. In the rest of this chapter, we will look first at the psychological characteristics and benefits of gratitude and then at several effective ways of developing this virtue by training our thoughts and (eventually) our emotional responses.

The Psychology of Gratitude

Robert Emmons and other psychologists have recently found several benefits of gratitude—some to be expected, others more surprising. Emmons summarizes the results of their studies as follows:

> Grateful people experience higher levels of positive emotions such as joy, enthusiasm, love, happiness, and optimism, and ... the practice of gratitude as a discipline protects a person from the destructive impulses of envy, resentment, greed, and bitterness. We have discovered that a person who experiences gratitude is able to cope more effectively with everyday stress, may show increased resilience in the face of trauma-induced stress, and may recover more quickly from illness and benefit from greater physical health. Our research has led us to conclude that experiencing gratitude leads to increased feelings of connectedness, improved relationships, and even altruism. We have also found that when people experience gratitude, they feel more loving, more forgiving, and closer to God. Gratitude, we have found, maximizes the enjoyment of the good.[27]

We'll further examine the cultivation of gratitude (what Emmons calls "the practice of gratitude as a discipline") below; first let us take a closer look at just a few recent studies of the sort Emmons references.

In a helpful review of research on gratitude and its implications for clinical practice, Alex Wood and colleagues analyze the results of various investigations regarding the emotional state of gratitude, the corresponding character trait, and the effectiveness of several common gratitude-inducing practices. In short, they argue that "gratitude is a key underappreciated trait in clinical psychology, of relevance due to a strong, unique, and causal relationship with wellbeing, and due to the potential to use simple and easy tasks to increase gratitude alongside existing clinical interventions."[28] While the authors are careful to emphasize that much more research remains to be done, they point to some very positive preliminary findings. First, grateful people tend to be "more extroverted, agreeable, open, and conscientious, and less neurotic" than less-grateful people; and gratitude as a stable personality trait predicts wellbeing in ways that go beyond this standard "Big Five" personality assessment. Gratitude is associated with decreased risk of depression, anxiety, substance addiction, and eating disorders; it is also linked to post-traumatic growth and to higher functioning among those with post-traumatic stress disorder.[29]

Analyzing gratitude as an emotion (rather than as a character trait), psychologists Michael McCullough and Jo-Ann Tsang propose three moral roles that it serves. First, it functions as a "moral barometer," alerting us when someone has done something especially nice on our behalf. Second, gratitude is a moral motive: if we're grateful to our benefactors, we'll want to benefit them—or maybe even third parties—in return. Third, they argue, it's a moral reinforcer: expressions of gratitude are rewarding for the benefactors, which makes them more likely to give in the future.[30]

Psychologist Dan McAdams, who studies generativity (the desire to leave a positive legacy for future generations), has found that highly generative people, such as the exemplars I interviewed, tend to have a sense of early advantage in life: that they have enjoyed especially good fortune—and that they should pass their blessings on to others.[31] I heard that sentiment come to life as I interviewed Toni Temporiti, who, as we saw earlier, was highly appreciative of her good (but not abnormally good) upbringing. In fact, when I asked a big-picture question about her philosophy of life, she replied:

When I was little, I always wondered why I was given so much. I came from a mom and dad who were older and from a family that struggled, but because we had a grocery store, we always had food. And they really showed me how whatever we have been given, it's not just for us—it's to be shared. And I just couldn't appreciate them more. And their example— never being lectured. It was in their living. I remember my mom telling the story how people could come to the store and could run a tab and pay at the end of the week. And my mom would put the bill in the bill place, and she'd come in on Monday and the bills would be gone. Especially if there were kids involved, my uncle Mike would just tear up people's bills, because he knew they couldn't pay them. And then my mom would be so funny, because she knew he would do that, but she would say, "Why don't you do that *before* I do all of the work?" [Laughs.] She'd make me laugh, you know, because she would do it too; but it was like, "Why do I have to do all the work and *then* you tear them up?" But that's the family I grew up in.

Whether we came from a similarly generous family or not, we can all work on appreciating (and, eventually, passing on), the blessings we do have. But first, of course, we'll have to recognize those blessings—this recognition is itself an essential part of gratitude. As we close this chapter, taking inspiration from both Emmons's research and Temporiti's example, we'll examine several effective ways of cultivating gratitude in ourselves.

Growing in Gratitude

As with any ethical virtue, even those predisposed toward gratitude (as Temporiti clearly was) must deliberately cultivate the mature, fully developed trait through repetition—of both internal thoughts and external actions. Also like other ethical virtues, the virtue of gratitude involves a disposition toward a particular emotional state—a *feeling* of gratitude or thankfulness—in response to appropriate situational triggers. And, psychologist Philip Watkins proposes, feelings of gratitude tend to be self-perpetuating. Feeling grateful completes and enhances our enjoyment of benefits, which makes us feel happier—and feeling happier makes us better at recognizing our blessings and others' good intentions.[32] But since emotions can't be trained directly in the way that our actions and even our thoughts can, psychologists and philosophers tend to focus on ways in which we can form habits of thought and action that eventually bring our feelings along for the ride. To that end, Robert Emmons ends his book on gratitude with a "top ten" list of tested, concrete ways in which we can begin to cultivate gratitude in ourselves;[33] I will summarize some of them here.

Practices 1–4 and 10 on Emmons' top ten list focus primarily on our mental lives—on reframing our thoughts about our relationships and experiences. First, he advises us to keep a gratitude journal—perhaps the most commonly studied gratitude-cultivation technique. Each day, we should take time to reflect on and write down at least three things for which we are grateful. If the process gets stale (e.g., if we find ourselves listing the same three things every day), we can vary it by analyzing our benefits into multiple components or by using variations on the gratitude theme. For example, in another book Emmons suggests having a different focus each day of the week: for example, thinking on Tuesdays about a good that is going to end soon, on Wednesdays about how our lives would be different if not for some blessing, and on Thursdays about those to whom we are grateful and for what.[34]

I was intrigued to hear that Temporiti herself uses a gratitude journal. In response to a question regarding challenges she has faced in life, she (like many of us) thought of the deaths of loved ones. But she immediately added, "That taught me how precious life is and not to take people for granted, that people come in and out of our life for some reason and their time with us is really a gift. I have a book of my own, and it's about people in my life who have really blessed me on my journey, and I look at it often and thank them."

Emmons also suggests that we cultivate gratitude by remembering the *bad* experiences in our lives and reflecting on how far we've come. Perhaps the most surprising of the practices Emmons suggests—its effectiveness was surprising to Emmons himself as well—is that we "think outside the box" by developing gratitude not only toward our beneficiaries, but even toward those who have hurt us, for giving us the opportunity to grow in virtue.

Emmons's remaining suggestions for cultivating gratitude, items 5–9 on his top-ten list, focus primarily on actions we can take to practice thankfulness. For example, he encourages us to create visual reminders on Post-it notes or our electronic devices, use accountability partners, spend more time with grateful people, and employ grateful self-talk. Finally, recognizing that emotions often are not under our direct control, he advises us to go through the motions of gratitude: "If we go through grateful motions, the emotion of gratitude should be triggered. What is a grateful motion? Saying thank you. Writing letters of gratitude. Isn't this the way we socialize our children to become grateful members of a civic society? ... So what if the motion has to be forced? The important thing is to do it. Do it now, and the feeling will come.... If we stand around waiting for a feeling to move us, we may never get going."[35]

Speaking with Toni Temporiti, one gets the feeling that she has seldom stood around waiting. During a sabbatical from her counseling practice, she did quite the opposite: she spent much of the year traveling throughout Africa. When she returned, she resumed counseling—but, as she told me, "I couldn't get Africa out of my heart. Tried, but could not. And all I could think about was that I wanted to go back. I started just dreaming, and I went online and I put the words in: 'Africa, women, small loans,' and this word came up—'microfinancing'—which I had heard but I didn't know much about." After attending a seminar on microfinancing, Temporiti was sure it was what she wanted to do:

> I came back home, and I gathered two Sisters—one who was a lawyer, and one who was in economics—and we started an organization called Microfinancing Partners in Africa, where we would partner with people all around Africa and help to get money for loans for them to start a small business so that they could bring themselves out of poverty—more of a hand up than a handout. We just celebrated eleven years of doing this wonderful work of microfinancing in Africa. We're in four countries, and I could not be more blessed and privileged to be a part of this. It's a small way to make a difference in people's lives.

Among the many blessings Temporiti has found in her microfinancing work is a personal and familial one:

> An unexpected outcome is that, two years into doing microfinancing, I realized the significance of a story that I had been told since I was a small

child. My grandfather died very young, leaving ten children. At that time, if the husband died, you'd send your children back to Italy and they'd be raised by aunts and uncles. But my grandmother decided not to do that but to keep the family together. And a business man and a Jewish merchant and a parish priest helped her: they gave her a loan to start a small grocery store, and all my mom's brothers and sisters worked in the grocery store. And they were able to feed the family, keep them together, and educate the kids—which is what we do now in Africa. So in the most unexpected way, it just came full circle. And it's been wonderful: I'm named after my grandmother, and I never met her—she died before I was born—but I feel like I'm so connected to her through this project.

––––––––––––

Indeed, Temporiti sees so many meaningful interpersonal connections woven throughout her life; those seem to be the main sources of her experiences of gratitude. For many of us who have also enjoyed some good relationships in our lives, perhaps we could begin to cultivate our own gratitude simply by taking a bit of time to notice and appreciate the blessings of those relationships.

At the end of Temporiti's interview, I asked whether she discerned a central theme in her life story. By now you can probably guess what she said; let's end this chapter by reflecting on how her words might apply to our own lives: "I think it's being blessed. Really feeling blessed, and having been given so much that it's impossible *not* to pass it on."

Part 6

EXTENDING GOODNESS

Next Door, across the World,
and Everywhere in Between

Chapter 16

FRIENDSHIP

Keeping Good Company

A S W E S A W in chapter 15, Sister Toni Temporiti of Microfinancing Partners in Africa is an amazingly grateful woman—in fact, she says the theme of her life story is how blessed she is. Just as striking, I think, is what she is grateful *for*: people and relationships. She has been blessed, she told me, by her parents and extended family, lifelong friendships that began in high school, the boyfriend she gave up when she became a nun, and the other women she joined in her religious community. When reading through Temporiti's descriptions of these blessings, I couldn't help but notice that they provide great examples not only of gratitude, but also of the best kinds of friendships. With some help from Aristotle, I'll show you what I mean.

Friends Are Good; Good Friends Are Best

As Aristotle reminds us in book 8 of *Nicomachean Ethics*, everyone needs friends: the rich and powerful need suitable recipients of their gifts; the poor need a refuge from their troubles. The young need someone to help keep them from straying, the old need care and support, and those in their prime need help performing great deeds. Friendship holds people together: families, cities, and humanity in general. Aristotle's words are echoed in the work of developmental psychologists, who only recently have begun to turn their attention to friendship across the lifespan. In their review of recent literature on friendship at various stages of life, Rosemary Blieszner and Karen Roberto found that even infants and toddlers benefit from social interaction with peers: it reduces inhibitions and promotes appropriate emotional responsiveness and "play skills." In middle childhood, we come to expect more closeness, loyalty, and emotional support from our friends. These roles and expectations become stronger in adolescence, which allows friends to "provide significant support to one another as they cope with the developmental challenges confronting them"; friends are increasingly important as confidants, and "experiences shared with friends shape and moderate social adaptation, enhance personal competence, and promote the development of identity."[1] And, as Aristotle would expect, close, supportive, and norm-following friends help keep young people from falling into problems like alcoholism and depression.[2]

In early adulthood, especially before marriage, we tend to rely primarily on our friends for support, companionship, and guidance; both marriage and parenting tend to reduce reliance on (other) friendships. By middle adulthood, when work and family responsibilities peak for most of us, we tend to have fewer friends and less time to spend with them. Still, Blieszner and Roberto make the Aristotelian-sounding observation that "friends may be directly involved in expressions of generativity [i.e., concern for leaving a positive legacy], either insofar as they require mentoring, or to the extent that they share in efforts to accomplish generative goals such as volunteering to help develop and manage community programs."[3] And, as we might expect, among older adults relationships provide an important form of social support and wellbeing; older people tend to concentrate their limited physical and emotional energy on a few close relationships. In this way, friendship continues to meet people's emotional and relational needs throughout the lifespan.

In addition to conferring emotional health advantages, Aristotle argues, friendship is both a fine thing in itself and a sign of a person's goodness. So if we want to live well (and we all do), we'll need to take the right approach to friendship. Aristotle devotes two of the ten books of his *Nicomachean Ethics* to friendship; there, he provides some strikingly concrete and helpful advice on its cultivation, maintenance, and dissolution.

To understand why friendship is desirable, Aristotle suggests, we should reflect on why *anything* is desirable. As it turns out, desirable things fall into three main categories: useful, pleasant, and good.[4] Useful things are useful *for* something else; only pleasant and good things are ends in themselves. As we'd expect, then, among kinds of friendship, Aristotle categorizes those that are merely useful—friendships of utility—as the lowest. Still, however, such friendships are desirable within their limits: for example, as long as everyone involved is on the same page regarding the nature of the relationship, it's great to have mutually beneficial business associates or study buddies.

Friendships of pleasure are somewhat higher than those of utility: we value these friends not for what they can do for us, but for what we enjoy about *them*. And since pleasure is desirable as an end in itself, we do well to befriend some people simply because we enjoy their company. For young children, almost all friendships tend to be of this nature—they choose companions who make them laugh and who enjoy similar activities; to some extent, we continue to use these criteria as we seek friends through adulthood. Such friends help us to relax and unwind from our work, distract us from our difficulties, and are just plain fun. As long as this fun is harmless and doesn't interfere with our exercise of virtue (our excellent activity), we can safely pursue it—in moderation, of course. Still, however, friendships of pleasure are not especially deep or noble: when it comes down to it, we value and wish well to these friends not for their own sake but because their company is pleasant for *us*.

The best and most complete or "perfect" friendships involve friends who value each other and want good things for each other for the other's own sake—not just for the sake of continuing to receive benefits or pleasure from their friend, although these good friends *do* also tend to be the most helpful and pleasant too. Because it is the other's good qualities—virtues—that we value in these complete friendships, they are sometimes known simply as "friendships of virtue." Their description as "perfect" also signals that these friendships are rare: they take time and effort—and virtue!—to cultivate.[5]

Interestingly, recent psychological research appears to confirm (at least in part) Aristotle's division of friendship into three types—with significant differences in their contribution to our wellbeing. In a large study of European adults, for example, Filip Agneessens and colleagues found that friendships could be categorized according to the type of support they provided: instrumental (useful), companionship (primarily pleasant), and/or emotional—the latter implying at least closeness, if not necessarily ethical excellence. As Aristotle might expect, long-term partners and best friends tended to provide all three types of support. The researchers looked also at relationships with colleagues; happily, their largest reported area of support was companionship—not mere utility.[6]

William Rawlins, a seasoned researcher in the area of adult friendship, has drawn similarly Aristotelian-sounding conclusions regarding types and functions of friendship. In what he calls the "dialectic of affection and instrumentality," he says that "friendship ideally involves fondness for another unique person and not as a member of some desirable category or to secure advantages for oneself. Viewing our friend primarily as a means to self-serving ends ... sullies the ideals" of friendship.[7] On the other hand, he notes, "being friends includes calling on others for assistance and support, as well as experiencing edifying opportunities to respond to serve the well-being of persons we hold dear"—so perhaps it is not surprising that "best friendships are viewed as more intimate *and* more useful than other friendship types."[8] Close friends, Rawlins has found, expect three main things of each other: to be "somebody I can talk to," "someone I can depend on to be there for me," and "someone I have fun with and enjoy"—again, qualities that seem related to goodness (or at least emotional closeness), utility, and pleasure. [9]

Mencius, much like Aristotle, says that true "friendship with a man is friendship with his virtue"—it "should be maintained without any presumption on the ground of one's superior age, or station, or the circumstances of his relatives ... and does not admit of assumptions of superiority."[10] Similarly, Rawlins observes that friendship "involves treating others as equals despite disparities in personal attributes or social standing" and that (citing Aristotle) "friendship embodies ideal qualities of human relationships, including trust, loyalty, generosity, and concern for the other's welfare for his or her sake"[11]—in other words, good friends are virtuous friends. While we are inclined to see the best in our friends, Rawlins notes, we also expect them to live up to certain moral standards and virtues—which, in part, are the reason we befriended them.[12]

Also like Aristotle, Mencius advises those of us who want to become and remain virtuous to keep good company: "The scholar whose virtue is most distinguished in a village shall make friends of all the virtuous scholars in the village. The scholar whose virtue is most distinguished through-out a State shall make friends of all the virtuous scholars of that State. The scholar whose virtue is most distinguished throughout the kingdom shall make friends of all the virtuous scholars of the kingdom"—and if that isn't enough, he should "make friends" with the great sages of history by reading their writings and biographies.[13]

Similarly, Xunzi repeatedly encourages us to be very careful about the people with whom we associate—in particular, he emphasizes the importance of the right company for helping us to learn about the Way of virtue:

> In learning, nothing is more important than to associate with those who are learned, and of the roads to learning, none is quicker than to love such men.... Only if a man has arrived where he is by the proper way should you have dealings with him; if not, avoid him. If he is respectful in his person, then you may discuss with him the approach to the Way. If his words are reasonable, you may discuss with him the principles of the Way. If his looks are gentle, you may discuss with him the highest aspects of the Way.[14]

As he goes on to point out, and as we saw in chapter 11, there is something to be learned from those who behave badly: namely, what *not* to do. But we learn so much more if we befriend people who can serve as positive role models—and as trusted advisors and even critics: "He who comes to you with censure is your teacher; he who comes to you with approbation is your friend; but he who flatters you is your enemy. Therefore the gentleman loves his teacher, draws close to his friends, but heartily hates his enemies. He loves good untiringly and can accept reprimand and warning from it."[15]

In fact, like both Aristotle and Mencius, Xunzi tells us that even after we overcome our original, flawed nature and become virtuous, we continue to need both teachers and friends to guide us: "A man, no matter how fine his nature or how keen his mind, must seek a worthy teacher to study under and good companions to associate with. If he studies under a worthy teacher, he will be able to hear about the ways of [legendary sages] Yau, Shun, Yu, and Tang; and if he associates with good companions, he will be able to observe conduct that is loyal and respectful. Then, although he is not aware of it, day by day he will progress in the practice of benevolence and righteousness."[16]

We, too, will have the best friendships possible if we become as virtuous as we can be—and befriend the best people we can find.

An Exemplar of Friendship

If we are fortunate enough to have virtuous friendships of the sort Aristotle, Mencius, and Xunzi recommend, they tend to last: the qualities we value in these friends are much more stable than the favors or pleasures our lesser friendships might bring. Aristotle's words about the need for friends and the longevity of good friendships are echoed in Toni Temporiti's descriptions of the friends she's had since high school:

> High school friends, even to this day, are touchstones: the idea of friendships being lifelong and so necessary in the good and bad times of life, and staying connected. There are some friends who, if you don't talk to them in a couple of months and reconnect, it's like seconds. And others who you haven't seen in years and then reconnect, and it's so fun to relive memories. So a foundation for who I am as I do this work in Africa and microfinancing, is how many of them have connected with me on Facebook and through my emails. And I'm in the middle of nowhere, in a sense, in Africa, and I get this email from a classmate saying how excited they are to live this through me, how excited they are to be a part, and it just means everything.

In addition to being lasting, friendships of virtue are of necessity rare for two main reasons. First, cultivating and maintaining them requires a lot of time and effort. As Aristotle explains, to develop a friendship of this sort we have to "live together" with our friends: we need a sustained pattern of substantial, shared activity. Second, they involve an "excess of feeling"—a serious emotional investment akin to falling in love.[17] In fact, Aristotle argues, love is friends' characteristic virtue. We will our friend's good for his or her own sake; and we share in his or her joys and sorrows as our own. Since we are mere human beings, the number of people toward whom we can direct such intense feeling is quite limited. Fortunately, however, as psychologists have recently discovered, when it comes to good friends less really may be more. For people with best friends, having even three "high-quality" (predominantly positive) relationships doesn't necessarily increase wellbeing compared to having two.[18]

Although they require a lot more investment of time and feeling than other friendships, our few good friendships are clearly worth the effort. In addition to being good in their own right, as Aristotle observed and Rawlins suggested above, these friendships are also the most pleasant and useful—or, as Agneessens and colleagues might put it, they provide the most companionship and instrumental benefits. Why? Because virtuous people are genuinely pleasant company—in fact, many of the virtues Aristotle discusses are related to good social interaction. And what could be more beneficial— more "useful"—than a friend who challenges us to achieve excellence? And, as Toni Temporiti's stories show, that is just what a good friend does. The friends she has had since high school continue to encourage her in her noble activities, and the same characteristics—and goodness—are found in her story of a more recently formed friendship with a now-deceased fellow nun:

> Sister Liz—she was, and is, a touchstone. She was tall and beautiful, in her 70s. We were going to supper one night, the night she died; she called and said, "I don't feel well; I don't know if I can make it to supper." About an hour later I got a call that she had an aneurism and died. And this woman just had been happy to be alive and had so much joy. She went with me twice to Africa, and she was fun. And she would just say, "You go, girl!"—and her encouragement and her love for me was life-changing. She just gave me joy, and continues to. And when I feel like, "Oh my gosh, I have to do another talk or another something," I think of Liz, who would turn it around. She did it with church stuff too, and she'd make me laugh when I'd go to Mass—she'd be prim and proper and she would nudge me. And I would start laughing and I couldn't stop, but she looked prim and proper, and so I was the one getting in trouble for laughing. So we had so much fun together.

I love the joyful image of nuns fidgeting and giggling in church; but of course the story was also a sad one, about a deep loss. When I asked how she had coped with the death of such a close friend, Temporiti gave a further testament to the goodness of Sister Liz and the friendship they had enjoyed: "The interesting thing is, Liz was not in my community; she was in another religious community—and her community, who loved her tremendously, their support of me was beyond imagination. Liz talked about Microfinancing Partners in Africa every day. And she would talk to her sisters about me, and their support in my grief was unprecedented. That's how open they were to me and to Liz as well—I mean, she had so many close friends in her community, and yet their openness to me really helped me get through it." Through Liz, Temporiti may have gained not just one loyal and supportive friend, but also the long-term friendship of several good women.[19]

Bad Friends and Ex-Friends

One main reason that virtuous friendships tend to last, as an Aristotle-inspired public service ad might put it, is that friends don't let friends go bad.[20] If our friends seem to be losing the good qualities that we admired in them, our job is to do all we can to help them recover their virtues. But of course we can't actually stop our friends from going bad if they're determined to do so: they're as free as we are to develop habits—even vices. So what do we do if, despite our best efforts to inspire and challenge them, our good friends do go bad? As we might expect Aristotle to point out, the answer to that question depends on the situation. If our friend becomes outright vicious while we become or remain good, maintaining the friendship becomes impossible: "The bad is not lovable, and must not be loved; for we ought neither to love the bad nor to become similar to a base person, and we have said that similar is friend to similar."[21] But we shouldn't break off the friendship until we determine that the friend has become *incurably* vicious: "If someone can be set right, we should try harder to rescue his character than his property, insofar as character is both better and more proper to friendship."[22] Similarly, when asked about friendship, Confucius advised, "Reprove your friend when dutifulness requires, but do so gently."[23]

On the other hand, as the Confucians argue, it can strain a friendship if we attempt to correct every minor flaw we see in our friends. (I'm still learning this lesson with my husband and teenage children, who don't always appreciate my self-improvement tips.) As Confucius puts it, being overbearing toward friends will lead to distance—even estrangement.[24] So unless a friend is interested in our criticism, we generally should save it for important situations and significant character defects.

What about the more common case in which, for reasons other than incurable vice, old friends grow apart? In some instances, the friends grow apart because one becomes more virtuous while the other's character remains the same. In such a situation, Aristotle advises, the two can no longer be close friends, although it is fitting "to accord something to past friends because of the former friendship":[25] to remain on good terms and, when appropriate, to do the former friend favors and offer friendly gestures.

Another general reason for which friendships are commonly dissolved is unmet expectations. Most often, these disappointments arise in friendships of utility: since each friend is in the relationship for benefit, each wants to get more and give less.[26] More serious disappointments can come from misunderstandings regarding the nature of the relationship and the other person's expectations. As Blieszner and Roberto note, such problems arise frequently during adolescence, when increased expectations can lead to "greater conflict, and possible dissolution, as a result of accusations of untrustworthy and disrespectful acts, lack of sufficient attention, and inadequate communication."[27] And that sort of thing can happen to any of us: for example, if you believe that your study buddy or junior colleague has befriended you because she enjoys your company or respects your character, you will feel unjustly used upon learning that she has befriended you only for the sake of her exam grades or career advancement. Or if your neighbor lends you his car out of what you believe to be an affectionate expression of generosity and goodwill, but you later learn that he lent it under the expectation that you would agree to mow his lawn all summer, you might reasonably complain of being deceived. What should you do in cases like these?

As the old saying goes, "an ounce of prevention is worth a pound of cure." Aristotle tells us, "We should consider at the beginning who is doing us a good turn, and on what conditions, so that we can put up with it on these conditions, or else decline it."[28] But if it's too late for the preventive approach, we should make a reasonable effort at returning the favor—and be wiser next time. In cases of outright deceit (e.g., if the study buddy really did lead you to believe she was befriending you for your character), the best approach is similar: adjust to the now-known expectations or dissolve the friendship as amicably as possible. Fortunately, doing good deeds—even for a not-especially-worthy recipient—was still good for your development of the virtues of character; and you may even have learned something that will increase your virtue of wisdom.

Virtuous Friendships and the Rest of Us

Because good friendships are established on the basis of the friends' virtues, according to Aristotle and Mencius, only virtuous people can have truly good friendships. And that seems basically right: people who are kind, fair, and trustworthy make good friends; those who are unkind, or who can't be trusted with our possessions or our secrets, make for lousy friends. So why does it seem to most of us that we've had good friends—even though most of us are not (and never were) fully virtuous?

Here are just a few possible answers: First, if we've been brought up in good (or good-enough) habits—which, Aristotle argues, is a prerequisite for benefitting from his lectures on ethics[29]—we probably have at least the beginnings of at least some of the virtues. Perhaps that is sufficient to make us suitable candidates for at least pretty-good friendships. Second, as Aristotle acknowledges, we may have natural, incomplete analogs of at least some virtues: For example, some people seem naturally giving or daring—traits akin to generosity and bravery.[30] These might also be sufficient to allow for fairly good friendships even in the absence of fully developed virtues. Finally, we may be overrating our friendships: we should be wary of assuming that our friendships have been as good as friendships get. It may be that the best friendships we've had—and the best friendships that (as far as we can tell) anyone we know has had—fall far short of being "perfect" or complete.

That last possibility may be easier to illustrate with the analogous experience of being in love; so in the hope that it will be illuminating, I'll summarize the mildly embarrassing story of my love life. I first thought I was in love—with my cousin—at age five. I was sorely disappointed to learn that my state didn't allow first cousins to marry. In fourth grade, I became thoroughly infatuated with a classmate, about whom I spent countless hours daydreaming. Sometime during sixth grade, I finally realized that I was not really in love with him, and I "fell in love" with no one else until my junior year in high school, when I became friends with a young man I met on a retreat. After a rather brief series of letters and phone calls, we were half-jokingly discussing marriage. (Rumors of my "engagement" circulated much more widely than I'd anticipated.) Eventually, that infatuation faded for lack of sufficient in-person interaction. After that, I "fell in love" twice more with young men I dated briefly (less than six months each) in high school and college before dating my husband—with whom, I am happy to report, I really did fall in love.

So what is the point of my mildly embarrassing story? Simply this: It is very easy to assume—wrongly—that your relationships are as good as they get. We are not capable of complete objectivity regarding our own experiences and relationships; and our limited experience can lead us to believe that the maximum state we have encountered is the maximum possible.[31]

How can you tell, then, if you really do have good, complete friendships? As my story of "falling in love" illustrates, it's not enough to assume you'll know the real thing when you see it—that may very well be true, but you'll likely also "know" a lot of less-than-real things before you see the real one. Given the limitations of human knowledge and experience, we will sometimes be uncertain of the character of our relationships—and perhaps we'll always be uncertain of their *exact* character: for instance, that this is the second-best friendship any two people have ever had, or that my best friend would abandon me only if I became an axe murderer. Still, with introspection, a bit of prudence, and some advice from Aristotle and the other classical philosophers we've studied, our knowledge can be considerably improved. First, as Aristotle has argued, the best friendships are those between the best people. So to know whether you're even capable of the best sort of friendship, you need to take an honest look at yourself (and perhaps at the rest of this book) to see whether you have the necessary excellences of character. Then you should ask yourself whether this friendship is helping you grow in virtue: a truly good friendship brings out and strengthens the best traits in both people.[32] You'll also need to look honestly at your motivations regarding the friendship: Are you in it primarily for pleasure or advantage, or do you love your friend for his or her own sake? Finally, you must (insofar as you are capable) try to answer these same questions regarding your friend: Is she or he a virtuous person and becoming an even better person as a result of your friendship; and does she or he love you for your own sake?

If both parties are increasingly virtuous and value each other for their own sake, the friendship is at least a candidate for completeness. If and when the relationship also has grown through much shared activity, the friendship becomes complete: a "friendship of goodness" or simply a good friendship. How much activity is enough? As with most practical matters, there isn't a set amount that can be specified in advance, but Aristotle gives us some helpful indicators: People know each other well enough to be good friends when they have "shared their salt" often (i.e., had many meals together), become lovable in themselves to each other, and have gained each other's confidence.[33] They have spent much time together pursuing activities that both enjoy.[34] Finally, a sign of good friendship is that the friends see one another as "other selves"; we'll turn next to the topic of friendship and self-love.

Be Your Own Best Friend

We've seen that Aristotle, like the Confucian authors, advises us to keep good company: since we tend to become like those with whom we associate, we need to be selective about whom we befriend. Have you noticed that there's one person who is always with you—from whom, try as you might, you can't escape? Right: It's you. As long as you're stuck with yourself for the rest of your life, you ought to make sure you're the sort of person you want to be around—as Aristotle advises, you should become your own best friend.

Interestingly, the defining features of a good friendship really are found in a good person's relationship to herself. A friend "wishes and does goods or apparent goods to his friend for the friend's own sake; ... wishes the friend to be and live for the friend's own sake[;] ... spends his time with his friend, and makes the same choices; ... [and] shares his friend's distress and enjoyment."[35] How do these features play out when your good friend is you? As Aristotle goes on to explain in an argument reminiscent of his teacher Plato (see chapter 8), you are of one mind with yourself when you desire the same things (i.e., goods) with your whole psyche. As a good person, you wish these things—including your own self-preservation—for your own sake: especially for the sake of your rational part. Further, you find yourself pleasant company because memories of your past actions don't bring regret; neither do your plans for the future bring anxiety.

On the other hand, if you are not a good person, you will be unable to befriend yourself. Base people are at odds with themselves: they "do not choose things that seem to be good for them, but instead choose pleasant things that are actually harmful; and cowardice or laziness causes others to shrink from doing what they think best for themselves."[36] And they can't stand to be alone with themselves; they need constant distraction from their regrets. Hence Aristotle wraps up his section on self-love and friendship with this advice: "If this state [of internal discord] is utterly miserable, everyone should earnestly shun vice and try to be decent; for that is how someone will have a friendly relation to himself and will become a friend to himself."[37] In fact, as he goes on to say in a later section, we should become our own *best* friend: in wishing the best things—excellent actions, not material possessions—to ourselves more than to anyone else, we demonstrate a virtuous kind of self-love.[38]

While Temporiti, as far as I could tell, had always been a good friend to herself, not all of my interviewees could say the same. Susan Burton, whose story we saw in chapter 6, provides a particularly vivid example of first being at odds with herself and later becoming her own best friend. Following a traumatic childhood and then the death of her son, Burton was constantly seeking distraction from her pain and regret—and soon became addicted to alcohol and drugs. Throughout six prison terms and several attempts to sober up and move on with life, Burton faced significant internal discord. Part of her really wanted to change her life, but another part felt too hopeless to follow through with those plans. Her situation was, just as Aristotle described it, "utterly miserable."

It was only after gaining the companionship of a woman who reached out offering help, along with that of her twelve-step program sponsor and a few other positive new influences, that Burton was able to "shun" substance abuse and the negative influences in her life, to make peace with herself through self-examination and self-forgiveness, and to work on developing a more virtuous character—one committed to helping other women and to a more just society. Now she works full time to help formerly incarcerated women escape the cycle of addiction and imprisonment. In doing so, Burton offers the women friendship and a positive role model while continuing to be her own best friend by offering herself something even better: virtuous actions.

Chapter 17

BEFRIENDING THE WORLD

ALTHOUGH many of us form satisfying and edifying personal connections with a few close friends and family members, Pam Koner's mission is to make those connections—and facilitate others' making connections—with people across the United States. A former dancer, fashion designer, and creative arts teacher, Koner founded and directs a nonprofit organization, Family-to-Family, which encourages and is the result of just that sort of personal connection. She tells the story like this:

> I was sitting on my deck in Hastings [on Hudson, New York], reading the *New York Times*, and I had a full refrigerator and two beautiful daughters. And I read this heart-wrenching story about families who didn't have enough food to eat, who lived in horrific conditions here in the U.S., and it was one of those touched-by-something-in-the-universe moments. As I was reading the article, I literally stopped and said, "I have to do something about this." I stood up, turned around, went to the phone and started try to track down the writer for the *New York Times* and the pastor of this church that he wrote his story about. And I relentlessly tried to contact him—*did* contact him, and Family-to-Family came about. I say that it was a "touched-by-the-universe moment" because, since I began it, there have been a number of people who have contacted me and said, "You know, I read that story in the *New York Times*; I just didn't know

what to do about it," or, "I read that story and I wanted to do something about it, but I didn't."[1]

_____

What, exactly, did Koner do? Well, the article's author put her in touch with the church pastor he had mentioned, who gave Koner the names and addresses of the seventeen families from his congregation who were in most need. Koner then recruited sixteen friends and acquaintances to join her in "adopting" a family each: mailing food and other basic necessities, along with personal letters, directly to the families' homes.

From that beginning, Family-to-Family has expanded to sponsorship of families, Holocaust survivors, and veterans across the country. As Koner reflected on the way in which she was inspired to found Family-to-Family, it was clear that she had been blessed at least as much as those she had assisted:

_____

Starting Family-to-Family was the most significant turning point in my life. And it put me on a path that changed my life and gave me purpose, so it's huge. The reality for me is that Family-to-Family was that thing in my life after my children—it so clearly was, and is, my purpose. If I reflect for a moment on what it has given me, I am so blessed by that, to have been touched by something that changed my life and allowed me to touch thousands of other peoples' lives in some small, tiny little way. It's an extraordinary gift for me.

_____

In this section we will examine philosophical and psychological explanations regarding just why Koner's reaching out to people has been such a gift to her—and how we can be similarly blessed.

Starting at Home

Koner's description of Family-to-Family as her purpose "after my children" is reminiscent of Mencius's theory: he argues that we develop—and should exercise—our virtues by a process he calls "extending." The main idea is quite simple: we start small and local, exercising kindness, for example, in small ways toward our families—doing so is natural even for young children, and a good home environment will allow this "sprout" of virtue to develop. Gradually, as our virtues and our social circles grow, we behave kindly toward friends and neighbors, acquaintances and classmates, strangers we encounter in our communities, and, eventually, "the world":

> That which people are capable of without learning is their genuine capability. That which they know without pondering is their genuine knowledge. Among babes in arms there are none that do not know to love their parents. When they grow older, there are none that do not know to revere their elder brothers. Treating one's parents as parents is benevolence. Revering one's elders is righteousness. There is nothing else to do but extend these to the world.[2]

So when we think of extension, we might visualize a set of concentric circles. As young children, we start with just the inner circle—our parents and other members of our immediate family. Gradually, our circles expand outward: we interact with—and exercise virtue toward—extended family, friends, and neighbors; then schoolmates, coworkers, and community members; and finally toward those we haven't met in our nation and, as Mencius says, the world. Each step outward in the set of concentric circles, then, represents increased relational distance.

Even as the reach of our virtue extends outward, however, it is natural and right that those in our inner circle of family and close friends receive more of our attention and care. When a rival philosopher criticizes Mencius's theory for suggesting that a fully virtuous person should not be fully impartial, Mencius suggests that this would be undesirable and perhaps psychologically impossible:

> Yi Zhi said, "According to the Way of the Confucians, the ancients treated the people 'like caring for a baby.' What does this saying mean? I take it to mean that love is without differentiations, but it is bestowed beginning with one's parents." ... Mencius said, "Does Yi Zhi truly hold that one's affection for one's own nephew is like one's affection for a neighbor's baby?"[3]

So we might think of the concentric circles as ripples in a pond. While the impact of great virtue, like that of a large stone, will be evident even quite far away from its source, its greatest effect will be felt by those who are nearest.

An interesting parallel to Mencius's theory can be found in empirical research regarding ingroup loyalty: the tendency to favor members of one's own social (e.g., ethnic, religious, or special interest) group. In an article reviewing the literature on this topic and explaining her own empirical work, psychologist Marilynn Brewer argues that ingroup preference need not be associated with negative attitudes toward, or poor treatment of, members of outgroups. She discusses G. W. Allport's Mencian-sounding theory of "concentric loyalties" in which "loyalties to more inclusive collectives (e.g., nations, humankind) are compatible with loyalties to subgroups (e.g., family, profession, religion)."[4]

Brewer argues that the achievement of concentric loyalties rather than prejudice against outgroups is indeed possible and is most achievable in "societies that are more complex and differentiated along multiple dimensions that are cross-cutting rather than perfectly correlated."[5] Further, she argues, the contemporary United States is an example of just such a society. In her own recent study of American college students, she found that (1) multiple group memberships are common, and most participants had no trouble naming at least four of their group identities; (2) combinations of group memberships vary widely, so that "memberships in religious, ethnic, gender, and political groupings were essentially uncorrelated"; and (3) "respondents do not see these identities as competing or mutually exclusive."[6] Brewer's literature analysis and empirical research, then, seems to favor the Mencian ideal of extension of one's positive (virtuous) attitudes and behaviors outward from the smaller ingroup (typically the nuclear family) to larger, more inclusive groups.

Because outward extension is the norm for virtue development, according to Mencius, we can infer from someone's extension to those more relationally distant that he or she is fully capable of behaving at least as virtuously toward those closer to home. In his most famous appeal to this sort of inference (quoted at greater length in chapter 2 of this book), Mencius chastises a king who takes pity on an ox destined for ritual slaughter but who fails to take care of his own people. Mencius comments, "Suppose there were someone who reported to Your Majesty, 'My strength is sufficient to lift five hundred pounds, but not sufficient to lift one feather. My eyesight is sufficient to examine the tip of an autumn hair, but I cannot see a wagon of firewood.' Would Your Majesty accept that?" After the king replies, "No," Mencius continues: "In the present case your kindness is sufficient to reach animals, but the effects do not reach the commoners. How is this different from the examples I just gave? Hence, one fails to lift a feather only because one does not use one's strength. One fails to see a wagon of firewood only because one does not use one's eyesight. The commoners fail to receive care only because one does not use one's kindness. Hence, Your Majesty fails to become King because you do not act, not because you are unable to act."[7] Like many of us, the king *chooses* not to exercise benevolence in some of his interactions with those closest to him.

Extension and Overextension

As an interesting corollary to his thought on the need for extension in the ethical life, in the passage we just discussed Mencius suggests that one's virtue may be *overextended*—that, especially in the early stages of virtue development, we may inappropriately direct our exercise of virtue toward too-distant others. In a much-discussed passage from his conversation with the king who spared the ox, Mencius says, "There was no harm. What you did was just a technique for (cultivating your) benevolence. You saw the ox but had not seen the sheep. Gentlemen cannot bear to see animals die if they have seen them living. If they hear their cries of suffering, they cannot bear to eat their flesh. Hence, gentlemen keep their distance from the kitchen."[8]

Whether or not we agree with Mencius about the necessity of animal slaughter and hence the need to limit extension in this particular case, I think we can all recognize that there are some cases in which over-empathizing with distant others can be problematic; for example, it can interfere with our ability to meet our obligations toward those in our care. And in fact, over-empathizing can even interfere with meeting the needs of the very people with whom we are empathizing: compassion fatigue is a real danger for those in caring professions such as nursing. And for all of us, as psychologist Nancy Eisenberg and her colleagues have shown, when observing another's predicament, empathizing—experiencing "vicarious negative emotion"—to the point at which we feel personal distress (as though we were actually the ones suffering) rather than sympathetic concern makes us *less* likely to help.[9]

So there are clearly limits regarding the extension of an ordinary person's compassion and even his or her virtue—especially at first. To that point, as

we saw in chapter 2, Mencius offers us some good advice regarding the gradual nature of virtue development and extension, in the form of this colorful
parable:

> One must work at it, but do not assume success. One should not forget
> the heart, but neither should one "help" it grow. Do not be like the man
> from Song. Among the people of the state of Song there was a farmer
> who, concerned lest his sprouts not grow, pulled on them. Obliviously,
> he returned home and said to his family, "Today I am worn out. I helped
> the sprouts to grow." His son rushed out and looked at them. The sprouts
> were withered.... Those who abandon them, thinking it will not help, are
> those who do not weed their sprouts. Those who "help" them grow are
> those who pull on the sprouts. Not only does this not help, but it even
> harms them.[10]

Similarly, if we focus too much on extending our virtues outward, especially
in their earlier stages of development, we may be in danger of *hindering* their
growth: if we fail to extend them as far as we'd hoped, our progress in virtue
may be hindered by discouragement; and even if we succeed in the outward
extension, the effort and willpower it takes to extend our virtue's reach before it is sufficiently mature may deplete our mental and moral resources.[11]

Depletion through overextension is a danger not only for those of us who,
like the king Mencius admonished, are just beginning to develop our virtues: Even in apparent moral exemplars, we occasionally see personal and
family problems arise when acts of virtue are concentrated too heavily in
the "outer rings" of their circles. For example, as I showed in more detail
elsewhere,[12] Virginia Durr—a Caucasian Alabama woman who dedicated
much of her adult life to the civil rights movement—followed this pattern,
extending her strong sense of justice outward to neighbors and strangers in
her community and beyond, but she did so at the expense of spending time
with her family. When interviewing Durr for their book on contemporary
moral exemplars, Anne Colby and William Damon noted that she lamented
this omission later in life:

> [The worst thing] was to have people say, "Well, now here, Virginia, I
> really don't see how you *can* do this. You *know* it's going to hurt [your

husband] and the children." And it *did* hurt the children. And I had to send them off to school. They were perfectly miserable. And none of them wants to come back to Montgomery now. Not one of them will even come back for a visit.... And so when your children feel that way about their home, it's very sad.[13]

Similarly, among my own interviewees, several who had been exceptionally kind and just toward strangers in their communities and beyond had to overcome difficulty exercising the same virtues within their family relationships: They described inability (or, Mencius would likely say, unwillingness) to maintain the level of caring and concern necessary to honor their obligations to their spouses, partners, or children. For example, as described in more detail in chapter 5, Captain James McCormick exercised heroic levels of self-sacrifice for the sake of his country over the course of his career in the U.S. Army, but he failed to sacrifice his personal interests for the sake of his family—a choice that resulted in two divorces and near-estrangement from his children by the time he was in his mid-thirties. It was a close brush with death (and, perhaps, a delayed response to the gentle admonishment of his grandmother) that finally convinced him to do what he'd been capable of doing all along: put more time and energy into being a father.

None of these observations about overextension, however, should be taken to mean that we do well to become complacent or lazy when it comes to extending our virtues. Much like striving for excellence in other areas such as athletics, training our character requires consistent, focused effort—and can be expected to yield significant results in the long run. But for the most part, progress is gradual. Although we may enjoy the occasional sudden breakthrough, it's the exception rather than the norm. When extending our virtues outward, character development tends to follow a similar pattern: only over a significant period of time, and with significant effort, can we expect significant results.

Underextension and Lack of Virtue

Although overextension of virtue is possible, as Mencius claims, *failing* to extend one's virtue—at least to a reasonable degree—is a sign that one doesn't have it at all. For example, he remarks: "If one extends one's kindness, it will be sufficient to care for all within the Four Seas. If one does not extend one's kindness, one will lack the wherewithal to care for one's wife and children."[14] So one who is unable or unwilling to extend kindness and care for those in his or her community, according to Mencius, will also fail to care for his or her own family. He makes a similar connection in more detail in a later passage:

> If one occupies a subordinate position but does not have the confidence of one's superiors, one cannot bring order to the people. There is a Way for gaining the confidence of one's superiors. If one does not have the faith of one's friends, one will not have the confidence of one's superiors. There is a Way for getting the faith of one's friends. If one serves one's parents but they are not happy, one will not have the faith of one's friends. There is a Way for making one's parents happy. If one examines oneself and one is not Genuine, one's parents will not be happy. There is a Way for making oneself Genuine. If one is not enlightened about goodness, one will not make oneself Genuine.... There has never been a case of one reaching the ultimate of Genuineness yet not inspiring others. There has never been a case of one not being Genuine yet being able to inspire others.[15]

Here we see a longer chain of inference: genuineness of character leads to pleasing one's parents, which leads to gaining the faith of one's friends, which in turn leads to having the confidence of one's superiors and ultimately being able to inspire order in one's community. So failure to extend one's good influence to the community seems to imply that one hasn't even extended it to one's immediate family—and, ultimately, that one lacks genuineness or integrity. To some degree, then, virtue is the sort of thing that *must* be extended outward if it is to thrive at all. If our sprouts of virtue don't grow, Mencius might say, they wither and die. From one's lack of extension, then, we can infer his or her lack of virtue more generally.

Extending Our Virtues: Some Practical Advice

As we have seen so far, our virtue should extend—with the same general theme but decreasing intensity—outward from our "inner circle" of family and close friends to our more-distant acquaintances and ultimately to the whole world. So if we are kind or compassionate only toward our in-group—or if we're good to strangers but *not* to our family—we have a problem with extension. In this section we will look at a few practical tips, inspired by philosophers, psychologists, and one of my interviewees, for extending our virtues in the right ways.

Take how you would treat loved ones as inspiration. Mencius's most prominent advice for outward extension of benevolence and righteousness is—like so many life lessons—simple but not necessarily easy: "Treat your elders as elders, and extend it to the elders of others; treat your young ones as young ones, and extend it to the young ones of others."[16] The principle expressed in that passage is a close cousin of the Golden Rule: just as we should generally treat others as we'd like to be treated, in a general sense we should treat others' family members as we would (or at least should) treat our own: with kindness and compassion, mindful of their age and ability.

A striking example of this extension "to the young ones of others" principle came in the form of a story I heard from James McCormick—my interviewee who had struggled to connect with his children. After the close brush with death in battle that I mentioned earlier, McCormick was determined to be a more caring father and to improve his relationships with his children; he resolved to come home alive for the sake of doing so. While still in Iraq recovering from his injuries, McCormick had a sudden opportunity to extend that newly resurfaced concern for his kids:

Easter Sunday following the battle, I was wounded and I had an infection. I was recovering in what we thought was the safest place in the camp, and it ended up being the place where the enemy attacked. There was nobody there to take charge of the defense, and I was the rankingest man, and so with a hand bandaged up, I grabbed my weapon and we ran to the perimeter. And until that day I had no issues whatsoever with standing, myself and the soldiers, firing on the enemy. It was just all a reaction that was natural; it just seemed right.

But there were houses right outside the compound, and during that battle, a group of eleven or twelve kids came running out of this house, right between us and the bad guys. So I told my soldiers to cease fire. And I can remember there was one little boy, looking back at me—they were probably fifty yards away—and I could see the terror in his face. I could see my kids in his face. And at that point, you know, we stopped shooting, but the enemy didn't. And the turning point came when there was a conscious decision: I could either sit there and let that boy die, or I could go get him—which I did. And it was the longest fifty yards of my life. But nobody could hit me. Nobody shot me. Bullets whizzed all past me, but there was this tremendous feeling of victory. I can't explain it to you. I had a bullet graze my helmet and everything, but nobody could ever hit me, and I knew they weren't going to hit me. I ran fifty yards out and ran fifty yards back. And then I got back up on my gun, and because the other kids had jumped down into a canal, they were well out of the line of fire. And the battle raged on, and the kid lived.

And you know, when the U.S. Army gave me a silver star, it wasn't for saving a little kid's life. It was because we cut down thirty insurgents. And I always had an issue with that. A real hero is not someone that wears a cape all the time and runs into the battle. A real hero is someone who makes a difference in someone else's life. You've never lived until you can really help someone who can never do anything to pay you back—you just do it because it's the right thing.[17]

Like McCormick, we may be able to extend our kindness and compassion by seeing our loved ones in the faces of acquaintances and strangers—the coworker or customer having a bad day, for example, or the homeless person seeking a meal.

"Share your fondness." Another piece of advice, also from Mencius, involves starting not only with the people closest to us, but also with the *things* of which we're especially fond. This theme comes up repeatedly in his conversation with the same king who spared the ox while failing to care for his subjects. When the king wonders why his people complain that his royal park is too large despite its being much smaller than that of the legendary sage king Wen, Mencius replies:

King Wen's preserve was seventy leagues square. Those who gathered kindling went there. Those who hunted wild chickens and rabbits went there. He shared it with the people. Was it not appropriate that the people regarded it as small? Now, when I first came to your borders, I only dared to enter after I had asked about the major prohibitions of this state. I heard that, within your borders is a preserve of forty leagues square, and that killing its deer is a crime as serious as killing a person. So this area of forty leagues square is a snare in the middle of the state. Is it not appropriate that the people regard it as large?[18]

The problem is not the size of the park; it is that the king refuses to share it. Similarly, in response to the king's confession that he is fond of war, Mencius replies that if he uses this fondness to rescue the oppressed, the people will be glad about his warlike tendencies.[19] And, most famously, when the king claims that he can't put Mencius's teachings regarding benevolent legal and economic policy into practice due to his fondness for money and women, Mencius responds in the same way: there is no harm in enjoying prosperity and romantic pursuits, he assures the king—as long as he ensures that the common people are able to enjoy them too.[20] As Mencius summarizes the point, "If Your Majesty shares the same delights as the people, then you will become King."[21]

So how can we begin to develop our budding virtues of benevolence and justice? Like the king, we can share the things that bring us the most joy. For example, like many people, I have a fondness for sweets—which gives me a lot of opportunities to share my fondness. At home, I can make a point of giving the last of the ice cream to my kids; at work, I can bring chocolate-covered espresso beans for the sleepy students in my 8:00 a.m. class. Extending beyond my social circle to people without reliable food sources, although it's generally not a good idea to send them empty calories, I can instead choose *not* to buy ice cream or chocolate this week and use the saved funds for a donation toward more nutritious food through my local food pantry or a global hunger-relief organization.

Practice deliberately—with benevolence and other virtues. As my example above shows, sharing our fondness can be a good opportunity to develop our temperance along with our benevolence. And in fact, the strategy of extending several virtues (not just benevolence) has been in play in the project I've assigned my Introductory Ethics students over the last few years. Each chooses a virtue he or she would like to study and (possibly) begin to develop; then, in addition to traditional academic research on the virtue, students practice exercising it at three levels of extension: for, toward, or with family or close friends, then more distant acquaintances, then the wider community. While the three short activities certainly aren't sufficient for habituation in the chosen virtue, my hope is that they provide a realistic model for future use. (And I participate in the project too—I can always use more practice extending my own virtues.)

Prevent overextension with emotional control. As we saw earlier, to extend benevolence we also need to be aware of the dangers of overextension—especially while our virtue "sprouts" are still immature. To react with sympathetic concern to others' suffering, rather than with help-inhibiting personal distress, Eisenberg and her colleagues have found, we need to develop our emotional control more generally. Although our initial ability to control our emotions is influenced by factors beyond our control, including genetics, our parents' warmth and disciplinary style, and the presence of role models, our emotional control can also be significantly improved by surrounding ourselves now with good role models and social reinforcement, through high expectations, and of course with practice.[22] Also, as we saw in chapter 3, emotional regulation is one aspect of willpower, which can be improved in the short term with adequate food, exercise, and sleep.

Beware of ingroup bias. Finally, when we are ready to extend our virtues outward to the next "circle," we need to be aware of—and work to eliminate—our harmful ingroup biases. As we saw at the beginning of this section, Brewer and Mencius rightly say that it is natural and even good to have more concern for those closer to us; but such concern is no excuse for biases against those who don't happen to fall into our closest social circles. While these biases may be natural—as we saw in chapter 2, even infants prefer people who share their trivial preferences—they can interfere with our development of benevolence and justice. Those same studies found that infants actually want to see those who *don't* share their preferences punished.[23] And in their seminal study of those who rescued Jewish victims of the Holocaust, Oliner and Oliner found that what separated rescuers from bystanders was that the rescuers lacked ingroup bias.[24]

And lest we think ingroup bias isn't a problem anymore, especially among educated adults in a diverse country such as the United States, here is one more disturbing study. College student participants in an fMRI machine were shown photos of various people and asked to report their emotions. Most of the results were along the lines we might expect: when viewing their home country's Olympic athletes they felt pride; when viewing wealthy-looking people they felt envy; when viewing people with severe disabilities they felt pity. In each of these cases, participants showed activity in the medial prefrontal cortex (mPfC), the area of the brain associated with social cognition. But when viewing homeless individuals, participants reported feeling disgust, and they *didn't* show mPfC activity—instead, they showed activity in the part of the brain associated with processing *objects*.[25] That's about as clear an empirical picture of dehumanization of an outgroup as we're likely to find.

So, what can we do to prevent this worst form of bias against those unlike us? Well, the same researchers suggest the general outlines of the way forward. We need to put people from our outgroups in their human context—to understand them as real people with thoughts and feelings, just as important as ourselves. Fortunately, there are many ways to do so, ranging from simple exercises of thought (researchers were able to trigger mPfC activity in people viewing photos of the homeless by asking questions about the photographed person's characteristics such as age), to reading novels or even watching TV shows featuring characters different from ourselves, to developing personal friendships across demographic and social lines. And this final, more personal, suggestion brings us back to Pam Koner—who did, and helped others to do, just that.

A Model of Extension

Pam Koner's extension of her benevolent activities from her family and local community outward toward members of other communities began with a compassionate response to a newspaper article and recruitment of other families to join her in a one-to-one (hence the name "Family-to-Family") pairing between families with extra resources and those who lacked basic necessities. Although the sponsoring families now donate financially so that Family-to-Family can arrange for sponsored families to receive their groceries fresher and more efficiently from local partner stores, sponsors still preserve the original hands-on, personal aspect of donation: they are encouraged to mail a non-food necessity such as toothpaste or winter gloves directly to "their" families each month. The families connected through these programs are also encouraged to write or email each other, often forming lasting friendships. For example, a testimonial on the organization's website reads, "I so look forward to the letters we receive each month from Iris. I feel I have truly met a life-long friend.... We have exchanged frustrations and joys just about everyday life. I feel we are truly friends across the miles."[26] These connections help families to understand each other in a personal way—one that, we might expect, increases compassion and decreases ingroup bias in both donors and recipients.

When I asked Koner about her plans for the future, her response reflected a deep concern for helping others grow in compassion and empathy—to continue to extend her benevolence outward and to help others do the same: "Part of what I'm really doing for this phase of my life is to live very much in the present, and continue to do what I do each day that makes my world better. I'll never not do what I do; I will die trying to feed hungry people. It's just like the mantra of my life now: finding ways to provide an outlet for compassion, empathy, and connection for as many people as I can. I love commonality and humanity, it's a part of my soul now. And there's always more ways to share, to help people share their bounties. I mean, it's endless." Or, as Mencius would say, "there is nothing else to do but extend these to the world."

Chapter 18

BENEVOLENCE AND GENEROSITY

The Most Lovable Virtues

VERY FEW things can amaze a room full of college seniors—especially during a four-hour evening class. But my students are amazed by the compassion of Gloria Lewis.

As we saw in chapter 7, Lewis left her home in Barbados to marry an American tourist. After enduring abuse and infidelity from her drug-addicted husband, Lewis realized the fairy-tale life she'd imagined would never be a reality; she left him and worked several low-paying jobs to support herself and her two young children. She eventually moved to Florida, remarried, and founded Care in Action USA, delivering to the homeless meals that she and her family cooked and packaged themselves. Beginning with twenty Sunday dinners, they now (with the help of volunteers) cook and serve hundreds of meals every week—while Lewis and her husband continue to hold working-class jobs. She describes her motivation this way:

For me, accomplishment is really asking, "Who have I helped? How have I made a difference in someone's life? Although I don't have much, how is it that I can do one little thing and still lift that person up?" It's not about me; it's about who I can lift today. Who can I be a shoulder to? Who I can give a kind word to? By doing that, it lifts you up. I learned that the less you worry about you, the more you're blessing yourself, and your problems just somehow take care of themselves.... And just a few kind words can really turn a person's life around.[1]

Soon after beginning to feed the homeless in their community, Lewis and her husband discovered—and felt called to meet—many other needs among the people they served: "We saw that everybody wanted to talk to us; everybody was needing someone. So then we started a Bible study. Now we've got forty or fifty people in the street in Bible studies. Now we've got people calling my husband whenever they're down and depressed. Now we've got people calling us just to give them hope." They help people find jobs, and then find a bicycle to get to work or clothing to wear—often from their own closets: "I don't need a mansion. I don't need a nice car while another person is struggling. That does nothing for me. It blesses me more to give that person the last five dollars in my pocket. It blesses me more to give away every outfit I have, because I have one on and I can wash it every day until I need another one. It blesses me more to know that I've just given that person hope by giving them something."

Lest you think Lewis was exaggerating, here's a story she shared with me about her son literally giving the shirt off his back just the previous day:

Yesterday I walked in the streets and a homeless guy was coming to ask me for some money, and he had on a t-shirt that said, "Homeless Lives Matter"; and I smiled and said, "I know that shirt." And he said, "No you don't—the person that gave it to me said it's one of a kind." I said right away, "Who gave it to you?" And he said, "A young man named Cedric took it right off his back and gave it to me. I was telling him about being homeless, and I cried to him, and he even did a video of me, and he gave me this shirt." I said, "That young man is my son."

After talking with Lewis, who gave him some bananas and a little money, the man asked why she and her family did that sort of thing. She told him, "It's all about that little bit of hope. You won't forget what my son did, and it has given you hope for tomorrow. That's why we do what we do."

Upon telling me that story—and before telling numerous others about how she has helped homeless people struggling with gang violence, mental illness, and drug addiction—Lewis reflected:

If we all lived like this, what a beautiful world this would be. It doesn't mean that we're not going to have problems, but we can all do something to help, and that's my motivation for doing this. It's for people to see that we can make a difference. It's for people to see that they can take that five minutes to say a kind word to a person. We need to be able to look at a person and see that they're in distress. We need to be able to stop in our busy lives and say, "How are you doing? What's going on?" And take five minutes out of our busy schedules, when we think that we have to do something, but that five minutes is a life that you can change.

Compassion and Benevolence

Like Gloria Lewis, classical Confucian philosopher Mencius advocates acting from compassion as a main key to virtuous living. As we saw in chapter 2, he argues that all of us are born with a sense of compassion for others' suffering—and that compassion, when cultivated and developed, can grow into an essential virtue: benevolence. In his most famous discussion of virtue, he puts his point like this: "Suppose someone suddenly saw a child about to fall into a well: anyone in such a situation would have a feeling of alarm and compassion—not because one sought to get in good with the child's parents, not because one wanted fame among one's neighbors and friends, and not because one would dislike the sound of the child's cries. From this we can see that if one is without the feeling of compassion, one is not human.... The feeling of compassion is the sprout of benevolence."[2]

Although virtue "sprouts" are a far cry from fully developed virtues, they are a good start. With the right environment and our efforts at "cultivation," over time the sprout of benevolence will grow to its full potential. We need to "weed" and "water" our sprouts with good actions and companions, and we must keep them away from negative or "freezing" external influences, but we must also avoid "pulling" on our sprouts by trying to force unrealistically rapid progress. Interestingly, Mencius observes, when our virtues are not yet developed, they are also threatened by difficult circumstances such as physical or economic hardship.[3] So if we are in a position to avoid that—and, better yet, to help others avoid it too—we can more easily nurture virtue sprouts into healthy, fully developed traits.

As we might begin to infer from Mencius's description of compassion as benevolence's sprout, he characterizes this important virtue in terms of love for our fellow human beings. Our benevolence, Mencius emphasizes, must be genuine. It cannot merely be pantomimed but must naturally flow from what is already within us. Of the great sage emperor Shun, for example, he says, "He acted *out of* benevolence and righteousness; he did not *act out* benevolence and righteousness."[4] So if you're still at the "fake it till you make it" stage of developing benevolent love of others, Mencius would be the first to tell you that you have some distance to go.

Of course, benevolence does have some external signs. For example, "The benevolent love others, and those who have propriety revere others. Those who love others are generally loved by others. Those who revere others are generally revered by others."[5] A rough external test of our benevolence, then, is others' responses to us: if people generally *don't* love us, that's a sign that we are not yet benevolent. Another external sign of our benevolence (or lack thereof), Mencius suggests, is that we choose to pursue activities whose success depends on the wellbeing (or detriment) of others—he illustrates the point with examples of professions that were common in his day: "'Is the arrow-maker less benevolent than the armor-maker? And yet, the arrow-maker only fears that he may not harm people; the armor-maker only fears that he may harm people.... Hence, one may not fail to be careful about one's choice of craft."[6]

When I asked my students recently whether they could think of any professions today in which there is a built-in conflict with others' interests, they had surprisingly little difficulty finding examples. One young man shared, "I'm thinking about going into the music industry, but I hesitate because it's so often been involved with the exploitation of women and children." Some mentioned business ventures that depend upon, and even work to cause, the failure of others' businesses. One student even suggested that my own profession—teaching—met this description because of the grading involved! (I think he meant that a fair grader inevitably assigns some students poor grades. As long as I'm not causing or hoping for my students' failure, though, I think teaching is an ethically safe profession in that regard.)

As we've seen with all of the virtues, the good news is that whether we develop benevolence is up to us—with enough effort, anyone can do it. But, also as with the other virtues, the news that we are capable of cultivating benevolence in ourselves comes with the inevitable corollary that there really is no one but ourselves to blame if our sprouts fail to grow: "Benevolence is like archery. An archer corrects himself and only then shoots. If he shoots but does not hit the mark, he does not resent the one who defeats him but simply turns and seeks [the cause] in himself."[7]

Just as with other virtues, then, the development of benevolence depends on commitment and practice. Although Xunzi disagrees with Mencius about our natural starting point—he thinks our nature tends toward evil rather than good—he agrees that we're all capable of developing virtue just as fully as the great sages: "The sage is a man who has arrived where he is through the accumulation of good acts," Xunzi says. "If the man in the street applies himself to training and study, concentrates his mind and will, and considers and examines things carefully, continuing his efforts over a long period of time and accumulating good acts,"[8] he can do the same—it's just that most of us don't choose to make the effort.

Mature benevolence, as Mencius repeatedly emphasizes throughout the *Mengzi*, is the key to success in caring for others and influencing them positively—whether those others are our disciples and subjects or our friends, family members, and coworkers. "If one is benevolent," he explains, "one will have glory. If one is not benevolent, one will have disgrace. Now, to dislike disgrace yet to dwell in what is not benevolent, this is like disliking wetness and dwelling in the damp."[9] So if we want interpersonal success as well as personal ethical excellence, our first priority should be to cultivate our sprouts of benevolence until they blossom into maturity.

As we undertake that task, Mencius provides one serious note of caution: While mature benevolence is key to excellent living, underdeveloped or underused benevolence is ineffective and can even be detrimental. As he rather dramatically puts the point: "Benevolence will overcome what is not benevolent just as water overcomes fire. Nowadays, those who practice benevolence are like someone who tries to save a wagonload of burning firewood with a single glass of water. When the fire is not extinguished, they claim that water cannot overcome fire. This aids what is not benevolent more than anything else does. In the end, all will be lost."[10]

In less dramatic ways (I hope) in your own life and perhaps in more dramatic ways when watching the news, you have probably seen several examples of situations like the one Mencius describes. A half-hearted attempt at "helping," whether it is with a routine household chore or a dramatic rescue effort, is not merely unhelpful—it can actively discourage others from stepping up, and it can even convince observers that really there was no point in helping at all. To be truly benevolent, we need to put our full effort—our whole heart (*xin*), as Mencius would say—into caring for those around us. That's a big task; in the next section we'll look at one main psychological suggestion for accomplishing it: development of empathy.

Empathy: The "Sprout" of Benevolence?

Some thinkers—both philosophers and psychologists—have suggested that there may be a link between empathy and the compassion-based virtue of benevolence.[11] And from a Confucian perspective, that proposal seems to make sense: even Mencius's description of the "feeling of alarm and compassion" we'd all have upon seeing a child about to fall might reasonably be interpreted as a feeling of empathy.

Further, empathy is an obvious example of what psychologists call a "prosocial emotion": one that tends toward benefitting others. For example, well-known empathy researcher Martin Hoffman points out that empathy—defined as "the vicarious affective response to another person"[12]—is associated with helping others. And the association is not just incidental. When an observer sees someone in "discomfort, pain, danger, or some other type of distress" and has "feelings that are more congruent with another's situation than with his own situation," he experiences "empathic distress."[13] Regarding empathic distress, Hoffman observers three things that point to its prosocial nature: Not only is it (a) positively correlated with helping, but it (b) precedes and contributes to the helping behavior and (c) is relieved when the observer succeeds in helping. Finally, as Hoffman also notes, empathy contributes to decreased aggression and manipulation—additional prosocial benefits.[14]

Although empathy can indeed encourage compassionate *behavior* in most of us, however, responding empathically is not the same as having the *trait* of benevolence. In fact, philosopher Christian Miller has argued that although empathy does give rise to altruistic motivation, it would be unnecessary for someone who is truly benevolent: "A genuinely compassionate person would not need to have a motive fostered by empathic feelings in order to reliably help others. Even without such a motive, a compassionate individual should be expected, other things being equal, to be able to recognize when someone is in need and try to do what he can to help."[15]

Further, as both Miller and Hoffman note, although empathy can move us toward compassionate behavior and away from aggression, it can also move us toward not-so-ethical responses. For example, as we saw in chapter 13 of this book, empathy has significant ethical limitations when it comes to justice: because empathy is felt most strongly toward those to whom we're most similar or most emotionally connected, an ethical approach based solely upon empathy will tend toward unfair ingroup bias. Further, empathizing with one person (e.g., through hearing her story presented in an emotional way, as in many studies) can lead us to place her needs and desires ahead of the greater needs of others.[16]

Another limitation of empathy as a basis of benevolence is that many of us avoid empathy entirely if we think it may motivate us to do something costly or inconvenient. For example, as researchers found, most people will choose to listen to an "objective" rather than an emotional, empathy-inducing account of a stranger's distress when warned that the story will be followed by a request for help.[17] Similarly, how many of us have changed the TV channel or scrolled past a social media post when confronted with stories of starving children or victims of natural disasters? Empathic distress is, well, *distressing*—and if the costs of alleviating our distress (i.e., by helping) strike us as too high, we'd rather avoid empathizing in the first place.

Further, even when directed appropriately, empathic motivation is highly fragile. Summarizing the results of several studies, Miller observes that empathic feelings "can be extremely fragile such that participants become easily distracted from thinking about what another person in need is feeling. When they are distracted, their altruistic motivation often simply vanishes."[18] And as Hoffman points out, even in the presence of empathy, competing self-interested motives such as avoidance of punishment, social condemnation, or even mere inconvenience often override any empathy-induced motivation to help. He cites an example from Oliner and Oliner's famous study of Holocaust rescuers and bystanders in which a normally compassionate doctor refused to help a Jewish man with a life-threatening illness.[19] Altruistic helping behavior, even among observers experiencing empathic distress, is also diminished by social effects such as "pluralistic ignorance" (concluding from others' failure to react that there is no emergency after all) and "diffusion of responsibility" (the assumption that someone else will help).

Even if empathy isn't equivalent to the virtue of benevolence (or what Miller calls "the virtue of compassion"), cultivating empathy may—with some limitations—be a useful step toward cultivating the virtue. As one might expect of a psychologist who has devoted much of his career to the study of empathy, Hoffman is optimistic about its potential ethical contributions: "Cognitive development (self-other differentiation, language mediation, role-taking, causal attribution) enables simple empathic distress to be transformed into increasingly sophisticated motives to consider the welfare of others, taking their life condition as well as their immediate feelings into account.... Empathy's amenity to cognitive influence is also important for another reason: It gives a potentially significant role to socialization and moral education, which may counteract empathic morality's limitations and magnify its capabilities."[20]

Hoffman suggests several ways in which parents, educators, and even juvenile corrections workers might help children strengthen and appropriately direct their empathy; here are just a few of his ideas:

1. Induction: Reasoning with children about their actions and how they affect others. As Hoffman notes, inductive parenting tends to be the preferred method among educated, middle-class Americans; sure enough, a lot of induction happens at my house—and it seems to be effective. ("What could happen if you throw your toy cars across the room?" "They could hit my sister." "What would happen if they hit her?" "She would get hurt." "Is it good or bad to hurt your sister?" Etc.)

2. Experience of a wide range of emotions: Overly sheltered children who have never experienced significant frustration, disappointment, or sadness may have a limited ability to empathize with others' distress. (Hoffman doesn't advocate exposing children to trauma, of course. But there's generally no need to "protect" them from ordinary

negative life events such as disagreements with siblings, disappointment about not getting a desired birthday present, or sadness at the
death of a pet.)
  3. Encouraging perspective-taking: Through pretend play, adults can
     demonstrate and encourage empathy with real or imagined people.[21]

This last method is also one we can all use on ourselves. As we saw in chapter
7, getting out of our own self-immersed perspective is a helpful way to avoid
rumination. Replacing our own perspective with that of someone affected
by our actions can also help us cultivate empathy. And when it's hardest
to imagine what could possibly be going through someone else's head, it's
probably the best time to imagine that very thing. (Really, what *could* she be
thinking and feeling?)

Because empathic bias, as we have seen, can be a real threat to our exercise of justice, Hoffman also suggests a few ways in which we can learn
to limit bias: (1) emphasize cross-group commonalities, such as emotional
responses to life experiences like praise and criticism, separation, and loss;
(2) look beyond the immediate situation to current or future others who may
be affected; and (3) think about how a loved one would feel in a stranger's or
victim's situation.[22] Perhaps, Hoffman suggests, if we work to moderate our
empathic biases, cultivating empathy can be a good route to developing our
sprouts of benevolence after all.

Interestingly, Hoffman ends his discussion of empathy and moral education by emphasizing that we need not eliminate empathic bias altogether.
As the Confucians would agree, it can be acceptable and even virtuous to
give more of our time and resources to those closest to us—as long as we
don't overstep the limits of justice or fail to help others. As a psychologist, he
doesn't give an in-depth analysis regarding how we should go about deciding
when and how much to help, however; for that sort of analysis, we'll turn to
Aristotle.

Generosity: The Virtue of Giving (and Taking)

Everyone who meets Gloria Lewis, it seems, wants to be her friend—
"everybody wanted to talk to us.... Now we've got forty, fifty people in the
street in Bible studies.... We've got people calling us just to give them hope."

And it's no wonder: as Aristotle points out in book 4 of his *Nicomachean Ethics*, generous people are "the most loved of all virtuous characters [because of] their giving."[23]

Although the description "giving" is sometimes used synonymously with "generous," the virtue of generosity is more complex than the term "giving" suggests. Like all virtues, generosity is a mean between extremes, primarily with regard to giving, but also with regard to taking:

> It is more characteristic of virtue to do good than to have good done to one, and more characteristic to do what is noble than not to do what is base; and it is not hard to see that giving implies doing good and doing what is noble, and taking implies having good done to one or not acting basely. And gratitude is felt towards him who gives, not towards him who does not take, and praise also is bestowed more on him. It is easier, also, not to take than to give; for men are apter to give away their own too little than to take what is another's.

A generous person, Aristotle explains, will give rightly and for the sake of goodness: "to the right people, the right amounts, and at the right time"[24]— and will not be pained upon parting with her possessions. Further, she will not take from the wrong sources (such as other people's possessions) nor even ask readily for contributions—at least, for contributions to her own wellbeing.

Even if you'll never be one of those famous philanthropists handing over an enormous donation to a fashionable cause, you can still be just as generous—and likely even more so: generosity depends on the means and the character of the giver rather than the monetary value of the donation. So if all you can afford to give to an important cause is ten dollars, but you do so happily and for the sake of improving others' lives, you may well be more generous than the billionaire who hands over a million-dollar check to the same charity. In fact, as Aristotle observes (and I observed in my interviewees' stories, too), generous people tend not to be very wealthy: they're better at giving away money and possessions than at accumulating them. But they don't give to everyone—they do their best to direct their limited funds to those who most need or merit them.[25] As we have seen, for example, in addition to Gloria Lewis's giving to the homeless, Andy Wells (chapter 10) provides training and jobs to those who are otherwise unemployable, Cathy Heying (chapters 2 and 19) provides low-cost car repair to those with low incomes, and Noah Levinson (chapters 11 and 12) provides medical care to at-risk children in India. All of these generous folks have limited resources; hence they all also have rather focused missions for their organizations.

Another feature of generous people is that, although they give a large proportion of their resources to worthy causes and beneficiaries, they don't give so excessively that they jeopardize their ability to contribute to worthy causes in the future. The practical problem with doing so is obvious; we'll touch on it and the associated vice of prodigality briefly before moving on to generosity's more common—and worse—opposing vice.

Prodigality: Yes, There Is a Wrong Way to Give

Although Aristotle's description of generosity leans much closer to giving too much than too little, it's possible to overdo any good thing. So, as with other virtues, there is a vice related to excessive giving: "prodigality," which simply means "wastefulness." When is giving wasteful? When it is directed to the wrong recipients—for example, toward those who flatter us rather than those who need or merit our assistance—or when it exceeds our means: that is, when it threatens our ability to meet obligations such as feeding our children or making our mortgage payment.

In addition to exceeding in giving, purely prodigal people are deficient in taking: they don't accept enough money even from legitimate sources such as employment. As Aristotle notes (and we can easily see), such people are rare: "It is not easy to give to all if you take from none; private persons soon exhaust their substance with giving."[26] Although prodigality is, technically speaking, a vice, people of this sort are really not so bad—certainly much better than stingy or "mean" people—for a few reasons:

1. They're easily cured: Age provides the right sort of life experience to help them see the limits of their means, and poverty prevents them from giving beyond those limits for very long.
2. They're close to the mean to begin with: The mean of generosity is much closer to giving too much than to giving too little. In fact, Aristotle even describes generous people as "exceeding in giving." And

combining excessive giving with deficient taking "is not the mark of a wicked or ignoble man ... but only of a foolish one."[27]

3. Their actions are much more beneficial than those of stingy people: The prodigal person "benefits many while the other benefits no one, not even himself."[28]

So while the vice of prodigality may be unwise, it's not malicious and is easily cured. As we'll see, the same can't be said of the opposite vice: meanness.

Being "Mean": The Vice of Stinginess

In contrast to prodigality, Aristotle argues, the vice of meanness—generosity's more obvious opposite—is common and "incurable." Why? It's common because it is more "innate" in ordinary human beings: as Aristotle bluntly puts it, "most men are fonder of getting money than of giving."[29] Another reason it is common is that it comes in a few different forms: deficient giving, excessive taking, and both together. Aristotle's descriptions of meanness's variations fit just as well today as they did thousands of years ago. He begins with the more typical stingy people, who "fall short in giving, but do not covet the possessions of others nor wish to get them. In some this is due to a sort of honesty and avoidance of what is disgraceful ... while others keep their hands off the property of others from fear" of retaliation—not wanting to risk having their own possessions taken, "they are therefore content neither to take nor to give."[30]

Another form of meanness, even worse than stinginess in some obvious ways, is that of the excessive taker, who will take "anything and from any source, e.g. those who ply sordid trades, pimps and all such people, and those who lend small sums and at high rates. For all of these take more than they ought and from wrong sources. What is common to them is evidently sordid love of gain."[31] As my students readily attest when I ask for modern-day examples, just as everyone loves a giver, everyone hates a taker—in addition to Aristotle's sadly still-relevant examples of pimps and loan sharks, they are annoyed by more common sorts of takers like roommates who don't do their share of the housework, friends who are always asking favors but never offering to return them, and acquaintances who routinely "forget" their wallets when going to restaurants.

Meanness is "incurable," according to Aristotle, because those with this vice get what they want: financial gain. So unless and until they come to see that accumulating wealth isn't making their lives meaningful or fulfilling, mean people are unlikely to change. And of course that *can* happen—think of Scrooge in Dickens's classic *A Christmas Carol*, for example—but it is unlikely to happen on its own. For Scrooge, it took supernatural visitors and the threat of tragedy to trigger reconsideration of his stingy ways.

Fortunately for most of us, life affords many less-dramatic opportunities to learn that wealth, as useful as it can be, is less important than more noble and meaningful pursuits—and is best used in their service. As I confessed in chapter 4, I naturally tend toward stinginess myself and have had to work against it consciously. It has helped to be married to someone I know to be more generous than I am: I can behave more generously by deferring to his judgment for the most part regarding things like how much to donate to good causes and how much to tip at restaurants. A second strategy, also a work-around of sorts, has been to set up automatic (and thus relatively painless) monthly donations to organizations whose work I especially admire. Third, and more directly combatting my stingy tendencies, I've tried to take Aristotle's advice about heading toward the less-bad extreme (prodigality) when I'm not sure where the mean lies. As we saw in chapter 1, that strategy tends to work pretty well, because for the majority of us—those who tend toward the worse extreme—the less-bad extreme is difficult to distinguish from the mean. So when in doubt about how much to do for others, I try to do what strikes me as slightly prodigal—and it usually turns out not to be.

When Prodigality Is Mean

Interestingly, though, just as an overly modest person actually can be a braggart in disguise (see chapter 6), one form of prodigality is also a form of meanness: "Most prodigal people ... also take from the wrong sources, and are in this respect mean. They become apt to take because they wish to spend and cannot do this easily; for their possessions soon run short. Thus they are forced to provide means from some other source. At the same time, because they care nothing for honour, they take recklessly and from any source; for they have an appetite for giving, and they do not mind how."[32] For example, a neighbor of mine lost thousands of dollars from his small business when an employee "gave" his friends discounted gas—by charging it to the company credit card and pocketing their cash. (As you can imagine, that sort of giving resulted in legal trouble for the employee as well as financial trouble for my neighbor.)

Although I hope most of us aren't tempted to outright steal for the sake of gift-giving, many of us *are* tempted by a more socially accepted but often problematic source: our own credit cards. Total U.S. consumer debt hovered around $4 trillion in 2018: over $12,000 for each man, woman, and child in the country, which was 45 percent higher than it had been ten years earlier.[33] The average American owes about 26 percent of her annual income in consumer debt—and spends about 10 percent of her income paying it off.[34]

Although consumer debt includes student and auto loans in addition to personal loans and credit cards, a major source of this debt for many Americans is excessive gift-giving—that is, giving beyond our means or other reasonable limits. In the United States, the average amount per person spent on holiday gifts in 2017 neared $1,000. A recent article provides some unsettling details:

> Parents are spending an average of $422 per child on holiday gifts, with 34% of parents spending $500 or more per child. Worse yet, an alarming number of parents are putting their finances at risk to make their kids' holiday wishes come true. An estimated 25% are taking drastic measures such as withdrawing money from their 401(k)s, dipping into their emergency savings, or taking out payday loans in order to purchase holiday gifts.[35]

Like excessive giving of gifts to others, "giving" excessively to ourselves can also be a form of prodigality—and a common source of consumer debt. (Indeed, "prodigality" or "wastefulness" is a very fitting description for indulging in luxuries that we can't afford—or whose price isn't justified by the benefits they provide.) For instance, many of us are tempted to buy more (or more expensive) cars, clothing, or vacations than is necessary or prudent—as Aristotle points out, prodigality is often combined with self-indulgence.

How do we avoid the vice of wrong-source prodigality—i.e., overspending—whether the beneficiaries are ourselves or others? Even if we wanted to wait for age and poverty to cure us, that probably wouldn't work with this form of the vice—since excessive taking replenishes the giving or spending source, we may be able to keep up the poor money management for decades. While financial planning is most definitely not my area of expertise—and the best advice I can offer is that you should find someone who *is* an expert—I'll briefly and humbly mention a few anti-wastefulness methods that have worked for my own family.

First, budget. As far as I can tell, that's the main thing on which all of the financial experts agree. Tracking spending can help us recognize and avoid waste, save money for necessary expenditures and long-term goals, and aid generosity by making our donations more automatic and painless. Being nerds, my husband and I have a budgeting spreadsheet that he developed himself; but there are many good, ready-made, easy-to-use budgeting programs—and some of them are available free of charge.

Second, determine relevant red flags (or "tripwires," as the Heath brothers call them)[36] that would signal a need to reevaluate spending habits. For example, you might reassess your situation when you owe more than 25 percent of your annual income in consumer (non-mortgage) debt, when you pay more in interest than in principal, or when you spend more than 10 percent of your paycheck just making the minimum payments. For my family, a tripwire came one year when my husband ran the year-end report on our budget—we saw that we had spent more on restaurants that year than on charitable donations. That was a sign that it was time to rethink the best use of our money.

Third, prioritize people over things. Spending—even unnecessary spending—on something that will mean a lot to a family member or a beloved friend is much less prodigal than spending on self-indulgence. Here is just one set of contrasting examples: while it is difficult for me to imagine ever having a good enough reason to spend three times as much as necessary on a purse or pair of boots just to own a particular brand-name version of the same quality, it strikes me as much more reasonable to spend a similar amount of "extra" money to commemorate a momentous occasion such as a wedding or to bring my children to the triennial family reunion.

While following those three bits of advice won't automatically make us generous, of course, you may find them a good start. Since the excessive taking of wrong-source prodigality is actually a form of meanness (the worse extreme), avoiding it is an important step in the direction of virtue.

Duties of Benevolence and Generosity?

Like my students, I'm amazed at Gloria Lewis's compassion: she gives so much of her time, income, and emotional resources to the homeless in her community, even as she struggles to provide for her own needs. Perhaps unlike my students, I'm amazed for philosophical reasons as well as human-interest ones. For one thing, at least on the surface, the extent of Lewis's giving looks more like the vice of prodigality than like the virtue of generosity as Aristotle describes it—the extent of her giving often seems to threaten her ability to keep providing for herself and those she is trying to help.

When we look more closely at Lewis's story, though, I think we can see that she is generous rather than prodigal. We might explain that conclusion in a few ways. First, we might appeal to her religious convictions: "exceeding in giving" makes sense in her life—it lies within the mean relative to her circumstances—largely because she believes that God is calling her to give and that he will make sure her basic needs are met. A second partial explanation, and a more religiously neutral one, is that Lewis has trained her perceptions—her ethical sensitivity—through repeated generous actions; perhaps that is why she "sees" the mean of generosity where most of us don't expect it. Third and perhaps most obviously (especially since I mentioned it earlier), because most of us tend toward stinginess ourselves, our perception of the mean may be distorted: even though we recognize the virtue of generosity in the big picture of Lewis's life, when it comes to her individual actions—especially if we imagine ourselves performing them—we can easily confuse generosity with prodigality.

As with all virtues, generosity is not just about the amount that we give; it's also about *how* we do it. Here is one striking feature of how Gloria Lewis and many other generous and benevolent people give: they don't think of giving as optional.

These days, I think most people *do* think of giving (at least when we have no obvious special obligation) as optional. A "duty to be generous" probably sounds paradoxical to most of us: Doesn't generosity mean going *beyond* the call of duty? How can it be "generous" of us to fulfill our obligations?

By this point in the book, though, perhaps you can already see why a virtue ethicist or a virtuous person like Lewis wouldn't think that way. If the goal of the ethical life isn't merely to do the bare minimum to repay what we owe to identifiable individuals—if, instead, the goal is to become ethically excellent people—then it is quite natural to suppose that generous giving and compassionate benevolence would be among the ethical life's most essential features. Far from being nice-but-not-necessary add-ons or afterthoughts to an ethical life focused on repaying debts, benevolence and generosity are indispensable core ethical excellences.

It is not surprising, then, that this perception that their work and sacrifices on behalf of others are a duty or responsibility—not just a nice idea—is common among ethically excellent people. Several of my interviewees, including James McCormick of Raising Cane Farms (chapter 5) and Lisa Nigro of the Inspiration Café (chapter 9), expressed this sense of necessity or duty by speaking of their benevolent and generous work in terms of justice, as did Cathey Brown of Rainbow Days (chapter 13), who also described her work in substance-abuse prevention as a God-given responsibility.

Similarly, in their fascinating studies of those who were rescuers and those who were bystanders during the Nazi Holocaust, Stephanie Fagin-Jones and Elizabeth Midlarsky found that rescuers "were, above all, distinguished from bystanders on the basis of their ability to subscribe to the personal norm that requires people to help others who are dependent on them without the expectation of gain, because it is the right thing to do."[37] And this description applies aptly to more famous Holocaust rescuers as well. For example, German businessman Oskar Schindler, whose story became known thanks to the award-winning film *Schindler's List*, is credited with saving the lives of twelve hundred Polish Jews by employing them in his factory—which, using his political influence, he had designated a "branch" of a Nazi concentration camp—to make (defective) bullets for the army. Irena Sendler, who rescued hundreds of Jewish children during World War II, said, "Every child saved with my help is the justification of my existence on this Earth, and not a title to glory."[38] And Raoul Wallenberg, a Swedish diplomat who saved thousands of Hungarian Jews before his arrest in 1945, dismissed a friend's urging to return to safety, saying, "To me there's no other choice. I've accepted this assignment and I could never return to Stockholm without the knowledge that I'd done everything in human power to save as many Jews as possible."[39]

Although we may not have the opportunity (or the courage?) to do something as dramatic as Schindler, Sendler, and Wallenberg did, we too can begin to grow toward ethical excellence if we can see helping others as morally required. And while the Holocaust rescuers had to overcome constant risks to their safety and frequent physical hardship, most of have to overcome more mundane temptations to ignore others' needs, such as busyness, distraction, or limited finances. Perhaps simply comparing our excuses with the much more legitimate ones these ethical heroes could have made will be enough to convince us that we have a long way to go in the generosity department. But just in case, lest we think we're too busy or too broke to help others, I'll close this chapter with Gloria Lewis's little pep talk about the ethical necessity of benevolence and generosity: having had "an abusive husband that almost took my life, having two kids with no dad, and being married to an ex-convicted felon who was on drugs, dealing with a son who drinks, which I don't like—in my struggles, with everything that we have going on, there's still room to bless another person. There's still no reason why you still can't give. There's no reason why you can't show compassion to others. There's no reason, period."

Part 7

PURSUING WISDOM—

and What to Do until You Find It

Chapter 19

TYING IT ALL TOGETHER

Practical Wisdom and Ethical Virtue

CATHY HEYING, the social worker whose story we previewed in chapter 2, was at a major life crossroad. Like many of us do at some point, she was contemplating a career change. Unlike most of us, though, she was thinking about leaving her dream job for one that didn't promise to be easy or enjoyable or even a good fit for her skill set: automotive repair. As she says, her frequent (and tempting) thought was, "I have this perfectly lovely life—why the hell would I mess with that? [Laughs.] Just leave well enough alone."[1] But in her direct service and public policy work surrounding poverty and homelessness, she frequently saw an unmet need for low-cost car repair—a service that could help prevent people from losing their jobs and prevent their families from ending up in homeless shelters. No one else was stepping forward. Maybe it was up to her.

Heying's decision to leave—or at least dramatically alter—her "perfectly lovely life" is striking in several ways: the magnitude of the change, for example, and the amount of sacrifice she was willing to endure. But it is also impressive for another reason: the process. As she considered her options and worked out the details, Heying showed admirable deliberation, reflection, and openness to good advice—marks of the virtue of prudence or practical wisdom.

Provide low-cost car repairs

Develop automotive repair skills

Acquire training at a technical college

Figure 19.1. Means-end pyramid: Car repair

As we illustrated in the first chapter of this book, our reasoning about how to achieve our goals can be represented (and facilitated) using what I called a "means-end pyramid": put a long-term goal at the top, then the immediate means to the goal just below, then the means to *those* means, until you reach action steps you can take today. Heying saw that to provide low-cost car repair, an essential means would be gaining the necessary skills— and the most obvious means to do that was to enroll in an automotive repair program at a local technical college. So her means-end pyramid would look (in part) like the one in figure 19.1.

But further deliberation was necessary before Heying could reasonably decide to leave her meaningful and satisfying dream job for tech school— and in general, the bigger the decision, the more carefully we should deliberate about it. In addition to continuing her internal consideration of her options and recognizing her own hopes and fears, Heying wisely reached out to people who knew her well and whose advice she trusted: family members, a long-term partner, friends, and coworkers. Their response, she says, was encouraging and supportive:

It was a huge shift in the trajectory of my life—having seen an unmet need and then thinking about meeting it. I had a lot of conversations with people: "Should I . . . ?"—like friends, partner I've been close to, lots of people in my life from my coworkers and folks at church to my mom— who, God bless her, has mostly with her seven kids tried to take a hands-off approach, not meddling in our lives too much. And I think even she was like, "Well, I can't say I saw this coming, but OK." [Laughs.]

I'm not good at failure. I don't allow it very much in myself, and so that was one of my biggest fears: "What if it doesn't work? What if I have to drop out? What if I fail?" That felt more horrifying to me in some ways than "What if I succeed?"—which sounds crazy, given the implications of succeeding. And people in my life said, "The worst thing that's going to happen is that you try it, it doesn't work, and then you need to move on. And then you'll stop wondering; otherwise you'll always wonder." And so that sort of encouragement was required to take the first steps.

The next step, then, was to visit the technical college and learn about the automotive program; so, still "a little reluctantly," that's what Heying did. She says, "I thought, 'I don't know anything about cars, but I'll go down to talk with them; that doesn't mean I have to do anything about it. I can just have the conversations.' And so I got a tour and talked to them, and at the end of it, the director says, 'Well, if you're thinking of starting in the fall, I've only got four slots left in the program before we're full. Probably those will be filled by the end of the week. So if you're at all serious, I need your application today.'" So, still reluctantly, Heying went ahead and filled out the application and started that fall. As she describes the decision, "I was like, 'I don't want to do this,' but I just couldn't *not*."

Another wise—and perhaps lucky—thing Heying did was find a good mentor when she was struggling early in the automotive program. Heying was finding the work itself difficult (it still does not come naturally to her, she says) and the instructional setting foreign: "It was such a different experience, and I suppose it had to be with eighteen-year-old boys, but it felt like what I imagined the Army to be like. They all called us by our last names and there was a lot of bellowing, for lack of better words." But one of those "bellowing" instructors that first semester took Heying under his wing. One day after class, having noticed that Heying obviously didn't fit the typical demographic for an automotive technician student, he asked what had brought her to the program. She explained her background and goals as well as her struggles, and he offered his unconditional support:

He looked me in the eye and he said, "You can do this, and I will do anything in my power to make sure you do this. So if that means we stay after class, if that means even if you're no longer in my class, when you need help, you need to talk, you're feeling overwhelmed, you come find me. I'm going to make sure you walk across that stage in two years." And he did everything he promised. He's been one of my biggest fans since the beginning, and I mean it very seriously when I say none of this would have happened without him, because I feel confident that I would have quit and none of it would have come to fruition.

As Heying's graduation from the automotive program neared, it was time to begin discerning the next steps toward providing low-cost car repair for those who most needed it. She had retained a part-time position in the human services organization affiliated with her church, and at first she was hopeful that the repair outreach she had in mind could be run under the auspices of her current employer. Also intrigued by the possibility, the organization increased Heying's employment to full-time, adding to her duties research into the feasibility of developing a car repair service in addition to their other poverty-relief efforts. In the way that she went about researching the best approach to not-for-profit car repair, Heying once again showed a lot of practical wisdom:

> I sat down and I made a list of the types of people that I thought I should talk to: lawyers, development people who raise money for nonprofits, nonprofits' executive directors, car mechanics and shop owners, and business people, and city council members. And then I went back to the list on the sheet and filled in names of people I knew who fit those descriptions— and so I started with them. I'd take them out for coffee and pick their brains and ask questions and get feedback, and then I'd ask, "Who else do you think I should be talking to?"

Several months and many cups of coffee later, Heying concluded that it wouldn't be feasible to run a repair shop under the umbrella of her current organization; she'd have to start a new nonprofit. She also (wisely again) realized she'd first need to gain some hands-on experience working in the automotive field—so, while still keeping her part-time job in housing services and policy, Heying worked at a nearby auto shop. Her two jobs made for a funny juxtaposition:

I picked up a part-time job working at Sears by the capitol: I figured if I want to run an automotive repair business, I should probably work in one for a while. Literally, there would be days when I would leave Sears, change out of my greasy uniform, with my greasy fingernails, and put on nice clothes and walk to the capitol and try to lobby on some sort of homeless or public benefits policy. And legislators would come in and get their oil changed, and they would be like, "Do I know you?" [Laughs.] "Yes. Yes, you do." So it was a weird, weird time.

From there, things started taking shape: within a few years, Heying had started The Lift, a nonprofit garage with several volunteer repair technicians, charging clients very little beyond the cost of parts. And as we saw in chapter 2, although Heying has been working full-time at the garage for several years, she has not stopped being a social worker—she continues to be attentive to her clients' needs and to do what she can to meet them: "It's so much more than fixing cars. I always say that we're social workers and grief counselors and financial counselors and resource specialists, and that we fix cars on the side. It's complicated, and people are coming to us with lots and lots of needs. Their car is just the presenting problem."

I've shared Cathy Heying's story at some length here because I think she did several things right—or, more to the point, wisely. She started with a worthy goal: helping people with an unmet need for affordable auto repair. She asked for advice from trusted friends and family members about whether the goal was something she was suited to pursue. She deliberated carefully about whether and how she could work toward it—and, after determining that she could, she went ahead and took the first steps. She found a trustworthy mentor with relevant experience, and she asked other knowledgeable people for their advice too. And she pursued the difficult good wholeheartedly—after gaining the necessary knowledge and skills to pursue it successfully. Although those features of practical wisdom can help us make good choices and develop good character, many of us (myself included) typically do not approach our decision making with nearly as much wisdom as Heying did. In the rest of this chapter we will consider some ways in which we might learn to do better.

Prudence, Intelligence, and Ethical Virtue

Do you ever wonder why some people who seem highly intelligent also seem to lack common sense? For example, they may earn top grades in school or succeed in careers requiring a great deal of knowledge or skill—while making a mess of their daily lives. To take just one example, because my university is in the middle of a curriculum review, hundreds of professors from dozens of academic fields are deliberating about the requirements of our undergraduate core curriculum. While everyone agrees in a very general way about the goal—the best possible education for our students—it's much harder to achieve consensus about the best means to that end.

This difficulty revealed itself in a humorous way during our Faculty Senate deliberations about a proposed one-credit course to be required for first-year students. The course would be a weekly seminar, taught by any faculty member from any discipline, on practical topics like time management, sleep habits, substance abuse, and relationships—you might call it a life skills class. At the senate meeting, one of my fellow senators voiced her concern: "I should *take* a class like this. There's no way I'm qualified to *teach* it!" Although my colleague got a predictable laugh from that comment, many of us saw the truth behind it—a PhD in Spanish or philosophy or even a "practical" discipline like economics or engineering is no guarantee of wisdom when it comes to managing our everyday lives. In other words, no amount of formal education could give this faculty member—or any of us—the virtue of practical wisdom or prudence.

So how *do* we develop practical wisdom—the ability "to deliberate well about what is good and ... about what sorts of thing conduce to the good life"?[2] As Aristotle and other philosophers argue, this vitally important virtue develops alongside the other ethical excellences. As we recall, Aristotle divides the excellences of the human psyche into two groups: virtues of thought and virtues of character—or, more simply, intellectual and moral virtues. Virtues of character always lie in a mean or middle ground between excess and deficiency: the mean as determined not by simple arithmetic but by correct practical reasoning. To achieve correct practical reasoning and locate the virtuous mean, we need to develop a virtue of thought: that's practical wisdom or prudence—a "higher-order virtue" which plays a "mediating, overseeing and orchestrating role" in adjudicating among competing options and values.[3]

In addition to being distinct from the ethical virtues whose mean it finds, practical wisdom also differs from theoretical wisdom. That's why it's common for people—like my senate colleague—to have one type of wisdom but lack the other. Theoretical wisdom deals with knowledge of what is unchangeable—of information that is outside of, and independent from, the knower's decision-making ability—for example, mathematical and scientific knowledge.[4] Prudence, on the other hand, is concerned with particular actions—and repeated actions form virtuous or vicious habits. Such actions, unlike the objects of scientific knowledge, can be otherwise than they are—they result from an agent's own choices. And unlike mere comprehension of what is good or bad in such actions, prudence is prescriptive.[5] For example, it doesn't just judge or discover that stealing from your parents is wrong; it also commands, "Don't steal from your parents." Prudence involves deliberating well: using our rational decision-making capacity excellently to achieve "rightness in respect both of the end, the manner, and the time."[6]

In its orientation toward actionable particulars, prudence is also like our desires—in fact, Aristotle describes decisions as "deliberative desires." As he explains, assertion and denial are related to thought in the same way that pursuit and avoidance are related to desire. "Since moral virtue is a state of character concerned with choice, and choice is deliberate desire, therefore both the *reasoning* must be true and the *desire* right, if the *choice* is to be good, and the latter [i.e., desire] must pursue just what [reason] asserts."[7] So unlike theoretical reason, which is aimed simply at truth, the function of practical reasoning—which deliberates about what actions to pursue or avoid—is "truth in agreement with right desire."[8] As he goes on to explain, desire and goal-directed reason jointly cause decision; decision, in turn, causes action. And training our desires to focus on the right objects is the job of the ethical virtues.

To be prudent, one must also be clever—i.e., good at reverse engineering his or her goals by reasoning backward (or downward on our means-end pyramid) from desired ends to the means that will best achieve them. But cleverness isn't enough for prudence: we could be quite clever at finding efficient means to all sorts of bad ends.[9] For example, suppose my goal in life is to become a super-villain. As I correctly reason (based on extensive cartoon-watching "research"), to achieve that end I'll need to do several things: (1) recruit a sidekick, (2) devise a nifty costume, (3) steal an impressive car and some high-tech gadgets (since I lack funds to buy them), and (4) undergo intensive training programs in both gadget usage and the martial arts. My figuring out these means to my bad end, and the further means to each of these means, may be clever—but it certainly isn't wise.

The necessity of good ends as well as of good means to achieve them shows the close connection between practical wisdom and the ethical virtues. The ends in various areas of our lives (e.g., health and social interaction) are discovered and pursued through exercise of virtues like temperance and friendliness. But without prudence, we can't reliably find the right means by which to pursue these ends—so just as practical wisdom depends on the ethical virtues for its ends, those virtues depend on practical wisdom to find the right means for their achievement. So prudence helps us find both the *mean* (right amount) with respect to a virtue and the *means* (necessary steps) to develop and exercise it. But because the virtues of character are habits formed by repeated action, these two "means" don't necessarily differ in practice: the right *means* to developing, say, the virtue of generosity is regularly doing actions that fall within the *mean* between giving too much and too little. At the end of his discussion of practical wisdom, Aristotle summarizes the synergy between wisdom and the virtues of character in this manner: "It is clear, then, from what has been said, that it is not possible to be good in the strict sense without practical wisdom, nor practically wise without moral virtue."[10] Practical wisdom and the ethical virtues are a package: because practical wisdom includes both the motivation to seek good ends and knowledge of the right means to do so, and to do good things for good ends is to be virtuous, a prudent person is a person who exercises not just cleverness but *all* of the virtues.

So to return to the question we asked toward the beginning of this chapter, how do we develop practical wisdom? In part, by developing the other virtues as well. And while (as with all virtues) the specific details will vary with one's life situation, the key seems to be attention to—and reflection on—what our life experience is "trying" to teach us. So in principle, just as was true of the other virtues, anyone capable of reading this book is capable of becoming prudent—but the process will take significant time and effort. It will also take good reasoning; we will look at that part next.

Reasoning Ethically

Because it involves not only knowledge of general principles concerning action but also knowledge of the particular situations and decisions to which the principles apply, prudence is more difficult to develop than are the other intellectual virtues. The type of knowledge it uses comes not just from theoretical learning but from experience of a significant range of relevantly similar situations. So while some young people certainly have more common sense than others, we wouldn't expect a child—even a highly intelligent one who can recite many true principles—to have practical wisdom. In fact, Aristotle thinks, sometimes older people have so much life experience that their practical judgments resemble those of someone with practical wisdom even if they haven't fully developed it either: they may know so many particulars that they almost seem to know the universal principles. So even when it doesn't rise to the level of practical wisdom, there is a lot to be said for the voice of experience.[11]

To perform ethical reasoning (or any practical reasoning) well, then, we need to correctly apply knowledge of two things: a more general principle and a more particular fact of the situation. As we saw in chapter 5, Aristotle describes this kind of reasoning—application of general principles to particular situations and actions—using what he calls a practical syllogism. Like the syllogisms of classical logic (which Aristotle also developed), practical syllogisms show how a more particular fact falls under a more general or universal rule. He starts us out with an easy example:

> General principle: Light meats are digestible and wholesome.
>
> Particular fact: Chicken is a light meat.
>
> Application: Therefore, chicken is digestible and wholesome.

To exercise practical wisdom, we must know both the general principle and the particular fact—and actually apply the one to the other. Although neither alone is sufficient for prudence—and an error in either can lead to poor deliberation about your options—if you had to choose between the general and the particular, it would be better to know just the particular.[12] For example, if we know from our or others' experience that dating our roommate's significant other is a bad idea, we'll avoid that interpersonal misstep even if we don't recognize it as an application of a more general principle like "It's unjust to date someone already in a committed relationship" or "It's unkind to hurt my roommate." (But we *will* likely make that mistake if we know the general principle but somehow fail to recognize that it applies to our situation.)

Practical syllogisms can also be helpful for understanding the reasoning (or, sometimes, lack thereof) behind our intuitions about difficult ethical issues—or even those that seem uncontroversial. When I teach my university's introductory ethics course, for example, sometimes I end the first class with a discussion of the ethical implications of stalking. It makes for an interesting lead-in to the practical syllogism because no one wants to say that it's OK—but when I ask my students why stalking people (with no intent to harm them) is wrong, they find it difficult at first to articulate ethical principles that apply. After a few attempts that don't really get at stalking's ethically problematic features (e.g., "You could go to jail"), though, they usually suggest general ethical principles related to things like fairness, privacy, and respect. From there, we can examine the proposed principles, applying them to other situations and rejecting or refining them when they lead to obviously problematic conclusions.[13]

Despite their simplicity, practical syllogisms can also be surprisingly helpful in ordering our ethical reasoning—or diagnosing problems with it. We can illustrate an impulsive or weak-willed person's reasoning by showing where the practical syllogism went wrong: substituting a suspicious "principle" for the inconvenient but true one, "forgetting" that the true principle applies to our own situation, or getting both the principle and the facts right but then ignoring our well-founded conclusion in favor of instant gratification—it's distressingly easy to ignore what we know when it conflicts with our desires. (Maybe we *really* like our roommate's significant other and feel like we cannot possibly wait to see if their relationship ends on its own.)

That last way we can go wrong with our practical syllogisms—by ignoring them—is where the motivational part of practical wisdom comes into play: a prudent person is more motivated to do the just or kind thing than to pursue short-term benefits. And that brings us back once again to the connection of practical wisdom to the ethical virtues: as Aristotle warned us, if we don't care more about being kind or just than about what we'll find pleasant in the moment, even our most skilled practical reasoning will not be prudence but mere cleverness—what Kristjánsson translates as "cunning capacity" or "unscrupulousness,"[14] and what one of my interviewees referred to as being "tricky." Her description of a family member's means-end reasoning might be a good cautionary tale for all of us:

> He took a tricky road. He engaged in behaviors that drew the line between raising money and making money—and raising money to make money. And as he raises it, he "made" it. Well, you didn't make the money: you raised it, and it's someone else's, and you use it for the purpose for which it's intended. So he engages in point A to point B [reasoning]; if there's some way that he can get over on somebody, then he'll go there.... And he actually had an epiphany once—I got him to start seeing a counselor, and the counselor had him write down all of his transgressions against women—and it took him weeks. And then the counselor had him call them up and apologize, and I watched him get his life back. People that wished he had dropped dead were wishing him well, and then his life just went and bloomed. But then [after a sudden career success that he used to manipulate people again] he started lying and so forth, and I saw his life go away. And I saw him bereaving his own choice.[15]

If we want to live without bereaving our choices, let's use our practical reasoning in service of virtuous ends. To help us do so, we'll turn next to the advice of some contemporary, Aristotle-inspired social scientists.

The Skill—and Will—of Practical Wisdom

According to psychologist Barry Schwartz and political scientist Kenneth Sharpe, there is much news about which to be hopeful. As they argue in their book *Practical Wisdom*—which they describe as an effort to provide an updated and empirically supported version of Aristotle's account of prudence—we are "born to be wise." With enough life experience and motivation, practical wisdom is as attainable as it is desperately needed in contemporary life. In fields ranging from medicine and law to education to banking and beyond, they observe, ordinary human beings are able to develop this moral skill, which is associated with acting well in our everyday personal and social activities. To develop practical wisdom, Schwartz and Sharpe (following Aristotle) note, we need to understand and adopt the *telos* (purpose) internal to those activities. For example, physicians need to value patients' health and understand how to promote it; and we could say similar things about teachers and students' learning, lifeguards and swimmers' safety, and hotel housekeepers and guests' comfort. "So practical wisdom combines will with skill. Skill without will—without the desire to achieve the proper aims of an activity—can lead to ruthless manipulation of others, to serve one's own interests, not theirs. And will without skill can lead to ineffectual fumbling around—the sort of thing we see in people who 'mean well' but leave situations in worse shape than they found them."[16]

To develop the necessary skills for practical wisdom, we ordinary human beings can capitalize on our impressive abilities to categorize things effectively by identifying the most important similarities and differences, to frame situations using relevant data and narratives, and to understand others' thoughts and feelings. And just as we get better with familiarity and practice at categorizing even in "fuzzy" situations (for example, are professional sports really "games"?), through experience and mentoring we can apply these same abilities in ethical contexts—to figure out, for example, whether a particular exaggeration or oversimplification counts as a lie.[17]

As several recent researchers suggest, learning from experience can give us an ethical expertise analogous to that of experts in other domains: expert jazz musicians, engineers, or teachers are guided primarily by highly developed intuitions and higher-order goals—the *teloi* of their activities—rather than by the rote features of the activities' "rules," as are novice practitioners. Similarly, practically wise people often tacitly—even effortlessly—recognize the salient features of the situation, the relevant underlying patterns, and the virtues needed to respond appropriately.

Inspired by the work of philosophers like Aristotle and Mencius, psychologist Darcia Narvaez argues that moral exemplars—ethically virtuous and practically wise people—are those who have developed "ethical expertise" in four domains: ethical sensitivity, ethical judgment, ethical focus, and ethical action. While the first two of these areas primarily address skill, the latter two concentrate mainly on will. Experts in ethical sensitivity quickly see the ethically relevant features of a situation and the roles those features might play—they are especially good at perspective-taking and responsiveness to others. Those with expert ethical judgment have a keen insight into how ethical principles involved should be interpreted and applied; they reason especially well about things like duties and consequences. Ethical focus experts consistently prioritize ethical values and goals highly—and regulate their own desires, emotions, and actions consistently with their ethical commitments. Finally, experts in ethical action are highly motivated to carry out the necessary actions to implement their ethical values and goals—they don't just *know* the good; they *do* the good.[18]

Narvaez goes on to suggest several less-encompassing skills (and "wills") related to each of these four areas. For example, to increase ethical sensitivity, we might work on perspective-taking or controlling our social biases; to refine our ethical judgment, we can reflect more on past processes and outcomes; for greater ethical focus, we could think in terms of respecting others or of our own identity and integrity; and to improve in the area of ethical action, we might practice taking initiative or planning to implement decisions.[19] For those of us who are still working on our practical wisdom, one or more of these skills might be a good place to start: they give us more specific (but still general enough to apply to each of our lives) ways in which to be more attentive to—and learn from—the kinds of life experiences that can grow into wisdom.

Thus far, the account offered by psychologists like Narvaez might sound suspiciously easy: most of us, they suggest, want to act well and make good decisions both in our everyday lives and in our careers—and with that will, most of us, given the right sort of environment in which to practice, will develop the skill of practical wisdom. So why do so many of us fail in this area?

Unfortunately, as Schwartz and Sharpe argue, the environment in which many of us live and work is exactly the *wrong* sort of environment in which to develop prudence. To protect the rest of us from people *without* the will to act well, institutions such as states, workplaces, and professional boards have set in place complex systems of rules and incentives—punishments and rewards. "Rules and incentives may improve the behavior of those who don't care, though they won't make them wiser. But in focusing on the people who don't care—the targets of our rules and incentives—we miss those who do care. We miss those who want to do the right things but lack the practical wisdom to do them well. Rules and incentives won't teach these people the moral skill and will they need. Even worse, rules can kill skill and incentives can kill will."[20] To take just one dramatic example from Schwartz and

Sharpe's book, wildland firefighters' survival rates decreased when the four general safety rules they had been taught were replaced with dozens of more detailed ones—firefighters lost the ability to interpret and improvise.[21]

Despite institutions that discourage practical wisdom, however, with a bit of extra effort and creativity ordinary people like us can still develop it. Sometimes we can work within or around overly scripted guidelines. For example, Schwartz and Sharpe tell stories of "canny outlaw" public school teachers who resist overstandardization by quietly—or, if necessary, not-so-quietly—abandoning the lockstep features of the required curriculum, using it instead as a general guide.[22] To avoid the undue external influences that can compete with our will to do good, we can decline incentives for doing the right thing—or decline to work in professions or companies that focus too heavily on external incentives. Better yet, those of us with leadership roles in our workplaces or community organizations (or the entrepreneurial skills to start new ones) can create organizational cultures that encourage wisdom—by emphasizing the *teloi* of our activities and by providing mentorship while leaving room for problem solving and improvisation. We'll turn next to the story of someone who did exactly that in his nonprofit organization.

Practical Wisdom: Pass It On

The most dramatic example of growth in practical wisdom among my interviewees—and also the most vivid illustration of the wisdom-killing features endemic in contemporary workplace cultures—was that of Mauricio Miller. As we saw in chapter 4, he perceived his work in the public social service sector as ineffective and even counterproductive: the overly rigid rules governing his work didn't leave the room for the discretion and problem solving that is needed for the growth and exercise of practical wisdom. For example, official guidelines required him to direct limited funds and opportunities toward those in the most trouble or "need"—usually meaning, in his experience, those least likely to be helped effectively by his programs. Although he saw and lamented this problem from the beginning of his career, Miller worked for decades in the traditional social service field—in fact, by the end of his career heading a public program, he found himself "helping" the adult children of those whose parents he had (apparently unsuccessfully) attempted to help escape gangs and poverty twenty years earlier. Continuing to use means that our experience tells us will not be successful in accomplishing our ends seems a significant failure to exercise prudence. (In fact, it exemplifies the informal definition of "insanity" often misattributed to Albert Einstein or Mark Twain: doing the same thing over and over and expecting different results.) Not finding a way to change the culture of his large governmental agency, or even the room to be a "canny outlaw" there, Miller played by the rules for decades.

Finally, after a long period of introspection and disillusionment, Miller had a sudden opportunity to try something else—something he thought would be more effective. With a one-month deadline to propose a new approach, he at first tried to think of a way to improve upon existing methods and programs; but, he says, "after two weeks, after a going through all of it and knowing social services for twenty years, I didn't know what I would do."[23] Then he thought about his own mother—a Mexican immigrant with a third-grade education who figured out how to lift her family from poverty—and about successful communities in U.S. history:

> People help their own social network—it's basic to all humanity. For poor communities, whether you were in the Jewish community, the Polish and the Irish, or the African American families in New Orleans, those communities that held together were the ones that made progress because they influenced each other so much.... And so that's when I started researching, well, how did African Americans come to build fifty townships in one state? How did Harlem get built? How were the New Orleans families doing it? How did the Polish do it? You know, how did the Cambodians come to own maybe ninety percent of the donut shops in California, or how did the Vietnamese own the manicure and nail shops? All these people held together and took pride in helping one another: that was the alternative.

Inspired by Malcolm Gladwell's popular social psychology book *The Tipping Point*,[24] as well as by his own background in engineering, Miller came to see community-based successes like the ones he had observed in terms of positive social epidemics. He explains:

Because I was an engineer, I knew chaos theory: everything is chaotic on the lower level, but out of that chaos comes patterns. And the social sector kept trying to make order out of the chaos by interjecting themselves at the family and individual levels, but they were disrupting what might be natural patterns—which was not right from the standpoint of engineering. And then I came to learn diffusion innovation theory or "tipping points": epidemic change happens because there's somebody or a small group that does something right. Other people start to join, and these are the early adopters. If there are enough early adopters, then a larger majority will say okay, and you'll get an epidemic change—you'll get this really fast change, like with Facebook. In technology, they totally know it. That's how social media spread.

With that knowledge and the examples of successful community efforts from the past, Miller knew what kind of program—or, rather, "*un*-program"—he wanted to propose: one that built on the hidden strengths in existing communities and that capitalized on people's tendencies to be influenced by their social networks. So he started the Family Independence Initiative (FII) "to see if proper deviance and epidemics was a more natural process, and if it could be resurrected."

The new organization, whose mission is to "trust and invest in low-income families across the nation so they can work individually and collectively to achieve prosperity,"[25] utilizes elegantly simple methods: families enroll in groups and are paid a small amount to journal each month for two years about their incomes, savings, goals, and progress. The Family Independence Initiative, true to its name, doesn't provide help in the usual sense. It doesn't subsidize housing, food, or anything else; in fact, any staff member caught helping clients is immediately fired. (They have fired four staff to date, Miller told me.) Instead, member families help and inspire others in their group by meeting monthly to share experiences and advice, sharing progress via a social media site, pooling funds for things like lending circles or college scholarships for their children, and even exchanging things like homegrown vegetables. The results have far exceeded those of traditional social service programs: over the two years during which the families journal, they average a 23 percent increase in monthly income, a 60 percent decrease in dependence on government assistance, and over a $5,000 increase in assets.[26]

One of Miller's most dramatic success stories—it was the story that came to mind when I asked him to recount a time when he'd done something wise—was that of a couple he called Jose and Maria, who joined FII with a group of other refugees from El Salvador. At first, like other members of their group, Jose and Maria were sending much of their income back to El Salvador, where their assets and extended family were located. But one day they decided to buy a house in the United States, and they got contributions from their group's other member families to pay the closing fees. Some FII staff who observed the group meeting were understandably concerned; they had reason to believe the couple had been misled by a predatory lender. The staff asked Miller if they could offer advice or sign the couple up for financial training. Miller agreed that the lender was taking advantage of Jose and Maria and that they would probably lose the house—but he insisted that the staff refrain from helping. And that turned out to be a wise decision:

All of a sudden I hear that these friends who loaned the money re-landscaped, retiled, and repainted the house, and the couple refinanced. With the new evaluation, they got the mortgage payment down to about forty percent of their income; and with this group of friends surrounding them, there's no way that they're going to lose this house. So the next thing that happens is that savings start going up for all of the other Salvadorian families—they're not sending their money back to El Salvador anymore. So I asked them, "How come you guys aren't sending money now?" And they said, "If they can buy a house, we can buy a house." Within eighteen months, all of the other families [in the group] owned homes in the United States. So it changed drastically.

Then I heard that it had a broader ripple effect in the refugee community: because of the early adopters, these four or five families owning homes, other families in that community were now buying homes in the United States. So if I had let my staff "save" that family, none of this change would have happened, because everyone would have thought that Jose and Maria screwed up. So my wise decision was not to help.

And there was one more thing that happened: this last December, I was presenting at Stanford and I told the Maria and Jose story; and afterwards a young Salvadorian man came up to me, and he said, "You know, my mother heard this story of your families buying homes. So my family tried buying a house, and it's the equity from that house that got me through Stanford." So that change had a ripple effect in the broader community; and fifteen years later, I see this kid coming out of Stanford because Jose and Maria took a chance and solved their own problems.

What is most interesting to me about Miller's growth in practical wisdom—from repeatedly trying what he observed not to work to developing seemingly radical but historically tested methods—is that his resulting organization seems to focus on encouraging others to develop and exercise their prudence too. And it does so in much the way that Schwartz and Sharpe (and Aristotle) would recommend: it encourages clients to set goals, to determine the best means to reach those ends, and to seek help and advice from those who know them best. Miller is confident—and the evidence thus far seems to show—that any family with the motivation and the social network to join FII can succeed. Toward the end of our interview, when I asked about his ethical approach to life, Miller summed it up like this:

> Everyone has innate talents, and given choices we build on them and share. If eighty percent of this world's population is living in poverty and they're ignored in terms of their talents, we're missing eighty percent of the capacity of the world to be productive, and have new talents, and have new artists—eighty percent of the world has something to contribute, but we won't even move to recognize it. If we did, it would bring us closer together. Imagine how productive we would be if that eighty percent of the world was actually accomplishing whatever their goals and capacities are. So, it makes no sense to me that we would ignore what all of these people have that they can share with society.

Perhaps to an even greater degree, it makes no sense for those of us who *have* the necessary opportunities and resources to fail to develop our own abilities—particularly, the practical wisdom that enables the rest of our virtues and activities to flourish.

As we have seen in this chapter, the practical wisdom needed for authentic ethical excellence requires time and effort: before we can develop the ethical expertise to make wise decisions intuitively, we will need to accumulate and reflect upon a significant range of life experiences and attentively apply their lessons to new situations. We will have to develop our reasoning abilities—and our motivation—to understand general ethical principles and apply them correctly to particular circumstances. And when faced with especially difficult decisions, we will need to seek advice from those wiser than ourselves. (Fortunately, much as we can recognize athletes without being athletic ourselves, we will usually know an especially wise person when we find one.) But what if even our wise mentors are stumped? Or what if they disagree with each other? In the final chapter of this book, we'll consider what to do when, despite our best efforts, we don't know what to do.

Chapter 20

WHEN ALL ELSE FAILS...

IF YOU ARE OBSERVANT (and if you read chapter 19 of this book), you may have noticed that Cathy Heying and Mauricio Miller—despite both having social service backgrounds and being among my favorite exemplars of practical wisdom—appear to disagree fundamentally regarding the best approach to alleviating poverty. Heying is all about helping: she left her dream job in social work and advocacy for one that directly meets a concrete need. And now, while providing low-cost car repair for low-income individuals and families, she continues to advocate for more help at the governmental level in areas like housing and even cash benefits. Miller, by contrast, was disillusioned with his social service work, which he saw as interfering with a more effective natural process of communities' lifting themselves out of poverty. In his organization, staff are immediately fired if they're caught giving direct aid to clients.

How should we make sense of the diverging views and advice, and sometimes no concrete advice at all, from seemingly wise and virtuous people—whether the "sages" are community exemplars like Heying and Miller, philosophers like Confucius and Plato, or our own trusted mentors and advisors?

First, consider this: if we think about it when we're not desperate for advice, it might be a relief to know that it's possible to be a wise and good person without having all of the answers to difficult ethical questions. Human life can be complicated, even for the best of us. So if we don't always have the answers either, we need not conclude that all of our ethical progress to date must have been an illusion.

Still, however, such considerations are less comforting when we are faced with a difficult decision. We'll end this book by considering what to do when we don't know what to do—when our own practical wisdom fails us and even our sages give us insufficient or conflicting guidance.

When Sages Disagree: Harmonize, Compromise, or Neutralize?

Suppose you have a difficult decision to make. Being humble enough to realize you need advice, you go to your go-to sources; but they seem to disagree entirely about what you should do. Mom will never speak to you again if you do not marry your suitor, but Dad won't speak to you if you do;[1] or your significant other thinks you should accept a job in his home town but your best friend advises you to go to graduate school abroad. Or Plato and Aristotle say punishing your children's misbehavior will cure the injustice (disorder) in their psyche and start to habituate them to behave themselves, but Confucius and Mencius say punishing your kids will just make them evasive and distant.[2]

If your sources really are good and trustworthy (and about equally so), a first step when they disagree is to figure out exactly what they disagree about—and what they *don't* disagree about—and why. Once you fully understand the reasoning behind their advice, you may find that (1) their disagreement is actually not very substantial, and their advice can be harmonized; or (2) although their disagreement is substantial, their advice contains some important common threads that can be honored; or (3) one piece of advice is significantly better than the other.

In the first case, when there really is no substantial disagreement, initially conflicting (or seemingly conflicting) advice can be harmonized. In an ideal world, for example, when you dig a bit deeper you find out that your significant other just wants to be near you and would be just as happy moving abroad too while you're in grad school—making your new university's town his temporary home town. Or maybe the Socratics and the Confucians agree that some kinds of punishments are ethical and effective while others are not.

In a second-best world, although your go-to sources of advice really do have significant disagreements, they also share some more fundamental values—and if so, there may be a reasonable compromise position that each advisor would find acceptable. For example, maybe your parents agree that you should get married and disagree about the merits of this particular suitor; but both would be happy enough to continue speaking to you if you married an alternate suitor whom you prefer—perhaps the one who just offered to move abroad with you. And surely the Socratics and Confucians agree that you should encourage your children to be virtuous and not to misbehave—are there methods other than punishment that could accomplish these ends?

If the world (or at least the part of your world needing good advice) is neither ideal nor second-best, you may still find a clear path forward thanks to an observation we made above: Not even the wisest sage has perfect judgment in all circumstances. When you clarify your advisors' diverging positions, you may find that one of them seems simply to be mistaken—perhaps his advice is inconsistent in itself or with his principles, as we saw in chapter 14 with some of the Confucians' more extreme advice about honoring our parents' wishes. Or maybe she's now made it clear that she really doesn't understand you or the situation well enough to make a reliable judgment. If you have a good reason (not a rationalization!—see chapter 5) to disregard a particular piece of advice, you should do so. And that will make your decision much easier.

Of course, it may turn out that you are not in any of those positions—not even the third-best one. The combined wisdom of your favorite sages may leave you without a clear direction—either because of inter-sage disagreements you cannot resolve or because they decline to give you concrete advice at all. I don't have all of the answers either. But thanks to the bigger-picture lessons we can take from the sources of wisdom we have seen in this book, when not even our wise mentors' guidance can point us down a well-lit path, we still have several tools at our disposal to help us sort things out in good faith.

Work-Arounds for the Not-Yet-Wise

Because (despite being a professional philosopher or "lover of wisdom") I am still among those working on the virtue of prudence, sometimes I find that I just don't have enough of it to be sure what to do in a particular situation—especially when the facts are not entirely clear. (For example, frequently there are multiple versions of the "facts" surrounding sibling squabbles.) As with so many decisions, what we should do when we reach the limits of our wisdom depends on the specifics of the situation—for example, the risks and potential benefits involved and how much time we can reasonably spend deliberating. Once in a while, we even find ourselves needing to make an important decision right away—with no time even to ask for the advice that we really seem to need. Let's start with a few work-arounds for situations requiring a quick decision and more wisdom than we possess.

Quick Advice

When time to deliberate is short, our best bet might be to return to Aristotle's advice from the first chapter of this book: beware of instant gratification and avoid the worse extreme. If we need to make an immediate decision ("Do you want the last piece of cheesecake?") and did not plan ahead, we can give ourselves this quick quiz: How will I feel about this decision tomorrow? Although it's not a fully rationalization-proof quiz ("I'll feel great about eating the cheesecake—that will save my spouse from temptation!"), it can at least prompt us to consider whether instant gratification is the only point in favor of one of our options.

Aristotle's other main piece of advice for finding the mean of virtue—first head toward the less-bad extreme—can also make for a quick quiz of sorts: We can ask, for example, "Does this option err on the side of cowardice or rashness? Toward prodigality or stinginess?" In fact, I had to do that sort of thing just this afternoon: when considering whether to spend a little more money on a long-term houseguest, I nearly said "no" automatically—having limited financial means, I generally try to slow money's outflow. But since I know myself to have a natural tendency toward stinginess, I am not confident in my automatic assessments of where the mean lies. So I had to ask myself whether my knee-jerk "no" decision would err on the side of stinginess or prodigality—and it clearly would tend toward stinginess. That's not to say that I should automatically say "yes" either, of course—there can be good reasons to decline. But lacking a compelling reason, I tried a second question—"Would he get at least twenty dollars' worth of use and enjoyment out of this item?"—and since he clearly would, buying it seemed the better thing to do both for my guest and for my character.

Finally, when short on time for deliberation, we should do a quick risk assessment, making sure we protect the people and values in most need of protection. Does one of the options—like letting the nine-year-old "babysit" himself—carry a small but significant risk of absolute disaster? Should the squabbling siblings, regardless of which one is most in the wrong, be sent to separate rooms to calm down? Is there any way you can protect your girlfriend's feelings without lying about how she looks in those pants? Just as Aristotle advises us to avoid the worse vice, we can do our best to avoid worst-case outcomes—the ones worst for our relationships, our character, and anything else we highly (and reasonably) value.

Slower Advice

When we have more time to make a decision—which is usually true if we had time to ask people for advice—there are several additional ethical analysis tools we can use. As we saw in chapter 19, many of the skills of practical wisdom can be used effectively even by non-experts: We can be more attentive to the likely consequences of various actions we could take, for example, and we can ask ourselves whether the situation calls for an emphasis on justice or on mercy. We can try to take the perspectives of the other people involved. And we can focus on honoring our core priorities and values as well as the *teloi* (purposes) of our activities. If we are still stuck after following that general advice, there are a couple more things we can try.

First, following philosopher Anthony Weston,[3] we can try a more creative approach—especially when we are stuck in what he calls "dilemma thinking": assuming that there are only two options and one "side" must be the sole winner. As I suggested we try with disagreeing advisors, even when deliberating alone we can approach an apparent dilemma by asking what assumptions and values the two or more options share—and whether there is another option that honors those while at least partly dissolving or bypassing the area of disagreement. Weston gives several more good ideas—my students love practicing them—for generating creative solutions to apparent dilemmas; in the interest of space, I'll just describe one of my favorites: "invite exotic associations." The idea is to generate a word or image randomly (by opening a dictionary, for example, or turning on the radio or TV for two seconds), pair it with your dilemma, and then free-associate from there. The more random the word or image, the better for purposes of getting you out of your mental rut—and, like many of Weston's creative suggestions, it really does work surprisingly well. (He gives a fun example of using the image of his houseplants to brainstorm several creative solutions to the problem of litter.)

When we have ample time to deliberate, we can also benefit from the good advice of Chip Heath and Dan Heath in their book *Decisive: How to Make Better Choices in Life and Work*. Among several other ideas, the Heath brothers suggest that if we don't know what to do, we may want to "multitrack"—pursue two or more possibilities. While multitracking is not always an option (you can't both marry and not marry your suitor, for example), it can work well in a wide range of situations. For example, if you are not sure whether you want to write your U.S. History term paper on the Civil War or the War on Drugs (and if it's still early enough in the term), take a few hours to write an outline of each. Another helpful suggestion from the Heaths involves fact-checking: we should ask ourselves what would have to be true for each potential solution or proposal to be the best one—and then do our best to find out whether any of those sets of facts *is* true. And, when feasible, we might test an option on a small scale.[4] College students actually try this option frequently when considering possible majors: If you think you might want to major in English literature, try taking a literature class and see how it goes. Similarly, if you're not sure whether to marry that suitor, first try dating him exclusively for a while.

Final Advice: Just Keep Trying

In some cases, even if we try all of the advice in this chapter (or as much of it as we have time to try), we still won't be sure what to do. As I have already admitted, that happens to me sometimes—and I do take a bit of comfort from knowing that even the exemplary people I interviewed don't always know exactly what to do either. As we saw in chapter 4, it took Mauricio Miller twenty years to change his approach to poverty—even though he thought from the beginning that the traditional system of public aid was counterproductive, he wasn't sure what would be a better alternative. And when Don Schoendorfer, whose story we saw in chapter 2, first tried to serve his fellow human beings, he chose activities that were a terrible fit for his personality and skill set: he describes this realization as being like a message from God saying "Don, what are you doing? ... You're terrible at this stuff. Why don't you use your tools that I gave you?"[5] So, like Miller, he tried something else—something he thought would work better. Sometimes that's what we need to do too: just keep trying. If what we tried isn't working, we need to adjust to the situation as it now is (perhaps even a bit worse than when we began), choose a course of action that we think will improve things, and do our best going forward. The good news is that, even if we aren't as successful with our revised attempts as Schoendorfer and Miller (eventually) were, reflecting upon and learning from our experiences will help us grow in practical wisdom—and probably in patience!

Sometimes the problem isn't so much that we don't *know* what we should do but that we don't *want* to do what we should do—and not necessarily for shallow or selfish reasons. Because we live in a flawed world with other flawed human beings, and because some goods are incompatible with others, upholding our most important values occasionally will require us to make non-trivial sacrifices: the right choice isn't necessarily the easy choice. In that case, the thing to do is take a deep breath and forge ahead with what we know is right—while bracing ourselves for its downside. For example, Rainbow Days founder Cathey Brown, whose story we saw in chapter 13, faced this sort of struggle when, to remain eligible for state grants, she was required to produce evidence—using a controlled study—that her alcohol- and drug-prevention programs were effective. The problem, from Brown's perspective, was the *controlled* aspect of the requirement: it meant that, in order to show how helpful her program was, she could *not* help a significant number of eligible children—instead, she would have to put them on a wait-list for a year so that she could show their outcomes were significantly worse than those of the kids her program admitted. For the sake of Rainbow Days' ability to help future children avoid alcoholism and drug abuse, Brown went ahead with the controlled study; but knowing that she had a good reason certainly did not make it easy to turn away children she could be helping already.

Similarly, Cathy Heying shared this reflection based on helpful advice she had once given a friend and later applied to her own life:

When we're the ones who pushed the ball, and it's going in the right direction, and it's going at the right speed, and we set it in motion, we somehow mistakenly believe that therefore it's all going to be easy because it's right. But that doesn't mean that it's always going to go smoothly, it's going to be painless, or it's going to be without fear, without angst. I think we often don't let ourselves feel the fear, or we get down on ourselves because it's like, "I did this; I have no one else to blame but myself." But just because it's a change we sought, doesn't mean it's not going to have its challenges or be hard or be lonely. And that doesn't mean that it's the wrong thing to do, and it doesn't mean I don't get to feel those feelings. Both of those things are true: You chose it, you made it happen; and it's hard, it's lonely, it's fearful—and they can stand true next to each other in equal weights at the same time. And, we shouldn't spend all of our energy denying that they're both true—the sooner we can just live with that tension, the better it'll be.

With the help of the philosophers, psychologists, and exemplars in this book, as well as our own mentors and sages, may we all develop both the wisdom to identify the ethical path forward in our lives and, even when it's difficult, the strength to follow it.

NOTES

Introduction

1. At least, it risks being useless for immediate tasks other than cultivating our minds. Although I'm a big fan of intellectual development for its own sake, I realize many people—including some of my students—don't share my enthusiasm.

2. I'll use the term "Socratic philosophers" to refer to classical Greek and Roman philosophers—including Plato, Aristotle, and the Stoics—who can trace their philosophical heritage to Socrates. The label, though not precise, is more informative than "Western" and roughly parallels "Confucian."

3. I do not mean to suggest, of course, that all—or even most—virtuous people become well known for their ethical excellence: no doubt many of us can point to unsung ethical heroes among our friends and relatives. However, as a reasonably objective method of finding people who are likely virtuous and have interesting life stories, seeking out winners of national awards for apparently virtuous behavior worked quite well.

4. I used the McAdams life story interview questions: Dan P. McAdams, *The Life Story Interview* (Foley Center for the Study of Lives, Northwestern University, 2008).

Chapter 1

1. For a helpful overview of the psychological literature on the (mostly negative) effect of extrinsic rewards on intrinsic motivation, see Christopher Peterson and Martin Seligman, *Character Strengths and Virtues: A Handbook and Classification* (Oxford: Oxford University Press, 2004), 241–44; and Robert Eisenberger and Michael Selbst, "Does Reward Increase or Decrease Creativity?," *Journal of Personality and Social Psychology* 66, no. 6 (1994): 1116–27.

2. Philosopher Alasdair MacIntyre coined the term "goods internal to practices" in *After Virtue*, 2nd ed. (Notre Dame, Ind.: University of Notre Dame Press, 1984). A practice is "any coherent and complex form of socially established cooperative human activity through

which goods internal to that form of activity are realized in the course of trying to achieve those standards of excellence which are appropriate to, and partially definitive of, that form of activity, with the result that human powers to achieve excellence, and human conceptions of the ends and goods involved, are systematically extended" (*After Virtue*, 187).

3. Interestingly, MacIntyre, strongly influenced by Aristotle, goes on to define "virtue" in terms of practices: "A virtue is an acquired human quality the possession and exercise of which tends to enable us to achieve those goods which are internal to practices and the lack of which effectively prevents us from achieving any such goods" (*After Virtue*, 191). And psychologists have recently noticed that virtues and related qualities tend to be related to at least certain aspects of a good human life; see, for instance, Jane Gillham et al., "Character Strengths Predict Subjective Well-Being During Adolescence," *The Journal of Positive Psychology* 6, no. 1 (2011): 31–44; and Willibald Ruch, A. Huber, Ursula Beermann, and Rene T. Proyer, "Character Strengths as Predictors of the 'Good Life' in Austria, Germany and Switzerland," in *Studies and Researches in Social Sciences*, vol. 16, ed. W. Ruch (Cluj-Napoca, Romania: Argonaut Press, 2007), 123–31.

4. Judy Berry, life story interview, June 24, 2016.

5. Gloria Lewis, life story interview, December 26, 2016.

6. Aristotle, *Nicomachean Ethics*, trans. W. D. Ross (Boston: Internet Classics Archive, 1994–2000), 1.1, 1094a8–10 http://classics.mit.edu/Aristotle/nicomachaen.html.

7. *Summa Theologica*, trans. Fathers of the English Dominican Province, 1920, www.newadvent.org/summa, I.4.

8. Aristotle, *Nicomachean Ethics*, 1.2, 1094a25–27.

9. Aristotle, *Nicomachean Ethics*, 1.7, 1097a33–b7.

10. Although I'll focus on Aristotle's own argument for now, the fact that philosophers like the Confucians arrived at similar answers to this and many other questions despite their cultural difference, as we'll see throughout the book, also seems to lend some support to Aristotle's conclusion. For a helpful analysis of the similarities between Aristotle and Confucian philosopher Mencius on this point in particular, see Benjamin Huff, "Eudaimonism in the *Mencius*: Fulfilling the Heart," *Dao: A Journal of Comparative Philosophy* 14, no. 3 (2015): 403–31.

11. These phrases are alternative translations of the same words in the original Greek text and should be interpreted synonymously. Since the Greek *arête*, typically translated "virtue," denotes excellence more generally, in my example above, we could describe a good pen as "virtuous" insofar as it has pen-relevant excellences, such as having well-flowing ink or being of a suitable size, shape, and weight for comfortable writing. Similarly, the Greek *ethika*, frequently translated "ethical" or "moral," refers to our dispositions or character quite broadly.

12. Aristotle, *Nicomachean Ethics*, 1.7, 1098a24–26. I've modified the translation slightly, using the original "psyche"—the Greek root of "psychology"—rather than the ambiguous English word "soul."

13. Viktor Frankl, "Postscript 1984: The Case for a Tragic Optimism," in *Man's Search for Meaning* (Boston: Beacon Press, 2006), 140.

14. Frankl, "Postscript 1984," in *Man's Search for Meaning*, 139–43.

15. Viktor Frankl, "Logotherapy in a Nutshell," in *Man's Search for Meaning*, 97–134, at 113.

16. A recent Gallup poll found that only 13 percent of workers worldwide are engaged in their jobs—that is, enjoying a "state of strong employee involvement, commitment and enthusiasm." See Annamarie Mann and Jim Harter, "The Worldwide Employee Engagement Crisis," *Gallup Business Journal*, January 7, 2016. While Gallup offers employers services to improve employee engagement, perhaps less-engaged (and career-mobile) employees would also do well to consider whether they are in the right line of work.

17. As Janet Smith argues, this principle applies even more generally to our activities, to other living beings, and even to artifacts. For example, if I put water in my car's engine and motor oil on my tomato plants, neither the car nor the plants will flourish—they will not be able to perform their functions. See Smith, "Natural Law and Sexual Ethics," in *Common Truths: New Perspectives on Natural Law*, ed. Edward B. McLean (Wilmington, Del.: ISI Books, 2000), 193–215.

18. Aristotle, *Nicomachean Ethics*, 1.13, 1102a4–5.

19. Aristotle, *Nicomachean Ethics*, 1.7, 1097b2.

20. The appetitive part of the human psyche in Aristotle's ethics is roughly equivalent to the combination of the spirited and desirous parts in Plato's; similarly, Xunzi categorizes emotions and desires together under the name of *qing*, or disposition. As these authors agree, each part of the psyche, and the psyche as a whole, flourishes only when we allow reason to take the lead.

21. Aristotle, *Nicomachean Ethics*, 2.1, 1103a25.

22. Aristotle, *Nicomachean Ethics*, 2.2, 1104a20–29. Confucians also discuss the means of various virtues and make suggestions for achieving them; for example, Xunzi says: "If you are too low-minded, lethargic, and greedy, lift yourself up with high ambitions.... If you are indolent and heedless, awaken yourself with the thought of imminent disaster." Xunzi, "Improving Yourself," in *Xunzi: Basic Writings*, trans. Burton Watson (New York: Columbia University Press, 2003), 25–33, at 27.

23. Xunzi, "Encouraging Learning," in *Xunzi: Basic Writings*, trans. Burton Watson (New York: Columbia University Press, 2003), 15–23, at 23. In ancient China it was believed that there were five colors (blue, red, black, white, and yellow), five flavors (salty, bitter, sour, pungent, sweet), and five musical notes (la, sol, mi, re, do). Each of these related to a specific element of the material world (water, fire, wood, metal, earth).

24. Aristotle, *Nicomachean Ethics*, 2.9, 1109a22–30.

25. Aristotle, *Nicomachean Ethics*, 2.9, 1109b19.

26. Mengzi [Mencius], *Mengzi*, trans. Bryan Van Norden (Indianapolis, Ind.: Hackett, 2008), 2A2.

27. Winnicott's theory regarding the good-enough mother can be found in his *Playing and Reality*, reprint ed. (New York: Basic Books, 1971).

28. Aristotle, *Nicomachean Ethics*, 2.9, 1109b2.

29. Aristotle, *Nicomachean Ethics*, 2.9, 1109b5–7. Although Aristotle's view of human nature doesn't seem to be nearly as pessimistic as Xunzi's, as we'll see later in this book, Aristotle does use the very same analogy that Xunzi used—warped wood—to explain moral development: If we have bad tendencies, both argue, we should "bend" ourselves in the opposite direction in the hope of straightening out.

Chapter 2

1. Don Schoendorfer, life story interview, January 13, 2017. All quotes from Schoendorfer are taken from this interview.

2. Mengzi [Mencius], *Mengzi*, trans. Bryan W. Van Norden (Indianapolis, Ind.: Hackett, 2008), 1A7. I've omitted the king's answer ("No") to Mencius's first question.

3. In fact, as scholars note, Mencius's references to "an innocent going to the execution ground" are telling: apparently such a scenario was far from unheard-of under this king's rule.

4. *Mengzi*, 2A6.

5. *Mengzi*, 6A6.

6. *Mengzi*, 2A2.

7. *Mengzi*, 6A8.

8. *Mengzi*, 6A9.

9. Xunzi, "Man's Nature is Evil," in *Xunzi: Basic Writings*, trans. Burton Watson (New York: Columbia University Press, 2003), 161–74, at 161.

10. Xunzi, "Man's Nature is Evil," in *Basic Writings*, 170.

11. Xunzi, "Man's Nature is Evil," in *Basic Writings*, 171.

12. Augustine, *Confessions*, trans. H. Chadwick (Oxford: Oxford World Classics, 2009), bk. 1. Although Augustine acknowledges that he doesn't remember his own infancy, he confesses that he (like all babies) was guilty of the "sin" of crying until he got what he wanted.

13. See, for example, J. Kiley Hamlin and Karen Wynn, "Young Infants Prefer Prosocial to Antisocial Others," *Cognitive Development* 26 (2011): 30–39; also Hamlin and Wynn, "Who Knows What's Good to Eat? Infants Fail to Match the Food Preferences of Antisocial Others," *Cognitive Development* 27, no. 3 (2012): 227–39.

14. See Amrisha Vaish, Manuela Missana, and Michael Tomasello, "Three-Year-Old Children Intervene in Third-Party Moral Transgressions," *The British Journal of Developmental Psychology* 29, no. 1 (2011): 124–30.

15. See Neha Mahajan and Karen Wynn, "Origins of 'Us' versus 'Them': Prelinguistic Infants Prefer Similar Others," *Cognition* 124 (2012): 227–33.

16. See, for example, Koleen McCrink, Paul Bloom, and Laurie Santos, "Children's and Adult's Judgments of Equitable Resource Distributions," *Developmental Science* 13, no. 1 (2010): 37–45. The good news is that older children and adults come to value things like equity and good intentions—and that even younger children seem to value such things when they don't stand to lose much; cf. J. Kiley Hamlin, "Failed Attempts to Help and Harm:

Intention versus Outcome in Preverbal Infants' Social Evaluations," *Cognition* 128, no. 3 (2013): 451–74.

17. Cathy Heying, life story interview, March 27, 2017. All quotes from Heying are taken from this interview.

18. Marcus Tullius Cicero, *De Officiis* [On duties], In *The Ethical Writings of Cicero*, trans. Andrew P. Peabody (Boston: Little, Brown, & Company, 1887), 1.28, http://oll.libertyfund .org/titles/cicero-on-moral-duties-de-officiis.

19. Cicero, *De Officiis*, 1.30–31. Aristotle says something similar in *Nicomachean Ethics* 6.13; and medieval Aristotelian philosopher Thomas Aquinas expresses a similar view with a bit more precision in the *Summa Theologica*, I-II.63.1.

20. Cicero, *De Officiis*, 1.31.

21. As of this writing, the survey can be found at www.viacharacter.org; you'll need to create an account (also free) to take the survey. (Although the researchers don't charge money for their service, they do receive some benefit from the use of survey data for their ongoing studies. But they also benefit other researchers by providing them with free access to their survey and data.)

22. Perhaps in an effort to remain positive, the VIA survey does not explicitly identify any weaknesses. Instead, it scores one's twenty-four "strengths" in descending order—so one's weakest area is identified as her "24th strength." For some doubts regarding Peterson and Seligman's suggestion that we can compensate for character weaknesses by developing our strengths, see Kristján Kristjánsson, *Virtues and Vices in Positive Psychology: A Philosophical Critique* (Cambridge: Cambridge University Press, 2013), chap. 7.

23. For a handy table listing their classification of virtues and strengths, see Christopher Peterson and Martin Seligman, *Character Strengths and Virtues: A Handbook and Classification* (New York: Oxford University Press, 2004), 29–30. Compare the second part of Thomas Aquinas's *Summa Theologica*, which categorizes the ethical domain according to seven main virtues (quite similar to the six mentioned by Peterson and Seligman). Under each of these is categorized other actions and traits that are part of, or similar to, the main virtue—some of these related qualities are also themselves ethical virtues. (Peterson and Seligman mention having included Aquinas among the philosophers whose texts they consulted; although they don't emphasize how similar their classification scheme is to his, they do note that their classification is highly compatible with the cardinal and Christian virtues.)

24. Peterson and Seligman, *Character Strengths and Virtues*, 16–28.

25. Jane Gillham et al., "Character Strengths Predict Subjective Well-Being During Adolescence," *The Journal of Positive Psychology* 6, no. 1 (2011): 31–44.

26. Nansook Park, Christopher Peterson, and Martin E. P. Seligman, "Strengths of Character and Well-Being," Journal of Social & Clinical Psychology 23 (2004): 603–19.

27. For more research on this topic, see http://www.viacharacter.org/www/Research/ Character-Strengths-and-Life-Satisfaction.

28. As we'll see later in this book, these strategies also fit well with Mencius's theory of virtue development via extension.

29. Daphna Oyserman and Leah James, "Possible Identities," in *Handbook of Identity Theory and Research*, ed. S. J. Schwartz et al. (Dordrecht, Netherlands: Springer, 2011), 117–45, at 119.

30. Oyserman and James, "Possible Identities," 135–39.

31. See, for example, Rene T. Proyer, Willibald Ruch, and Claudia Buschor, "Testing Strengths-Based Interventions: A Preliminary Study of the Effectiveness of a Program Targeting Curiosity, Gratitude, Hope, Humor, and Zest for Enhancing Life Satisfaction," *Journal of Happiness Studies* 14 (2013): 275–92; Jo Ann Mitchell, Rosanna Stanimirovic, Britt Klein, and Dianne Vella-Brodrick, "A Randomized Controlled Trial of a Self-Guided Internet Intervention Promoting Well-Being," *Computers in Human Behavior* (2009), doi:10.1016/j.chb.2009.02.003; and Martin Seligman, Tracy Steen, Nansook Park, and Christopher Peterson, "Positive Psychology Progress: Empirical Validation of Interventions," *American Psychologist* (2005), doi:10.0137/0003–099X.60.5.410.

Chapter 3

1. Estella Mims Pyfrom, life story interview, January 11, 2017. All quotes from Pyfrom are taken from this interview.

2. See Kelly McGonigal, *The Willpower Instinct: How Self-Control Works, Why It Matters, and What You Can Do to Get More of It* (New York: Penguin, 2012), 3–5.

3. Xunzi, "Dispelling Obsession," in *Xunzi: Basic Writings*, trans. Burton Watson (New York: Columbia University Press, 2003), 125–42, at 133. As the use of the word "volition" indicates, it can be difficult to translate ancient passages like this one without using explicitly will-related language ("volition" being derived from the Latin *"voluntas,"* or "will"). Hutton translates this sentence more neutrally as follows: *"it* [the mind] restrains itself, *it* employs itself; *it* lets itself go, *it* takes itself in hand; *it* makes itself proceed, *it* makes itself stop." Xunzi, *Xunzi: The Complete Text*, trans. Eric L. Hutton (Princeton, N.J.: Princeton University Press, 2014), 229. As we'll soon see, although Aristotle doesn't possess a developed notion of the will either, his work is (quite reasonably) translated as discussing "voluntariness"—another will-related term.

4. See Aaron Stalnaker, *Overcoming Our Evil: Human Nature and Spiritual Exercises in Xunzi and Augustine* (Washington, D.C.: Georgetown University Press, 2006), chap. 5.

5. See Aristotle, *Nicomachean Ethics*, trans. W. D. Ross (Boston: Internet Classics Archive, 1994–2000), 3.1.

6. John Searle, *Minds, Brains, and Science* (Cambridge, Mass.: Harvard University Press, 1984), 95.

7. Here, I am adapting Aristotle's own examples from *Nicomachean Ethics* 3.1. As he later notes, strictly speaking, these latter examples are of *non*voluntariness; they're also *in*voluntary if my going to class is *against* my will. (So if I really wanted to go to class and was pleasantly surprised to find myself carried there by the wind, my going there through compulsion would be nonvoluntary but not involuntary.)

8. See Thomas Aquinas, *Summa Theologica*, trans. the Fathers of the English Dominican Province, www.newadvent.org/summa, I-II.6.8. Aquinas calls ignorance of this sort "consequent ignorance" because it is a consequence of a voluntary omission. While this ignorance is itself voluntary, the actions issuing from it, though not involuntary (i.e., against the agent's will), are not voluntary (i.e., from her will) either—they are nonvoluntary.

9. Aristotle, *Nicomachean Ethics*, 3.1, 1110b32–1111a3, emphasis mine.

10. Aristotle, *Nicomachean Ethics*, 3.1, 1111a13–14. As Aristotle notes, no sane person can be ignorant of all of these particulars at once—or even of some particular ones such as who he is, although he can be ignorant of who *else* is involved in his action. For instance, in medieval writings a popular example of this sort was involuntary commission of adultery by someone who—through no fault of his own—mistakenly believed his partner to be his wife. As it turns out, however, not all ignorance of relevant circumstances causes involuntariness—even excluding deliberate and negligent ignorance. Occasionally we end up doing through ignorance what we might have done anyway: "The man who has done something owing to ignorance, and feels not the least vexation at his action, has not acted voluntarily, since he did not know what he was doing, nor yet involuntarily, since he is not pained" (*Nicomachean Ethics*, 1110b19–21). So to adapt that medieval example, suppose the man in question has been looking for an opportunity to commit adultery and mistakenly believes himself to be "settling" for his own wife. Aquinas terms this sort of ignorance "concomitant ignorance"—like "consequent" or negligent ignorance, it causes nonvoluntariness but not involuntariness (see *Summa Theologica*, I-II.6.8).

11. Aristotle, *Nicomachean Ethics*, 3.5, 1114b33–1115a1.

12. Since "willpower" and "strength of will" are so much more familiar to us than is "continence," I'll use them throughout.

13. Aristotle, *Nicomachean Ethics*, 7.4.

14. See Wilhelm Hofmann, Kathleen Vohs, and Roy F. Baumeister, "What People Desire, Feel Conflicted About, and Try to Resist in Everyday Life," *Psychological Science* 23, no. 6 (2012), 582–88.

15. Roy F. Baumeister and John Tierney, *Willpower: Rediscovering the Greatest Human Strength* (New York: Penguin, 2011), 36–37.

16. See Baumeister and Tierney, *Willpower*, chap. 10. For a more optimistic view regarding the limits of our willpower, see Walter Mischel, *The Marshmallow Test: Mastering Self-Control* (New York: Little, Brown, & Company, 2014), 216–20. See also McGonigal, *The Willpower Instinct*, chap. 3.

17. Actually, in *Nicomachean Ethics* 7.7, Aristotle adds to incontinence another related phenomenon: "softness," which involves abandoning our best judgment to escape pain rather than to pursue pleasure. Like incontinence, softness can come in both impetuous and weak varieties; so we actually have four possible states among those who act against their best judgment: impetuous incontinence, weak incontinence, impetuous softness, and weak softness. To avoid unnecessary complexity, though, I will (as Aristotle generally does) treat softness as a type of incontinence—broadly defined as defeat of reason by a strong appetite.

18. Aristotle, *Nicomachean Ethics*, 7.7, 1150b21–24.

19. McGonigal, *The Willpower Instinct*, 40.

20. I borrow the terms "actual knowledge" and "habitual knowledge" from John Locke; see *Essay Concerning Human Understanding* 4.1.8–9. Aristotle simply describes the two states as "using" and "not using" the knowledge; see *Nicomachean Ethics*, 7.3.

21. See Aristotle, *Nicomachean Ethics*, 7.3, 7, 10.

22. Lisa Nigro, life story interview, January 12, 2017.

23. As we'll see again later, although in theory the first premise could state that all acts of certain kind are to be done (rather than avoided), cases of act-types that are *always* to be done are few and general—e.g., "All acts that are the best choice under the circumstances are to be done." But there are plenty of more specific universal "don'ts."

24. Baumeister and Tierney, *Willpower*, 129–33; see also M. Muraven, R. F. Baumeister, and D. M. Tice, "Longitudinal Improvement of Self-Regulation through Practice: Building Self-Control through Repeated Exercise," *Journal of Social Psychology* 139 (1999): 446–57. While both writing down what they eat and using good posture are examples of perseverance rather than self-denial, as I note later in this section, the former might also *encourage* self-denial if it motivates someone not to eat things she wants to avoid recording.

25. See McGonigal, *The Willpower Instinct*, chaps. 1–2.

26. Baumeister and Tierney, *Willpower*, 227–31.

27. See Baumeister and Tierney, *Willpower*, chap. 4.

28. See Baumeister and Tierney, *Willpower*, 171–78.

29. Baumeister and Tierney, *Willpower*, 234–37; see also Nicole Mead and Vanessa Patrick, "In Praise of Putting Things Off: Postponing Consumption Pleasures Facilitates Self-Control," in *Advances in Consumer Research*, vol. 39, ed. Rohini Ahluwalia, Tanya L. Chartrand, and Rebecca K. Ratner (Duluth, Minn.: Association for Consumer Research, 2011), 30–31.

30. Baumeister and Tierney, *Willpower*, 159–66; see also K. Fujita, Y. Trope, N. Liberman, and M. Levin-Sagi, "Construal Levels and Self-Control," *Journal of Personality and Social Psychology* 90 (2006): 351–67.

31. Baumeister and Tierney, *Willpower*, 151.

32. See Baumeister and Tierney, *Willpower*, 157–58; see also D. T. De Ridder, G. Lensvelt-Mulders, C. Finkenauer, F. M. Stok, and R. F. Baumeister, "Taking Stock of Self-Control: A Meta-analysis of How Trait Self-Control Relates to a Wide Range of Behaviors," *Personality and Social Psychology Review* 16 (2012): 76–99.

33. Baumeister and Tierney, *Willpower*, 156; see also K. D. Vohs, J. P. Redden, and R. Rahinel, "Physical Order Produces Healthy Choices, Generosity, and Conventionality, Whereas Disorder Produces Creativity," *Psychological Science* 24 (2013): 1860–67.

Chapter 4

1. Mauricio Lim Miller, life story interview, March 29, 2017. All quotes from Miller are from this interview. Since the time of the interview, Miller has self-published a book on poverty that also includes parts of his life story: *The Alternative: Most of What You Believe about Poverty Is Wrong* (Morrisville, N.C.: Lulu Publishing Services, 2017).

2. Plato, *Apology*, trans. Benjamin Jowett, http://classics.mit.edu/Plato/apology.html. It's a short work (about seventeen pages) and a good read—and it will give you a good sense of why many prominent Athenians had it in for Socrates.

3. Plato, *Apology*, 37b–38a, emphasis added.

4. Confucius, *Analects*, trans. Edward Slingerland (Indianapolis, Ind.: Hackett, 2003), 4.26.

5. Mencius [Mengzi], *Mengzi*, trans. B. Van Norden (Indianapolis, Ind.: Hackett, 2008), 4A18. Interestingly, however, Confucius's own son studied under him without apparent ill effects.

6. Just as there are aptitude and interest tests to help people with career planning, psychologists have developed assessments to help us identify our strengths and weaknesses of character; we discussed one assessment of this sort, the VIA strengths survey, in chapters 1 and 2.

7. See Ignatius Loyola, *Spiritual Exercises*, trans. Louis J. Puhl (Chicago: Loyola Press, 1968). The Liturgy of the Hours, a recommended practice for all Catholics, also includes a brief daily examination of conscience as part of night prayer. See *The Liturgy of the Hours*, 4 vols. (Totowa, N.J.: Catholic Book Publishing Company, 1976).

8. Confucius, *Analects*, 1.4.

9. Confucius, *Analects*, 4.17.

10. Xunzi, "Improving Yourself," in *Xunzi: Basic Writings*, trans. Burton Watson (New York: Columbia University Press, 2003), 25–33, at 25.

11. Mencius, *Mengzi*, 2A2.7.

12. See Lewis R. Goldberg, "The Development of Markers for the Big-Five Factor Structure," *Psychological Assessment* 4 (1992): 26–42.

13. See, for example, Robert Wicklund, "Objective Self-Awareness," *Advances in Experimental Social Psychology* 8 (1975): 233–75; and, for more detail, T. Shelley Duval and Robert Wicklund, *A Theory of Objective Self-Awareness* (New York: Academic Press, 1972). More recently, researchers have found that this self-evaluation takes place even when the self-awareness isn't explicit—for instance, when there is a mirror in the room: see Paul J. Silva and Ann G. Philips, "Self Awareness without Awareness? Implicit Self-Focused Attention and Behavioral Self-Regulation," *Self Identity* 12, no. 2 (2013): 114–27.

14. See, for example, Daniel Goleman, *Emotional Intelligence: Why It Can Matter More than IQ* (New York: Bantam Books, 2005).

15. James Bennett-Levy, "Reflection: A Blind Spot in Psychology?" *Clinical Psychology* 27 (July 2003): 16–19, at 17.

16. See Ursula Staudinger, "Social Cognition and a Psychological Approach to an Art of Life," in *Social Cognition and Aging*, ed. T. M. Hess and F. Blanchard-Fields (New York: Academic Press, 1999), 343–75.

17. Julie J. Park and Melissa L. Millora, "The Relevance of Reflection: An Empirical Examination of the Role of Reflection in Ethic of Caring, Leadership, and Psychological Well-Being," *Journal of College Student Development* 53, no. 2 (2012): 221–42.

18. See Wally P., "The Early History of 'How It Works,'" http://bigbooksponsorship. org/articles-alcoholism-addiction-12-step-program-recovery/aa-history/early-history-works-wally/. I thank my friend Mary Jo Steffes for pointing me to moral inventory resources.

19. http://holisticrecoverycenters.com/wp-content/uploads/2016/06/Daily-Inventory-Canva.jpg.

20. Tasha Eurich, *Insight: Why We're Not as Self-Aware as We Think, and How Seeing Ourselves Clearly Helps Us Succeed at Work and in Life* (New York: Crown Publishing, 2017), 98.

21. See, for example, Daniel Stein and Anthony M. Grant, "Disentangling the Relationships among Self-Reflection, Insight, and Subjective Well-Being: The Role of Dysfunctional Attitudes and Core Self-Evaluations," *Journal of Psychology* 104, no. 5 (2014): 505–22.

22. See, for example, Paul D. Trapnell and Jennifer D. Campbell, "Private Self-Consciousness and the Five-Factor Model of Personality: Distinguishing Rumination from Reflection," *Journal of Personality and Social Psychology* 76, no. 2 (1999): 284–304. We'll discuss rumination and its remedies in chapter 7.

23. For a thorough analysis, see Timothy D. Wilson, *Strangers to Ourselves: Discovering the Adaptive Unconscious* (Cambridge, Mass.: Belknap Press, 2004).

24. Eurich, *Insight*, 100.

25. Tasha Eurich, "To Make Better Decisions, Ask Yourself 'What,' Not 'Why,'" *Science of Us*, May 2, 2017..

26. For a summary, see her interview: Melissa Dahl, "Do You Have Any Idea What Other People Think of You?" *Science of Us*, May 8, 2017.

27. William Damon and Anne Colby, *The Power of Ideals: The Real Story of Moral Choice* (New York: Oxford University Press, 2015), 104.

28. https://www.fii.org/. We'll discuss the Family Independence Initiative in more detail in chapter 7; for now, suffice it to say that it has achieved impressive results in families' incomes, assets, and education—all without "helping."

Chapter 5

1. James McCormick, life story interview, January 5, 2017. All quotes from McCormick are taken from this interview.

2. http://www.raisingcanefarms.com/ourmission.html

3. Plato, *Crito*, trans. Benjamin Jowett (Boston: Internet Classics Archive, 1994–2000), http://classics.mit.edu/Plato/crito.html. (You should pause and read it right now. Really. It's a good story, and it's quite short—I just reread it myself, and it took about ten minutes.)

4. William Damon and Anne Colby briefly mention most of these strategies in *The Power of Ideals: The Real Story of Moral Choice* (New York: Oxford University Press, 2015), 100–101; Robert Hoyk and Paul Hersey also describe most of them briefly (though not always by the same names) in *The Ethical Executive* (Stanford, Calif.: Stanford University Press, 2008), 68–74. For a more thorough treatment of rationalization (also called moral disengagement), see Albert Bandura's research: for example, *Moral Disengagement: How People Do Harm and Live with Themselves* (New York: Worth Publishers, 2016); "Selective Activation and Disengagement of Moral Control," *Personality and Social Psychology Review* 3, no. 3 (1999): 193–209; and "Mechanisms of Moral Disengagement in the Exercise of Moral Agency," *Journal of Personality and Social Psychology* 71, no. 2 (1996): 364–74.

5. For a recent investigation of moral licensing, see Sonya Sachdeva, Rumen Iliev, and Douglas L. Medin, "Sinning Saints and Saintly Sinners: The Paradoxes of Moral Regulation," *Psychological Science* 20 (2009): 523–28.

6. Damon and Colby, *The Power of Ideals*, 85.

7. Plato, *Crito*, 52d–e.

8. Some philosophers refer to this as the "ratcheting-up effect." The idea is that our obligations depend upon what is possible, and the existence of exemplary people demonstrates that it's possible to be much better than we actually are. See Vanessa Carbonell, "The Ratcheting-Up Effect," *Pacific Philosophical Quarterly* 93 (2012): 228–54. For more general discussion of the place of role models in ethics, see Linda Zagzebski's work: for example, "Exemplarist Virtue Theory," *Metaphilosophy* 41, no. 1–2 (2010): 41–57; and "The Moral Authority of Exemplars," in *Theology and the Science of Moral Action*, ed. James Van Slyke et al. (New York: Routledge, 2013), 117–29.

9. See, for instance, Chalene Johnson, *Push: 30 Days to Turbocharged Habits, a Bangin' Body, and the Life You Deserve!*, rev. ed. (New York: Rodale Books, 2017), chap. 28.

10. See, for instance, Tara Gray, *Publish & Flourish: Become a Prolific Scholar*, 3rd ed. (Las Cruces, N.M.: Teaching Academy, 2005).

11. Damon and Colby, *The Power of Ideals*, 104.

12. We touched on the practical syllogism in chapter 3 and will discuss it again (when looking at good practical reasoning) in chapter 19. For a more detailed analysis of Aristotle's practical syllogism, including discussion of some controversies surrounding its role and interpretation, see the classic article by F. C. S. Schiller, "Aristotle and the Practical Syllogism," *The Journal of Philosophy, Psychology and Scientific Methods* 14 (1917), 645–53.

13. See Aristotle, *Nicomachean Ethics* bk. 7; cf. Aristotle's *De Anima* 3 and *De Motu Animalium* 6–8.

14. I borrow this example from Mary Midgley, *Heart and Mind: The Varieties of Moral Experience*, 3rd ed. (New York: Routledge, 2003), chap. 3. As I have argued elsewhere, real life is a bit more complicated yet, in that all sorts of descriptions of things the agent does without intending to do are also accurate but are generally less relevant. For example, this same act could also be described as "Creating a small air current" or "Reflecting sunlight." See my "On Why and How Intention Matters," *American Catholic Philosophical Quarterly* 89 (2015): 369–95. For present purposes, however, we'll stick to the more obvious descriptors.

15. This example is from Ragnar Rommetveit's "Outlines of a Dialogically Based Social-Cognitive Approach to Human Cognition and Communication," in *The Dialogical Alternative: Towards a Theory of Language and Mind*, ed. A. H. Wold (Oslo: Scandinavian University Press, 1992), 19–44, at 25–26.

Chapter 6

1. Susan Burton, life story interview, January 16, 2017. All quotes from Burton are taken from this interview. Since that time, Burton and coauthor Cari Lynn have published a book telling her life story: *Becoming Ms. Burton* (New York: The New Press, 2017).

2. William Damon and Anne Colby, *The Power of Ideals* (New York: Oxford University Press, 2015) 94–95; cf. Damon, *Greater Expectations: Overcoming the Culture of Indulgence in America's Homes and Schools* (New York: Free Press, 1995).

3. These two variations of weakness of will apply more generally to any poor choice we make even though we (should) know better; for more on weakness of will, see chapter 3 of this book.

4. A succinct list of the twelve steps can be found at http://www.12step.org/the-12-steps/.

5. Aristotle, *Nicomachean Ethics*, trans. W. D. Ross (Boston: Internet Classics Archive, 199 4–2000), 4.7, 1127b13.

6. Marcus Tullius Cicero, *De Officiis* [On duties], trans. Andrew P. Peabody (Boston: Little, Brown, & Company, 1887), 1.13.

7. Aristotle, *Nicomachean Ethics*, 1127a30.

8. Aristotle, *Nicomachean Ethics*, 1127a33–1127b7.

9. Aristotle, *Nicomachean Ethics*, 1127a23–31.

10. Of course, there may be any number of people who are at least as virtuous as the exemplars that I interviewed, except that they are overly modest—likely with the result that I've never heard of them. (I won't say that *all* of my interviewees hit the virtuous mean of truthfulness about their own characteristics, though—a few of them were more self-promoting or more self-deprecating than truthfulness would seem to call for.)

11. Plato, *Gorgias*, trans. Donald J. Zeyl (Indianapolis, Ind.: Hackett Publishing Company, 1986), 479e–480b.

12. Plato, *Gorgias*, 477d, 504d.

13. For example, Summit Behavioral Health argues that "More often than not, it happens that the anticipation of having to deal with [legal issues] is far worse than the consequences you have to endure": https://www.serenityatsummit.com/recovery/part-addiction-treatment-clearing-wreckage-past-recovery/.

14. My dad always insisted that the statement is not a lie as long as your friend really *is* fat: that is, as long as you don't think it's the *pants* that are making her look that way. But even if he's right that it's not technically lying, such a statement is still deceptive—at least, assuming your friend means to ask whether she looks fat in the pants.

15. Delroy L. Paulhus and Oliver P. John, "Egoistic and Moralistic Biases in Self-

Perception: The Interplay of Self-Deceptive Styles with Basic Traits and Motives," *Journal of Personality* 66, no. 6 (1998): 1025–60, at 1026.

16. Delroy L. Paulhus and Douglas B. Reid, "Enhancement and Denial in Socially Desirable Responding," *Journal of Personality and Social Psychology* 60 (1991): 307–17. The authors studied the relationship between enhancement (claiming positive attributes) and denial (denying negative ones), and they looked at the relationship of each to deception both of ourselves and of others. As they found, self-deceptive denial was closely related to both types of impression management: other-deceptive denial and other-deceptive enhancement. Although they did not refer specifically to egoistic and moralistic bias in this article, it seems clear that both biases could be at work in self-deceptive denial, that is, one could deny having low intelligence or influence just as easily as she could deny being unkind or ungrateful.

17. See Daniel N. Jones and Delroy L. Paulhus, "Duplicity among the Dark Triad: Three Faces of Deceit," *Journal of Personality and Social Psychology* 113, no. 2 (2017): 329–42.

18. See Angela D. Evans, Allison M. O'Connor, and Kang Lee, "Verbalizing a Commitment Reduces Cheating in Young Children," *Social Development* 27 (2018): 87–94.

19. See Roy Baumeister, Kenneth Cairns, and Russell Geen, "Repression and Self-Presentation: When Audiences Interfere with Self-Deceptive Strategies," *Journal of Personality and Social Psychology* 62 (1992): 851–62.

20. Xunzi, "Man's Nature is Evil," in *Xunzi: Basic Writings*, trans. Burton Watson (New York: Columbia University Press, 2003), 161–74, at 174.

21. Mencius [Mengzi], *Mengzi*, trans. B. Van Norden (Indianapolis, Ind.: Hackett, 2008), e.g., 2A2, 6A9.

22. Chelsea Hays and Leslie J. Carver, "Follow the Liar: The Effects of Adult Lies on Children's Honesty," *Developmental Science* 17 (2014): 977–83.

23. Mencius, *Mengzi*, 5B8.

24. Damon and Colby, *The Power of Ideals*, chap. 4. We'll examine another of Damon and Colby's themes, open-mindedness, in chapter 12, in conjunction with the virtue of humility.

25. Damon and Colby, *The Power of Ideals*, 106–8. Bonhoeffer's diary is available, along with letters and other documents arranged in chronological order, in volumes 9–16 of the English version of his collected works. See especially *Conspiracy and Imprisonment: 1940–1945*, vol. 16 of *Dietrich Bonhoeffer Works*, ed. Mark S. Brocker, trans. Lisa E. Dahill (Minneapolis: Fortress, 2006).

26. Mauricio Lim Miller, life story interview, March 29, 2017.

27. Damon and Colby, *The Power of Ideals*, 111.

28. Damon and Colby, *The Power of Ideals*, 39–40, 115.

29. Michelle Alexander, *The New Jim Crow: Mass Incarceration in the Age of Colorblindness* (New York: The New Press, 2012).

30. "Connie," life story interview, 2017. (Although she has given me permission to use her name, for the sake of family privacy I've left real names out of this part of her story.)

31. Cathy Heying, life story interview, March 27, 2017. We see more of Heying's story in chapters 2 and 19.

Chapter 7

1. Xunzi, "Dispelling Obsession," in *Xunzi: Basic Writings*, trans. Burton Watson (New York: Columbia University Press, 2003), 125–42, at 125.

2. Xunzi, "Dispelling Obsession," in *Basic Writings*, 125.

3. Xunzi, "Dispelling Obsession," in *Basic Writings*, 130.

4. There is psychological research on one form of obsession—rejection sensitivity—and its tie to relationship drama: when coupled with low self-control, rejection sensitivity results in a destructive escalation of hostility in response to any negativity or criticism by one's partner. For a helpful summary of findings in this area, see Walter Mischel, *The Marshmallow Test: Mastering Self-Control* (New York: Little, Brown, & Company, 2014), chaps. 11–12.

5. Xunzi, "Dispelling Obsession," in *Basic Writings*, 126.

6. See Plato, *Republic*, trans. Benjamin Jowett (Boston: Internet Classics Archive, 1994–2000), book 9. Mischel summarizes his own relevant findings and those of his colleagues in the first chapter of *The Marshmallow Test*.

7. Xunzi, "Dispelling Obsession," in *Basic Writings*, 131.

8. Xunzi, "Dispelling Obsession," in *Basic Writings*, 132.

9. Xunzi, "Dispelling Obsession," in *Basic Writings*, 132.

10. For a fascinating take on the intellectual climate of medieval Europe upon this rediscovery, see Richard E. Rubenstein, *Aristotle's Children* (New York: Harcourt, 2003).

11. The literature on this bias is plentiful; for an interesting and accessible explanation with plenty of helpful examples, see Chip Heath and Dan Heath, *Decisive: How to Make Better Choices in Life and Work* (New York: Crown Publishing, 2013), especially chap. 5.

12. Xunzi, "Dispelling Obsession," in *Basic Writings*, 132.

13. A handy psychological definition is this: "passive and repetitive focus on the negative and damaging features of a stressful transaction." Ellen A. Skinner et al., "Searching for the Structure of Coping," *Psychological Bulletin* 129 (2003): 216–69, at 242.

14. See Norman Miller et al., "A Theoretical Model of Triggered Displaced Aggression," *Personality and Social Psychology Review* 7 (2003): 75–97.

15. Tasha Eurich, *Insight: Why We're Not as Self-Aware as We Think, and How Seeing Ourselves Clearly Helps Us Succeed at Work and in Life* (New York: Crown Publishing, 2017).

16. See Ethan Kross et al., "Self-Talk as a Regulatory Mechanism: How You Do It Matters," *Journal of Personality and Social Psychology* 106 (2014): 304–24.

17. Dominik Mischkowski, Ethan Kross, and Brad Bushman, "Flies on the Wall Are Less Aggressive: Self-Distancing 'In the Heat of the Moment' Reduces Aggressive Thoughts, Angry Feelings, and Aggressive Behavior," *Journal of Experimental Social Psychology* 48 (2012): 1187–91.

18. Ethan Kross and Ozlem Ayduk, "Making Meaning out of Negative Experiences by Self-Distancing," *Current Directions in Psychological Science* 20, no. 3 (2011): 187–191, at 188.

19. Studies have in fact shown self-distancing to be effective in children. See, for exam-

ple, Ethan Kross et al., "The Effect of Self-Distancing on Adaptive versus Maladaptive Self-Reflection in Children," *Emotion* 11, no. 5 (2011): 1032–39.

20. Gloria Lewis, life story interview, December 26, 2016. All quotes from Lewis are taken from this interview.

Chapter 8

1. Yuichi Shoda, Walter Mischel, and Philip K. Peake, "Predicting Adolescent Cognitive and Self-Regulatory Competencies from Preschool Delay of Gratification," *Developmental Psychology* 26, no. 6 (1990): 978–86. Mischel presents and applies much of his and his colleagues' research in *The Marshmallow Test: Mastering Self-Control* (New York: Little, Brown, & Company, 2014). As he notes there, the researchers were just as surprised as the rest of us to see these sorts of outcomes. They had simply been trying to find out at what age self-restraint typically develops.

2. Mischel, *The Marshmallow Test*, 24.

3. Confucius, *The Analects of Confucius*, trans. Edward Slingerland (Indianapolis, Ind.: Hackett, 2003), 1.14; cf. 6.11, 7.16, 17.22.

4. Confucius, *Analects*, 4.23; cf. 12.1.

5. Confucius, *Analects*, 14.13.

6. For a great biography of Kolbe, see Patricia Treece, *A Man for Others* (New York: Harper & Row, 1982). Of course, I'm not claiming that temperance requires that one be willing to starve to death, even for a good cause—clearly, Kolbe's heroic self-sacrifice went well beyond the demands of temperance.

7. Kristján Kristjánsson, *Virtues and Vices in Positive Psychology: A Philosophical Critique* (Cambridge: Cambridge University Press, 2013), 152.

8. "Anthony Weiner Gets 21 Months in Prison in Sexting Case," *CNN Politics*, Sept. 25, 2017, http://www.cnn.com/2017/09/25/politics/anthony-weiner-sentencing/index.html.

9. Aristotle, *Nicomachean Ethics*, trans. W. D. Ross (Boston: Internet Classics Archive, 1994–2009), 3.10, 1118a25–1118b3.

10. Aristotle, *Nicomachean Ethics*, 3.11.

11. Lucius Annaeus Seneca, *De Beneficiis*, in *Moral Essays*, 3 vols., trans. John W. Basore. The Loeb Classical Library (London: W. Heinemann, 1928–1935), 4.12–13.

12. Marcus Tullius Cicero, *De Officiis* [On duties], ed. W. Miller (Cambridge, Mass.: Harvard University Press, 1913), 1.2.

13. Plato, *Republic*, trans. Benjamin Jowett (Boston: Internet Classics Archive, 1994–2000), bk. 2, 360b–c.

14. Plato, *Republic*, bk. 9, 572d, 573d–574e, 576a, 580a. For brevity, I've included only Socrates's lines, omitting Glaucon's expressions of agreement.

15. Plato, *Republic*, bk. 9, 588c–e.

16. Plato, *Republic*, bk. 9, 588e–589a.

17. Plato, *Republic*, bk. 9, 589d, 591a.

18. See, for example, Jane Gillham et al., "Character Strengths Predict Subjective Well-Being during Adolescence," *Journal of Positive Psychology* 6, no. 1 (2011): 31–44.

19. For a thorough account of this phenomenon, see Allan Luks, *The Healing Power of Doing Good* (Bloomington, Ind.: iUniverse, 2001).

20. Plato, *Republic*, bk. 9, 589a–b.

21. For an interesting article on contemporary lion training, see Robin Finn, "The Island: The Wild Kingdom of a Lady Lion Tamer," *New York Times*, June 25, 2006.

22. Haidt, *The Happiness Hypothesis: Finding Modern Truth in Ancient Wisdom* (New York: Basic Books, 2006).

23. See Chip Heath and Dan Heath, *Switch: How to Change Things When Change is Hard* (New York: Broadway Books, 2010), esp. 5–6.

24. Jonathan L. Freedman and Scott C. Fraser, "Compliance without Pressure: The Foot-in-the-Door Technique," *Journal of Personality and Social Psychology* 4 (1966): 195–203; see also Heath and Heath, *Switch*, 158–61.

25. Katie Nodjimbadem, "The Trashy Beginnings of 'Don't Mess with Texas,'" *Smithsonian*, March 10, 2017.

26. Kelly McGonigal, *The Willpower Instinct: How Self-Control Works, Why It Matters, and What You Can Do to Get More of It* (New York: Avery, 2012), 10; see also chap. 4.

27. McGonigal, *The Willpower Instinct*, 113.

28. For an interesting—and disturbing—look at how that sort of marketing works, see Nir Eyal and Ryan Hoover, *Hooked: How to Build Habit-Forming Products* (New York: Portfolio, 2014).

29. McGonigal, *The Willpower Instinct*, chap. 5.

30. Xunzi, "A Discussion of Rites," in *Xunzi: Basic Writings*, trans. Burton Watson (New York: Columbia University Press, 2003), 93–113, at 93, translation modified to use the untranslated "*li*" instead of "ritual" and "principles."

31. Xunzi, "A Discussion of Rites," in *Basic Writings*, 94–95.

32. As Aaron Stalnaker observes, Xunzi seems to agree with Christian philosopher Augustine that people are "caught between desires for pleasure, dominance, and safety that seem to preclude mutual satisfaction." Stalnaker, *Overcoming Our Evil: Human Nature and Spiritual Exercises in Xunzi and Augustine* (Washington, D.C.: Georgetown University Press, 2009), 257.

33. Introducing quantity may blur the distinction between necessary and unnecessary desires. For example, while we clearly need food and clearly do *not* need to eat a whole cheesecake in one sitting, how much and what kind of food counts as "necessary"? Answering with any precision requires both prudence—a virtue we'll discuss later—and knowledge of the particulars of the situation. As an approximation, though, we can start with health as the determining factor: healthy food in healthy amounts counts as a "tame" or "necessary" desire, and unhealthy types and quantities of food count as "wild" or "unnecessary."

34. Confucius, *Analects*, 2.4. Lest we despair, it's worth noting that he also described ethical development as coming more easily to some others—most notably his disciple Yan Hui, who seemed to have been born virtuous: see *Analects*, 2.9, 9.20, 11.4, and especially 16.9.

Chapter 9

1. Lisa Nigro, life story interview, January 12, 2017. All quotes from Nigro are taken from this interview.

2. See Thomas Aquinas, *Summa Theologica*, trans. Fathers of the English Dominican Province, 1920, http://www.newadvent.org/summa/2051.htm, I-II.51.3. Interestingly, as he points out, changing our habits of belief—using active reasoning to persuade habitual reason or opinion—is different: one conclusive demonstration can be enough to change our minds. Similarly, one strong physical stimulus can occasion a new bodily habit—as in the case of addiction, or, in Aquinas's own example, a single dose of a powerful medicine.

3. Confucius, *The Analects of Confucius*, trans. Edward Slingerland (Indianapolis, Ind.: Hackett, 2003), 9.19.

4. Xunzi, "Encouraging Learning," in *Xunzi: Basic Writings*, trans. Burton Watson (New York: Columbia University Press, 2003), 15–23, at 18. (At the time, a *li* was about 400 meters—so a journey of a thousand *li* would be about 400 kilometers or about 250 miles.)

5. Aquinas, *Summa Theologica*, II-II.137.1. I've removed an internal citation, which is to Aristotle's *Nicomachean Ethics*, 2.3.

6. Christopher Peterson and Martin Seligman, *Character Strengths and Virtues: A Handbook and Classification* (Oxford: Oxford University Press, 2004), 29.

7. Peterson and Seligman, *Character Strengths and Virtues*, 229.

8. Peterson and Seligman, *Character Strengths and Virtues*, 229.

9. Peterson and Seligman, *Character Strengths and Virtues*, 238–39.

10. Roy F. Baumeister and John Tierney, *Willpower: Rediscovering the Greatest Human Strength* (New York: Penguin, 2011), 36–37.

11. Angela Duckworth et al., "Grit: Perseverance and Passion for Long-Term Goals," *Journal of Personality and Social Psychology* 92, no. 6 (2007): 1087–1101, at 1089.

12. Duckworth et al., "Grit," 1087–88.

13. Peterson and Seligman, *Character Strengths and Virtues*, 240.

14. Xunzi, "Encouraging Learning," in *Basic Writings*, 16.

15. Xunzi, "Encouraging Learning," in *Basic Writings*, 17. The terms translated "gentleman" and "men of breeding" refer to the good character (rather than to the social class or gender) of the people they describe. In the next essay, "Improving Yourself," Xunzi describes the gentleman as "sincere, obedient, and brotherly," and as having "a love of learning, modesty, and alertness." Xunzi, "Improving Yourself," in *Basic Writings*, 25–33, at 31.

16. Xunzi, "Improving Yourself," in *Basic Writings*, 31.

17. Xunzi, "Improving Yourself," in *Basic Writings*, 25; cf. Confucius, *Analects*, 16.4.

18. Xunzi, "Improving Yourself," in *Basic Writings*, 30.

19. Xunzi, "Improving Yourself," in *Basic Writings*, 29.

20. Carol S. Dweck, "The Role of Expectations and Attributions in the Alleviation of Learned Helplessness," *Journal of Personality and Social Psychology* 31, no. 4, (1975): 674–85, at 674. For a helpful explanation of learned helplessness and of attribution styles more gen-

erally, see Lyn Abramson, Martin Seligman, and John Teasdale, "Learned Helplessness in Humans: Critique and Reformulation," *Journal of Abnormal Psychology* 87, no. 1 (1978): 49–74, especially the table on p. 57.

21. Debi Starnes and Otto Zinser, "The Effect of Problem Difficulty, Locus of Control, and Sex on Task Persistence," *The Journal of General Psychology* 108, no. 2 (1983): 249–55.

22. Robert Eisenberger and Michael Selbst, "Does Reward Increase or Decrease Creativity?" *Journal of Personality and Social Psychology* 66, no. 6 (1994): 1116–1127, at 1118. For brevity, I've removed several internal citations, which are mainly to Eisenberger's own work. See also Robert Eisenberger, "Learned Industriousness." *Psychological Review* 99, no. 2 (1992): 248–67.

23. Albert Bandura, "Self-Efficacy: Toward a Unifying Theory of Behavioral Change," *Psychological Review* 84, no. 2 (1977): 191–215, at 193.

24. Bandura, "Self-Efficacy," 193–94.

25. Albert Bandura, "On the Functional Properties of Perceived Self-Efficacy Revisited," *Journal of Management* 38, no. 1 (2012): 9–44, at 19. Bandura cites several studies here but relies especially on the work of Bouffard-Bouchard: see T. Bouffard-Bouchard, "Influence of Self-Efficacy on Performance in a Cognitive Task," *Journal of Social Psychology* 130 (1990): 353–63; and T. Bouffard-Bouchard, S. Parent, and S. Larivee, "Influence of Self-Efficacy on Self-Regulation and Performance among Junior and Senior High-School Age Students," *International Journal of Behavioral Development* 14 (1991): 153–64.

26. Bandura, "On the Functional Properties," 13. Bandura also discusses these techniques, sometimes by different names, in "Self-Efficacy: Toward a Unifying Theory," 195–200; see especially the chart on p. 195.

27. Sarah A. Schnitker, "An Examination of Patience and Well-Being," *The Journal of Positive Psychology* 7, no. 4, (2012): 263–80, at 270–74.

28. Peterson and Seligman, *Character Strengths and Virtues*, 236.

29. Schnitker, "Patience and Well-Being," 242–43.

30. And, assuming the role models are relevantly similar to us (as role models should be), observing and imitating them can also be a type of social modeling of the sort Bandura advocates for increasing self-efficacy.

31. Although stories abound regarding people who were "all there" but unable to communicate due to brain injury, a particularly interesting one is that of Martin Pistorius: a young man who spent over a decade aware but unable to move or speak. See his book, *Ghost Boy* (Nashville, Tenn.: Thomas Nelson, 2013); or search YouTube for his TED talk. For a more academic study of brain injury and disability rights, see Joseph J. Fins, *Rights Come to Mind: Brain Injury, Ethics, and the Struggle for Consciousness* (New York: Cambridge University Press, 2015). I thank Lisa Nigro for directing me to this latter book.

Chapter 10

1. Andy Wells, life story interview, July 9, 2016. All quotes from Wells are taken from this interview.

2. Marcus Tullius Cicero, *De Officiis* [On duties], in *The Ethical Writings of Cicero*, trans. Andrew P. Peabody (Boston: Little, Brown, & Company, 1887), 1.41.

3. See, e.g., Confucius, *Analects*, trans. Edward Slingerland (Indianapolis, Ind.: Hackett, 2003), 4.17; Xunzi, "Improving Yourself," in *Xunzi: Basic Writings*, trans. Burton Watson (New York: Columbia University Press, 2003), 25–33, at 25.

4. Cicero, *De Officiis*, 1.41.

5. Confucius, *Analects*, 2.10.

6. Mencius [Mengzi], *Mengzi*, trans. Bryan W. Van Norden (Indianapolis, Ind.: Hackett, 2008), 2A2, 2A7.

7. Confucius, *Analects*, 4.7.

8. Confucius, *Analects*, 5.10.

9. Confucius, *Analects*, 2.9; cf. 6.7, 6.11, and 9.20.

10. Confucius, *Analects*, 2.5–8; cf. 12.1–3.

11. To be clear, I don't take this development to be conclusive evidence that my guess was correct. Surely it's strong evidence that he was suffering from *some* sort of mental illness; but I'm obviously unqualified to diagnose it.

12. For a helpful overview of the literature on the development of this life skill, see Nicholas Epley and Adam Waytz, "Mind Perception," in *Handbook of Social Psychology*, ed. S. T. Fiske, D. T. Gilbert, and G. Lindzey (New York: John Wiley & Sons, 2010), 498–541.

13. Nalini Ambady and Max Weisbuch, "Nonverbal Behavior," in Fiske, Gilbert, and Lindzey, *Handbook of Social Psychology*, 464–97, at 482. In fact, the authors report, hearing the person speak often led to *reduced* accuracy of observers' judgments.

14. Epley and Waytz, "Mind Perception," 502; cf. Roy F. Baumeister and Mark R. Leary, "The Need to Belong: Desire for Interpersonal Attachments as a Fundamental Human Motivation," *Psychological Bulletin* 117 (1995): 497–529.

15. Ambady and Weisbuch, "Nonverbal Behavior," 483.

16. C. Neil Macrae and Suzanne Quadflieg, "Perceiving People," in Fiske, Gilbert, and Lindzey, *Handbook of Social Psychology*, 428–63, esp. 433, 439.

17. Joachim Kruger and Thomas Gilovich, "Actions, Intentions, and Trait Assessment: The Road to Self-Enhancement is Paved with Good Intentions," *Personality and Social Psychology Bulletin* 30 (2004): 328–39.

18. Macrae and Quadflieg, "Perceiving People," 435. Or at least, we make assumptions based on the appearance of age: as the authors note on p. 437, baby-faced individuals are perceived to be submissive, naïve, and lovable—and are less likely than individuals with more mature-looking faces to be convicted when tried for violent crimes.

19. Confucius, *Analects*, 9.23.

20. See https://www.viacharacter.org/character-strengths for the list of twenty-four strengths, divided into six virtue categories. See chapter 2 of this book for further discussion of the VIA survey.

21. See Deborah J. Mitchell, J. Edward, Russo, and Nancy Pennington, "Back to the Future: Temporal Perspective in the Explanation of Events," *Journal of Behavioral Decision Making* 2 (1989): 25–38.

22. Confucius, *Analects*, 12.22.

23. Confucius, *Analects*, 12.16.

24. Confucius, *Analects*, 1.16.

25. Confucius, *Analects*, 12.20.

26. Confucius, *Analects*, 7.8; cf. 15.16.

27. Confucius, *Analects*, 15.8.

28. Confucius, *Analects*, 15.17.

29. Cicero, *De Officiis*, 1.15. Compare Socrates's charitable approach to others' semblance of intellectual virtue in Plato's *Euthydemus*: "We should be friendly to anyone who has anything at all sensible to say and makes a robust effort to follow through on their line of thought" (306c8–d1), as quoted (and translated) by Don Adams in "Socratic *Agape* Without Irony in the *Euthydemus*," *American Catholic Philosophical Quarterly* 91, no. 3 (2017): 273–98.

30. Cicero, *De Officiis*, 1.15.

31. Confucius, *Analects*, 4.15.

32. Confucius, *Analects*, 15.24. As Slingerland explains, the classical Chinese character for understanding is made of up two component characters indicating "comparing" and "heart-mind"; thus understanding involves "an ability to show sympathy, through putting oneself imaginatively in another's place" and "an intuitive ability to amend or suspend the dictates of dutifulness—or to apply them flexibly," combining propriety with context-sensitivity when rigidity would be unreasonable. See Edward Slingerland, "Appendix I: Glossary of Terms," in Confucius, *Analects*, 242.

33. Confucius, *Analects*, 6.30; cf. 12.16.

34. See Mencius, *Mengzi*, 2A6.

35. Christian Miller, *Moral Character: An Empirical Theory* (Oxford: Oxford University Press, 2013), chap. 5. Deliberately limiting empathy isn't always a bad thing: as with all emotions, excessive empathy can be a problem. (For example, burnout is a strong possibility for over-empathizing nurses and caregivers: feeling every patient's suffering as though it were one's own is clearly unsustainable.) So while most of us should develop *more* empathy and compassion in at least some situations, we shouldn't aim for *unlimited* compassion.

36. Confucius, *Analects*, 15.15.

37. Mencius, *Mengzi*, 4B28; cf. 4A4.

38. Mencius, *Mengzi*, 1A7, 2A6.

39. Confucius, *Analects*, 12.23.

Chapter 11

1. Xunzi, "Improving Yourself," in *Xunzi*, trans. Burton Watson (New York: Columbia University Press, 2003), 25–33, at 30.

2. Confucius, *Analects*, trans. Edward Slingerland (Indianapolis, Ind.: Hackett, 2003), 7.22.

3. Brandon Dahm, personal communication.

4. Margaret Martin, life story interview, February 17, 2017. All quotes from Martin are taken from this interview.

5. Gloria Lewis, life story interview, December 26, 2016.

6. Aristotle, *Nicomachean Ethics*, trans. W. D. Ross (Boston: Internet Classics Archive, 1994–2009), 1.4, 1095b1–6.

7. There has been considerable debate among psychologists regarding the effectiveness of role modeling through children's literature. See, for example, James S. Leming, "Tell Me a Story: An Evaluation of a Literature-Based Character Education Programme," *Journal of Moral Education* 29 (2000): 413–27; Kevser Koc and Cary A. Buzzelli, "The Moral of the Story Is...: Using Children's Literature in Character Education," *Young Children* 59 (2004): 92–97; and Darcia Narvaez, "Does Reading Moral Stories Build Character?" *Educational Psychology Review* 14 (2002): 155–77. For a fascinating group of studies using classic children's stories—with mixed results—to discourage children's lying behaviors, see Kang Lee et al., "Can Classic Moral Stories Promote Honesty in Children?" *Psychological Science* 25 (2014): 1630–36; and Victoria Talwar et al., "Promoting Honesty: The Influence of Stories on Children's Lie-Telling Behaviors and Moral Understanding," *Infant and Child Development* 25 (2016): 484–501.

8. See the classic article by Albert Bandura, Dorothea Ross, and Sheila A. Ross, "Imitation of Film-Mediated Aggressive Models," *Journal of Abnormal and Social Psychology* 66 (1963): 3–11; and his more recent summary of related studies, Albert Bandura, "Bobo Doll Studies," *Encyclopedia of Media Violence*, ed. Matthew S. Eastin (Thousand Oaks, Calif.: SAGE Reference, 2013), 53–55.

9. Confucius, *Analects*, 15.10.

10. Confucius, *Analects*, 13.21.

11. See Mengzi [Mencius], *Mengzi*, trans. Bryan Van Norden (Indianapolis, Ind.: Hackett, 2008), 5B8.

12. Noah Levinson, life story interview, February 13, 2017. Unless otherwise noted, all quotes from Levinson are taken from this interview.

13. Noah Levinson, "Genesis," http://calcuttakids.org/about-us/calcutta-kids-timeline/genesis/

14. Confucius, *Analects*, 7.22.

15. Confucius, *Analects*, 4.17.

16. Kristján Kristjánsson, "Emulation and the Use of Role Models in Moral Education," *Journal of Moral Education* 35 (2006): 37–49, at 44.

17. Vanessa Carbonell, "The Ratcheting-Up Effect," *Pacific Philosophical Quarterly* 93 (2012): 228–54.

18. Jonah Berger and Lindsay Rand, "Shifting Signals to Help Health: Using Identity Signaling to Reduce Risky Health Behaviors," *Journal of Consumer Research* 35 (2008): 509–18, esp. 512–14.

19. For more on Mary Jo Copeland and her work, see http://www.sharingandcaring hands.org/meet-mary-jo. Or for a full biography, see Michelle Hinck, *Great Love: The Mary Jo Copeland Story* (Berea, Ohio: Quixote, 2013).

20. Meghan Sullivan, "Moral Saints and Moral Failure," (lecture, Philosophy Department Outside Speaker Series, University of St. Thomas, St. Paul, Minnesota, March 9, 2017).

21. Susan Wolf, "Moral Saints," *The Journal of Philosophy* 79, no. 8 (1982): 419–39.

22. Vanessa Carbonell, "What Moral Saints Look Like," *Canadian Journal of Philosophy* 39, no. 3 (2009), 371–98.

23. Robert Merrihew Adams, "Saints," *The Journal of Philosophy* 81, no. 7 (1984): 392–401, at 398.

24. Wolf, "Moral Saints," 421–22. Perhaps in response to my observations—and those of Adams and Carbonell—Wolf would reply that these people aren't the sort she meant by "moral saints." And maybe they're not—but they're the sort most of us *do* mean by the term, and I as far as I'm aware the sort of person she describes as a moral saint doesn't exist.

25. Wolf, "Moral Saints," 424.

26. Wolf, "Moral Saints," 420. This quality only *partly* resembles her characterization because her description exaggerates the extent to which moral concerns would interfere with other human goods such as "the opportunity to engage in the physical and intellectual activities of our choice, and the love, respect, and companionship of people whom we love, respect, and enjoy" (420), and thus it seems to go beyond moral centrality to something more like moral exclusivity.

27. Anne Colby and William Damon, *Some Do Care: Contemporary Lives of Moral Commitment* (New York: Free Press, 1992), 300.

28. Jeremy A. Frimer and Lawrence J. Walker, "Reconciling the Self and Morality: An Empirical Model of Moral Centrality Development," *Developmental Psychology* 45, no. 6 (2009): 1669–81.

29. Lawrence J. Walker and Jeremy A. Frimer, "Moral Personality of Brave and Caring Exemplars," *Journal of Personality and Social Psychology* 93, no. 5 (2007): 845–60.

30. I actually learned about this idea from Chip Heath and Dan Heath's book *Decisive: How to Make Better Choices in Life and Work* (New York: Crown, 2013), 108. The original source is Aaron T. Beck, *Love Is Never Enough* (New York: HarperPerennial, 1989), 245–46.

31. I used a version of McAdams's life narrative interview with my exemplars as well; it can be found here: https://www.sesp.northwestern.edu/foley/instruments/interview/.

32. Walker and Frimer, "Brave and Caring Exemplars," esp. 850; see table 2 on p. 853.

33. Jen Guo, Miriam Klevan, and Dan P. McAdams, "Personality Traits, Ego Development, and the Redemptive Self," *Personality and Social Psychology Bulletin* 42, no. 11 (2011): 1551–63, at 1551; for a full treatment of the redemptive self in historical exemplars, see McAdams, *The Redemptive Self: Stories Americans Live By* (New York: Oxford University Press, 2013).

34. Guo, Klevan, and McAdams, "Redemptive Self," 1551.

Chapter 12

1. Noah Levinson, life story interview, February 13, 2017. All quotes from Levinson in this chapter are taken from this interview.

2. Mencius [Mengzi], *Mengzi*, trans. Bryan Van Norden (Indianapolis, Ind.: Hackett, 2008), 2A8.

3. Plato, *Apology*, trans. Benjamin Jowett (Boston: Internet Classics Archive, 1994–2000), 23b; cf. Plato, *Euthydemus*, trans. Benjamin Jowett (Boston: Internet Classics Archive, 1994–2000), 293b, in which Socrates says that he knows a lot of things, but nothing that's worth much; and Plato, *Phaedrus*, trans. Benjamin Jowett (Boston: Internet Classics Archive, 1994–2000), 235c, in which Socrates says he knows only his own ignorance.

4. Xenophon, *Memorabilia*, in *Xenophon in Seven Volumes*, vol. 4, trans. E. C. Marchant (Cambridge, Mass.: Harvard University Press, 1923), 4.2.

5. Plato, *Gorgias*, trans. Benjamin Jowett (Boston: Internet Classics Archive, 1994–2000), 458a.

6. For an accessible discussion of Socrates's humility, see Glenn Rawson, "Socratic Humility," *Philosophy Now* 53, https://philosophynow.org/issues/53/Socratic_Humility.

7. Aristotle, *Nicomachean Ethics*, trans. W. D. Ross (Boston: Internet Classics Archive, 1994–2000), 4.3.

8. See both Plato's *Apology* and book 4 of Xenophon's *Memorabilia*.

9. Marcus Tullius Cicero, *De Officiis* [On duties], trans. Andrew P. Peabody (Boston: Little, Brown, & Company, 1887), 1.41.

10. Cicero, *De Officiis*, 1.19, 24, 26, 34.

11. Augustine, Letter 118 to Dioscorus, trans. J. G. Cunningham, in *The Confessions and Letters of St. Augustine*, Nicene and Post-Nicene Fathers, 1st ser., vol. 1, ed. Philip Schaff (Buffalo, N.Y.: Christian Literature Publishing Co., 1887), section 22, 445–46.

12. Aquinas, *Summa Theologica*, trans. Fathers of the English Dominican Province, 1920, http://www.newadvent.org/summa/2051.htm, II-II.161. Aquinas argues that humility is "knowledge of one's own deficiency" (a. 2) and "praiseworthy self-abasement to the lowest place" (a. 1 ad 2): its function is "to temper and restrain the mind, lest it tend to high things immoderately" (a. 1).

13. Sara Rushing, "Comparative Humilities: Christian, Contemporary, and Confucian Conceptions of a Political Virtue," *Polity* 45, no. 2 (2013): 198–222, at 216.

14. Rushing, "Comparative Humilities," 217.

15. Confucius, *Analects*, trans. Edward Slingerland (Indianapolis, Ind.: Hackett, 2003) 4.14; see also *Analects*, 1.16, 14.29, 14.30, 15.19, and 15.21.

16. Confucius, *Analects*, 12.21; cf. 6.22, 9.11, and 15.38.

17. Confucius, *Analects*, 14.20; cf. 2.13, 4.22, 4.24, 12.3, and 14.27.

18. Confucius, *Analects*, 17.8.

19. Xunzi, "Encouraging Learning," in *Xunzi: Basic Writings*, trans. Burton Watson (New York: Columbia University Press, 2003), 13–23, at 19. "Man of breeding" represents a beginner's level of virtue; "sage" is the highest level possible.

20. Xunzi, "Encouraging Learning," in *Basic Writings*, 22.

21. Confucius, *Analects*, 6.15. Although Aristotle might have called such action excessively modest, it clearly was intended not to deceive but to deflect praise—Meng's courage was obvious.

22. Confucius, *Analects*, 8.1. Propriety required that rulership be offered to the immediate successor three times before being offered to the next heir in line. The Great Uncle's deference to his more worthy nephew also involved realistic self-assessment, another aspect of humility.

23. Confucius, *Analects*, 11.26.

24. Confucius, *Analects*, 7.33; cf. 9.12.

25. Confucius, *Analects*, 8.21.

26. Mencius, *Mengzi*, 5A.

27. Confucius, *Analects*, 6.11.

28. Confucius, *Analects*, 12.2.

29. Confucius, *Analects*, 8.11.

30. Confucius, *Analects*, 8.5.

31. Confucius, *Analects*, 1.10.

32. Iris Murdoch, *The Sovereignty of Good* (London: Routledge & Kegan Paul, 2013), 101.

33. Jin Li, "Humility in Learning: A Confucian Perspective," *Journal of Moral Education* 45 (2016): 147–55.

34. Michael C. Ashton and Kibeom Lee, "Empirical, Theoretical, and Practical Advantages of the HEXACO Model of Personality Structure," *Personality and Social Psychology Review* 11 (2007): 150–66, at 157; see also tables 2 and 3 on pp. 154 and 156.

35. Christopher Peterson and Martin Seligman, *Character Strengths and Virtues: A Handbook and Classification* (Oxford: Oxford University Press, 2004), 470.

36. Jordan P. LaBouff et al., "Humble Persons Are More Helpful than Less Humble Persons: Evidence from Three Studies," *The Journal of Positive Psychology* 7 (2012): 16–29.

37. June Price Tangney, "Humility: Theoretical Perspectives, Empirical Findings and Directions for Future Research," *Journal of Social and Clinical Psychology* 19 (2000): 70–82.

38. Anne Colby and William Damon, *Some Do Care: Contemporary Lives of Moral Commitment* (New York: Free Press, 1992), 29; for further description of the nominating process, see chap. 2 and appendix A of the same work.

39. William Damon and Anne Colby, *The Power of Ideals: The Real Story of Moral Choice* (New York: Oxford University Press, 2015), 137–49.

40. Damon and Colby, *The Power of Ideals*, 117, 191–97.

41. The Serenity Prayer was originally written by American theologian Reinhold Neibuhr around 1930 and popularized by twelve-step programs like Alcoholics Anonymous.

Chapter 13

1. Cathey Brown, life story interview, February 15, 2017. All quotes from Brown are taken from this interview.

2. Susan Burton, life story interview, January 16, 2017. All quotes from Burton are taken from this interview.

3. Michelle Alexander, *The New Jim Crow: Mass Incarceration in the Age of Colorblindness* (New York: The New Press, 2012).

4. See Aristotle, *Nicomachean Ethics*, trans. W. D. Ross (Boston: Internet Classics Archive, 1994–2000), 5.3.

5. See Aristotle, *Nicomachean Ethics*, 5.4.

6. Aristotle, *Nicomachean Ethics*, 5.9, 1137a4–16. (Hellebore, a plant used for medicinal purposes in ancient times, turned out to be poisonous. But that just serves to highlight the difficulty of being a good physician—and the even greater difficulty of being a just judge.)

7. The Chinese term for this virtue, *yi*, is often translated "righteousness." To avoid misleading religious connotations, I'll modify my favorite translation to use "rightness" instead. We'll discuss the virtue of benevolence, *ren*, in chapter 18.

8. Mencius, *Mengzi*, trans. Bryan Van Norden (Indianapolis, Ind.: Hackett, 2008), 2A6.

9. Mencius, *Mengzi*, 7B31; cf. 6A10.

10. Barry R. Schlenker, "Integrity and Character: Implications of Principled and Expedient Ethical Ideologies," *Journal of Clinical and Social Psychology* 27 (2008): 1078–1125, at 1081.

11. Schlenker, "Integrity and Character," 1085.

12. Schlenker, "Integrity and Character," 1099.

13. See Schlenker, "Integrity and Character," 1102–11.

14. See Schlenker, "Integrity and Character," 1116–17.

15. Plato, *Republic*, trans. Benjamin Jowett (Boston: Internet Classics Archive, 1994–2000), esp. bk. 4.

16. Wilhelm Hofmann, Kathleen Vohs, and Roy F. Baumeister, "What People Desire, Feel Conflicted About, and Try to Resist in Everyday Life," *Psychological Science* 23, no. 6 (2012), 582–88.

17. Plato, *Republic*, bk. 2.

18. Ben Kenward and Matilda Dahl, "Preschoolers Distribute Scarce Resources according to the Moral Valence of Recipients' Previous Actions," *Developmental Psychology* 47, no. 4 (2011): 1054–64.

19. Alessandra Geraci and Luca Surian, "The Developmental Roots of Fairness: Infants' Reactions to Equal and Unequal Distributions of Resources," *Developmental Science* 14 (2011): 1012–20.

20. Koleen McCrink, Paul Bloom, and Laurie R. Santos, "Children's and Adult's Judgments of Equitable Resource Distributions," *Developmental Science* 13, no. 1, (2010): 37–45.

21. Martin Hoffman, *Empathy and Moral Development: Implications for Caring and Justice* (Cambridge: Cambridge University Press, 2000), 107.

22. Robert Coles, *The Moral Life of Children* (Boston: Atlantic Monthly Press, 1986), 27–28.

23. Amrisha Vaish, Manuela Missana, and Michael Tomasello, "Three-Year-Old Children Intervene in Third-Party Moral Transgressions," *The British Journal of Developmental Psychology* 29, no. 1 (2011): 124–30.

24. Arber Tasimi and Karen Wynn, "Costly Rejection of Wrongdoers by Infants and Children," *Cognition* 151 (2016): 76–79. This result holds unless the wrongdoer's gift is *much* larger—then self-interest takes over.

25. Hoffman, *Empathy and Moral Development*, 198.

26. See Hoffman, *Empathy and Moral Development*, chap. 8.

27. For a detailed account of modern slavery, see any of Kevin Bales's books, including *Disposable People*, 3rd ed. (Berkeley: University of California Press, 2012).

28. Even this method is far from fool-proof, though, as I've recently learned. Many prisons "employ" inmates or "lease" them out to private companies for little or no pay. For an overview article on prison labor, see https://returntonow.net/2016/06/13/prison-labor-is-the-new-american-slavery/; for a list of companies employing it, see https://www.buycott.com/campaign/companies/504/boycott-companies-that-use-prison-labor.

29. This duty of justice is more difficult to fulfill than it sounds, however. Frequently, representatives who promote justice in one area also promote unjust policies in others.

30. Patty Webster, life story interview, February 10, 2017. All quotes from Webster are taken from this interview.

31. Immaculee Ilibagiza, *Left to Tell: Discovering God amidst the Rwandan Holocaust* (Carlsbad, Calif.: Hay House, 2006).

32. See Aristotle, *Nicomachean Ethics*, 5.3. For more on restorative justice, see Daniel Van Ness and Karen Heetderks Strong, *Restoring Justice*, 2nd. ed. (Cincinnati, Ohio: Anderson Publishing, 2003).

33. See, e.g., Jeff Latimer, Craig Dowden, and Danielle Muise, "The Effectiveness of Restorative Justice: A Meta-Analysis," *The Prison Journal* 85, no. 2 (2005): 127–44.

34. Katelyn Beaty, "I Met the Man Who Killed My Entire Family: How Rwandan Genocide Survivor Immaculee Ilibagiza Found Forgiveness," *Christianity Today* (August 2017).

35. Aristotle, *Nicomachean Ethics*, 4.5.

36. Radhi H. Al-Mabuk, Robert D. Enright, and Paul A. Cardis, "Forgiveness Education with Parentally Love-Deprived Late Adolescents," *Journal of Moral Education* 24, no. 4 (1995): 427–44; esp. tables 1–3. For more on Enright's forgiveness programs and research, see the International Forgiveness Institute's website, https://internationalforgiveness.com/.

37. Al-Mabuk, Enright, and Cardis, "Forgiveness Education," 427.

38. For a helpful discussion, see Paul M. Hughes and Brandon Warmke, "Forgiveness," The Stanford Encyclopedia of Philosophy (Summer 2017 Edition), ed. Edward N. Zalta, https://plato.stanford.edu/archives/sum2017/entries/forgiveness/.

39. Robert Enright, *Eight Keys to Forgiveness* (New York: W. W. Norton, 2015); cf. https://internationalforgiveness.com/need-to-forgive.htm.

40. Reconciliation frequently works the other way around as well: when the offender first apologizes, it is much easier for the offended party to offer forgiveness and goodwill. See, e.g., Michael E. McCullough, "Forgiveness as a Human Strength: Theory, Measurement, and Links to Well-Being," *Journal of Social and Clinical Psychology*, 19, no. 1 (2000), 43–55.

41. Cathy Heying, life story interview, March 27, 2017. See chapters 2 and 19 for more of Heying's story.

Chapter 14

1. Judy Berry, life story interview, June 24, 2016. All quotes from Berry are taken from this interview.

2. David Finkelhor, Heather Turner, Anne Shattuck, and Sherry L. Hamby, "Violence, Crime, and Abuse Exposure in a National Sample of Children and Youth," *JAMA Pediatrics* 167, no. 7 (July 2013): 614–21.

3. I owe this point to David McPherson.

4. Mencius [Mengzi], *Mengzi*, trans. B. Van Norden (Indianapolis, Ind.: Hackett, 2008), 7A15; cf. 3A5.

5. Philip J. Ivanhoe, *Confucian Reflections: Ancient Wisdom for Modern Times* (New York: Routledge, 2013), 59–60.

6. Mencius, *Mengzi*, 7A45.

7. Marcus Tullius Cicero, *De Officiis* [On duties], in *The Ethical Writings of Cicero*, trans. Andrew P. Peabody (Boston: Little, Brown, & Company, 1887), 1.17. As he makes clear elsewhere, Mencius also affirms the primacy of the relationship between spouses or co-parents: "For a man and a woman to live together is the greatest of human roles" (*Mengzi*, 5A2). Interestingly, while also recognizing them as basic and natural human tendencies and seeming to advocate them for common citizens, Plato portrays strong spousal and parent-child bonds as potential threats to rulers' and soldiers' loyalty toward their city-state: see *Republic*, trans. Benjamin Jowett (Boston: Internet Classics Archive, 1994–2000), book 5.

8. Cicero, *De Officiis*, 1.16–17.

9. Confucius, *Analects*, trans. Edward Slingerland (Indianapolis, Ind.: Hackett, 2003), 1.2. See also 2.21, in which Confucius argues that engaging in filial behavior is "taking part in government" because it influences those who govern.

10. See especially Mencius, *Mengzi*, 3A3 and 1A2–5; and Confucius, *Analects*, 12.1, and *Analects*, 12.19, where Confucius describes a virtuous leader's influence as being like the wind on grass: "when the wind moves over the grass, the grass is sure to bend." See also, e.g., *Analects*, 2.1, 2.3, 2.19–20, 8.2, and 12.16–18.

11. Confucius, *Analects*, 1.2, 1.6.

12. Cicero, *De Officiis*, 1.33.

13. Marcus Tullius Cicero, *Pro Plancio*, in *The Orations of Marcus Tullius Cicero*, vol. 3, trans. C. D. Yonge (London: George Bell & Sons, 1891), 12.29.

14. Philip J. Ivanhoe, "Filial Piety as a Virtue," in *Working Virtue: Virtue Ethics and Contemporary Moral Problems*, ed. R. L. Walker and P. J. Ivanhoe (New York: Clarendon, 2007), 297–312, at 304–5.

15. Confucius, *Analects*, 4.19; see also 2.6. The fixed itinerary presumably serves to reduce parents' anxiety.

16. Confucius, *Analects*, 2.7; see also 2.8.

17. Confucius, *Analects*, 1.11; see also 2.5, 4.20; cf. 17.21, in which Confucius advocates a three-year mourning period for parents.

18. It is possible, and sometimes desirable, to separate your parents' causal role in your existence from their role as caregivers—this is especially obvious in cases of infant adoption, in which (as I trust seems obvious to most of us) the bulk of our filial piety is owed to the adoptive parents. Still, there can be *some* room for appreciation and respect for one's birth parents as well. For a helpful analysis of this point, see Ivanhoe, "Filial Piety as a Virtue." We also saw Gloria Lewis express a similar point regarding her son's absentee father in chapter 7.

19. Mencius, *Mengzi*, 5A1.

20. Mencius, *Mengzi*, 5A2. As Mencius explains in the following passage, Shun honored his older brother, Xiang, by giving him a territory to "rule"; but he directed other officials to administer it (and, no doubt, to keep Xiang out of trouble).

21. Mencius, *Mengzi*, 7A35.

22. Confucius, *Analects*, 13.18; cf. 11.5.

23. Cicero briefly discusses this connection between justice and piety in *De Inventione*, found in *The Orations of Marcus Tullius Cicero*, trans. C. D. Yonge, vol. 4 (London: George Bell & Sons, 1888), 2.53. Thomas Aquinas, who cites Cicero when categorizing filiality under justice, explains the connection more fully: "A special virtue is one that regards an object under a special aspect. Since, then, the nature of justice consists in rendering another person his due, wherever there is a special aspect of something due to a person, there is a special virtue. Now a thing is indebted in a special way to that which is its connatural principle of being and government. And piety regards this principle, inasmuch as it pays duty and homage to our parents and country" (Thomas Aquinas, *Summa Theologica*, trans. Fathers of the English Dominican Province, 1920, www.newadvent.org/summa, II-II.101.3).

24. Confucius, *Analects*, 2.5.

25. Although today we tend to reserve "ritual" and "rite" for symbolic actions we perform in formal contexts on special occasions, such as weddings or funerals, the Confucians used the term more broadly to refer to any action used to convey meaning. In this broader sense, we engage in rituals all the time. To take just one set of examples, our greeting rituals may include shaking hands, asking how the other is doing, and saying we're doing well when asked—whether or not we're actually doing well.

26. Confucius, *Analects*, 4.18.

27. Interestingly, while advocating strong loyalty to one's parents even in the face of serious misbehavior (including theft and murder!), the Confucians do seem to allow distancing oneself from one's family in some extreme circumstances. For example, when Shun married Emperor Yao's two daughters, he didn't tell his parents; Mencius argues that this seemingly unfilial course of action was justified because he couldn't have gotten married had he informed them beforehand (*Mengzi* 5A2). When Sima Niu, whose older brothers had attempted a political revolt and were subsequently exiled, complains that he alone has no brothers, Confucius's disciple and apparent successor Zixia doesn't chastise him for denying that his brothers exist. Instead, he encourages Sima Niu to think of everyone as his brother (*Analects*, 12.5).

28. Ivanhoe expresses a similar view in "Filial Piety as a Virtue," 310–11.

Chapter 15

1. See chapter 2 for more on the survey, or find the survey itself at www.viacharacter.org.

2. Sister Toni Temporiti, life story interview, March 21, 2017. All quotes from Temporiti are taken from this interview. (I use the term "nun" here in its popular, nontechnical sense, to designate a Catholic woman who has taken vows of poverty, chastity, and obedience within a religious order. Technically speaking, most religious sisters, including Temporiti, actually are not nuns: that term is reserved for those who live cloistered away from the world.)

3. Philip J. Ivanhoe, "Filial Piety as a Virtue," in *Working Virtue: Virtue Ethics and Contemporary Moral Problems*, ed. R. L. Walker and P. J. Ivanhoe (New York: Clarendon, 2007), 297–312, at 299. As Ivanhoe acknowledges, traditional Confucian arguments also frequently base filial piety on the parents' causal role in bringing about the child's existence; but he considers this role insufficient to ground the virtue of piety. For more on filial piety, see chapter 14 of this book.

4. Some may doubt Aristotle's recognition of a need for gratitude in the ideally virtuous person: he describes someone with the virtue of magnanimity or "greatness of soul" as "the sort of man to confer benefits, but he is ashamed of receiving them.... And he is apt to confer greater benefits in return; for thus the original benefactor besides being paid will incur a debt to him, and will be the gainer by the transaction." Aristotle, *Nicomachean Ethics*, trans. W. D. Ross (Boston: Internet Classics Archive, 1994–2000), 4.3, 1124b9–13. While it certainly sounds as though Aristotle is ascribing ingratitude to highly virtuous people, however, Aquinas argues that Aristotle's words here should be interpreted in light of his discussion of the common good and the end of human life—particularly in his discussion of the outward, common-good focus of the benefit-conferring virtue of magnificence (*Nicomachean Ethics*, 4.2) and the reciprocity of friendship (*Nicomachean Ethics*, 8–9). See Aquinas, *Commentary on the Nicomachean Ethics*, trans. C. I. Litzinger, OP (Chicago: Henry Regnery Company, 1964), 4.3; and *Summa Theologica*, trans. Fathers of the English Dominican Province, 1920, www.newadvent.org/summa, II-II.106.129. For a helpful analysis of Aquinas's interpretation of, and revisions to, Aristotle's treatment of magnanimity, see Mary M. Keys, *Aquinas, Aristotle, and the Promise of the Common Good* (New York: Cambridge University Press, 2006), chap. 6.

5. Marcus Tullius Cicero, *De Officiis* [On duties], in *The Ethical Writings of Cicero*, trans. Andrew P. Peabody (Boston: Little, Brown, & Company, 1887), 1.15.

6. Marcus Tullius Cicero, *Pro Plancio*, in *The Orations of Marcus Tullius Cicero*, vol. 3, trans. C. D. Yonge (London: George Bell & Sons, 1891), 33.80–1.

7. Lucius Annasus Seneca, *De Beneficiis* [On benefits], in *Moral Essays*, trans. John W. Basore, 3 vols., The Loeb Classical Library (London: W. Heinemann, 1928–1935), 3:1.10.

8. Seneca, *De Beneficiis*, 2.27.

9. Robert Emmons, *Thanks! How the New Science of Gratitude Can Make You Happier* (New York: Houghton-Mifflin, 2007), 4–5.

10. Some philosophers have struggled a bit with gratitude as a three-term relation: pri-

marily, it seems, because a person can experience a gratitude-like emotion of gladness or appreciation regarding her existence or her whole life without believing that there is a supreme being who has given her these things. For a brief and thoughtful account of this struggle, see Robert C. Solomon, foreword to *The Psychology of Gratitude*, ed. Robert A. Emmons and Michael E. McCullough (New York: Oxford, 2004), v–xi. For an overview of philosophical accounts of gratitude (including its distinction from mere gladness or appreciation), see Tony Manela, "Gratitude," in *The Stanford Encyclopedia of Philosophy*, Spring 2015 edition, ed. Edward N. Zalta, https://plato.stanford.edu/archives/spr2015/entries/gratitude/.

11. Robert C. Roberts, "The Blessings of Gratitude: A Conceptual Analysis." In Emmons and McCullough, *The Psychology of Gratitude*, 58–80.

12. Seneca, *De Beneficiis*, 2.31.

13. Seneca, *De Beneficiis*, 3.17.

14. Seneca, *De Beneficiis*, 2.35.

15. Seneca, *De Beneficiis*, 2.23.

16. See, e.g., Seneca, *De Beneficiis*, 3.8: "Though the gifts are the same, if they are differently given their weight is not the same. A man may have bestowed on me a benefit, but suppose he did not do it willingly, suppose he complained about having bestowed it, suppose he regarded me more haughtily than was his wont, suppose he was so slow to give that he would have conferred a greater service if he had been quick to refuse." Surprisingly, Mencius occasionally accepted but didn't acknowledge gifts that were given in an inappropriate manner: see Mencius, *Mengzi*, trans. Bryan Van Norden (Indianapolis, Ind.: Hackett, 2008), 6B5.

17. See, e.g., Confucius, *Analects*, trans. Edward Slingerland (Indianapolis, Ind.: Hackett, 2003), 14.34.

18. Seneca, *De Beneficiis*, 4.40.

19. Seneca, *De Beneficiis*, 4.37.

20. Psychologists tend to refer to this phenomenon as the "hedonic treadmill"; for a helpful overview, see Jonathan Haidt, *The Happiness Hypothesis* (New York: Basic Books, 2006), chap. 5.

21. Strictly speaking, the virtue of gratitude (like all ethical virtues) has two opposing vices: one of excess and one of deficiency. But sometimes one vice is so rare that it doesn't even have a name—such is the case with the excess opposing gratitude. Some philosophers have recently tried "over-gratitude" as a description for excessive thankfulness—e.g., excessive effusiveness toward benefactors, or thankfulness toward people (or even things) other than benefactors: see Manela, "Gratitude"; see also Claudia Card, "Gratitude and Obligation," *American Philosophical Quarterly* 25, no. 2 (1988): 115–27. While this term and its description do seem to provide a decent theoretical account of the relevant vice of excess, I don't expect "over-gratitude" to catch on in everyday speech: there are too few cases of it to justify adding the word to our working vocabulary.

22. As Seneca notes (*De Beneficiis* 3.1–2), forgetfulness can have the same effect: if I fail to call to mind the benefits I have received, I'll sooner or later forget them entirely and hence fail to be grateful for them. Seneca considers this sort of forgetfulness to be the worst sort of ingratitude because there is no hope of later becoming grateful for something I don't

even remember. He does not comment on whether pride tends to cause such forgetfulness, but that hypothesis seems plausible: pride can easily motivate me not to think about benefits I've received from others. Emmons (*Thanks!*, 127–31, 139–40) agrees that pride ("inability to acknowledge dependency") can be an obstacle to gratitude; he also mentions two forgetfulness-related psychological phenomena: negativity bias (tendency to disproportionately perceive and remember bad experiences) and busyness or distraction.

23. Seneca, *De Beneficiis*, 2.27.

24. Seneca, *De Beneficiis*, 4.20.

25. Seneca, *De Beneficiis*, 3.3.

26. See Emmons, *Thanks!*, 136–37.

27. Emmons, *Thanks!*, 11–12.

28. Alex M. Wood, Jeffrey J. Froh, and Adam W. A. Geraghty, "Gratitude and Well-Being: A Review and Theoretical Integration," *Clinical Psychology Review* 30, no. 7 (2010), 890–905, at 891.

29. Wood, Froh, and Geraghty, "Gratitude and Well-Being," 893–94.

30. Michael McCullough and Jo-Ann Tsang, "Parent of the Virtues? The Prosocial Contours of Gratitude," in Emmons and McCullough, *The Psychology of Gratitude*, 123–44, at 125–29.

31. See, e.g., Jen Guo, Miriam Klevan, and Dan P. McAdams, "Personality Traits, Ego Development, and the Redemptive Self," *Personality and Social Psychology Bulletin* 42, no. 11 (2016): 1551–63. For a more detailed account, see Dan P. McAdams, *The Redemptive Self: Stories Americans Live By*, rev. ed. (New York: Oxford, 2013).

32. Philip Watkins, "Gratitude and Subjective Well-Being," in Emmons and McCullough, *The Psychology of Gratitude*, 167–94, esp. 184–85.

33. Emmons, *Thanks!*, chap. 7.

34. Robert Emmons, *Gratitude Works!: A 21-Day Program for Creating Emotional Prosperity* (San Francisco: Jossey-Bass, 2013), 30.

35. Emmons, *Thanks!*, 205–6. Chapter 16

Chapter 16

1. Rosemary Blieszner and Karen A. Roberto, "Friendship across the Life Span: Reciprocity in Individual and Relationship Development," in *Growing Together: Personal Relationships across the Lifespan*, ed. F. R. Lang and K. L. Fingerman (Cambridge: Cambridge University Press, 2004), 159–82, at 169.

2. Blieszner and Roberto, "Friendship across the Life Span," 170.

3. Blieszner and Roberto, "Friendship across the Life Span," 172.

4. Aristotle, *Nicomachean Ethics*, trans. W. D. Ross (Boston: Internet Classics Archive, 1994–2009), 8.2.

5. Aristotle, *Nicomachean Ethics*, 8.3.

6. Filip Agneessens, Hans Waege, and John Lievens, "Diversity in Social Support by Role Relations: A Typology," *Social Networks* 28, no. 4 (2006): 427–41.

7. William K. Rawlins and Laura D. Russell, "Friendship, Positive Being-with-Others, and the Edifying Practices of Storytelling and Dialogue," in *Positive Psychology of Love*, ed. Mahzad Hojjat and Duncan Cramer (New York: Oxford University Press, 2013), 30–43, at 33.

8. Rawlins and Russell, "Friendship, Being-with-Others, and Dialogue," 33.

9. Rawlins and Russell, "Friendship, Being-with-Others, and Dialogue," 39.

10. Mencius, *Mengzi*, trans. Bryan Van Norden (Indianapolis, Ind.: Hackett, 2008), 5B12.

11. Rawlins and Russell, "Friendship, Being-with-Others, and Dialogue," 32.

12. Rawlins and Russell, "Friendship, Being-with-Others, and Dialogue," 34.

13. Mencius, *Mengzi*, 5B17.

14. Xunzi, "Encouraging Learning," in *Xunzi: Basic Writings*, trans. Burton Watson (New York: Columbia University Press, 2003), 15–23, at 21–22.

15. Xunzi, "Improving Yourself," in *Basic Writings*, 25–33, at 25.

16. Xunzi, "Man's Nature is Evil," in *Basic Writings*, 161–74, at 174.

17. Aristotle, *Nicomachean Ethics*, 8.6, 1158a14.

18. See Kira S. Birditt and Toni C. Antonucci, "Relationship Quality Profiles and Well-Being among Married Adults," *Journal of Family Psychology* 2, no. 14 (2007): 595–604.

19. As you may notice, this result seems to contradict Aristotle's claim that it's possible to be good friends with very few people. I think living in community is what facilitates the exception: Just as you could (I hope) develop close friendships with several family members who lived in your house, presumably it's possible to develop similarly close friendships in "families" living in close-knit religious communities.

20. The reference is to a campaign by the Ad Council; in case you don't remember the "Friends Don't Let Friends" ads, you can find them here: https://www.adcouncil.org/Our-Campaigns/The-Classics/Drunk-Driving-Prevention.

21. Aristotle, *Nicomachean Ethics*, 9.3, 1165b15–17.

22. Aristotle, *Nicomachean Ethics*, 9.3, 1165b19–21.

23. Confucius, *Analects*, trans. E. Slingerland (Indianapolis, Ind.: Hackett, 2003), 12.23.

24. Confucius, *Analects*, 4.26.

25. Aristotle, *Nicomachean Ethics*, 9.3, 1165b34–35.

26. Aristotle, *Nicomachean Ethics*, 8.13.

27. Blieszner and Roberto, "Friendship across the Life Span," 169.

28. Aristotle, *Nicomachean Ethics*, 8.13, 1163a8–9.

29. Aristotle, *Nicomachean Ethics*, 1.4.

30. See, e.g., Aristotle, *Nicomachean Ethics*, 3.6–9, and 4.1.

31. We can relate this observation to the development of virtue and the experience of pleasure as well: see Plato's discussion of pleasure in the *Republic*, book 9.

32. Aristotle, *Nicomachean Ethics*, 9.6–7.

33. Aristotle, *Nicomachean Ethics*, 8.3.

34. Aristotle, *Nicomachean Ethics*, 9.2.

35. Aristotle, *Nicomachean Ethics*, 9.4, 1166a3–8.

36. Aristotle, *Nicomachean Ethics*, 9.4, 1166b7–11.

37. Aristotle, *Nicomachean Ethics*, 9.4, 1166b27–29.

38. Aristotle, *Nicomachean Ethics*, 9.8.

Chapter 17

1. Pam Koner, life story interview, January 28, 2017. All quotations from Koner are taken from this interview.

2. Mencius [Mengzi], *Mengzi*, trans. Bryan Van Norden (Indianapolis, Ind.: Hackett, 2008), 7A15. For more on our "sprouts" of virtue, see *Mengzi*, 2A6, and chapter 2 of this book.

3. Mencius, *Mengzi*, 3A5.

4. Marilynn Brewer, "The Psychology of Prejudice: Ingroup Love or Outgroup Hate?" *Journal of Social Issues* 55 (1999): 429–44, at 434. See G. W. Allport, *The Nature of Prejudice* (Cambridge, Mass.: Addison-Wesley, 1954), 44.

5. Brewer, "The Psychology of Prejudice," 439.

6. Brewer, "The Psychology of Prejudice," 440–41.

7. Mencius, *Mengzi*, 1A7.

8. Mencius, *Mengzi*, 1A7.

9. See, e.g., Nancy Eisenberg, "Empathy-Related Emotional Responses, Altruism, and Their Socialization," in *Visions of Compassion: Western Scientists and Tibetan Buddhists Examine Human Nature*, ed. R. J. Davidson and A. Harrington (London: Oxford University Press, 2002), 131–64, at 138. Eisenberg and her colleagues measured the extent of vicarious response, leading to either personal distress or sympathetic concern, using self-report, heart rate, skin conductivity, and facial reactions.

10. Mencius, *Mengzi*, 2A2.

11. For more on willpower and its depletion, see chapter 3 of this book.

12. Heidi Giebel, "Extend Your Benevolence: Kindness and Generosity in the Family and Beyond." In *Virtues in Action: New Essays in Applied Virtue Ethics*, ed. M. Austin (New York: Palgrave Macmillan, 2013), 70–85.

13. Anne Colby and William Damon, *Some Do Care: Contemporary Lives of Moral Commitment* (New York: Free Press, 1992), 126–27.

14. Mencius, *Mengzi*, 1A7.

15. Mencius, *Mengzi*, 4A12.

16. Mencius, *Mengzi*, 1A7.

17. James McCormick, life story interview, January 5, 2017.

18. Mencius, *Mengzi*, 1B2.

19. Mencius, *Mengzi*, 1B3.

20. Mencius, *Mengzi*, 1B5.

21. Mencius, *Mengzi*, 1B1.

22. Eisenberg, "Empathy-Related Emotional Responses," 137–39.

23. Neha Mahajan and Karen Wynn, "Origins of 'Us' versus 'Them': Prelinguistic Infants Prefer Similar Others," *Cognition* 124 (2012): 227–33.

24. Samuel P. Oliner and Pearl M. Oliner, *The Altruistic Personality: Rescuers of Jews in Nazi Europe* (New York: Free Press, 1988).

25. Lasana T. Harris and Susan T. Fiske, "Dehumanizing the Lowest of the Low: Neuroimaging Responses to Extreme Outgroups," *Psychological Science* 17, no. 10 (2006): 847–53. The researchers verified the disgust part by having other participants look at photos of things like overflowing toilets—sure enough, their pattern of brain activity was about the same.

26. https://www.family-to-family.org/sponsor-a-family/one-to-one/

Chapter 18

1. Gloria Lewis, life story interview, December 26, 2016. All quotes from Lewis are taken from this interview.

2. Mencius [Mengzi], *Mengzi*, trans. Bryan Van Norden (Indianapolis, Ind.: Hackett, 2008), 2A6.

3. See, e.g., *Mengzi*, 1A7: "Only a noble is capable of having a constant heart while lacking a constant livelihood. As for the people, if they lack a constant livelihood, it follows that they will lack a constant heart. No one who lacks a constant heart will avoid dissipation and evil." Mencius's observation fits well with Christian Miller's account of mixed character traits in *Moral Character: An Empirical Theory* (New York: Oxford University Press, 2013). As Miller shows repeatedly throughout the book, most of us tend to act well when circumstances are favorable, but we drop our "good" behavior when there are competing priorities.

4. Mencius, *Mengzi*, 4B19, emphasis mine.

5. Mencius, *Mengzi*, 4B28.

6. Mencius, *Mengzi*, 2A7. Mencius also contrasts the shaman-healer and the coffin-maker in this passage; but that contrast strikes me as less plausible—burying the (already) dead seems an important service to the family and perhaps even to the deceased himself. Still, he does have a point: the coffin-maker would be out of business if people stopped dying.

7. Mencius, *Mengzi*, 2A7.

8. Xunzi, "Man's Nature is Evil," in *Xunzi: Basic Writings*, trans. Burton Watson (New York: Columbia University Press, 2003), 161–74, at 171.

9. Mencius, *Mengzi*, 2A4.

10. Mencius, *Mengzi*, 6A18.

11. For a fascinating effort to construct a philosophical theory of ethics based on empathy, see Michael Slote, *The Ethics of Care and Empathy* (New York: Routledge, 2007). Although analysis of Slote's work is beyond my scope here, for an interesting critique see Marion Hourdequin, "The Limits of Empathy," in *Virtue Ethics and Confucianism*, ed. Stephen C. Angle and Michael Slote (New York: Routledge, 2015), 209–18. We'll focus here on psychological approaches to empathy.

12. Martin L. Hoffman, *Empathy and Moral Development: Implications for Caring and Justice* (Cambridge: Cambridge University Press, 2000), 29.

13. Hoffman, *Empathy and Moral Development*, 30.

14. Hoffman, *Empathy and Moral Development*, 30–36; see also chap. 6.

15. Miller, *Moral Character*, 122; cf. 113–18. As Hoffman's analysis (*Empathy and Moral Development*, chap. 2) seems to suggest, a bonus of Miller's interpretation is that even people with empathic disorders such as Asperger's Syndrome would be capable of developing the virtue of benevolence. For more detail regarding the "empathy-altruism hypothesis," see the work of C. Daniel Batson, who summarizes his decades of research in *Altruism in Humans* (New York: Oxford University Press, 2011).

16. See, e.g., Batson, *Altruism in Humans*, 195–98.

17. For one interesting example, see Laura Shaw, C. Daniel Batson, and R. Todd, "Empathy Avoidance: Forestalling Feeling for Another in Order to Escape the Motivational Consequences," *Journal of Personality and Social Psychology* 67 (1994): 879–87. Hoffman (*Empathy and Moral Development*, 34–35) and Miller (*Moral Character*, 123–25) also summarize these and similar results.

18. Miller, *Moral Character*, 125.

19. Hoffman, *Empathy and Moral Development*, 33–34; see Samuel P. Oliner and Pearl M. Oliner, *The Altruistic Personality: Rescuers of Jews in Nazi Europe* (New York: Free Press, 1988).

20. Hoffman, *Empathy and Moral Development*, 287. For a dissenting voice, arguing that these limitations are so serious that they make empathy morally disadvantageous, see Paul Bloom, *Against Empathy: The Case for Rational Compassion* (New York: HarperCollins, 2016).

21. Hoffman, *Empathy and Moral Development*, 288–92. Relatedly, as Hoffman notes, role-playing exercises have also been effective for fostering empathy and discouraging victim-blaming among older juvenile offenders in state correctional programs.

22. Hoffman, *Empathy and Moral Development*, 293–97.

23. Aristotle, *Nicomachean Ethics*, trans. W. D. Ross (Boston: Internet Classics Archive, 1994–2000), 4.1, 1120a21.

24. Aristotle, *Nicomachean Ethics*, 4.1, 1120a25.

25. Aristotle, *Nicomachean Ethics*, 4.1.

26. Aristotle, *Nicomachean Ethics*, 4.1, 1121a17.

27. Aristotle, *Nicomachean Ethics*, 4.1, 1121a26–27.

28. Aristotle, *Nicomachean Ethics*, 4.1, 1121a29.

29. Aristotle, *Nicomachean Ethics*, 4.1, 1121b14–17.

30. Aristotle, *Nicomachean Ethics*, 4.1, 1121b21–28.

31. Aristotle, *Nicomachean Ethics*, 4.1, 1121b30.

32. Aristotle, *Nicomachean Ethics*, 4.1, 1121a30.

33. Wolf Richter, "America's Consumer Debt Keeps Skyrocketing," *Business Insider*, February 8, 2018, http://www.businessinsider.com/americas-consumer-debt-keeps-skyrocketing-2018-2.

34. Lorie Konish, "Consumer Debt Is Set to Reach $4 Trillion by the End of 2018," *CNBC*, May 21, 2018, https://www.cnbc.com/2018/05/21/consumer-debt-is-set-to-reach-4-trillion-by-the-end-of-2018.html.

35. Maurie Backman, "Here's What the Average American Spends on Holiday Gifts," *The Motley Fool*, December 1, 2016 (updated October 2, 2018), https://www.fool.com/retirement/2016/12/01/heres-what-the-average-american-spends-on-holiday.aspx.

36. See Chip Heath and Dan Heath, *Decisive: How to Make Better Choices in Life and Work* (New York: Crown Publishing, 2013), chap. 11.

37. Stephanie Fagin-Jones and Elizabeth Midlarsky. "Courageous Altruism: Personal and Situational Correlates of Rescue During the Holocaust." *Journal of Positive Psychology* 2, no. 2 (2007): 136–47, at 144.

38. Scott T. Allison and George R. Goethals, *Heroes: What They Do and Why We Need Them* (New York: Oxford University Press, 2011), 24.

39. "Raoul Wallenberg: A Man Who Made a Difference," https://sweden.se/society/raoul-wallenberg-a-man-who-made-a-difference/.

Chapter 19

1. Cathy Heying, life story interview, March 27, 2017. All quotes from Heying are taken from this interview.

2. Aristotle, *Nicomachean Ethics*, trans. W. D. Ross (Boston: Internet Classics Archive, 1994–2000), 6.5, 1140a26–28.

3. Kristján Kristjánsson, *Virtues and Vices in Positive Psychology: A Philosophical Critique* (Cambridge: Cambridge University Press, 2013), 156. For longer but very helpful recent Aristotelian accounts of practical wisdom and practical reasoning more generally, see Alasdair MacIntyre, *Ethics in the Conflicts of Modernity: An Essay on Desire, Practical Reasoning, and Narrative* (Cambridge: Cambridge University Press, 2016); and Daniel C. Russell, *Practical Intelligence and the Virtues* (Oxford: Oxford University Press, 2009).

4. Aristotle, *Nicomachean Ethics*, 6.6–7.

5. Aristotle, *Nicomachean Ethics*, 6.10.

6. Aristotle, *Nicomachean Ethics*, 6.9, 1142b28.

7. Aristotle, *Nicomachean Ethics*, 6.2, 1139a24–25, emphasis added.

8. Aristotle, *Nicomachean Ethics*, 6.2, 1139a30.

9. See Aristotle, *Nicomachean Ethics*, 6.12.

10. Aristotle, *Nicomachean Ethics*, 6.13, 1144b30–31.

11. Aristotle, *Nicomachean Ethics*, 6.11.

12. Aristotle, *Nicomachean Ethics*, 6.7–8.

13. Philosophers may see the resemblance of this exercise to John Rawls's description of reflective equilibrium in *A Theory of Justice* (Cambridge, Mass.: Harvard University Press, 1971).

14. Kristjánsson, *Virtues and Vices in Positive Psychology*, 157.

15. Although all of my interviewees gave me permission to use their names, for the sake of family privacy I've omitted identifying details here.

16. Barry Schwartz and Kenneth Sharpe, *Practical Wisdom: The Right Way to Do the Right Thing* (New York: Riverhead Books, 2010), 8.

17. Schwartz and Sharpe, *Practical Wisdom*, 54–56.

18. Darcia Narvaez, "Human Flourishing and Moral Development: Cognitive and Neurobiological Perspectives on Virtue Development," in *Handbook of Moral and Character Education*, ed. L. P. Nucci and D. Narvaez (New York: Routledge, 2008), 310–27, at 312. Although Narvaez suggests that exemplars are experts in "one or more" of these areas, it seems to me that a practically wise person must have at least *some* expertise in all four.

19. Narvaez, "Human Flourishing and Moral Development," 319.

20. Schwartz and Sharpe, *Practical Wisdom*, 12.

21. Schwartz and Sharpe, *Practical Wisdom*, 41–42.

22. Schwartz and Sharpe, *Practical Wisdom*, chap. 9.

23. Mauricio Lim Miller, life story interview, March 29, 2017. All quotes from Miller are taken from this interview.

24. Malcolm Gladwell, *The Tipping Point: How Little Things Can Make a Big Difference* (New York: Little, Brown & Company, 2006).

25. Family Independence Initiative, https://www.fii.org/about/.

26. Family Independence Initiative, https://www.fii.org/approach/impact/.

Chapter 20

1. This conflicting advice is borrowed from Jane Austen's *Pride and Prejudice*.

2. See, e.g., Plato, *Gorgias*, 479e; Aristotle, *Nicomachean Ethics*, 1180a; Confucius, *Analects*, 2.3; and Mencius [Mengzi], *Mengzi*, 4A18.

3. Anthony Weston, *Creative Problem Solving in Ethics* (Oxford: Oxford University Press, 2006).

4. Chip Heath and Dan Heath, *Decisive: How to Make Better Choices in Life and Work* (New York: Crown Publishing, 2013), chaps. 3 and 7.

5. Don Schoendorfer, life story interview, January 13, 2017.

BIBLIOGRAPHY

Abramson, Lyn, Martin Seligman, and John Teasdale. "Learned Helplessness in Humans: Critique and Reformulation." *Journal of Abnormal Psychology* 87, no. 1 (1978): 49–74.

Adams, Don. "Socratic *Agape* Without Irony in the *Euthydemus*." *American Catholic Philosophical Quarterly* 91, no. 2 (Spring 2017): 273–98.

Adams, Robert Merrihew. "Saints." *The Journal of Philosophy* 81, no. 7 (1984): 392–401.

Agneessens, Filip, Hans Waege, and John Lievens. "Diversity in Social Support by Role Relations: A Typology." Social Networks 28, no. 4 (2006): 427–41.

Alexander, Michelle. *The New Jim Crow: Mass Incarceration in the Age of Colorblindness.* New York: The New Press, 2012.

Allison, Scott T., and George R. Goethals. *Heroes: What They Do and Why We Need Them.* New York: Oxford University Press, 2011.

Allport, Gordon W. *The Nature of Prejudice.* Cambridge, Mass.: Addison-Wesley, 1954.

Al-Mabuk, Radhi H., Robert D. Enright, and Paul A. Cardis. "Forgiveness Education with Parentally Love-Deprived Late Adolescents." *Journal of Moral Education* 24, no. 4 (1995): 427–44.

Ambady, Nalini, and Max Weisbuch. "Nonverbal Behavior." In Fiske, Gilbert, and Lindzey, *Handbook of Social Psychology*, 464–97.

Angle, Stephen, and Michael Slote, eds. *Virtue Ethics and Confucianism.* New York: Routledge, 2013.

Aristotle. *Nicomachean Ethics.* Translated by W. D. Ross. Boston: Internet Classics Archive, 1994–2009.

Ashton, Michael C., and Kibeom Lee. "Empirical, Theoretical, and Practical Advantages of the HEXACO Model of Personality Structure." *Personality and Social Psychology Review* 11 (2007): 150–66.

Augustine. *Confessions.* Translated by H. Chadwick. Oxford: Oxford World Classics, 2009.

———. Letter 118 to Dioscorus. Translated by J. G. Cunningham. In *Augustine: Prolegomena: St. Augustine's Life and Work, Confessions, Letters*, 437–38. Nicene and Post-

Nicene Fathers, 1st ser., vol. 1, ed. Philip Schaff. Buffalo, N.Y.: Christian Literature Publishing Co., 1887.

Bales, Kevin. *Disposable People*. 3rd ed. Berkeley: University of California Press, 2012.

Bandura, Albert. "Self-Efficacy: Toward a Unifying Theory of Behavioral Change." *Psychological Review* 84, no. 2 (1977): 191–215.

———. "Mechanisms of Moral Disengagement in the Exercise of Moral Agency." *Journal of Personality and Social Psychology* 71, no. 2 (1996): 364–74.

———. "Selective Activation and Disengagement of Moral Control." *Personality and Social Psychology Review* 3, no. 3 (1999): 193–209.

———. "On the Functional Properties of Perceived Self-Efficacy Revisited." *Journal of Management* 38, no. 1 (2012): 9–44.

———. "Bobo Doll Studies." In *Encyclopedia of Media Violence*, edited by Matthew S. Eastin, 53–55. Thousand Oaks, Calif.: SAGE Reference, 2013.

———. *Moral Disengagement: How People Do Harm and Live with Themselves*. New York: Worth Publishers, 2015.

Bandura, Albert, Dorothea Ross, and Sheila A. Ross. "Imitation of Film-Mediated Aggressive Models." *Journal of Abnormal and Social Psychology* 66 (1963): 3–11.

Batson, C. Daniel. *Altruism in Humans*. New York: Oxford University Press, 2011.

Baumeister, Roy, Kenneth Cairns, and Russell Geen. "Repression and Self-Presentation: When Audiences Interfere with Self-Deceptive Strategies." *Journal of Personality and Social Psychology* 62, no. 5 (1992): 851–62.

Baumeister, Roy F., and Mark R. Leary. "The Need to Belong: Desire for Interpersonal Attachments as a Fundamental Human Motivation." *Psychological Bulletin* 117 (1995): 497–529.

Baumeister, Roy F., and John Tierney. *Willpower: Rediscovering the Greatest Human Strength*. New York: Penguin, 2011.

Beaty, Katelyn. "I Met the Man Who Killed My Entire Family: How Rwandan Genocide Survivor Immaculee Ilibagiza Found Forgiveness." *Christianity Today* (August 2017).

Beck, Aaron T. *Love Is Never Enough*. New York: HarperPerennial, 1989.

Bennett-Levy, James. "Reflection: A Blind Spot in Psychology?" *Clinical Psychology* 27 (July 2003): 16–19.

Berger, Jonah, and Lindsay Rand. "Shifting Signals to Help Health: Using Identity Signaling to Reduce Risky Health Behaviors." *Journal of Consumer Research* 35, no. 3 (2008): 509–18.

Birditt, Kira S., and Toni C Antonucci. "Relationship Quality Profiles and Well-Being among Married Adults." *Journal of Family Psychology* 21, no. 4 (2007): 595–604.

Blieszner, Rosemary, and Karen A. Roberto, "Friendship across the Life Span: Reciprocity in Individual and Relationship Development." In *Growing Together: Personal Relationships across the Lifespan*, edited by F. R. Lang and K. L. Fingerman, 159–82. Cambridge: Cambridge University Press, 2004.

Bloom, Paul. *Against Empathy: The Case for Rational Compassion*. New York: HarperCollins, 2016.

Bock, Tonia, Logan Tufte, and Heidi Giebel. "A New Moral Identity Measure: Integrating Thomistic Virtue Ethics with an Ericksonian Identity Development Perspective." Third Annual Conference of the Jubilee Centre for Character and Virtues. Oriel College, Oxford, United Kingdom, 2015.

Bonhoffer, Dietrich. *Conspiracy and Imprisonment: 1940–1945*. Vol. 16 of *Dietrich Bonhoeffer Works*. Edited by Mark S. Brocker, translated by Lisa E. Dahill. Minneapolis, Minn.: Fortress, 2006.

Bouffard-Bouchard, Therese. "Influence of Self-Efficacy on Performance in a Cognitive Task." *Journal of Social Psychology* 130, no. 3 (1990): 353–63.

Bouffard-Bouchard, Therese, Sophie Parent, and Serge Larivee. "Influence of Self-Efficacy on Self-Regulation and Performance among Junior and Senior High-School Age Students." *International Journal of Behavioral Development* 14, no. 2 (1991): 153–64.

Brewer, Marilynn. "The Psychology of Prejudice: Ingroup Love or Outgroup Hate?" *Journal of Social Issues* 55 (1999): 429–44.

Burton, Susan. *Becoming Ms. Burton*. With Cari Lynn. New York: The New Press, 2017.

Carbonell, Vanessa. "What Moral Saints Look Like." *Canadian Journal of Philosophy* 39, no. 3 (2009): 371–98.

———. "The Ratcheting-Up Effect." *Pacific Philosophical Quarterly* 93, no. 2 (2012): 228–54.

Card, Claudia. "Gratitude and Obligation." *American Philosophical Quarterly* 25, no. 2 (1988): 115–27.

Cicero, Marcus Tullius. *De Officiis* [On duties]. In *The Ethical Writings of Cicero*, translated by Andrew P. Peabody. Boston: Little, Brown, & Company, 1887.

———. *The Orations of Marcus Tullius Cicero*. Translated by C. D. Yonge. London: George Bell & Sons, 1891.

Colby, Anne, and William Damon. *Some Do Care: Contemporary Lives of Moral Commitment*. New York: Free Press, 1992.

Coles, Robert. *The Moral Life of Children*. Boston: Atlantic Monthly Press, 1986.

Confucius. *The Analects of Confucius*. Translated by Edward Slingerland. Indianapolis, Ind.: Hackett, 2003.

Dahl, Melissa. "Do You Have Any Idea What Other People Think of You?" *Science of Us*, May 8, 2017.

Damon, William. *Greater Expectations: Overcoming the Culture of Indulgence in America's Homes and Schools*. New York: Free Press, 1995.

Damon, William, and Anne Colby. *The Power of Ideals: The Real Story of Moral Choice*. New York: Oxford University Press, 2015.

De Ridder, D. T., G. Lensvelt-Mulders, C. Finkenauer, F. M. Stok, and R. F. Baumeister. "Taking Stock of Self-Control: A Meta-analysis of How Trait Self-Control Relates to a Wide Range of Behaviors." Personality and Social Psychology Review, 16 (2012): 76–99.

Duckworth, Angela, Christopher Peterson, Michael D. Matthews, and Dennis R. Kelly. "Grit: Perseverance and Passion for Long-Term Goals." *Journal of Personality and Social Psychology* 92, no. 6 (2007): 1087–1101.

Duval, T. Shelley, and Robert Wicklund. *A Theory of Objective Self-Awareness*. New York: Academic Press, 1972.

Dweck, Carol S. "The Role of Expectations and Attributions in the Alleviation of Learned Helplessness." *Journal of Personality and Social Psychology* 31, no. 4 (1975): 674–85.

Eisenberg, Nancy. "Empathy-Related Emotional Responses, Altruism, and Their Socialization." In *Visions of Compassion: Western Scientists and Tibetan Buddhists Examine Human Nature*, edited by R. J. Davidson and A. Harrington, 131–64. London: Oxford University Press, 2002.

Eisenberger, Robert. "Learned Industriousness." *Psychological Review* 99, no. 2 (1992): 248–67.

Eisenberger, Robert, and Michael Selbst. "Does Reward Increase or Decrease Creativity?" *Journal of Personality and Social Psychology* 66, no. 6 (1994): 1116–27.

Emmons, Robert. *Thanks! How the New Science of Gratitude Can Make You Happier*. New York: Houghton Mifflin, 2007.

———. *Gratitude Works! A 21-Day Program for Creating Emotional Prosperity*. San Francisco: Jossey-Bass, 2011.

Emmons, Robert, and Michael McCullough, eds. *The Psychology of Gratitude*. Oxford: Oxford University Press, 2004.

Enright, Robert. *Eight Keys to Forgiveness*. New York: W. W. Norton, 2015.

Epley, Nicholas, and Adam Waytz. "Mind Perception." In Fiske, Gilbert, and Lindzey, *Handbook of Social Psychology*, 498–541.

Eurich, Tasha. *Insight: Why We're Not as Self-Aware as We Think, and How Seeing Ourselves Clearly Helps Us Succeed at Work and in Life*. New York: Crown Publishing, 2017.

———. "To Make Better Decisions, Ask Yourself 'What,' Not 'Why.'" *Science of Us*, May 2, 2017. https://www.thecut.com/2017/05/to-make-better-decisions-ask-yourself-what-not-why.html.

Evans, Angela D., Allison M. O'Connor, and Kang Lee. "Verbalizing a Commitment Reduces Cheating in Young Children." *Social Development* 27, no. 1 (2018): 87–94.

Eyal, Nir, and Ryan Hoover. *Hooked: How to Build Habit-Forming Products*. New York: Portfolio, 2014.

Fagin-Jones, Stephanie, and Elizabeth Midlarsky. "Courageous Altruism: Personal and Situational Correlates of Rescue During the Holocaust." *Journal of Positive Psychology* 2, no. 2 (2007): 136–47.

Finkelhor, David, Heather Turner, Anne Shattuck, and Sherry L. Hamby. "Violence, Crime, and Abuse Exposure in a National Sample of Children and Youth." *JAMA Pediatrics* 167, no. 7 (2013): 614–21.

Fins, Joseph J. *Rights Come to Mind: Brain Injury, Ethics, and the Struggle for Consciousness*. New York: Cambridge University Press, 2015.

Fiske, S. T., D. T. Gilbert, and G. Lindzey, eds. *Handbook of Social Psychology*. New York: John Wiley & Sons, 2010.

Frankl, Viktor. *Man's Search for Meaning*. Boston: Beacon Press, 2006.

Freedman, Jonathan L., and Scott C. Fraser. "Compliance without Pressure: The Foot-in-the-Door Technique." *Journal of Personality and Social Psychology* 4, no. 2 (1966): 195–203.

Frimer, Jeremy, and Lawrence Walker. "Reconciling the Self and Morality: An Empirical Model of Moral Centrality Development." *Developmental Psychology* 45, no. 6 (2009): 1669–81.

Fujita, Kentaro, Yaacov Trope, Nira Liberman, and Maya Levin-Sagi. "Construal Levels and Self-Control." *Journal of Personality and Social Psychology* 90, no. 3 (2006): 351–67.

Gerachi, Alessandra, and Luca Surian. "The Developmental Roots of Fairness: Infants' Reactions to Equal and Unequal Distributions of Resources." *Developmental Science* 14, no. 5 (2011): 1012–20.

Giebel, Heidi M. "Extend Your Benevolence: Kindness and Generosity in the Family and Beyond." In *Virtues in Action: New Essays in Applied Virtue Ethics*, edited by Michael W. Austin, 70–85. New York: Palgrave Macmillan, 2013.

———. "On Why and How Intention Matters." *American Catholic Philosophical Quarterly* 89, no. 3 (2015): 369–95.

Giebel, Heidi, and Benjamin Huff. "Justice, Benevolence, and Friendship: A Confucian Addition to Thomistic Ethics?" In *The Wisdom of Youth: Essays Inspired by the Early Work of Jacques and Raissa Maritain*, edited by Travis Dumsday, 310–28. Washington, D.C.: The Catholic University of America Press, 2016.

Gillham, Jane, Zoe Adams-Deutsch, Jaclyn Werner, Karen Reivich, Virginia Coulter-Heindl, Mark Linkins, Breanna Winder, et al. "Character Strengths Predict Subjective Well-Being During Adolescence." *Journal of Positive Psychology* 6, no. 1 (2011): 31–44.

Gladwell, Malcolm. *The Tipping Point: How Little Things Can Make a Big Difference*. New York: Little, Brown & Company, 2006.

Goldberg, Lewis R. "The Development of Markers for the Big-Five Factor Structure," *Psychological Assessment* 4 (1992): 26–42.

Goleman, Daniel. *Emotional Intelligence: Why It Can Matter More Than IQ*. New York: Bantam Books, 2005.

Gray, Tara. *Publish and Flourish: Become a Prolific Scholar*. 3rd ed. Las Cruces, N.M.: Teaching Academy, 2005.

Guo, Jen, Miriam Klevan, and Dan P. McAdams. "Personality Traits, Ego Development, and the Redemptive Self." *Personality and Social Psychology Bulletin* 42, no. 11 (2016): 1551–63.

Haidt, Jonathan. *The Happiness Hypothesis*. New York: Basic Books, 2006.

Hamlin, J. Kiley. "Failed Attempts to Help and Harm: Intention versus Outcome in Preverbal Infants' Social Evaluations." *Cognition* 128, no. 3 (2013): 451–74.

Hamlin, J. Kiley, and Karen Wynn. "Young Infants Prefer Prosocial to Antisocial Others." *Cognitive Development* 26, no. 1 (2011): 30–39.

———. "Who Knows What's Good to Eat? Infants Fail to Match the Food Preferences of Antisocial Others." *Cognitive Development* 27, no. 3 (2012): 227–39.

Harris, Lasana T., and Susan T. Fiske. "Dehumanizing the Lowest of the Low: Neuroimaging Responses to Extreme Outgroups." *Psychological Science* 17, no. 10 (2006): 847–53.

Hays, Chelsea, and Leslie J. Carver. "Follow the Liar: The Effects of Adult Lies on Children's Honesty." *Developmental Science* 17, no. 6 (2014): 977–83.

Heath, Chip, and Dan Heath. *Switch: How to Change Things When Change Is Hard*. New York: Broadway Books, 2010.

———. *Decisive: How to Make Better Choices in Life and Work*. New York: Crown Publishing, 2013.

Hinck, Michelle. *Great Love: The Mary Jo Copeland Story*. Berea, Ohio: Quixote, 2013.

Hoffman, Martin. *Empathy and Moral Development: Implications for Caring and Justice*. Cambridge: Cambridge University Press, 2000.

Hofmann, Wilhelm, Kathleen Vohs, and Roy F. Baumeister. "What People Desire, Feel Conflicted About, and Try to Resist in Everyday Life." *Psychological Science* 23, no. 6 (2012): 582–88.

Hourdequin, Marion. "The Limits of Empathy." In Angle and Slote, *Virtue Ethics and Confucianism*, 209–18.

Hoyk, Robert, and Paul Hersey. "Minimizing." In *The Ethical Executive*, 68–74. Stanford, Calif.: Stanford University Press, 2008.

Huff, Benjamin. "Eudaimonism in the *Mencius*: Fulfilling the Heart," *Dao: A Journal of Comparative Philosophy* 14, no. 3 (2015): 403–31.

Hughes, Paul M., and Brandon Warmke. "Forgiveness." *The Stanford Encyclopedia of Philosophy* (Summer 2017 Edition), edited by Edward N. Zalta, https://plato.stanford.edu/archives/sum2017/entries/forgiveness/.

Ignatius Loyola. *Spiritual Exercises*. Translated by Louis J. Puhl. Chicago: Loyola Press, 1968.

Ilibagiza, Immaculee. *Left to Tell: Discovering God amidst the Rwandan Holocaust*. Carlsbad, Calif.: Hay House, 2006.

Ivanhoe, Philip J. *Confucian Reflections: Ancient Wisdom for Modern Times*. New York: Routledge, 2013.

———. "Filial Piety as a Virtue." In *Working Virtue: Virtue Ethics and Contemporary Moral Problems*, edited by R. L. Walker and P. J. Ivanhoe, 297–312. New York: Clarendon, 2007.

Johnson, Chalene. *Push: 30 Days to Turbocharged Habits, a Bangin' Body, and the Life You Deserve!* Rev. ed. New York: Rodale Books, 2017.

Jones, Daniel N., and Delroy L. Paulhus. "Duplicity among the Dark Triad: Three Faces of Deceit." *Journal of Personality and Social Psychology*, 113, no. 2 (2017): 329–42.

Kenward, Ben, and Matilda Dahl. "Preschoolers Distribute Scarce Resources According to the Moral Valence of Recipients' Previous Actions." *Developmental Psychology* 47, no. 4 (2011): 1054–64.

Keys, Mary M. *Aquinas, Aristotle, and the Promise of the Common Good*. New York: Cambridge University Press, 2006.

Koc, Kevser, and Cary A. Buzzelli, "The Moral of the Story Is … : Using Children's Literature in Character Education." *Young Children* 59, no. 1 (2004): 92–97.

Kristjánsson, Kristján. "Emulation and the Use of Role Models in Moral Education." *Journal of Moral Education* 35, no. 1 (2006): 37–49.

———. *Virtues and Vices in Positive Psychology: A Philosophical Critique.* Cambridge: Cambridge University Press, 2006.

Kross, Ethan, and Ozlem Ayduk. "Making Meaning out of Negative Experiences by Self-Distancing." *Current Directions in Psychological Science* 20, no. 3 (2011): 187–91.

Kross, Ethan, Emma Bruehlman-Senecal, Jiyoung Park, Aleah Burson, Adrienne Dougherty, Holly Shablack, et al. "Self-Talk as a Regulatory Mechanism: How You Do It Matters." *Journal of Personality and Social Psychology* 106, no. 2 (2014): 304–24.

Kross, Ethan, Angela Duckworth, Ozlem Ayduk, Eli Tsukayama, and Walter Mischel. "The Effect of Self-Distancing on Adaptive versus Maladaptive Self-Reflection in Children." *Emotion* 11, no. 5 (2011): 1032–39.

Kruger, Joachim, and Thomas Gilovich. "Actions, Intentions, and Self-Assessment: The Road to Self-Enhancement Is Paved with Good Intentions." *Personality and Social Psychology Bulletin*, 30, no. 3 (2004): 328–39.

LaBouff, Jordan P., Wade C. Rowatt, Megan K. Johnson, Jo-Ann Tsang, and Grace M. Willerton. "Humble Persons Are More Helpful Than Less Humble Persons: Evidence from Three Studies." *The Journal of Positive Psychology* 7 (2012): 16–29.

Latimer, Jeff, Craig Dowden, and Danielle Muise. "The Effectiveness of Restorative Justice: A Meta-Analysis." *The Prison Journal* 85, no. 2 (2005): 127–44.

Lee, Kang, Victoria Talwar, Anjanie McCarthy, Ilana Ross, Angela Evans, and Cindy Arruda. "Can Classic Moral Stories Promote Honesty in Children?" *Psychological Science* 25, no. 8 (2014): 1630–36.

Leming, James S. "Tell Me a Story: An Evaluation of a Literature-Based Character Education Programme." *Journal of Moral Education* 29 (2000): 413–27.

Li, Jin. "Humility in Learning: A Confucian Perspective." *Journal of Moral Education* 45, no. 2 (2016): 147–65.

Locke, John. *An Essay Concerning Human Understanding.* Ed. Kenneth P. Winkler. Indianapolis: Hackett, 1996.

Luks, Allan. *The Healing Power of Doing Good.* Bloomington, Ind.: iUniverse, 2001.

MacIntyre, Alasdair. *After Virtue.* 2nd ed. Notre Dame, Ind.: University of Notre Dame Press, 1984.

———. *Ethics in the Conflicts of Modernity: An Essay on Desire, Practical Reasoning, and Narrative.* Cambridge: Cambridge University Press, 2016.

Macrae, C. Neil, and Suzanne Quadflieg. "Perceiving People." In Fiske, Gilbert, and Lindzey, *Handbook of Social Psychology,* 428–63.

Mahajan, Neha, and Karen Wynn. "Origins of 'Us' versus 'Them': Prelinguistic Infants Prefer Similar Others." *Cognition* 124 (2012): 227–33.

Manela, Tony. "Gratitude." In *The Stanford Encyclopedia of Philosophy,* edited by Edward N. Zalta. Spring 2015 Edition. https://plato.stanford.edu/archives/spr2015/entries/gratitude/.

Mann, Annamarie, and Jim Harter. "The Worldwide Employee Engagement Crisis." *Gallup Business Journal*, January 7, 2016.

McAdams, Dan P. *The Life Story Interview*. Foley Center for the Study of Lives, Northwestern University, 2008.

———. *The Redemptive Self: Stories Americans Live By*. Rev. ed. New York: Oxford, 2013.

———. "Psychological Science and the *Nicomachean Ethics*: Virtuous Actors, Agents, and Authors." In *Cultivating Virtue: Perspectives from Philosophy, Theology, and Psychology*, edited by Nancy Snow, 307–36. New York: Oxford University Press, 2015.

McAdams, Dan, and Jack Bauer. "Gratitude in Modern Life: Its Manifestations and Development." In Emmons and McCullough, *The Psychology of Gratitude*, 81–99.

McCrink, Koleen, Paul Bloom, and Laurie R. Santos. "Children's and Adults' Judgments of Equitable Resource Distributions." *Developmental Science* 13, no. 1 (2010): 37–45.

McCullough, Michael E. "Forgiveness as a Human Strength: Theory, Measurement, and Links to Well-Being." *Journal of Social and Clinical Psychology* 19, no. 1 (2000): 43–55.

McCullough, Michael, and Jo-Ann Tsang. "Parent of the Virtues? The Prosocial Contours of Gratitude." In Emmons and McCullough, *The Psychology of Gratitude*, 123–44.

McGonigal, Kelly. *The Willpower Instinct: How Self-Control Works, Why It Matters, and What You Can Do to Get More of It*. New York: Penguin, 2012.

Mead, Nicole, and Vanessa Patrick. "In Praise of Putting Things Off: Postponing Consumption Pleasures Facilitates Self-Control." In *Advances in Consumer Research*, vol. 39, edited by Rohini Ahluwalia, Tanya L. Chartrand, and Rebecca K. Ratner, 30–31. Duluth, Minn.: Association for Consumer Research, 2011.

Mencius [Mengzi]. *Mengzi*. Translated by Bryan Van Norden. Indianapolis, Ind.: Hackett, 2008.

Midgley, Mary. *Heart and Mind: Varieties of Moral Experience*. 3rd ed. New York: Routledge, 2003.

Miller, Christian. *Moral Character: An Empirical Theory*. Oxford: Oxford University Press, 2013.

Miller, Mauricio Lim. *The Alternative: Most of What You Believe about Poverty Is Wrong*. Morrisville, N.C.: Lulu Publishing Services, 2017.

Miller, Norman, William C. Pedersen, Mitchell Earleywine, and Vicki E. Pollock. "A Theoretical Model of Triggered Displaced Aggression." *Personality and Social Psychology Review* 7, no. 1 (2003): 75–97.

Mischel, W. *The Marshmallow Test: Mastering Self-Control*. New York: Little, Brown, & Company, 2014.

Mischkowski, Dominik, Ethan Kross, and Brad Bushman. "Flies on the Wall Are Less Aggressive: Self-Distancing 'In the Heat of the Moment' Reduces Aggressive Thoughts, Angry Feelings, and Aggressive Behavior." *Journal of Experimental Social Psychology* 48, no. 5 (2012): 1187–91.

Mitchell, Deborah J., J. Edward Russo, and Nancy Pennington. "Back to the Future: Temporal Perspective in the Explanation of Events." *Journal of Behavioral Decision Making* 2, no. 1 (1989): 25–38.

Mitchell, Jo Ann, Rosanna Stanimirovic, Britt Klein, and Dianne Vella-Brodrick. "A Randomized Controlled Trial of a Self-Guided Internet Intervention Promoting Well-Being." *Computers in Human Behavior* 25, no. 3 (2009). doi:10.1016/j.chb.2009 .02.003.

Monroe, Kristen R. "Cracking the Code of Genocide: The Moral Psychology of Nazis, Bystanders, and Rescuers during the Holocaust." *Political Psychology* 29, no. 5 (2008): 699–736.

Muraven, M., R. F. Baumeister, and D. M. Tice. "Longitudinal Improvement of Self-Regulation through Practice: Building Self-Control through Repeated Exercise." *Journal of Social Psychology* 139 (1999): 446–57.

Murdoch, Iris. *The Sovereignty of Good*. London: Routledge & Kegan Paul, 2013.

Naifeh, Steven, and Gregory White Smith. *A Stranger in the Family*. New York: Penguin, 1996.

Narvaez, Darcia. "Does Reading Moral Stories Build Character?" *Educational Psychology Review* 14, no. 2 (2002): 155–77.

———. "Human Flourishing and Moral Development: Cognitive and Neurobiological Perspectives of Virtue Development." In *Handbook of Moral and Character Education*, edited by L. P. Nucci and D. Narvaez, 310–27. New York: Routledge, 2008.

Oliner, Samuel P., and Pearl M. Oliner. *The Altruistic Personality: Rescuers of Jews in Nazi Europe*. New York: Free Press, 1988.

Oyserman, Daphna, and Leah James. "Possible Identities." In *Handbook of Identity Theory and Research*, edited by S. J. Schwartz et al., 117–45. Dordrecht, Netherlands: Springer, 2011.

Park, Julie J., and Melissa L. Millora. "The Relevance of Reflection: An Empirical Examination of the Role of Reflection in Ethic of Caring, Leadership, and Psychological Well-Being." *Journal of College Student Development* 53, no. 2 (2012): 221–42.

Park, Nansook, Christopher Peterson, and Martin E. P. Seligman. "Strengths of Character and Well-Being." *Journal of Social & Clinical Psychology* 23, no. 5 (2004): 603–19.

Paulhus, Delroy L., and Oliver P. John. "Egoistic and Moralistic Biases in Self-Perception: The Interplay of Self-Deceptive Styles with Basic Traits and Motives." *Journal of Personality*, 66, no. 6 (1998): 1025–60.

Paulhus, Delroy L., and Douglas B. Reid. "Enhancement and Denial in Socially Desirable Responding." *Journal of Personality and Social Psychology*, 60, no. 2 (1991): 307–17.

Peterson, Christopher, and Martin Seligman. *Character Strengths and Virtues: A Handbook and Classification*. Oxford: Oxford University Press, 2004.

Pistorius, Martin. *Ghost Boy*. Nashville, Tenn.: Thomas Nelson, 2013.

Plato. *Apology*. Translated by Benjamin Jowett. Boston: Internet Classics Archive, 1994–2000.

———. *Crito*. Translated by Benjamin Jowett. Boston: Internet Classics Archive, 1994–2000.

———. *Euthydemus*. Translated by Benjamin Jowett. Boston: Internet Classics Archive, 1994–2000.

———. *Gorgias*. Translated by Benjamin Jowett. Boston: Internet Classics Archive, 1994–2000.

———. *Phaedrus*. Translated by Benjamin Jowett. Boston: Internet Classics Archive, 1994–2000.

———. *Republic*. Translated by Benjamin Jowett. Boston: Internet Classics Archive, 1994–2000.

Proyer, Rene, Willibald Ruch, and Claudia Buschor. "Testing Strengths-Based Interventions: A Preliminary Study on the Effectiveness of a Program Targeting Curiosity, Gratitude, Hope, Humor, and Zest for Enhancing Life Satisfaction." *Journal of Happiness Studies* 14, no. 1 (2013): 275–92.

Rawlins, William K., and Laura D. Russell. "Friendship, Positive Being-with-Others, and the Edifying Practices of Storytelling and Dialogue." In *Positive Psychology of Love*, edited by Mahzad Hojjat and Duncan Cramer, 30–43. New York: Oxford University Press, 2013.

Rawls, John. *A Theory of Justice*. Cambridge, Mass.: Harvard University Press, 1971.

Rawson, Glenn. "Socratic Humility." *Philosophy Now* no. 53 (2005): 31–33.

Roberts, Robert C. "The Blessings of Gratitude: A Conceptual Analysis." In Emmons and McCullough, *The Psychology of Gratitude*, 58–80.

Rommetveit, Ragnar. "Outlines of a Dialogically Based Social-Cognitive Approach to Human Cognition and Communication." In *The Dialogical Alternative: Towards a Theory of Language and Mind*, edited by A. H. Wold, 19–44. Oslo, Norway: Scandinavian University Press, 1992.

Rubenstein, Richard. *Aristotle's Children*. New York: Harcourt, 2003.

Ruch, Willibald, A. Huber, Ursula Beermann, and Rene T. Proyer. "Character Strengths as Predictors of the 'Good Life' in Austria, Germany and Switzerland." In *Studies and Researches in Social Sciences*, vol. 16, edited by Romanian Academy, George Barit Institute of History, Department of Social Research, 123–31. Cluj-Napoca, Romania: Argonaut Press, 2007.

Rushing, Sara. "Comparative Humilities: Christian, Contemporary, and Confucian Conceptions of a Political Virtue." *Polity* 45, no. 2 (2013): 198–222.

Russell, Daniel. *Practical Intelligence and the Virtues*. Oxford: Oxford University Press, 2009.

Sachdeva, Sonya, Rumen Iliev, and Douglas Medin. "Sinning Saints and Saintly Sinners: The Paradox of Moral Self-Regulation." *Psychological Science* 20 (2009): 523–28.

Schiller, F. C. S. "Aristotle and the Practical Syllogism." *The Journal of Philosophy, Psychology and Scientific Methods* 14, no. 24 (1917): 645–53.

Schlenker, Barry R. "Integrity and Character: Implications of Principled and Expedient Ethical Ideologies." *Journal of Clinical and Social Psychology* 27 (2008): 1078–125.

Schnitker, Sarah A. "An Examination of Patience and Well-Being." *The Journal of Positive Psychology*, 7, no. 4 (2012): 263–80.

Schwartz, Barry, and Kenneth Sharpe. *Practical Wisdom: The Right Way to Do the Right Thing*. New York: Riverhead Books, 2010.

Searle, John. *Minds, Brains, and Science*. Cambridge, Mass.: Harvard University Press, 1984.

Seligman, Martin, Tracy Steen, Nansook Park, and Christopher Peterson. "Positive Psychology Progress: Empirical Validation of Interventions." *American Psychologist* 60, no. 5 (2005): 410–21.

Seneca, Lucius Annasus. *De Beneficiis* [On benefits]. In *Moral Essays*. 3 vols. Translated by John W. Basore. The Loeb Classical Library. London: W. Heinemann, 1928–1935.

Shaw, Laura, C. Daniel Batson, and R. Todd. "Empathy Avoidance: Forestalling Feeling for Another in Order to Escape the Motivational Consequences." *Journal of Personality and Social Psychology* 67 (1994): 879–87.

Shoda, Yuichi, Walter Mischel, and Philip K. Peake. "Predicting Adolescent Cognitive and Self-Regulatory Competencies from Preschool Delay of Gratification." *Developmental Psychology* 26, no. 6 (1990): 978–86.

Silva, Paul J., and Ann G. Philips. "Self Awareness without Awareness? Implicit Self-Focused Attention and Behavioral Self-Regulation." *Self Identity* 12, no. 2 (2013): 114–27.

Skinner, Ellen A., Kathleen Edge, Jeffrey Altman, and Hayley Sherwood. "Searching for the Structure of Coping." *Psychological Bulletin* 129, no. 2 (2003): 216–69.

Slingerland, Edward. "The Situationist Critique and Early Confucian Virtue Ethics." In *Cultivating Virtue: Perspectives from Philosophy, Theology, and Psychology*, edited by Nancy Snow, 135–70. New York: Oxford University Press, 2015.

Slote, Michael. *The Ethics of Care and Empathy*. New York: Routledge, 2007.

Smith, Janet. "Natural Law and Sexual Ethics." In *Common Truths: New Perspectives on Natural Law*, edited by Edward B. McLean, 193–215. Wilmington, Del.: ISI Books, 2000.

Solomon, R. Foreword to *The Psychology of Gratitude*, edited by Emmons and McCullough, v–xi.

Stalnaker, Aaron. *Overcoming Our Evil: Human Nature and Spiritual Exercises in Xunzi and Augustine*. Washington, D.C.: Georgetown University Press, 2009.

Starnes, Debi, and Otto Zinser. "The Effect of Problem Difficulty, Locus of Control, and Sex on Task Persistence." *The Journal of General Psychology* 108, no. 2 (1983): 249–55.

Staudinger, Ursula. "Social Cognition and a Psychological Approach to an Art of Life." In *Social Cognition and Aging*, edited by T. M. Hess and F. Blanchard-Fields, 343–75. New York: Academic Press, 1999.

Stein, Daniel, and Anthony M. Grant. "Disentangling the Relationships among Self-Reflection, Insight, and Subjective Well-Being: The Role of Dysfunctional Attitudes and Core Self-Evaluations." *Journal of Psychology* 104, no. 5 (2014): 505–22.

Sullivan, Meghan. "Moral Saints and Moral Failure." Lecture, Philosophy Department Outside Speaker Series, University of St. Thomas, St. Paul, Minnesota, March 9, 2017.

Talwar, Victoria, Sarah Yachison, and Karissa Leduc. "Promoting Honesty: The Influence of Stories on Children's Lie-Telling Behaviors and Moral Understanding." *Infant and Child Development* 25, no. 6 (2016): 484–501.

Tangney, June Price. "Humility: Theoretical Perspectives, Empirical Findings and Directions for Future Research." *Journal of Social and Clinical Psychology* 19, no. 1 (2000): 70–82.

Tasimi, Arber, and Karen Wynn. "Costly Rejection of Wrongdoers by Infants and Children." *Cognition* 151 (2016): 76–79.

Thomas Aquinas. *Summa Theologica.* Translated by the Fathers of the English Dominican Province. Online version of original 1920 edition. www.newadvent.org/summa.

———. *Commentary on the Nicomachean Ethics.* Translated by C. I. Litzinger, OP. Chicago: Henry Regnery, 1964.

Trapnell, Paul D., and Jennifer D. Campbell. "Private Self-Consciousness and the Five-Factor Model of Personality: Distinguishing Rumination from Reflection." *Journal of Personality and Social Psychology* 76, no. 2 (1999): 284–304.

Treece, Patricia. *A Man for Others.* New York: Harper & Row, 1982.

Vaish, Amrisha, Manuela Missana, and Michael Tomasello. "Three-Year-Old Children Intervene in Third-Party Moral Transgressions." *The British Journal of Developmental Psychology* 29, no. 1 (2011): 124–30.

Van Ness, Daniel, and Karen Heetderks Strong. *Restoring Justice.* 2nd. ed. Cincinnati, Ohio: Anderson Publishing, 2003.

Vohs, Kathleen D., Joseph P. Redden, and Ryan Rahinel. "Physical Order Produces Healthy Choices, Generosity, and Conventionality, Whereas Disorder Produces Creativity." *Psychological Science* 24, no. 9 (2013): 1860–67.

Walker, Lawrence J., and Jeremy A. Frimer. "Moral Personality of Brave and Caring Exemplars." *Journal of Personality and Social Psychology* 93, no. 5 (2007): 845–60.

Watkins, Philip. "Gratitude and Subjective Well-Being." In Emmons and McCullough, *The Psychology of Gratitude,* 167–94.

Weston, Anthony. *Creative Problem Solving in Ethics.* Oxford: Oxford University Press, 2006.

Wicklund, Robert. "Objective Self-Awareness." *Advances in Experimental Social Psychology* 8 (1975): 233–75.

Wilson, Timothy D. *Strangers to Ourselves: Discovering the Adaptive Unconscious.* Cambridge, Mass.: Belknap Press, 2004.

Winnicott, Donald. *Playing and Reality.* New York: Basic Books, 1971.

Wolf, Susan. "Moral Saints." *The Journal of Philosophy* 79, no. 8 (1982): 419–39.

Wood, Alex M., Jeffrey Froh, and Adam Geraghty. "Gratitude and Well-Being: A Review and Theoretical Integration." *Clinical Psychology Review* 30, no. 7 (2010): 890–905.

Xenophon. *Memorabilia.* In *Xenophon in Seven Volumes,* vol. 4, translated by E. C. Marchant. Cambridge, Mass.: Harvard University Press, 1923.

Xunzi. *Xunzi: Basic Writings.* Translated by Burton Watson. New York: Columbia University Press, 2004.

———. *Xunzi: The Complete Text.* Translated by Eric L. Hutton. Princeton, N.J.: Princeton University Press, 2016.

Zagzebski, Linda. "Exemplarist Virtue Theory." *Metaphilosophy* 41, no. 1–2 (2010): 41–57.

———. "The Moral Authority of Exemplars." In *Theology and the Science of Moral Action,* edited by James Van Slyke, Gregory Peterson, Kevin Reimer, Michael Spezio, and Warren Brown, 117–29. New York: Routledge, 2013.

INDEX

Ethical Excellence: Philosophers, Psychologists, and Real-Life Exemplars Show Us How to Achieve It was designed in Garamond Premier Pro and composed by Kachergis Book Design of Pittsboro, North Carolina. It was printed on 60-pound Natural Smooth Web and bound by Sheridan of Chelsea, Michigan.